SOCIAL MOBILITY IN CONTEMPORARY JAPAN

Social Mobility in Contemporary Japan

Educational Credentials, Class and the Labour Market in a Cross-National Perspective

Hiroshi Ishida

Foreword by John H. Goldthorpe

Stanford University Press
Stanford, California

Stanford University Press
Stanford, California

Originating publisher: Macmillan Press Ltd,
Hampshire and London
First published in the U.S.A. by
Stanford University Press, 1993
Printed in Great Britain
Cloth ISBN 0–8047–2087–8
Paper ISBN 0–8047–2523–3
Original printing 1993
Last figure below indicates year of this printing:
04 03 02 01 00 99 98 97 96 95
This book is printed on acid-free paper.

For my family, nuclear and extended

Contents

List of Figures

List of Tables

Foreword

In recent years interest in Japanese society has steadily mounted. For the public at large, the central questions are those posed by Japan's outstanding economic performance. Why has Japan been so successful? Why have the Japanese been apparently able to avoid, or to respond more effectively to, the economic difficulties that have beset their European and North American competitors? What lessons can the West learn from Japanese economic institutions, business practices and managerial techniques? For the academic community, such questions have fallen within – and have given new life to – a long-standing debate on the very nature of industrial society. Has Japan, as the first nation outside the European cultural sphere to reach the stage of advanced industrialism, thereby created a new form of industrial society? Does the Japanese case show that there are ways of combining 'modern' economic and technical rationality with 'traditional' values and norms that diverge from those followed in the west – and that western theorists of industrialism have wished to see as functionally imperative?

In response to this interest, books on Japanese society, both 'popular' and academic, have of late been written in some number. However, while these have often been enthusiastically received, it is important not to overlook the fact that the research base of this literature still leaves much to be desired. All too frequently, large issues have been addressed – and large conclusions reached – by reference to a miscellaneous collection of official statistics and reports, case studies, journalism and, where all else fails, personal impressions. Apart from the inevitably patchy nature of evidence of this kind, it imposes little scholarly or scientific discipline. The danger is ever-present that the selection from it that is made reflects as much the needs of an individual author's case as the intrinsic value of particular items.

The resort to such a scissors-and-paste methodology can of course be defended as *faute de mieux*. However, if social scientists in the West are to treat the Japanese experience with the seriousness that it deserves, it is now surely time for them to start to create far more secure foundations for its understanding than have thus far existed. The present study – by a Japanese sociologist with in part a Western training and now teaching in the United States – will, I hope, be seen in retrospect as marking a significant pioneering contribution to this end.

In contrast with books of the kind earlier referred to, Hiroshi Ishida's work is both less and more ambitious: less, in that it concentrates on just one aspect of Japanese society – the forms and processes of its stratification; more, because it seeks to treat this topic through the analysis of evidence that relates to Japanese society as a whole, that exists as a fully documented and publicly accessible data-set, and that allows systematic, rather than merely impressionistic, comparisons to be made between Japan and other industrial nations.

The value of Ishida's work is apparent in two main ways. First, it reveals that certain beliefs concerning the distinctiveness of Japanese society that are widely held in the West – and sometimes among the Japanese themselves – are quite groundless or, at all events, are in need of rather radical qualification: for example, the belief that Japan is a highly 'meritocratic' society in which educational qualifications play a greater role than in the West in determining occupational and socioeconomic achievement; or again, that in Japan social class plays no significant part in the shaping of life-chances and life-styles. Such demolition of accumulated myths – for which there never *was* any strong empirical support – is an essential ground-clearing operation. But secondly, and more constructively, Ishida's rigorous yet subtle comparative analyses enable him to show how Japanese social stratification has in fact a clear generic similarity with that of the United States and Great Britain, while at the same time allowing him to identify a number of more detailed respects in which Japan does display its own specific features – and ones, it may be added, that are not apparently waning under the influence of some universally operative 'logic of industrialism'.

Ishida's work is representative of a style of macro-sociology, at once comparative, quantitative and historically-orientated, that has developed rapidly over the last decade or so in several centres in the United States and Europe, including his own universities of Harvard and Oxford. It is, however, one which many Japanese 'area specialists' – and still, in Britain at least, not a few sociologists – will find unfamiliar and, perhaps, in the technical demands that it makes upon them, somewhat forbidding and uncongenial. I urge them not to be too easily put off, and especially not through prejudice against what is often referred to in a dismissive – yet typically ill-informed – way as 'number-crunching'. To those unacquainted, or still unhappy, with sociology in this style, I would make two points which they may find of help as they seek to come to better terms with it.

First, while quantitative techniques of the kind that Ishida employs do indeed generate many numbers, such numerical results, in the form of coefficients, parameters, etc. should be regarded as of only secondary importance. The primary advantage offered by such techniques is *conceptual*. To give but one example, when loglinear models are applied in the study of social mobility, the major gain in sociological understanding that is achieved comes from the distinction that can then be made between absolute and relative rates – and, in turn, from the possibility of testing hypotheses concerning the latter – rather than from any estimation of models that may be attempted. It is therefore on the conceptual argument for which a quantitative technique serves as vehicle that the reader's attention should always focus: the numbers that may follow are complement and elaboration.

Secondly, when as may often occur in considering an exercise in 'quantitative' sociology, one has doubts about the indicators through which the phenomena of interest have been represented and measured, it is important to be clear as to the exact nature and implications of one's response. It is one thing to object that the particular indicators used are unreliable or invalid – implying that other, better ones might be found. To be able to offer, and to evaluate, such criticism is in fact part of the craft of quantitative analysis. It is, however, quite another thing to claim that the phenomena in question simply cannot be quantified at all. For, if this is indeed so, then the extent to which we will be able to talk in any way about the sociological issues that are associated with them is likely to be severely curtailed. For most such issues – and in fact all of those central to the present study – are ones that possess an inescapably quantitative aspect. How can one discuss whether one society is more 'open' or 'meritocratic' than another, whether rates of social mobility are rising or falling, whether status hierarchies are consistent or inconsistent, without in the end engaging in quantitative analysis of some kind? To offer under the banner of a 'qualitative' sociology what amount to no more than quantitative accounts but with the numbers and the key analytical concepts left out, is neither productive nor, indeed, honest.

Hiroshi Ishida's book is one which, in an entirely legitimate way, requires an effort from its readers. The author does not expect them to take his conclusions on trust. Rather, he invites them to follow him through all the stages of his analysis, and offers them every opportunity to check and query his procedures. Those who respond positively to this invitation will be amply rewarded. They will learn a great deal about Japan, about social stratification, and about sociology itself.

JOHN H. GOLDTHORPE

Acknowledgements

The intellectual roots of this study may be traced back to my encounter with two sociologists in my undergraduate days. Kazuko Tsurumi of Sophia University in Tokyo taught me how to ask big sociological questions, and which questions are worth attacking. Her concern with the issues of class and inequality had a profound influence on my intellectual development. It was Otis Dudley Duncan, then of the University of Arizona, who first introduced me to quantitative study in sociology. By observing him close up, I learned a great deal about what sociological research is, and what kind of work is worth imitating. He later took time to read my writings and answered a number of questions on loglinear modelling by mail. Many other thoughtful and stimulating teachers during my undergraduate days contributed to my thinking and the present state of this study: Gail Bernstein, the late Beverly Duncan, and I. Roger Yoshino of the University of Arizona; and Shuichi Kato, Yoriko Meguro, Iwao Munakata, Hideo Okamoto, Joji Watanuki and Hiroshi Yoshida of Sophia University.

This study grew out of my Ph.D. thesis written at Harvard, and I have benefited from the comments and suggestions of my supervisors there: James A. Davis, Jerry Karabel, Lee Rainwater and Ezra Vogel. Ronald Breiger, Mark Granovetter and Harrison White helped me set up this project and inspired me with their good example. My graduate student colleagues at Harvard were a critical resource in developing my ideas of social stratification and mobility. Among a number of friends who provided a supportive and intellectually lively atmosphere, Julie Brines, Sara Freed, Anne Hornsby, Peter Hedstrom, John Lie and Michael Macy patiently listened to my initial findings and made editorial and substantive suggestions on the numerous drafts of my thesis.

The final writing of this work took place after I moved to the University of Oxford. I was able to meet two sociologists who shared my interest in social mobility: John H. Goldthorpe and John M. Ridge. Countless conversations over tea and lunch with them helped me understand not only the British data-set but also the nature of British society. I am especially grateful to John Goldthorpe for opening my eyes to the 'European orientation' to the study of social mobility. I also gained great intellectual advantage from my interactions with fellows, associates and visitors of Nuffield and St Antony's

College including Duncan Gallie, Roger Goodman, Jon Jonsson, A.H. Halsey, Anthony Heath, Colin Mills, Clyde Mitchell, Susan McRae, Clive and Joan Payne, J.A.A. Stockwin and Rosemary Thorp.

I owe an enormous debt to many researchers who collected the national survey data sets which were used in this study. In addition, Professors Ken'ichi Tominaga, Atsushi Naoi and Hideo Okamoto and Mrs Sachiko Imada explained to me the details of the Japanese data-set and provided useful insights into stratification in Japanese society. David Featherman, Aage Sørensen and Erik Olin Wright gave me advice on the weighting and coding scheme for the American data-sets. Computer assistance was provided by Scott Bradner, Cheri Minton and Nancy Williamson at Harvard and by Clive Payne at Oxford. I also benefited from advice on statistical analyses from various experts including Arthur P. Dempster, Robert Erikson, Harry Ganzeboom, Clive Payne, Steve Rytina and Wout Ultee.

Many people kindly read parts or all of the manuscript and helped enormously to improve it, or made useful suggestions concerning the papers which were eventually included in this book: Gary Allison, Steve Anderson, Gerry Curtis, Ronald Dore, Carol Gluck, John Goldthorpe, Roger Goodman, Takeshi Inagami, Takeshi Ishida, Hideo Kojima, Colin Mills, James Morley, David Morris, Hugh Patrick, Susan Pharr, Canice Prendergast, Sawako Shirahase and J.A.A. Stockwin. I am also grateful to Keith Povey for his editorial assistance and to Muriel Bell for her help in the US publication of the book.

Financial and institutional support was provided by Harvard University (Department of Sociology and the Edwin O. Reischauer Institute of Japanese Studies), the Toyota Foundation, John Swire and Sons (Japan), the National Academy of Education (Spencer Fellowship), the University of Oxford (Nuffield College, St Antony's College and the Nissan Institute of Japanese Studies) and Columbia University (Department of Sociology and the East Asian Institute).

Earlier versions of the analyses reported in Chapters 3 and 4 appeared in *Japanese Sociological Review* and *International Journal of Comparative Sociology*. Parts of Chapter 7 were presented at the Nissan Institute of Japanese Studies in February 1987 and at the annual meeting of the Association for Asian Studies in April 1987 and appeared in *European Sociological Review*. Parts of Chapter 6 were presented at the annual meeting of the British Sociological Association in April 1987.

Finally, I would like to thank the members of my family for their continuous support and encouragement. Having been brought up in an academic family, I feel very fortunate that I inherited a lot of 'cultural capital'. My parents always had great confidence in me and rescued me financially, emotionally and intellectually on a number of occasions when I needed help. My wife, Sawako Shirahase, has been a colleague, typist, editor, research assistant and counsellor. Without her technical expertise and emotional and intellectual support, this book would not have been completed.

HIROSHI ISHIDA

The author and publishers also wish to thank the following for permission to reproduce copyright material:

Sekai Shisosha, Tokyo, for data in Table 5.6, from Hiroshi Takeuchi, *Kyoso no Shakaigaku* (1981).

Nihon Keizai newspaper, for data in Table 5.7 (1986).

Yuhikaku, Tokyo, for data in Table 5.8, from Shigeki Koyama, 'Kanryo to Gakureki', in Hiroshi Takeuchi and Makoto Aso (eds), *Nihon no Gakureki Shakai wa Kawaru* (1981).

Michael Useem and Jerome Karabel, for data in Table 5.9, from unpublished draft of Michael Useem and Jerome Karabel, 'Pathways to Top Corporate Management' (1986).

Standard and Poor's, for data in Table 5.10, from Standard and Poor's *Executive/College Survey* (1982).

David Boyd, for data in Table 5.11, from David Boyd, *Elites and Their Education* (1973).

1 Social Mobility in Contemporary Japan

One of the important questions in industrial societies is how people attain their socioeconomic position. It is a question of who gets ahead, and what determines individual success in industrial societies. It is also a question of social mobility. If fathers simply hand over their position to their sons and the allocation of social position is determined by social origin, there will be no mobility between generations. In contrast, a society is relatively 'open' and 'mobile' when social position is allocated independent of social origin, and people can attain positions regardless of their background characteristics. This study attempts to understand the process through which individuals attain socioeconomic status and to examine the pattern of change in class position between generations in Japan through a cross-national comparison with the United States and Britain.

In approaching the issue of status attainment and class mobility in Japan two diverging lines of argument are present. One emphasizes uniformity and convergence, the other distinctiveness. A central proposition of theories of industrial society is that industrial technology and economy have determinate effects on social structure and process; a large measure of uniformity is therefore expected among all industrial nations (Kerr *et al.*, 1960). Of particular interest here is the claim that cross-national similarity in the process of status attainment and in patterns of social mobility will emerge (Treiman, 1970). It is therefore important to see whether these 'genetic features' of industrial societies have emerged in the Japanese case. As the first nation outside the European cultural context to have achieved a high level of industrialization, Japan represents a critical case for theories of industrial society to prove their predictive power.

The second line of argument focuses on national distinctiveness. Ideas stressing cultural and historical peculiarities of stratification and mobility pattern appear to be present in every nation. For example, there exist popular images that America is a land of opportunity and that Britain is a rigid class society (e.g., Morishima, 1977). As early as the writings of Tocqueville ([1835] 1969), America was characterized as an exceptionally fluid society where the lines of class demarcation were blurred. In contrast, nineteenth-century English society was generally considered to have the rigid class structure of the capitalist society (Marx [1867] 1967), and it is often believed that a rigid class barrier continues to characterize modern British society.[1] The idea of Japanese distinctiveness in the process of status attainment can be found in the thesis of 'educational credentialism' in Japan. This thesis highlights the importance of educational credentials in status attainment. In essence, it suggests that opportunities for education are more open in Japan, and that education has much more determinate consequences for socioeconomic success in Japan than in other societies.

The main contribution of this study is to address these two lines of argument using a comparative perspective. Cross-national comparison is essential in evaluating claims both of uniformity and of distinctiveness. An isolated study of mobility in a particular society cannot alone address the question of whether a rate of mobility is high or low, and of whether a process of status attainment is typical or anomalous. Through comparative studies, it becomes possible to identify what is common and what is distinctive about patterns and processes of mobility. The key to comparative study is to assure a high degree of comparability of data-sets. Failure to achieve comparability endangers any conclusions derived from the analysis, since we cannot exclude the possibility that differences in the status attainment processes arise from differences in the data-sets attributable to artefacts of measurement and variable construction. This study therefore works with unit record-level data of social surveys conducted in Japan, the United States and Britain.[2] Instead of relying on already published data sources, efforts are made to construct variables in a highly comparable fashion from the original data. This extensive process of recording is fundamental to comparative analysis and distinguishes this work from many other comparative studies which used published results reported in government statistics and professional journals.

When the thesis of 'educational credentialism' is evaluated within a comparative framework using data of high quality, it receives little empirical support: what was claimed to be distinctive in Japan is not substantiated. Opportunities for education are not particularly open in Japan, and education plays an important role in socioeconomic success not only in Japan but also in the United States and Britain. Furthermore, the process of status attainment is not always uniform across the three industrial nations. For example, the socioeconomic benefits of a college degree show a wide variation; the increase in occupational status and income following the attainment of a BA degree is much larger in the United States than in Japan and Britain. Our comparative analysis, therefore, provides an empirical assessment both of theories of industrial society and the argument about Japanese distinctiveness.

In the following sections of this chapter, we will elaborate various hypotheses and propositions which can be derived from theories of industrial society – in particular, theories concerning the status attainment process and intergenerational mobility in industrial nations. We will also review a number of propositions which claim a 'Japanese distinctiveness' in the process of status attainment.

1.1 STATUS ATTAINMENT RESEARCH AND INDUSTRIALISM

The question of who gets ahead and how status is attained became the primary focus of studies on stratification and mobility in the United States in the 1960s and 1970s. Following the publication of Blau and Duncan's *The American Occupational Structure* (1967), the study of social mobility became an examination of the status attainment process and thus concerned with the process through which individuals attain educational and socioeconomic status throughout their life-course. Blau and Duncan conceived of social mobility as a movement of individuals along a continuum of status hierarchy, and the central aim of the study was the modelling of the causal influence determining the individuals' present positions in the social hierarchy.

One of the most innovative aspects of status attainment research has been the incorporation of intergenerational and intragenerational mobility processes into a single conceptual framework of the socioeconomic life-cycle (Bielby, 1981). The father's status is only one of the relevant factors which affect the individuals' ranked status in a hierarchical system. Characteristics determined at the individuals' birth, including the father's status, are taken as the antecedents of educational attainment, which in turn influences the attainment of occupational and economic statuses throughout the individual's working life. Intergenerational and intragenerational mobility is portrayed as a process through which the status attained either by birth or by achievement at one stage of the life-cycle affects the prospects for all subsequent stages.

The study of the status attainment process derives from the

innovative use of the structural equation model (Duncan, 1966; 1975) which provides quantitative estimates of the relative influences of social origin and of later achieved educational status on socioeconomic attainment. The most prominent theme in the study of status attainment is the comparison of the effect of ascribed forces (that is, factors determined at birth) with the effect of opportunities (that is, factors which are achieved throughout the life-course) on the allocation of individuals in the socioeconomic hierarchy (Featherman and Hauser, 1978). Using a national survey (Occupational Change in a Generation Survey I), Blau and Duncan (1967, p. 241) concluded: '[T]he American occupational structure is largely governed by universalistic criteria of performance and achievement, with the notable exception of the influence of race'.

By the mid-1970s the issue of status attainment had moved to the centre of intellectual discourse among Japanese social scientists working on stratification and mobility. Tominaga and his associates (Tominaga, 1979) collected data on social stratification and mobility in Japan in 1975, a survey similar to the Occupational Change in a Generation Survey (OCGI) in the United States. They also employed the quantitative techniques developed in American sociology (see, for example, Tominaga, 1979; Fujita, 1978). After discussing the relative impact of social origin and of achieved education on the attainment of socioeconomic status, Tominaga (1979, p. 483) concluded:

> Since the effect of respondents' education is greater than that of social origin in determining status attainment, Japanese society is clearly based on the achievement principle of allocation. However, since educational attainment is not independent of social background and educational aspiration which affects educational attainment is also affected by social origin, the effect of ascription is present in the society.

These conclusions about the ascribed versus achieved principles in status allocation are related to the idea of 'industrialism' and the 'convergence thesis'. The idea of industrialism predicted that since industrializing nations were subject to a common set of technological imperatives, in the long run their core structures would become increasingly similar (Kerr *et al.*, 1960; Feldman and Moore, 1962), and that the principle in allocation of social positions would shift from particularistic to universalistic criteria (Parsons, 1951; Levy, 1966).

Japan, the United States and Britain are among the leading industrialized countries in the world. Britain has the longest history of industrialization while Japan is a late starter who achieved rapid economic growth in the post-war period. These three nations had different courses of industrialization, but there is no doubt that they have all achieved the level of 'mature' industrial societies. What then follows from the idea of industrialism is that the three societies should converge to a similar pattern of status attainment, namely the dominance of universalistic over particularistic principles in the allocation of social position. Furthermore, since these countries experienced continuous economic growth and an increasing level of industrialization in the twentieth century, the thesis of industrialism also predicts a declining influence of particularism and a corresponding increase of universalism in the process of status attainment over the period.

It is this thesis of industrialism which underlies this comparative study of social mobility in Japan, the United States and Britain. The process of the attainment of educational credentials and socioeconomic status in the three countries will, accordingly, be subject to detailed examination and comparison. The findings from the subsequent chapters provide only partial support for the thesis. A cross-national similarity is found in the trend toward increasing relative importance of universalistic criteria, namely educational credentials, in the allocation of socioeconomic position. However, uniformity and convergence do not always prevail; a substantial cross-national variation is found in the socioeconomic benefits of education and the relative weight of education, as compared with that of social origin, in determining socioeconomic status.

1.2 EDUCATIONAL CREDENTIALISM IN JAPAN

In the context of Japanese studies, the most provocative hypothesis advocating a Japanese distinctiveness in the process of status attainment probably comes from the idea of 'Japan as an educational credential society'.[3] Six main propositions about the process of status attainment in Japan can be derived directly or indirectly from this idea of 'educational credentialism' (*gakureki-shakai-ron* in Japanese). These six propositions are discussed in detail below. However, as the empirical examination in subsequent chapters will show, they receive little empirical support.

Proposition One: Educational attainment is largely independent of social background in Japan: opportunities for education are in general open to all the members of society, and individuals who are talented and work hard will achieve higher levels of education.

Proposition Two: The effect of educational credentials on the attainment of socioeconomic status is larger in Japan than in other societies. Since the process of educational selection is more competitive in Japan, it is believed that the benefits of obtaining educational credentials are larger in Japan.

Proposition Three: The impact of educational credentials is greater than the effect of social background on socioeconomic achievement in Japan: the universalistic criterion of performance dominates the particularistic criterion of social origin in the allocation of socioeconomic status. And the dominance of education is more pronounced in Japan than in other nations.

Proposition Four: In Japan the effect of higher education on socioeconomic attainment depends on the quality of institution awarding the degree. The effect of college quality on labour market outcomes is stronger in Japan than in other societies.

Proposition Five: The effect of educational credentials is long-lasting in Japan, so that credentials affect not only the initial labour market status at the time of entry into the labour force but also later socioeconomic achievement throughout the entire career. And this long-term effect of education is particularly strong in Japanese society.

Proposition Six: The effect of educational credentials on socioeconomic attainment is homogeneous across all segments of Japanese society: the attainment of educational credentials is assumed to produce an increase in socioeconomic status for all members. All individuals in the society benefit from the investment in an increased level of education.

The first proposition concerns the relationship between social background and education. Although the Japanese general public acknowledges the fact that the students of the University of Tokyo come disproportionately from wealthier families (e.g., Ushiogi, 1978; Sengoku and Matsubara, 1978), since entrance to the higher level of education beyond the compulsory education is exclusively determined by the results of entrance examinations, it is generally believed that opportunities for education are open to all members of society and that merit and hard work determine the outcome of educational competition (Ushiogi, 1980, p. 13; Reischauer, 1977). However, more recent scholarly works by Japanese social scientists (Fujita, 1978, 1981; Ehara, 1977, 1984; Ushiogi, 1975) have documented the dependence of educational attainment on social origin.

The topic of the relationship between social background and education also concerns the role of education in social mobility. If educational opportunities are open to all individuals regardless of their social background characteristics, as the idea of 'educational credentialism' implies, then education holds the key to social mobility to the extent that it affects socioeconomic attainment. On the other hand, if educational attainment is largely influenced by various resources of the family, as some American and European studies appear to suggest (Bowles and Gintis, 1976; Apple, 1979, 1982a, 1982b; Giroux, 1983; DiMaggio, 1982; Bernstein, 1977; Bourdieu and Passeron, 1977), then education plays a role of reproducing inequality and class structure from one generation to the next.

The comparative study of the process of educational attainment in Chapter 3 reports empirical evidence of differential access to education by social origin in all three societies. The findings suggest that the overall effect of social background on educational attainment is by no means weaker in Japan than in the United States and Britain.

The second proposition concerns a comparison of the socioeconomic benefits of education. The advocates of the thesis of 'educational credentialism' in Japan appear to believe that the socioeconomic returns to credentials are greatest in Japan. In reviewing the past literature on the effects of education on the attainment of socioeconomic status, Kadowaki (1978, p. 8) claimed: 'The international comparisons concluded that the estimates of the effect of education were particularly high in Japan. If we assume that the social function of education is to select and allocate individuals with varying ability and skill into different social positions, the Japanese educational system performs this function most efficiently'.

In contrast, Koike and Watanabe (1979) in *Gakureki Shakai no Kyozo* (The Illusion of the Educational Credential Society), argued against 'educational credentialism'. Using the US Census and European Community Earnings data, they showed that the wage gaps between different levels of education were smaller in Japan than in the EC countries and the United States. They concluded that no empirical evidence supported the notion that 'the Japanese society is an educational credential society and therefore wage differentials by different levels of education are large' (Koike and Watanabe, 1979, p. 73).

However, these studies making an international comparison of the socioeconomic benefits of education were based on data-sets which were not strictly comparable. This study uses the national survey data-sets from Japan, the United States and Britain, recodes the original data into measurements with a high degree of comparability, and compares the effect of educational credentials on occupational status and income. The results of the cross-national comparison suggest that the socioeconomic benefits of educational credentials, especially those of college education, are not necessarily larger in Japan than in the United States and Britain.

The third proposition concerning the dominance of achieved over ascribed criteria in the allocation of socioeconomic benefits is in effect a restatement of the thesis of industrialism. The idea of 'educational credentialism' in Japan implicitly accepts the hypothesis of industrialism which states that social position is more likely to be determined by educational qualifications (universalistic criteria) than by social origin (particularistic criteria) in industrial nations (Fujita, 1977).

Previous studies (Tominaga, 1979; Yasuda, 1971; Fujita, 1977, 1983) which claimed the dominance of universalistic over particularistic principles in the allocation of social position compared the effect of education with that of the father's occupational status. However, the father's status is only one of the relevant factors of social background which affect men's socioeconomic success. This study encompasses a wide range of social background characteristics, including the father's occupational status, and examines individual impacts and the overall effect on men's occupational and income attainment. When various factors of social background (such as family income, urban origin and the father's and mother's education) are included in the model, these background characteristics together play at least as important a role as education in the process of socioeconomic attainment in Japan.

The fourth proposition focuses upon the relationship between stratification in higher education and socioeconomic attainment. The difference among middle school, high school and college graduates is only one of the relevant dimensions of educational stratification. Even among men who complete higher education, graduates of prestigious universities occupy a distinctively more advantaged position in the labour market than those from less competitive institutions. Since there is a tremendous competition among high school students in Japan for entrance to prestigious universities (Rohlen, 1983; White, 1987), it is believed that graduating from these prestigious institutions guarantees socioeconomic success and that such benefits must be greater in Japan than in other nations. This issue is discussed in detail in the following section of this chapter and subsequently in Chapter 5.

The fifth proposition, about the long-lasting effect of educational credentials in Japan, is considered to be one of the most serious problems of 'educational credentialism'. As claimed by sociologists of education such as Tomoda (1977) and Hashizume (1976a), the effect of credentials tends to persist over men's entire careers, as if, once acquired, they become an ascribed characteristic. The strongest version of this argument can be found in the OECD (1971) report on the Japanese educational system.

> It is essentially an ascriptive system in the sense that once one is allocated to a group it is very difficult to change one's class. It is like being born into a class, only that in a *degreeocracy social birth takes place later than biological birth*. More precisely it takes place at the time of the various entrance examinations, and like all births it has its pain (Galtung, 1971, p. 139, emphasis in original).

Galtung (1971) characterized Japanese society as a system of 'degreeocracy' in which educational degrees determine later socioeconomic life, as class of origin did in the aristocracy. Highly credentialized men tend to be rewarded in pay and promotion regardless of their job performance, and the effect of credentials persists throughout the career, independent of what men actually do in the workplace.

In order to examine the long-term effect of education, this study (Chapter 4) estimates the net effect of educational credentials on current occupational status in Japan, the United States and Britain, independent of its effect on initial occupational status at the time of entry into the labour market. If the net effect of education on later occupational status is larger than its effect through the first occupation, the results imply that educational credentials affect later occupational achievement long after labour market entry. Furthermore, age–income profiles for different levels of education are compared in order to examine whether the income gaps between levels of education widen as men proceed in their career. As shown in Chapter 4, these exercises provide empirical evidence which is not always consistent with the proposition of educational credentialism that the effect of credentials is long-lasting, and that this long-lasting effect is particularly strong in Japan.

The sixth proposition concerns the homogeneity of the returns to education among members of the different segments of society. None of the Japanese studies on the relationship between education and labour market outcomes specifies the structural context in which education affects socioeconomic attainment.[4] The socioeconomic benefits of education are assumed to be homogeneous among all members of society; no single study questioned whether the effect of education on socioeconomic attainment was different among various groups within it. Chapter 7 examines the effect of education on income, home ownership and stock investment separately for different classes. The analysis shows that investment in education yields different amounts of income returns depending upon class position.

1.3 HIGHER EDUCATION AND THE LABOUR MARKET

The process of status attainment among college graduates deserves special attention. One of the most significant social structural transformations in post-Second World War Japan and the United States has been the development of the educational system, especially the expansion of higher education (Trow, 1970; Ushiogi, 1978). Japan and the United States are among the leading countries in the world in terms of the number of students enrolled in institutions of higher learning and the proportion of the population that is college-educated (Monbusho, 1988).

With a large number of young people now attending college, two significant consequences related to the process of status attainment among college graduates can be expected. The first is that the socioeconomic benefits of college education may decline because of a larger supply of college-educated population (cf. Dore, 1976). The second is that stratification *within* the higher education system may have a significant effect on labour market outcomes.

The decline in the returns to college education is discussed under the issue of 'overeducation' or 'underemployment' (Rumberger, 1981; 1982) of college graduates in the United States. According to Freeman (1971; 1976), the market value of college education declined in the 1970s in the United States due to a downturn in the labour market for college graduates. While the supply of college-going population expanded in the late 1960s, the demand for college and professional graduates began to slow down in the 1970s. The college-educated population was consequently 'overeducated' in the marketplace. In Japan, imbalance between the increase in the college-educated population and that in managerial and professional employment is called 'employment substitution' by college graduates (Koike and Watanabe, 1979; Watanabe, 1976, 1982; Yano, 1980).

This term implies that occupations normally occupied by high school graduates are now being taken by college graduates.

The issue of 'overeducation' has so far received little attention in British society. Although the number of university students increased dramatically in the 1960s, the graduates of institutions of higher education are still a small minority in contemporary British society, and we should expect that the market value of a higher education has not as yet declined.

The issue of the declining market value of a college education is discussed in detail in Chapter 5, using intercohort analysis. The trends in the returns to a college education in the first occupational status report that the benefits of a college education have been generally stable over the period to which our data-sets relate in all three societies despite the increase in the college-educated labour force and the changing historical and economic contexts.

Stratification in higher education and its impact on labour market outcomes are the second issue related to the process of status attainment among college graduates. In Japan, the quality or rank of institutions of higher learning has received much attention both from the general public and from social scientists (Aso, 1983; Takeuchi and Aso, 1981; Hashizume, 1976a, 1976b; Iwauchi, 1980; Takeuchi, 1981; Ogata, 1976). The advocates of 'educational credentialism' in Japan often claim that the impact of stratification in higher education on labour market outcomes is evidence of the strong correlation between educational credentials and socioeconomic attainment.

College quality appears to influence various labour market outcomes in Japan. Ando (1979) has shown that the distribution of income and occupational status is dependent upon the ranking of the college. In addition, the graduates of 'prestigious' colleges are more likely to get jobs in large firms and more likely to occupy managerial positions than the graduates of 'non-prestigious' schools (Hashizume, 1976a; Koike and Watanabe, 1979; Iwauchi, 1980; cf. Takeuchi, 1981).

Many large firms recruit candidates exclusively from the 'prestigious' universities, especially high-ranking national universities and two prestigious private schools. Graduates of less competitive schools are not even considered for job interviews and examinations. The practice of preselecting job applicants according to the quality of their colleges is called the 'school designation system' (*shiteiko seido* in Japanese). A 1975 survey by the Japan Recruiting Centre (Nihon Rikuruto Senta, 1975) showed that approximately one-third of the large firms (which employ more than 5000 employees) adopt this system and that larger firms are more likely to prefer this system than smaller ones. Many researchers (for example, Matsuura, 1978, p. 146; Hashizume, 1976a, p. 11) claimed that the practice of 'school designation' was much more prevalent than the responses of the surveys showed.

The recruitment practices of large firms reflect the public recognition of the relationship between college quality and career success. According to the cross-national survey reported by the Prime Minister's Office of Japan (Sorifu, 1978), 63 per cent of Japanese respondents stated that graduation from 'top-ranking' colleges would become a more important aspect of a college degree in obtaining better pay and status, while only 8 per cent of American and 7 per cent of British respondents did so.[5] Both scholarly studies and public opinion thus suggest that the effect of college quality on socioeconomic attainment among college graduates in Japan is a particularly strong one.

In the United States, stratification in higher education and its impact on labour market outcomes appear to have attracted less attention than in Japan. However, a few studies of the status attainment process have paid direct attention to the institutional rankings in higher education. These studies (Solmon and Wachtel, 1975; Solmon, 1975; Trusheim and Crouse, 1981; Tinto, 1980; Karabel and McClelland, 1987) have in general shown that graduates of prestigious colleges are more successful in the attainment of higher socioeconomic status than the graduates of lower-status institutions, and that this effect of college quality persists even after controlling for such factors as social background, ability and aspirations. Since almost 50 per cent of all American young people attend institutions of higher learning and a pattern of 'overeducation' or 'underemployment' of college graduates has been demonstrated by scholarly studies, stratification within American higher education is likely to have a significant impact on the alumni's achievement (Karabel, 1972; Clark, 1962).

While the institutional rankings of the colleges independently affect the alumni's bargaining power in the labour market, some argue that elite institutions are disproportionately attended by individuals from already advantaged backgrounds, and that the apparent effect of college quality may overestimate the independent direct effect (Karabel and Astin, 1975; Useem and Miller, 1975; Bowles and Gintis, 1976). To the extent, however, that institutional quality has an independent effect, it operates so as to reinforce the advantages of the already privileged.

In Britain, the relationship between stratification in higher education and the labour market is highlighted by the dominance of two ancient universities, Oxford and Cambridge, in access to elite positions in British society (e.g., Sampson, 1982). The privileged access of Oxbridge seems to cover all major institutional spheres in Britain: the Church of England, the military, the judiciary, politics, the civil service and the private sector. Furthermore, Stanworth (1984) has shown that the role of Oxbridge in elite recruitment has become more important during the century: 'Oxford or Cambridge educations have become more common amongst most elites in the last eighty years or so' (Stanworth, 1984, p. 261).

Chapter 5 of this study proposes to examine the relationship between stratification in higher education and labour market outcomes within a comparative framework. While studies in all three societies document the impact of college quality on labour market outcomes, no cross-national studies have been conducted to estimate the relative magnitude and strength of its effect. The major aim of this study is to compare the effect of institutional rankings on the attainment of occupational status and income in Japan and the United States;[6] it tests the proposition derived from the thesis of 'educational credentialism' in Japan that the college quality effect is greater there than in the United States. The analysis also compares the extent to which stratification in higher education reproduces inequality between generations in the two societies. While such a reproduction function is reported in the United States, none of the studies on the impact of college quality in Japan controls for the effect of social background. It is thus important to examine whether the apparent college quality effect documented by Japanese social scientists overestimates its independent impact. Finally, Chapter 5 sheds light on the relationship between stratification in higher education and the process of recruitment and formation of elite groups in Japan, the United States and Britain. We propose to examine educational origins of the top corporate and bureaucratic elites in the three societies.

1.4 CLASS STRUCTURE, CLASS MOBILITY AND INDUSTRIALISM

The study of the status attainment process dominated American research on social stratification and mobility in the 1960s and 1970s. It has now become the major paradigm in the field, at least in the United States (Featherman, 1981; Bielby, 1981; Sørensen, 1986).

Status attainment research also had a considerable impact on studies of social stratification and mobility in Japan (e.g., Tominaga, 1979) and continues to influence many cross-national researches (e.g., Treiman and Terrell, 1975; Lin and Yauger, 1975; Kerckhoff, 1974). However, there is different orientation to the study of social mobility.

Partly in reaction to the prevalence of status attainment research, there has been a revival, especially among European sociologists, of the tradition of studying social mobility from the perspective of class structure and class formation. The difference between the two orientations, as Goldthorpe (1984; 1987) has pointed out, lies mainly in the context of stratification within which mobility takes place. Status attainment research defines 'mobility' within the context of a status hierarchy. The primary focus of status attainment research is the movement of individuals along the status hierarchy across the successive stages of the life-cycle. Social mobility is conceived as occurring along the continuum of a status hierarchy which can be ranked by different status characteristics, such as occupational prestige and income (Goldthorpe, 1984).

The alternative orientation defines 'mobility' within the context of class structure. Individuals are located within a structure of interrelated social collectivities which can be defined by market and production relations. Social mobility is conceived as movements of individuals which involve detachment from, and attachment to, distinguishable social collectivities (Goldthorpe, 1987).

While status attainment research conceives of mobility as an upward and downward movement of individuals along the status hierarchy, mobility research from the class structure perspective does not necessarily imply that mobility be upward or downward. Goldthorpe (1984, p. 3) summarizes the sociological significance of mobility research from the two diverging orientations:

> [W]here the context of mobility is seen as that of a class structure, it is in any event unlikely that what happens to individuals will be the only focus of attention: the implications of mobility for classes as collectivities will tend to be of at least comparable concern. However, where the context is that of a social hierarchy, it is indeed the rate and pattern – and the determinants – of the movement of individuals within that hierarchy that must represent the issues of paramount importance.

It is crucial, therefore, to recognize the importance of studying mobility from the perspective of class structure, rather than from that of status hierarchy. 'Class structure' is defined in terms of the social relations of production and marketable skills.[7] Two fundamentally qualitative dimensions in the social relations of production are pivotal in determining class: control over the means of production and control over labour (Wright, 1978; 1979).

Control over the means of production divides the workers from the capitalists. However, defining class by the possession of, or separation from, the means of production ignores the role of top managers and boards of directors in the corporations. Under advanced capitalism, as more and more business becomes incorporated, the form of ownership is transformed to collective and institutional ownership (Miyazaki, 1976; Okumura, 1978, 1984; Berle and Means, 1932; Useem, 1984). The location of the power of control over the means of production resides not only in individual owners but also in the top executives who may or may not own stock in the corporation. The class which has control over the means of production thus encompasses boards of directors as well as individual owners.

The second qualitative dimension which defines class involves control over labour. Control over labour differentiates the professional–managerial class from other workers (Ehrenreich and Ehrenreich, 1979; Abercrombie and Urry, 1983). Members of the professional–managerial class have the capacity to organize their own labour and are relatively free of direct supervision. In the case of the managers, they have the capacity to supervise other people's labour. The professional–managerial class occupies a distinct position in terms of the relationship to its own labour process and the labour process of others. In contrast, workers are those who have control neither over the means of production nor of labour. However, workers can be further differentiated by the nature of their work and the extent of the marketable skills they possess. They can be broken down into three categories: non-manual working class, skilled working class, and semi-and non-skilled working class (see Chapter 6 for a detailed discussion of the definition and operationalization of class).

Using class categories defined in terms of social relations of production and marketable skills, this study examines the patterns of intergenerational class mobility in Japan, the United States and Britain. Although the studies of class structure informed by the Neo-Marxist or Marxist perspective have appeared both in Japan (Ohashi, 1971; Shoji, 1977, 1982; Hara, 1979; Steven, 1983) and the United States (Wright *et al.*, 1982; Wright, 1985), none of these studies examined class mobility (but, see Griffin and Kalleberg, 1981; Robinson, 1984a, 1984b). The examination of patterns of class mobility addresses questions not answered by the analysis of class structure: what is the extent of class inheritance for different class categories in the three societies? Is mobility mainly induced by changes in the class structure between the generations in the three societies? Are the patterns of class fluidity, or the patterns of mobility net of the structural shifts in class distribution, similar in the three societies?

Mobility research (Erikson *et al.*, 1979, 1982, 1983; Portocarero, 1983a, 1983b, 1985; Erikson and Goldthorpe, 1987a, 1987b) which was guided by the class structure and class formation perspective and undertaken in modern European societies has shown considerable cross-national variation in the patterns of observed gross mobility – or, as it is often called, absolute mobility. This variation was primarily accounted for by 'historically-determined differences' in the shape of the class structures (Erikson *et al.*, 1982, p. 1). In contrast, the same studies showed that the patterns of mobility net of structural changes – often called relative mobility or class fluidity – were remarkably similar among European societies. Erikson and Goldthorpe (1987a) even proposed a model of core class fluidity which characterized the basic pattern of relative mobility among nine European nations. These studies appear to support the thesis proposed by Featherman, Jones and Hauser (1975) concerning the similarity in the patterns of social mobility across industrial societies (hereafter the FJH thesis). These authors claim that an essential similarity in mobility patterns cannot be found at the observed 'phenotypical' level of absolute mobility but is present at the 'genotypical' level of relative mobility or class fluidity (cf. Erikson *et al.*, 1983).

The examination of the patterns of class mobility in Japan, the United States and Britain is directly relevant to this thesis. Since all three countries are highly industrialized capitalist societies, this thesis predicts that the three societies show very similar patterns of relative mobility but not of observed absolute mobility. Chapter 6 of this study focuses on the patterns of observed mobility by estimating the extent of total mobility and by analyzing inflow and outflow mobility matrices which respectively indicate the patterns of class trajectory and class recruitment. Chapter 6 also describes the features of class fluidity – that is, the patterns of mobility net of structural shifts in class distribution between generations. These exercises appear to emphasize the importance of the insights of the FJH thesis.

Another substantive theme discussed in Chapter 6 concerns the issue of trends in intergenerational class mobility. Featherman, Jones and Hauser (1975) recognized that mobility rates might change during the transition period from a pre-industrial to an industrial society, but they agreed that, once a 'mature' industrial society had been reached, it would show stability and cross-national similarity (cf. Grusky and Hauser, 1984; Hauser *et al.*, 1975a, 1975b; Tyree *et al.*, 1979; Erikson and Goldthorpe, 1987a). In contrast to this 'threshold theory', a more dynamic prediction is proposed by some advocates of the thesis of industrialism or 'post-industrialism' (Treiman, 1970; Bell, 1973).

Treiman (1970; cf. Treiman and Yip, 1987) claims that a natural tendency towards greater 'openness' and equality is inherent in industrialism. As societies increase the level of industrialization, according to Treiman, there is a tendency for class fluidity (or relative chances of mobility) steadily to increase. Industrial societies have '(a) more extensive education, (b) more pervasive mass communications, (c) greater urbanization, and (d) increased geographical mobility', and these factors function to 'break down the rigidity of class structure of traditional society' (Treiman, 1970, p. 219).

Tominaga (1979) applied this thesis of industrialism to the Japanese case. He analyzed intergenerational occupational mobility tables which were constructed from three national surveys of social mobility conducted in 1955, 1965, and 1975. By using the Yasuda index (Yasuda, 1964) as the measure of relative chances of mobility, he showed a trend of a 'rapid and consistent increase' in relative mobility chances and concluded that this trend suggested 'the fact that structural changes produced by industrialization promote equal opportunities' (1979, p. 83).

Chapter 6 examines trends in class mobility in Japan using a cross-cohort comparison. It evaluates empirically the claim of increasing 'openness' in the class structure of post-war Japan and examines stability and change in relative chances of mobility across successive cohorts. These analyses lead us to question the notion of increasing 'openness' in Japanese society.

1.5 CLASS STRUCTURE, STATUS HIERARCHIES AND LABOUR MARKET INEQUALITY

Although there are two divergent orientations to the study of social mobility, status hierarchies and class structures are closely interrelated at the empirical level. A 'class' can be composed of individuals with various status characteristics. While differences in class position can be reflected in the socioeconomic status variations of the individuals occupying class positions, class positions themselves need not be perfectly correlated with other characteristics, such as occupational status and income.

In the United States, as we have argued above, status hierarchies have occupied the central location in the study of stratification. Occupational status and class were recognized as conceptually and empirically distinct notions and included in statistical analyses only relatively recently (Kalleberg and Griffin, 1980; Wright, 1980b; Wright *et al.*, 1982). Furthermore, Wright (1979; 1985) claims that class plays a central role in explaining income inequality and has a stronger predictive power than occupational status in determining income attainment. Wright (1979) concludes that class appears to be a dominant variable in the explanation of inequality in contemporary American society.

In Japan, the intellectual tradition (especially that of Marxism) emphasized the centrality of class in the structure of inequality (Yamada, 1934; Noro, 1930; Hirano, 1967; Ouchi, 1971). However, many social scientists came to question the notion that class structure constitutes the basis of stratification in Japan. One of the debates which centred around the issue of class structures and status hierarchies was the intellectual exchange among three prominent social scientists on the issue of 'the new middle class'.[8]

Murakami (1977), a theoretical economist, sparked off the debate by arguing for the emergence of 'the new middle mass' (Murakami, 1984). He first cited the result of a social attitude survey conducted by the Prime Minister's Office: over 90 per cent of the respondents stated that their standard of living was in the middle level. While he recognized that such surveys were of only limited significance, he further claimed that living standards had rapidly risen in post-war Japan and that there had appeared in contemporary Japanese society a huge intermediate stratum which belonged neither to the lower nor the upper class and whose members were highly homogeneous in their life-styles and attitudes. There was no clear class structure as such, but what had emerged in post-war industrial Japan was the tendency of 'non-structuration in various dimensions of status hierarchies' (Murakami, 1984, p. 188). In virtually every dimension of status hierarchies, class boundaries were blurred: 'There are no longer any fundamental differences in life styles – ways of talking, dressing or living – among lower managers, clerks, factory foremen, manual workers, shopholders, shop assistants or farmers' (Murakami, 1977, p. 7).

Kishimoto (1977), writing from a Marxist point of view, reacted with scepticism to Murakami's claim about the emergence of a new middle mass. He showed that the people who identified themselves as middle class in the attitude survey did not in fact occupy a middle position within the distribution of income, savings and home ownership. For example, 62 per cent of those with an annual income of less than US$ 5000 in 1984 responded that their standard of living was in the middle level (Sorifu, 1984, p. 11). Kishimoto claimed that increased consumption and homogeneity of life-style were surface phenomena and that the basic principle of the society as a whole was the 'bipolarity between capitalists and workers' (Kishimoto, 1978, p. 151). The middle class, according to Kishimoto's definition, was composed of people who possessed sufficient personal assets to be able to support themselves by disposing of those assets. In particular, land and home ownership, and stock, securities and bank savings were crucial assets for self-sufficiency, especially in case of a sudden change of economic conditions. He concluded that since the majority of the Japanese people did not possess these crucial assets and were vulnerable to economic change, 'the emergence of the new middle class with sufficient personal assets is a total illusion in contemporary Japan' (Kishimoto, 1978, p. 247).

Tominaga (1977) joined the debate over the new middle class by reporting empirical findings from an analysis of a social stratification and mobility survey.[9] He rejected Murakami's claim of a trend toward homogeneity but also disagreed with Kishimoto's idea of bipolarity between capitalists and workers. According to Tominaga (1977; 1989), stratification in contemporary Japan is marked by a tendency towards status inconsistency. Because rewards and resources are distributed by pluralistic criteria, only a small proportion of the population can be characterized as occupying consistently low or high statuses. The majority of the population cannot be called unequivocally high or low, and therefore when viewed from a macro-perspective, what can be termed a 'diverse middle class' has emerged.

In addition to the ideas proposed by these three scholars, there is another perspective which contributes to the debate on the relationship between class structure and status hierarchies. The dual structure hypothesis which is found in the work of labour economists (e.g., Ujihara and Takanashi, 1971; Odaka, 1984; cf. Koike, 1988) focuses on the differentiation among employees according to firm size. This hypothesis claims that various rewards and resources are differentially distributed by firm size even among workers who belong to the same class. For example, differences in wage, range of fringe benefits and working conditions are found between manual workers in large firms and those in small and medium-sized firms. This hypothesis emphasizes the importance of firm size in labour market stratification among employees.

In order to demonstrate the relationship between class structure and status hierarchies, this study examines the distribution of various status characteristics among classes. Four hypotheses about the status composition of classes can be derived from the four perspectives noted above. First, the hypothesis of homogeneity of status attributes, which is derived from the work of Murakami, states that since class boundaries are blurred in virtually every dimension of status hierarchies, the status composition of various classes will be highly homogeneous. Second, the hypothesis of bipolarity endorsed by Kishimoto predicts that classes will be polarized into two basic groups of capitalists and workers with respect to their status characteristics. Third, the hypothesis of status inconsistency proposed by Tominaga predicts that various status characteristics of classes will be inconsistent, so that classes cannot be characterized by consistently high or low status attributes. Fourth, the dual structure hypothesis predicts that the status characteristics of employees will be differentiated not only by their class positions but also by the size of the firm in which they are employed. These hypotheses are empirically examined in Chapter 7.

Chapter 7 also takes up the issue of the importance of class in determining the distribution of rewards in society. In the United States, many sociologists (Wright, 1979, 1985; Wright and Perrone, 1977; Kalleberg and Griffin, 1980; Griffin and Kalleberg, 1981; Robinson and Kelley, 1979) have documented that class affects income and other job rewards, independent of occupational status. Wright (1979) claimed that the effect of class on income was stronger than that of occupational status.

However, none of the Japanese studies which argued for the centrality of class in the determination of rewards in the society showed that the differential distribution of various rewards among classes could not be explained by the difference among these categories in status characteristics, such as education and occupational status.[10] In other words, they have not shown that income differences between the capitalists and the workers, for example, are not the result of the higher level of education and occupational prestige of the capitalists. In order to demonstrate the importance of class in determining the distribution of rewards in society, it is crucial to document that class affects the attainment of income and other rewards, independent of education and occupational status. This study therefore estimates the predictive power of class in explaining inequality of income, home ownership and stock holdings in Japan and the United States, independent of the effect of education and occupational status.[11]

The final issue to be examined in the interplay among class structure, status hierarchies and inequality of rewards in a society is the structural effect of class on the status attainment process. This issue derives from the critical appraisal of the intellectual basis of status attainment research that has emerged in American studies on stratification. Critics (e.g., Spilerman, 1977; Baron and Bielby, 1980; Horan, 1978) claimed that status attainment research had been preoccupied with the effects of individual characteristics, and paid little attention to structural features of society that might mould the process of status attainment. American studies of stratification (Beck, Horan and Tolbert, 1978; Tolbert, Horan and Beck, 1980; Bibb and Form, 1977; Stolzenberg, 1978) incorporated various structural variables – such as indicators of labour market segmentation or of class relationship – into their structural equation models of the status attainment process.

Following these studies, it is important to place the process of status attainment within the structural context of class. In other words, the effect of education on attainment of income, home ownership and stock investment should be analyzed separately for different classes. The returns to education may vary considerably from one class to another. Wright (1979) and Winn (1984) have already shown that individuals who occupy different class positions receive different income returns to education in the United States and Sweden. There is therefore no reason to assume that the structural effect of class on the relationship between education and income and other rewards is absent in Japan (cf. Hashimoto, 1986).

This analysis has profound implications for the hypothesis of 'educational credentialism' in Japan. As discussed above, one of the propositions derived from the idea of 'Japan as an educational credential society' is that the effect of educational credentials on socioeconomic attainment is homogeneous across all segments of Japanese society: educational achievement will benefit everyone who works hard enough to obtain qualifications, regardless of his class position. The homogeneous socioeconomic benefits of education have been taken for granted among the advocates of 'educational credentialism'; it is thus crucial to test this proposition in order to assess the validity of the thesis in Japan.

In sum, the interplay among class structure, status hierarchies and inequality of labour market rewards is analyzed in three basic ways in this study. First, various status characteristics of classes are investigated in detail. The examination of the status composition of classes is concerned with testing four hypotheses about the relationship between class structure and status hierarchies. Second, the effect of class on the attainment of income, home ownership and stock holdings is estimated. The analysis assesses the relative explanatory power of class as compared with the power of education and of occupation in determining inequality of labour market rewards. Third, the process of status attainment is placed within the structural context of class; it examines how class conditions the way education affects attainment of rewards in the labour market.

1.6 OUTLINE OF THE BOOK

Having described the various issues that this study will address, it may be useful to outline briefly the chapters which follow. Chapter 2 describes in detail the Japanese, American and British data-sets used in this study and the questionnaire questions and coding scheme for variables. Chapters 3–5 examine the process of status attainment in Japan, the United States and Britain. Chapter 3 focuses on the determinants of educational attainment, and Chapter 4 discusses occupational and income attainment. Chapter 5 focuses on college graduates and their socioeconomic attainment, with a special emphasis on the effect of college quality. Chapters 6 and 7 place class at the centre of analysis. Chapter 6 discusses class structure and intergenerational class mobility, and Chapter 7 examines the interplay among class structure, status hierarchies and labour market rewards. Finally, Chapter 8 attempts to bring together the major findings in the preceding chapters and to arrive at some general conclusions about social mobility in Japan.[12]

Notes

1. However, these ideas of national distinctiveness have not been substantiated by empirical studies (Lipset and Bendix, 1959; Miller, 1960; Blau and Duncan, 1967; Treiman and Terrell, 1975; Goldthorpe, 1987; Erikson and Goldthorpe, 1985, 1987a, 1987b; Kerckhoff *et al.*, 1985).
2. It is important to remind the readers at the very beginning of this study that this comparative analysis will examine men aged between 20 and 64 in the three countries. It is not our intention to exclude women from the analysis, but the limitation of the data-sets available for the analysis makes this inevitable (see Chapter 2 for details).
3. For an extensive literature review of the studies on 'educational credentialism' in Japan, see Yamazaki *et al.* (1983).
4. The only exception is a study by Hashimoto (1986). Grusky (1983) also showed regional variation in the process of status attainment.
5. The results come from national surveys of men and women working in organizations (thereby excluding employers, self-employed workers, farmers, students, and those not in the labour force) aged 35 or over in Japan, the United States and Great Britain in 1976. The surveys were planned by the Prime Minister's Office of Japan and conducted by independent research institutions in the three countries (for details, see Sorifu, 1978, Chapter 2).
6. The British survey did not ask the names of the university which the respondents had attended. Our analysis on the effect of college quality on socioeconomic attainment is therefore restricted to Japan and the United States.
7. For a variety of Neo-Marxist and Neo-Weberian conceptions of class, see, for example, Giddens (1973), Parkin (1979), Goldthorpe (1987), Wright (1979, Chapter 1; 1980a), Calvert (1982), and Marshall *et al.* (1988).
8. The debate originally took place in a series of articles on the new middle class which were published in *The Asahi* newspaper in 1977. Three scholars who took part in the debate later published books expanding their ideas (Murakami, 1984; Kishimoto, 1978; Tominaga, 1979). The summary of their arguments is taken from both the original articles and the expanded versions. Some other Japanese scholars made various comments on this issue (e.g., Naoi, 1979; Ariyoshi and Hamaguchi, 1982; Goto, 1985).
9. He relies especially on the work by Imada and Hara (1979) which empirically documented the tendency towards status inconsistency in Japanese society.
10. The only exception is a study of Hashimoto (1986) which showed that income differential by class was not explained by education and occupational status.
11. Since the British Survey did not ask for information on home ownership and stock investment, our analysis is restricted to Japan and the United States.
12. It may be appropriate here to add two comments regarding the format of the text. First, the Japanese language requires that some vowels be

pronounced short and others long. When Japanese is written in roman script, the long vowels are sometimes shown by a line drawn above them for example, *hōhō* which means methods in English. We have not, however, adopted this format; this is first because there is no agreement among Japanese linguists about which vowels should be pronounced long and which ones short, and secondly because it is simpler to read in unstressed orthography, especially for those not familiar with the language. The second comment regarding format deals with the tables, the sources for which are not shown when the data in the table are constructed from the social survey data-sets described in Chapter 2. Sources are indicated only when the data in the table come from sources other than our own social survey data sets.

2 Data and Variables

2.1 DATA

The Japanese data used in this study came from the 1975 Social Stratification and Mobility National Survey (hereafter SSM).[1] The first national survey on stratification in Japan was conducted in 1955 as a part of a project of 'comparative social stratification and mobility' by the International Sociological Association. Since then, a national survey on stratification has been conducted every decade to facilitate trend analysis. The 1975 SSM constitutes the third survey, and is the only survey which provides a public-use tape. The 1975 SSM was designed by 29 1975 SSM committee members who included sociologists, statisticians and scholars in other fields. They were responsible for constructing questionnaires and a pre-test, and for survey design and analysis; the actual fieldwork was conducted by the Public Opinion Science Society (*Yoron Kagaku Kyokai*), an independent survey organization.

The 1975 SSM is a sample consisting of men between the ages of 20 and 69 residing in Japan in 1975. The sample design was a stratified two-stage one. Groups of wards, towns, villages and cities were used as primary sampling units, selected in strata from 3309 national electoral blocks by population size, industry characteristics and geographical proximity. Resident registers for each primary unit were used to select random individuals. The design provided 303 primary units, and the male sample initially drawn was 4001. Personal interviews and follow-ups were conducted between 15 October and 30 November 1975. The response rate of 68.1 per cent yielded a usable sample of 2724 (for details of sample design, see Ando, 1978). The response rate was somewhat lower than that of the American and British data-sets.[2] This lower rate can be explained in part by the fact that SSM was not carried out by the Census Statistics Bureau or other government organization which people are more likely to trust. Another possible explanation is that since surveys of this kind which ask for detailed information about family background and income are rarely conducted in Japan, some of the people contacted declined to participate in the survey (see Tominaga, 1979, p. 27).

The 1975 SSM collected detailed information on (1) the occupations held by respondents at various work life-stages and their employment status, industry, size of firm and managerial status, (2) education, income and assets, (3) social background, such as father's education and occupation and the number of siblings, and (4) attitudes such as job satisfaction, party preference and class consciousness. We will not reproduce the entire text of the survey questionnaires, but we will describe in detail the variables used in this study in the following section (for a complete list of survey items, see Tominaga, 1979 or SSM National Survey Committee, 1976).

The American data came from two sources: the 1973 Occupational Change in a Generation II Survey (hereafter OCG) and the 1980 Class Structure and Class Consciousness Survey (hereafter CSCC).[3] David Featherman and Robert Hauser were the principal investigators for OCG and Erik Olin Wright organized the CSCC survey. The details of the sampling procedure are described elsewhere (US Bureau of the Census, 1978; Hauser and Featherman, 1977; Featherman and Hauser, 1978; Wright 1982; Wright *et al.*, 1982). It is sufficient to note the following points: (1) the 1973 OCG consists of 33 613 (weighted sample) men aged 20–65 representing about 53 million men in the civilian non-institutional population in the United States. The survey was carried out by the US Bureau of the Census as an adjunct to the March 1973 Current Population Survey (CPS). The sample comes from a stratified, multi-stage cluster sample, and the data were collected by a mailout survey with telephone and personal follow-up by CPS interviewers. (2) The 1980 CSCC contains a total of 1499 respondents in the labour force, 92 unemployed men and 170 housewives not in the labour force. The data were collected in a national telephone survey conducted by the Survey Research Center at the University of Michigan. The sample comes from a two-stage systematic cluster sample of telephone numbers in the coterminous United States.

The British data came from the 1972 Oxford Mobility Survey (hereafter OMS).[4] The survey was undertaken by the members of the Oxford Social Mobility Group based at Nuffield College, University of Oxford. The details of the sampling procedure can be found elsewhere (Goldthorpe, 1980; Halsey, Heath and Ridge, 1980). The 1972 OMS is a sample consisting of men aged between 20 and 64 resident in England and Wales in 1972.[5] A stratified two-stage sample design was used to draw male electors from Electoral Registers, and a usable sample size was 10 309. Respondents who were not resident in England and Wales at age 14 were excluded because it was not possible to recode the educational experience of these respondents into the educational qualification categories described below.[6]

2.2 SAMPLE RESTRICTIONS

This study is restricted to the employed male labour force between the ages of 20 and 64.[7] The age range is determined by OMS which has the smallest age range of all the samples.[8] SSM, OCG and OMS include only male respondents, thus female respondents are excluded from CSCC. Students, unemployed persons, retirees and house husbands are all excluded from this analysis. In the Japanese data, students were not asked any of the labour market questions including personal income and occupation. SSM also grouped unemployed, retired, house husbands and all others who were not actively in the labour force in a 'no occupation' category for the employment status question. Consequently, for Japanese not actively in the labour force, there is no labour market information available. The comparative sample considered here can thus include only active labour force members. After incorporating these restrictions, the total sample size was 2467 for SSM, 29 086 for OCG, 739 for CSCC and 9482 for OMS.[9]

2.3 WEIGHTING

The US Bureau of the Census (1978) has developed elaborate weights for the Current Population Survey (CPS), so that weighted sample counts will sum to population counts by age, sex, or race/ethnicity. The weights also adjust for coverage errors, non-interviews and sampling variability in the CPS. The 1973 OCG, which is a supplement of CPS, therefore uses weights to inflate the sample counts. The average weight was 1576.46, and the weighted sample size was 33 613 (Featherman and Hauser, 1978).

The CSCC data set was weighted by a post-hoc weight factor. According to Wright (Wright *et al.*, 1982, p. 717), the CSCC data-set is 'overrepresented both in higher status occupations and in higher levels of education'. He recommends weighting because without it the sample will not reproduce the Census distribution for education and occupation.

The SSM raw data tape does not contain a weight factor; the SSM committee did not calculate weights for the data. When we compare age, occupational and educational distributions of the sample with the comparable distributions in the 1970 and 1975 Japanese Census, a slight discrepancy is found. Tables 2.1–2.3 show the comparison of the two distributions. SSM oversampled managers by 3.1 per cent and farmers by 4.5 per cent, while it undersampled elementary school graduates by 4.6 per cent and the youngest cohort (20–29) members by 3.6 per cent. The ideal situation would have been to employ a similar weighting used in OCG, so that sample counts would have summed to population counts, and coverage error, non-response, and sampling variability would then have been corrected for. However, the US Bureau of the Census (1978, Chapter 5) weight estimation procedure is extraordinarily complicated. Furthermore, the absence of detailed technical information on the SSM survey design precludes the possibility of replicating even a crude version of the weighting procedure employed for OCG. Given the lack of technical information and the minimum departure from the Census distributions, we will use the unweighted sample. This decision is consistent with the approach of Japanese researchers who have already analyzed SSM (e.g. Tominaga, 1979; Fujita, 1978).

Table 2.1 Percentage distribution of occupation in 1975 SSM and 1975 Japanese Census among men aged 20–69

Japanese Census major occupation groups	*1975 SSM*	*1975 Census*	*Difference*
Professional and technical workers	7.0	7.3	−0.3
Managerial workers	9.6	6.5	+3.1
Clerical workers	13.7	13.3	+0.4
Sales workers	11.5	13.0	−1.5
Farmers, lumbermen and fishermen	15.1	10.6	+4.5
Workers in mining	0.3	0.3	0.0
Workers in transport and communication	6.2	6.9	−0.7
Skilled and production workers	32.0	36.0	−4.0
Protective workers	1.3	2.1	−0.8
Service workers	3.2	3.9	−0.7
Non-classified workers	0.1	0.1	0.0

Source: 1975 SSM Survey and 1975 Population Census of Japan, vol. 5, Table 8.

Table 2.2 Percentage distribution of education in 1975 SSM and 1970 Japanese Census among men aged 20–69

Education	*1975 SSM*	*1970 Census*	*Difference*
No education	0.6	0.2	+0.4
Elementary, junior high and old system higher elementary school	47.0	51.6	−4.6
Senior high school and old system middle school	34.6	31.0	+3.6
Junior college and higher professional school	4.4	4.1	+0.3
University and graduate school	10.6	9.9	+0.7
Still in school	2.8	3.1	−0.3

Source: 1975 SSM Survey and 1970 Population Census of Japan, vol. 2, Table 9.

Table 2.3 Percentage distribution of age cohort in 1975 SSM and 1975 Japanese Census among men aged 20–69

Age cohort	*1975 SSM*	*1975 Census*	*Difference*
20–29	25.1	28.7	−3.6
30–39	26.0	25.4	+0.6
40–49	23.8	22.3	+1.5
50–59	15.2	13.5	+1.7
60–69	9.9	10.1	−0.2

Source: 1975 SSM Survey and 1975 Population Census of Japan, vol. 2, Table 2.

The British OMS data set is not weighted either. The distribution of the respondents in OMS by age and by region showed a very small difference from that of the 1971 Census (Goldthorpe, 1980, pp. 285–6), and the Oxford researchers did not recommend weighting because the weight factor made no significant difference to the data-set (Goldthorpe, 1980, p. 282). We will therefore use the OMS data in its unweighted form.

2.4 VARIABLES

This section describes the questions and coding scheme for the variables used in this study. Comparability among the three societies was the primary locus in constructing variables. We tried to employ an identical coding scheme for the same variables in various surveys. Consequently, not all the available information in a specific survey was used to construct a variable (see, for example, the description of the education variable below). Loss of information, however, should be compensated by the effort to ensure comparable measurements.

Race

The variable race exists only in the American data. This does not, however, preclude the existence of a so-called 'minority group' in Japanese society. There are two major minority groups: Korean and Chinese who live in Japan permanently, and the *burakumin* (the descendants of the outcastes) people, who are Japanese in racial and ethnic origin but are treated as a minority group for historical reasons. According to the Ministry of Justice (Sorifu, 1986), about 758 000 Koreans and Chinese were living in Japan in 1985 as aliens (about 0.6 per cent of the total population). Aliens are those who do not hold Japanese citizenship and are thus not entitled to most government benefits. Koreans and Chinese constituted about 90 per cent of all aliens in 1985, and most of them were born in Japan and were permanent residents while still holding alien status (cf. Lie, 1987; Lee and DeVos, 1981). They are excluded from the SSM survey population since they do not have Japanese citizenship; they nonetheless occupy a distinct minority status, and are often engaged in lower-status occupations.

According to the official government statistics (Hirasawa, 1983, p. 6), the *burakumin* population exceeded 1 million in 1975. The Buraku Liberation League, one of the *burakumin* organizations, claims that the *burakumin* population is over 3 million. It is, however, widely agreed that the *burakumin* people occupy a disadvantaged position in Japanese society; they are overrepresented in the lower end of the occupational ladder, and are often engaged in leather crafts (Yoshino and Murakoshi, 1977, Chapter 5). The average educational attainment among *burakumin* people is known to be lower than that of the entire population, and the status attainment process of these minority people is probably different from the rest of the population (Hirasawa, 1983).[10] Besides the *burakumin* population, a very small number of the *Ainu* minority group resides in the northern part of Japan, Hokkaido. Unfortunately SSM does not provide minority status information; we have therefore to bear in mind that some minority group members were probably included in the survey without being identified.

In the British OMS data, there were a small number of respondents who were of non-white ethnic origin; they were mostly from the former British colonies. However, these respondents accounted for a very small proportion of our sample (0.2 per cent), primarily because we excluded the respondents who were not resident in England and Wales at age 14. The number was so small that it was not possible to construct a separate race/ethnic variable.

In the American data, 'white' respondents were assigned a score of 1 on this variable and all others were assigned 0. This variable thus measures the advantage of being white rather than non-white. We decided to include this variable in the American analysis, even though a comparable variable did not exist in the Japanese and British data-sets. This decision was based on the notion that we should not restrict our analysis to common factors in different societies by discarding what was peculiar to one country (cf. Treiman and Terrell, 1975). Eliminating a crucial internal variation might result in an artificial homogeneous pattern of status attainment (Burawoy, 1977).

Education

Education is one of the variables which it is difficult to make comparable across societies. SSM asked the respondents, 'Which kind of school in the list did you last attend?' and then 'Did you graduate from that school?' The list purports to include most types of schools from both the old pre-war and the new post-war educational system. They are: old system elementary school (6), old system higher elementary school (8), old system middle school (11), old system high school (14), old system university and graduate school (16), new system middle school (9), new system high school (12), new system junior college and technical college (14), new system university and graduate school (16) and no education (0).[11] The numbers in parentheses indicate years of schooling which were assigned to each category. If the respondent did not graduate from the school, he was assigned a score for the preceding level. The variable for years of schooling is thus a quasi-continuous one ranging from 0 to 16. These questions on educational attainment reflect the Japanese notion that educational qualifications obtained by graduating from the institution, not simply years of schooling, affect socioeconomic success.

Educational credential dummy variables were also constructed. They are a middle school diploma dummy, a high school diploma dummy and a bachelor's degree (hereafter BA) dummy. Respondents with old system or new system middle school diplomas and those with higher educational attainment were assigned a score of 1 and otherwise 0 for the middle school diploma dummy. The high school diploma dummy assigned a score of 1 to those who received old or new high school diplomas and a score of 0 otherwise. The BA dummy gave a score of 1 to college degree holders and 0 otherwise.

OCG and CSCC asked for the highest grade the respondent had completed, and recoded in single years except for the highest category which included all people with 17 or more years of schooling.[12] In order to assure comparability with the Japanese data-set, single years were recoded into a quasi-years of schooling variable as follows: 0 through 5 = 0, 6 and 7 = 6, 8 = 8, 9 and 10 = 9, 11 = 11, 12 and 13 = 12, 14 and 15 = 14, 16 or more = 16. The diploma dummies were constructed in a similar fashion. The middle school diploma dummy assigned a score of 1 to those with 8 years' or more schooling and otherwise 0. The high school diploma dummy gave a score of 1 to respondents with 12 years' schooling or more and a score of 0 to those with 11 years' or less. The BA dummy assigned a score of 1 to respondents with 16 years' or more and a score of 0 to those with less than 16 years' schooling.

The correlation between quasi-years of schooling and original single years is 0.980 for OCG and 0.986 for CSCC, and mean and variance for quasi-years are virtually identical to those for original single years.[13] Recoding neither changed the mean nor reduced the variance. Although the effects of education measured by single years on occupational status and income are slightly higher than the effects of education measured by quasi-years, the differences are minimal. We will therefore refer hereafter to quasi-years of schooling as years of schooling.

The diploma dummies will be used to allow non-linear relationships between education and socioeconomic status. The percentages of variance in occupational status and income explained by the three diploma dummies are significantly higher than the percentages explained by years of schooling. We will use these diploma dummies as much as possible to assess the differential impacts of various educational credentials on socioeconomic attainment. Years of schooling will be used as a summary measure of the effect of education on labour market outcomes.[14]

The British educational system differs markedly from its Japanese and American counterparts, and it is therefore difficult to construct a comparable education variable. In order to have some degree of comparability, two dimensions of educational qualification are distinguished in Britain: academic and vocational/professional qualifications. Academic qualifications can be compared with a high school diploma and a bachelor degree in Japan and the United States while vocational and professional qualifications do not have comparable counterparts. Academic qualifications are determined by the question on school exams. Three levels of academic qualification are distinguished: (1) respondents who had an Ordinary School Certificates or Matriculation or at least one O-level General Certificate of Education (hereafter O-level),[15] (2) respondents who had a Higher School Certificate or an A-level GCE (hereafter A-level), and (3) respondents who obtained a bachelor's degree or a Diploma of Technology (hereafter BA degree).[16]

OMS also collected detailed information on vocational/professional qualifications obtained by the respondents. The responses are grouped into the following four groups: (1) Ordinary National Certificate and Intermediate Certificate of the City and Guilds of London Institute (hereafter ONC), (2) Higher National Certificate and Final Certificate of the City and Guilds (hereafter HNC), (3) lower professional qualifications, such as nursing and primary and secondary school teaching (hereafter Level C), and (4) higher professional qualifications, such as accounting, architecture, medicine and law (hereafter Level B). ONC-level certificates were obtained normally after 2 to 3 years of part-time study at technical college or other establishment of further education while the students were concurrently in employment. HNC-level certificates ordinarily required a further 2 years of study.

Professional qualifications are divided into two groups according to the classification of Qualifications in *Qualified Manpower Tables, Sample Census 1966, Great Britain* (OPCS, 1970b, Appendix C). Lower-grade professional qualifications are called 'Level C' qualifications and are determined by membership of certain professional associations and by certificates awarded by such associations. Examples of these associations are: British School of Osteopathy, Central

Midwives' Board, General Nursing Council, Institution of Electrical and Electronic Tehnicians and Royal Institute of Public Health and Hygiene. Higher-grade professional qualifications are called 'Level B' qualifications; examples of professional associations in this category are: Architectural Association, Association for Medical Workers, Institute of Chartered Accountants, Institution of Mechanical Engineers and Law Society.

These academic and vocational/professional qualifications are used in our study as a number of dummy variables representing a specific qualification category. There is no equivalent of the 'years of schooling' variable in the British data-set. Education is measured by distinct qualification categories along the two dimensions.

College quality

In addition to vertical differentiation (primary, secondary and higher education), stratification in higher education is measured by survey items in Japan and the United States. SSM asked the respondents who had attended four-year colleges and universities their school's name and their affiliated department (or their major). College names were recoded into three categories indicating college quality. The highest category includes all 'imperial' universities, Tokyo Kogyo University, Hitotsubashi, Kobe, and two most prestigious private schools, Waseda and Keio. The second category includes other national and public universities, and major private schools such as the Tokyo *Rokudaigaku* (five prestigious private schools in Tokyo), Doshisha and Ritsumeikan. The third category contains all other universities.[17] The graduates of highly selective schools comprise slightly less than 20 per cent, the graduates of selective school 48 per cent, and the rest of the college graduates 32 per cent of all college graduates.

These three categories were constructed because they reflect the popular conception of stratification in Japanese higher education. It was a common practice among Japanese companies until the late 1970s openly to limit applicants by accepting only those who had attended certain specified schools (Hashizume, 1976a). Large companies interviewed only students who went to one of the 'first-rank universities'. Less prestigious companies sought job applicants from the so-called 'second-rank schools'. The ranking usually reflects the difficulty of the entrance examination, but the older schools generally have advantages over the newer ones. The ranking of institutions of higher education in Japan is thus made conspicuously clear by the college entrance examination and employers' preference. There is probably little disagreement among Japanese people about the ranking of the three categories and the schools included in each category.

The ranking of the colleges in the United States is not as clear as in Japan. The best available measure, and the one which is used most often, is the Astin's college selectivity score, a rank based on the average SAT scores (verbal and mathematical) of college freshmen for over 1600 institutions (Astin, 1971). This takes values from 400 to 1600. Astin's selectivity score is further recoded to three categories: 1154 and above, 998 to 1153 and less than 998. The cutting points are based on a schema from Astin (1971), and this three-category version is adopted so as to have the same number of categories and approximately the same distribution as in Japan. The graduates of highly selective institutions, those of selective institutions, and those of non-selective institutions account for 16 per cent, 45 per cent and 39 per cent of all college graduates, respectively.

In the regression analysis reported in Chapter 5, the category for non-selective institutions is used as a base category, and two dummy variables are included in the equation. The dummy variable for highly selective institutions measures the socioeconomic advantage of graduating from highly selective institutions rather than from non-selective ones, and the dummy variable for selective institutions measures the advantage of graduating from selective institutions rather than from non-selective ones.

Current occupation

SSM coded responses to 'what kind of work are you doing?' into 289 detailed occupational categories developed by the 1975 SSM committee (Yasuda and Hara, 1982). These occupational categories were then recoded to (1) Japanese Occupational Prestige Scores which were constructed by Japanese sociologists (Okamoto and Hara, 1979; Naoi, 1979), (2) Standard International Occupational Prestige Scores (Treiman, 1977), and (3) the SSM major occupation groups.

Japanese Prestige Scores (hereafter JPS) for the 288 detailed occupational categories had already been provided by prior research (Tominaga, 1979, Appendix 1). The recoding procedure for assigning International Occupational Prestige Scores (hereafter IPS) to the Japanese occupational categories was carried out in a straightforward way. Following Treiman's 'Coding Rules for Assigning Standard

Scale Scores' (1977, Appendix 9.1), each Japanese occupational category was matched to the most specific occupational category of the International Standard Classification of Occupation for which the IPS is estimated. Generally there was no difficulty in assigning a standard classification category.[18] IPS scores for 288 detailed occupational categories are shown in the Appendix, p. 265. JPS ranged from 26.7 and 83.5 with a mean of 45.28 and a standard deviation of 10.99. IPS ranged from 13 and 78 with a mean of 41.54 and a standard deviation of 11.73. The correlation between IPS and JPS was 0.894.[19]

Finally, the detailed 288 initial occupational categories in SSM were recoded to eight SSM major occupation groups: professional and technical workers, managers and administrators, clerical workers, sales workers, skilled workers, semi-skilled workers, unskilled workers, and farmers.

The British OMS asked the respondents the kind of work they were doing at the time of interview and coded the responses into 222 occupational unit groups of the 1970 Population Census Classification of Occupations (OPCS, 1970a). These detailed categories were then recoded to (1) the Hope–Goldthorpe scale of occupations (which used both occupation and employment status to assign scores), (2) IPS, and (3) the SSM major occupation groups. The construction of a Hope–Goldthorpe scale (hereafter H–G scale) had already been undertaken by the members of the Oxford Social Mobility Group (Goldthorpe and Hope, 1974). The assignment of IPS to 222 occupations was done exactly the same way as the procedure used in the Japanese survey. The IPS scores are shown in the Appendix, p. 274. The correlation between the H–G scores and the IPS scores was 0.852. The correlation is lower than that in Japan and the United States, primarily because the H–G scale uses occupational and employment status in its construction.

To determine the current occupation, OCG and CSCC asked the respondents 'what kind of work are you doing or do you do?' The responses were coded into 1970 Census three-digit occupational codes and then recoded to (1) Hodge–Siegel–Rossi Prestige Scores (hereafter HSR), (2) IPS, and (3) the SSM major occupation groups. The HSR scores were taken from the rating system developed at the National Opinion Research Center of the University of Chicago (see Davis, 1982, Appendix F and G; Siegel, 1971). The IPS scores for the 1970 Census three-digit codes were provided by Treiman (1977, Appendix C.2.).[20] Finally, the detailed 1970 Census occupational classification was recoded to the eight SSM major occupation groups described above. Eight occupational groups were used for constructing class categories (see Chapter 6).

The correlation between IPS and HSR was 0.934 in both OCG and CSCC. The figure seems to correspond with the correlation (0.963) estimated by Treiman's early study (1977, p. 176; see also Inkels and Rossi, 1956; Hodge, Treiman, and Rossi, 1966). The high correlations between IPS and prestige scores developed in each country indicate that there is strong agreement in occupational prestige assessment among the three countries, and that occupations in the three countries can be ranked on a comparable scale. We will thus in this study use IPS as a measure of occupational status. Using a standard scale allows us to compare occupational movement along the same dimension and compare the increment in occupational status produced by independent variables in the three countries. For example, if a BA degree would increase IPS by 28 points, the increase in occupational prestige would correspond to the same occupational movement of, say, a carpenter becoming an electrical engineer in the three countries.

It is also legitimate and interesting to use prestige scores defined separately by each country. Some researchers claim that the term 'prestige' differs from one country to another, and that we cannot compare directly the 'prestige' of a certain occupation in one country to that of the same occupation in another.[21] While there are some virtues in using the separate occupational status scale, there is a major drawback: we would not be able to compare directly, for example, the effect of education on occupational status in Japan and the United States because a point increase in occupation status would not reflect an equivalent movement along the same dimension in the three societies. Since the major concern of this study is to compare the impact of education on occupational status in the three countries, we *do* need a comparable measurement of occupational status.

First occupation

OCG asked the respondents, 'Describe the first, full-time civilian job you had after you completed your highest grade in school'. CSCC did not contain questions related to first occupation. OMS asked the question 'What was your very first full-time job after you finished your full-time education?' SSM asked the respondents, 'We would like to ask you about your occupational career. What kind of work were you doing in your first occupation?'

The question in SSM did not specify that the first occupation be a full-time occupation after the completion of education. This poses a problem of comparability. The failure to specify the occupation after the completion of education, however, does not result in a major distortion in comparability since very few men in Japan return to school after entering regular employment. Many Americans interrupt their schooling to enter full-time employment and some years later return to school to complete a degree (cf. Hogan, 1978) and some of the British attend further education while they are in employment. In contrast, the linkage between education and the labour market is fairly rigid in Japan, and the life-course sequence from education to occupation is seldom reversed. The failure to specify full-time occupation poses a much more serious problem. Some SSM respondents might have reported a part-time job or a school vacation job as their first occupation. The first occupation in the Japanese data-set is consequently more likely to be concentrated in lower-entry jobs and to have lower prestige scores than the first occupation in OCG and OMS. However, the members of the 1975 SSM Committee believe that the probability of reporting a part-time job is very small.[22]

There is a possibility of underreporting of first occupation in OCG as well. Featherman and Hauser (1978, Appendix C and p. 272, n. 14) reported that approximately 12 per cent of all men in the 1973 OCG replicate was subject to such misreporting. A large fraction of them appeared to be young men who were still in school, so our sample restriction presumably excludes them from the analysis. Nonetheless, there might be a small portion of respondents in our sample who reported part-time or school vacation jobs as their first occupation and this would consequently lower their prestige scores.

While OCG may be subject to such misreporting and there may be a possibility that the first occupation reported in SSM is not limited to full-time occupation after school completion, we have no way of eliminating the part-time and school vacation jobs and jobs before school completion. For the purposes of this analysis, we will thus consider first occupation in SSM, OCG, and OMS as if they were comparable, without mentioning this potential built-in discrepancy of the variable further. Readers should, however, be aware of the possibility of a non-comparable element in this variable.

The responses to the first occupation questions were coded into detailed occupational categories, and then into (1) Japanese or HSR prestige scores or a H–G scale of occupations, (2) IPS, and (3) eight

SSM major occupation groups. The correlations between IPS and JPS, between IPS and HSR, and between IPS and the H–G scale were 0.856, 0.939 and 0.904, respectively. We will use IPS to measure occupational status as we did for current occupation.

Managerial status

SSM asked the respondents who were employees their formal managerial status. The detailed formal managerial titles were recoded into three categories: managerial positions, supervisory positions, and non-management. CSCC asked the respondents who were employed by someone else to report their position within his business or organization. The three possible responses were the same as the SSM recoding. OMS classified the respondents who were not self-employed into managers, supervisors/foremen, and other employees in the employment status variable. The managerial status variable will be used to operationalize class categories (see Chapter 6 for detailed procedure).

Employment status

The employment status in OCG and CSCC is straightforward. It contains three basic categories: self-employed, employed by someone else, and work without pay. The employment status in OMS is more detailed: (1) self-employed with 25 or more employees, (2) self-employed with less than 25 employees, (3) self-employed without employees, (4) managers, (5) foremen/supervisors, (6) apprentices and trainees, (7) family employees, and (8) other employees.[23] The employment status in SSM is rather complicated. There are five categories: (1) owners and top executives, (2) small employers who employ one to four employees, (3) self-employed independent workers, (4) family workers, and (5) general employees. The most problematic category is the 'owners and top executives' category. It is composed of owners who are self-employed and top executives who are not self-employed but have a substantial control over the business and probably own stock in the company. The 'employer' category in SSM thus contains a small number of people who are not self-employed. CSCC asked the respondents who were employed by someone else for a profit-making business whether or not they were an owner or part-owner of the firm. If the firm were incorporated, he would be an owner but classified as not self-employed. By including these employee owners in the 'employer' category, the employment status in SSM and CSCC will be reasonably comparable.

Income

SSM asked the respondents to report their total individual income before taxes in the past year. The 'total individual income' includes wage and salary income, income from assets, interest and other sources of unearned income, and income from part-time and temporary jobs. The SSM respondents were asked to choose one of bracketed income categories rather than to report actual income amount. Fortunately, the income interval for each bracket was identical (500 000 yen or $1667 when $1US=300 yen in 1975), except for the first one which was less than 250 000 yen or $833. There was no open-ended category. The mid-point for each bracket was used as an estimate of the actual raw income for the individual. For the first category, a mid-point of 125 000 yen (mid-point between 0 and 250 000 yen) or $466 was used. Finally, yen were converted into dollars by applying the average exchange rate of 300 yen=$1 US in 1975.[24] The mean income was $7167 and the standard deviation was $4441.

OCG coded the total annual individual income in raw dollars in the past year. It was then recoded into income brackets identical to SSM and then assigned mid-points. 'No income' and 'negative income' people were grouped into the lowest income bracket, because the lowest category in SSM included everyone whose income was less than 250 000 yen or $833. The mean for the raw dollar individual income was $10 848, with a standard deviation of $8488, while the mean for the recoded income was $10 866 with a standard deviation of $8487. A slight increase in the mean is due to the fact that all respondents in the lowest category, including those with no and with negative income, were assigned $417 in the recoded income variable. This recoding procedure unfortunately discards some detailed information available in the original coding, but it does assure that the income variable is measured in a comparable way in both societies.

CSCC asked for the total individual earning before taxes in 1979. CSCC did not ask for the total individual income. The total individual income was estimated by summing four sources of income: the total individual earning, income from social security or any other government programme, income from rented or sold property, and income from investments.[25] The responses were coded into one of 11 income brackets which ranged from 'under $5000' to '$75 000 or over'. The actual dollar amount of income was estimated by taking the mid-point and extrapolating in the open-ended category. The extrapolation method was based on the Pareto curve.[26] After estimating the actual dollar amount of income in 1979, the amount was converted to constant units of 1972 dollars by applying the Consumer Price Index to deflate the 1979 income.[27] Four sources of income (in 1972 dollars) were summed to estimate the total individual income. Finally, as in OCG, the 1972 dollars were recoded into income brackets identical to SSM and then assigned mid-points. The mean income was $13 400 and the standard deviation was $12 587.[28]

OMS asked for the total individual earnings (including ordinary overtime pay) from the respondent's main job before taxes in 1972. The responses were coded to one of 13 income brackets and the mid-points were assigned by the Oxford Social Mobility group. The original income brackets were not available in the coding book, so these mid-points were used and converted into US dollars by applying the average exchange rate of £2.606=$1 US. It is important to notice, however, that OMS asked for the total individual earnings income rather than for the total individual income from all sources including non-wage income. The income variable in OMS is therefore not strictly comparable with that in the Japanese and American data-sets. Consequently, the distribution of earnings income in Britain is more equal than that of total income in Japan and the United States, and the difference in income variation among the three societies has a significant impact on the effect of educational credentials on income (see Chapter 4).

Work experience and decay

The 'cumulative work experience' variable was calculated from age and education in OCG and CSCC. The formula, age − total years of school completed − 6, purports to measure time potentially spent working since age 6. The 'work experience' is estimated in OMS using age of respondents and age when respondents left school. The 'work experience' variable in SSM is constructed by age and age at first job. There were 85 respondents who did not report age at first job. The formula for the American data was used for these respondents to rescue some cases. We also calculated 'work experience' in SSM from age and education. This correlated 0.985 with 'work experience' constructed by age at first job. The 'work experience' variable is not a direct measure of work experience nor job tenure; some respondents worked while they were in school, and others did not work even when they had left school.

'Decay of work experience' refers to the square of 'work experience'. It will estimate the non-linear function of income by age when introduced with 'work experience'. A significant negative coefficient for 'decay', along with a positive slope of income on 'experience', will reflect reduction in income at older ages as productive capacities are likely to decline or 'decay'.

Assets

Two kinds of assets are included in the comparative analysis: home ownership and investment in stocks and bonds. SSM and CSCC asked the respondents whether they owned their home. SSM also asked the respondents whether they invested in stocks and bonds. CSCC asked the respondents whether they received 'any income from investments other than real estate or savings, such as from stocks, bonds, profits from business, and so on'. While CSCC asked for income from investments, rather than for investments themselves, it is very unlikely that those who invested in stocks and bonds did not receive any income from them. The respondents who owned their home and invested in stocks and bonds were assigned a score of 1 and a score of 0 otherwise.

SSM also asked the respondents whether they owned land, possessed sports club membership, and had air-conditioned homes. These three additional items can be used as an indicator of total assets and wealth. OMS asked no questions on assets.

Parental education

SSM asked the respondents 'which school in the list did your father (or mother) last attend?' The same list used for respondent's education was provided to identify the educational level. The same coding scheme for education was thus used to transform the level of school to years of schooling. However, since the respondents were not asked whether or not their father (or mother) had graduated from the school, each level includes those who completed the level and those who did not.

OCG asked for the highest grade of school the respondent's father (or mother) had completed. When the respondents were not living with their father when they were 16 (or when they were 'growing up'), the highest grade of school completed by the head of their household (or father substitute) was reported.[29] The responses were coded into single years of schooling as was the respondent's education. Single years of schooling was further recoded into quasi-years of schooling to retain the comparability, though the recoding procedure was different from that of the respondent's education. Since SSM did not ask a question about graduation or completion of the school they reported, the following recoding scheme was used: 0 = 0, 1 through 6 = 6, 7 and 8 = 8, 9 = 9, 10 and 11 = 11, 12 = 12, 13 and 14 = 14, 15 or more = 16. CSCC asked no questions on parental education.

The parental education in OMS was determined based upon parents' school exams and qualifications, and type of secondary school which they attended. Parents with any school exams (including GCE O-level and A-level, School Certificate Matriculation, and Higher School Certificate) or with Level C and Level B qualifications or with BA degrees were assigned to the highest level of education. Since there was only a small proportion of fathers (6 per cent) and mothers (5 per cent) in our sample who fell into this category, it was not possible to make further distinction between academic and vocational qualifications. Among those who had no academic and vocational qualifications, the parents who attended selective secondary schools were assigned to the middle level of education.[30] The rest of the parents who did not attend selective secondary schools and had no qualifications were assigned to the lowest level of education. As in the case of the respondent's education, the parental education variable in the British data is coded differently from that in the Japanese and American data sets.

Father's occupation

SSM asked respondents about the kind of work their father did when they were 15 years old. OCG and OMS asked about the kind of work their father (or the head of the household if the father was absent) did when they were 16 years old (OCG) or 14 years old (OMS). CSCC asked 'what kind of work did your father (or father substitute) generally do while you were growing up?' Despite a slight difference in wording, these questions can be thought of as measuring the same variable.[31] The responses were coded to detailed Japanese occupational categories (SSM), the 1970 US Census three-digit occupational categories (OCG and CSCC), and the 1970 Population Census Classification of Occupations (OMS). These occupational categories were then assigned to (1) JPS or an HSR or H–G scale, (2) IPS, and (3) eight SSM major occupation groups. The correlation between JPS and IPS was 0.889. The correlation between the HSR scale and IPS was 0.926 in OCG and 0.933 in CSCC. The correlation between the H–G scale and IPS was 0.806.

Siblings

OCG and OMS asked about the number of brothers and sisters including stepbrothers, stepsisters, and children adopted by the parents and asked the respondents to exclude siblings who had lived but were now deceased.[32] The responses were recoded and the range was from 0 to 10 or more.

SSM asked 'how many brothers and sisters do you have including yourself? Please exclude those who are now deceased'. The response to this question minus 1 was recoded as the 'number of siblings' which ranged from 0 to 10 or more. The SSM coding instruction did not specify whether stepbrothers and stepsisters were included. But the number of stepsiblings in Japan is probably very small because of the low divorce rate and has a negligible impact on the analysis. CSCC asked no question about the number of siblings.

Family income and well-being at the age of 15

OCG asked for the family income when the respondent was about 16 years old. OCG asked its respondents to choose one of 13 income brackets ranging from 'no income' to '15 000 dollars or more'. These 13 categories were recoded into five groups as follows: far below average (less than $500), below average ($500–2999), average ($3000–7999), above average ($8000–14 999), and far above average ($15 000 or more). These categories were determined so that the distribution of respondents would be almost identical to SSM relative categories.

OMS asked the respondents whether they had the following amenities at home when they were aged 14: a telephone, a refrigerator, an inside flush lavatory, and a fixed bath or shower. The responses were coded on a five-point scale from none of these (0) to all of these (4). The possession of these amenities is a good indicator of living standard of the family in which the respondent grew up.

SSM asked the respondents what was 'the well-being or living standard of the family at the age of fifteen, compared with the average family then'. The respondents were asked to select one of five responses: far below average, below average, average, above average, and far above average. Family well-being at about age 15 is therefore a five-point scale ordinal variable in three data-sets. CSCC asked no questions on economic well-being of the family when the respondent was growing up.

Farm upbringing and urban origin

Farm upbringing is determined by the father's occupation. If the father (or the father substitute in the American and British data) engaged in farm occupation, the respondents were assigned a score of 1 and otherwise 0. Urban origin is determined by a place of residence when the respondent was about 15 years old. In SSM, the respondents who grew up in a town, city, and metropolitan area were assigned a score 1 and otherwise 0. In CSCC, the response of 'city and suburban area' was assigned a score of 1 and otherwise 0. OCG allowed respondents to answer 'the same place I do now'. A score of 1 was therefore assigned to the respondents who reported city or suburban area and those who responded 'the same place' and the current residence was city or suburban. Farm upbringing and urban/rural origin are not the same thing. Some men work on farms without living in rural areas, while some others live in rural areas and are engaged in non-farm occupations. The correlations between farm upbringing and urban origin were not high: 0.299 in SSM, 0.490 in OCG, 0.496 in CSCC, and 0.335 in OMS.

Age and cohort

All surveys asked the respondents their birth date and coded their age. Three age cohorts were then constructed as follows: age 20–34, age 35–49, and age 50–64.[33] Each age cohort entered the labour market at different periods, and experienced different job opportunities and career trajectories. This study will examine the process of status attainment separately for each age cohort.

Notes

1. I am indebted to the 1975 SSM Committee for access to the data tape and to Professors Ken'ichi Tominaga, Atsushi Naoi, and Hideo Okamoto and to Mrs Sachiko Imada for advice on the coding scheme.
2. The Occupational Change in a Generation II Survey had a response rate of 88 per cent and the Class Structure and Class Consciousness Survey had a response rate of 78 per cent. The British survey had a response rate of 82 per cent.
3. For access to these American data-sets and advice on the weighting and coding scheme, I am grateful to Professors David Featherman, Aage Sørensen, Jerry Karabel and Erik Olin Wright.
4. I am indebted to the Oxford Social Mobility Group for access to the OMS data-set.
5. We will hereafter refer to the OMS data-set as the 'British' data-set even though the survey covered only England and Wales.
6. It was even difficult to recode education of the respondents who were educated in Scotland and Ireland because the Scottish and Irish educational systems were different enough from the English one to cause problems in codings. I am grateful to Mr John Ridge in helping me understand the details of the educational systems and survey items of the OMS.
7. In Chapter 3 where we analyze the determinants of educational attainment, we include individuals who were not in the labour force. Lack of labour market information does not necessarily exclude these non-active labour force members from the analysis of educational attainment.
8. In Chapter 7 where we analyze only the Japanese and American data-sets, the age range is 20 to 65.
9. The sample size was further reduced when some of the variables included in the analysis had missing cases.
10. DeVos and Wagatsuma (1966) and Yoshino and Murakoshi (1977) provide an introduction on *burakumin* in English.
11. For the details of the school system in Japan written in English, see Passin (1965), Cummings (1980), and Rohlen (1983).
12. OCG obtained information on the respondent's education, current occupation and income from a March 1973 Current Population Survey interview which was conducted with the most responsible adult who happened to be at home when the interviewer arrived at the household. So most of these data probably came from wives rather than male respondents (US Bureau of the Census, 1978). The accuracy of the information is probably less than it would have been had it been obtained from the respondent himself.
13. In the OCG data, mean and variance for quasi-years are 11.46 and 3.66 while those for original single years are 11.83 and 3.46, respectively. In the CSCC data, mean and variance for quasi-years are 12.42 and 2.72 and those for original single years are 12.66 and 2.75, respectively.
14. The years of schooling and high school diploma dummy were highly correlated in all surveys. This high correlation forces us to preclude the possibility of including both years of schooling and diploma dummies in

predicting labour market outcomes. In other words, it is not possible to test the effect of obtaining a diploma or a degree over and above single years of schooling.

15. A small number of respondents who had a Certificate of Secondary Education (CSE) and clerical and commercial qualifications, such as typing, shorthand, book-keeping, or a RSA commercial certificate, are classified into the 'no academic qualification' category. Matriculation was technically distinct from the Ordinary School Certificate, but no distinction is made here.
16. The BA degree category also includes respondents with a master's and doctor's degree.
17. See Ando (1979) for recoding college names to college ranking.
18. Some occupational categories such as 'miso and soy sauce makers' did not have substantive matches to a specific standard category; In these cases the closest unit group (aggregate of specific occupational categories) was assigned. For 'miso and soy sauce makers', the unit group 'food preservers' was assigned.
19. This figure is slightly lower than the Treiman's estimate (1977, p. 176) of 0.96 using IPS and the Japanese Prestige Scores developed in the 1955 SSM survey.
20. I used the IPS scores for the 1970 Census occupational classification created by Treiman except for 'school administrators (college)' category. Treiman assigned the IPS of 86 which was the highest IPS among the 1970 Census occupations. He matched 'school administrator (college)' with the 'university president, dean' category in the international standard classification of occupation. I used my own judgement to match the same Census category with 'university and higher education teachers' which is the unit group for 'university president, dean'. The associated IPS score was 78. My decision was based on the idea that most 'school administrators (college)' were not university presidents or deans and that the score of 86 overestimated the amount of prestige conferred to this category.
21. For example, carpenters are considered an above-average prestige occupation in Japan (JPS is 45) while the HSR score for carpenters is about an average of 40. Similarly, a carpenter becoming an electrical engineer would result in a 29 point increase in the HSR prestige scores in the United States, while the corresponding occupational movement in Japan would produce only a 16 point increase (notice that the corresponding change in the IPS was a 28 point increase). However, this is an extreme example; generally the same occupational movement results in an almost equivalent increase or decrease in prestige scores in the three countries. Moreover, as we have seen, the correlations between the prestige scores developed independently in each country and the IPS were extremely high (see also Treiman, 1977, Chapter 5).
22. This observation is based upon personal communications with a number of 1975 SSM Committee members.
23. Apprentices and trainees are classified as 'other employees' for our coding purpose.
24. The annual average exchange rate between yen and dollar was 299 yen

= $1 US in 1975 and 292 yen in 1974. We have used 300 yen = $1 US as a rule of thumb in this analysis.

25. These non-earning incomes were received either by the respondent or by the respondent's family. There was no way to distinguish the two. The total amount of individual income in CSCC is thus slightly overestimated. The mean and the standard deviation are higher in CSCC than in OCG.
26. Miller (1971, Appendix B) provides a basic exposition of the Pareto curve and estimation procedure. The estimated mid-point for the highest category in CSCC was 153 081.
27. Compared with a dollar in 1972, the purchasing power of a dollar in 1979 was about 58 cents according to the Consumer Price Index (US Bureau of the Census, 1979, p. 474).
28. SSM and OCG asked for the income in the past 12 months. CSCC asked for the income for the previous year. This means that the income year does not necessarily coincide with the survey year.
29. Including father substitutes slightly increases valid cases. But the non-response rate (9 per cent) of SSM is not particularly higher than that of OCG (6 per cent), and the inclusion of substitutes should not have a significant impact on comparability.
30. Selective secondary schools include all independent (both HMC and non-HMC), direct grant, and technical/central schools.
31. As in the case of father's education, SSM did not ask for information on father substitutes when the respondent's father was absent. Since the head of the household when the father was absent tended to be the mother who was more likely to be in the lower end of the occupational ladder, the exclusion of these father substitutes probably increased the mean occupational status for father's occupational prestige. However, we do not know the exact impact of this exclusion on our analysis. Readers should thus bear in mind a slight difference in the measurement of father's occupation and father's education variables in the three countries.
32. OMS did not ask respondents to exclude siblings who were not alive at the time of interview.
33. Since the survey years are different among the four surveys and we have not adjusted for this difference, the same age cohorts among the three surveys do not imply that they entered the labour market at the same period.

3 The Process of Educational Attainment

3.1 INTRODUCTION

This chapter examines the classic topic of social background and education within a comparative framework. Three overriding substantive concerns govern our analysis. The first is the issue of the equality of educational opportunities. The idea of 'educational credentialism' in Japan implies that opportunities for education are in general open to all members of the society, and that individuals are competing on an equal basis to achieve higher levels of education. Education therefore holds the key to social mobility to the extent that it affects the attainment of socioeconomic status. Traditional status attainment research in the United States also focused on the mobility function of education. Treiman and Terrell (1975, p. 577), for example, found that 'in both countries [the United States and Great Britain] education is largely independent of social origins and thus serves mainly as a channel of social mobility'.

However, studies by sociologists of education in Japan (e.g., Ushiogi, 1975; Yamamoto, 1979) reported evidence which casts doubt on the idea of educational credentialism. Ehara (1977; 1984), for example, showed that college plans among high school graduates were affected by the father's occupation, net of types of high school attended, high school grades, and sex. The relationship between social background and education has also received renewed attention under the rubric of 'economic and cultural reproduction of education' (for an overview, see Apple, 1978; Apple, 1982a; Giroux, 1983). Contrary to the liberal view that education equalizes opportunity, radical researchers have claimed that inequality of schooling reproduces class structure from one generation to the next: people who occupy positions at the top of the socioeconomic hierarchy pass on their advantaged position to their children by assuring them a better education (Bowles, 1971; 1972).

Other critics have argued that not only socioeconomic but also cultural resources are an important component of perpetuating class inequality between generations; the children of highly-educated parents who are likely to be endowed with cultural resources are more likely to advance their educational attainment, and consequently their socioeconomic attainment (Bernstein, 1977; Bourdieu and Passeron, 1977; Halsey *et al.*, 1980). While some critics focused on economic reproduction and others on cultural reproduction, both agreed that educational opportunities were limited by the various resources with which individuals grew up; educational attainment was largely determined by the amount of the family's economic and cultural capital.

According to the thesis of 'educational credentialism', Japanese society should show a relatively weak effect of social background, if the effect is not entirely absent. Cross-national comparison with American and British societies will enable us to assess this prediction; we will compare the overall effect of social background on educational attainment in three countries.

The second substantive concern governing this chapter pertains to the thesis of industrialism. According to Treiman (1970), this thesis predicts that the effect of social origin on educational attainment diminishes as societies industrialize (cf. Boudon, 1974). Industrialization facilitates the development of a free mass educational system which opens up the opportunity for everyone to continue with schooling regardless of the family's financial resources. Urbanization also reduces the effect of social origin on educational attainment, 'since educational opportunities are more readily available to urban children and since there is less pressure upon the children of urban industrial workers to leave school at an early age to go to work' (Treiman, 1970, p. 218).

Empirical studies on educational attainment in Japan, the United States and Britain, however, are generally not consistent with the thesis of industrialism. Despite the prevalence of the idea of 'Japan as an educational credential society', scholarly work in Japan often demonstrates evidence of a constant effect of social background on college attendance across different cohorts. Fujita (1981, pp. 34–5), for example, claims that the difference in the rates of attendance in higher education varies according to the occupation of the fathers concerned, and that this has remained unchanged in the twentieth century although there has been a general increase in the college attendance rate regardless of social origin. Similarly in the United States, differences in years of schooling among individuals from different socioeconomic origins were found to be stable during the twentieth century (Duncan, 1968; Hauser, 1970; Hauser and Featherman, 1976). Halsey *et al.* (1980) also reported in their cross-cohort analysis of educational attainment in Britain that social class differentials in access to secondary and post-secondary education remained unchanged. Although direct comparisons of these studies are unwarranted because of the differences in method and measurement of education and social background, one must cast doubt on the prediction of the industrialism thesis.

One of the most crucial methodological requirements in cross-cohort comparison of the effect of social origin on educational attainment is to separate cross-cohort change in the distribution of education from that in the allocation of education. During the twentieth century all three societies experienced an expansion of their educational system. However, the expansion of the system does not necessarily mean a weakening of the effect of social origin on educational attainment: 'Over cohorts, even if the principles by which schooling is allocated are invariant, the distribution of schooling may become more equal. Conversely, even if the degree of variation in the formal schooling distribution were completely fixed over cohorts, the principles by which individuals are allocated places in the distribution could radically change' (Mare, 1981, pp. 73–4). Our analysis in this chapter will therefore focus on cross-cohort change in the allocation of education – that is, change in social background differentials in educational attainment, net of change in the marginal distribution of schooling. The results of our cross-cohort comparison should determine whether there is a decreasing effect of social origin on education, as suggested by the thesis of industrialism.

The third substantive concern of this chapter pertains to the multidimensional aspect of social background. Recent critics of traditional status attainment models emphasize that a distinction should be made among the different resources from which men can benefit in their social background. Apple (1978; 1982a; 1982b) criticized past research on economic reproduction of education for ignoring the cultural component. According to him, economic reproduction theories, often referred to as correspondence theses, have often neglected 'the *cultural* reproduction of class relations, its role in recreating and legitimating the form and content of the communicative and symbolic resources, the "cultural capital", of dominant groups' (Apple, 1982a, p. 9, emphasis in original).

A man's social background is not unidimensional. It subsumes characteristics of the parents and of the family and of all the accompanying influences of the environment in which he is brought up. We will focus on three distinct resources from which men can benefit in their social background and analyze separately the effects on educational attainment; these three resources are economic capital, social capital and cultural capital.

'Economic capital' refers to the total amount of property and wealth that a family can utilize to help its children secure a better education. Children from wealthy backgrounds have much better access to private educational institutions and individual private tutors. Pre- and post-compulsory education in Japan is largely offered by private institutions; 59 per cent of all kindergartens, 24 per cent of high schools, and 78 per cent of institutions of higher learning was private in 1982 (Monbusho, 1983). In the United States, 18 per cent of elementary education, 10 per cent of secondary education, and 54 per cent of higher education was private in 1982 (US Department of Education, 1982). The dependence of higher education on the private sector is larger in Japan than in the United States. In 1980, the total educational spending including tuition and living expenses was about 1.4 times higher in the private than in the public sector in Japan (Monbusho, 1983, p. 302), and 2.4 times higher in the United States (US Bureau of the Census, 1983, p. 163).[1] College attendance is thus most likely to be affected by the amount of economic capital that a family possesses.

Economic capital is also crucial in what is called 'after-school programmes' in Japan. Private tutoring and cram schools have become extremely popular in Japan, even starting in the very early years of formal education (Rohlen, 1980). One survey showed that in 1980 almost 55 per cent of sixth grade students attended some kind of after-school programme in Tokyo, Osaka and Nagoya.[2] The household expenditures for after-school programmes increased from about 5 per cent of total expenditures in 1965 to close to 20 per cent in 1982 (Sorifu, 1982). The widespread social phenomenon of *ran juku* (cram school proliferation) suggests the rising importance of the effect of economic capital on educational achievement; the children from less wealthy families are becoming more deprived of access to these after-school programmes. If success in education is becoming increasingly dependent on cram schools, we should expect to see an increase in the effect of economic capital in present-day Japan.

The fact that economic capital can influence the degree of educational attainment is by and large considered socially undesirable and unacceptable in many societies. The idea that a wealthy family can 'buy' schooling for its children disturbs many people. We are therefore particularly concerned with the extent to which wealth and property determine educational success. We will examine whether the amount of economic capital significantly affects the educational achievement of men after other background characteristics have been controlled for.

The advantages and disadvantages associated with social background are not necessarily only economic in nature. 'Social capital' – the social circumstances surrounding childhood development – is as important a factor as economic capital in influencing educational achievement.[3] Differences in the 'amount' of social capital come mainly from variations in three major life circumstances: urban and farm background, number of siblings, and father's occupational status.

The disadvantages faced by men from rural and farm origins have been well-documented in all countries (e.g., Sewell, 1964, 1971; Haller and Sewell, 1957; Tsukahara and Kobayashi, 1979). Educational and occupational opportunity structures in the rural and farm communities are clearly less favourable to individual educational development. Access to higher levels of education, especially post-secondary education, is limited in rural and farm areas. Colleges and universities are concentrated in urban areas, in the large cities in Japan.[4] The urban environment also offers a wider range of occupational opportunities, and some of these require a college education. Rural men tend to gather information on occupational opportunities from a restricted local setting and are less likely to aspire to occupations which require substantial education; rural and farm settings provide a less favourable social environment for the development of educational aspirations (Sewell, 1964).

Educational and occupational aspirations are also influenced by the father's occupation. Previous studies (Sewell *et al.*, 1970; Haller and Portes, 1973; Nakayama and Kojima, 1979) have shown that children whose fathers engaged in higher-status occupations are more likely to have higher aspirations and eventually more likely to advance in their own education. Their favourable home environment influences these children's choices regarding occupational opportunities. Parents' social networks and contacts sometimes help the educational advancement of their children (Bourdieu and Passeron, 1977; 1979). Professional fathers, for example, are more likely to have friends who will be influential in their children's education. These friends can range from college professors who may directly influence the decision on admission to business executives who themselves went to prestigious colleges and can offer some advice to the college applicant.

The size of the family in which men were brought up also constitutes an important element of social capital (Blake, 1985; Mare and Chen, 1986). Large families have to divide up the wealth among many children; investment per child will consequently be smaller than in a single-child family. Hauser and Featherman (1976) found that an additional sibling resulted in about a one-quarter year decrease in years of schooling. In traditional Japanese society, it is commonly believed that the eldest son receives much greater attention and support than the rest of his brothers and sisters. While our analysis does not include birth order, the general tendency would be that the larger the family, the lower the educational attainment.

The third resource from which men can benefit in their social background is cultural capital. The notion of 'cultural capital' has been refined and elaborated above all by Pierre Bourdieu (1973, 1974, 1977; Bourdieu and Passeron, 1977, 1979). According to Bourdieu, men from varying cultural backgrounds inherit different amounts of cultural capital – an instrument to de-code 'symbolic wealth socially designated as worthy of being sought and possessed' (Bourdieu, 1977, p. 488; cf. Bernstein, 1977). Cultural capital refers to an inherited linguistic and cultural competence – a refined and elegant style of language and speech, an appropriate manner and demeanour, and general cultural awareness, for example, are essential components. Japanese society in particular requires a mastery of honorific and polite forms of language, as well as an understanding of social position determined by age and experience. An appropriate use of an honorific form of language and an awareness of social relationships between senior and junior positions, especially between teachers and students, may be interpreted as an essential element of cultural capital in the Japanese context.

Success in school is dependent on the possession of this rare capital which will be converted to educational credentials or 'scholastic capital' in Bourdieu's term. Schools are ostensibly fair and meritocratic but in fact do not give every child an equal chance of success. The children who can benefit most from what the school has to offer them are those who are already endowed with the means of appropriating what is offered for themselves – that is, with the requisite cultural capital (Bourdieu, 1974; 1977).

The possession of economic and social capital does not necessarily coincide with the possession of cultural capital. Bourdieu showed that the children from non-propertied, but highly-educated, parents were the ones who had inherited the appropriate cultural capital. Highly-educated parents who have gone through academic institutions themselves have a better understanding of the educational system and its mechanisms, and will probably be better equipped to help their children go through the same system (Bourdieu and Passeron, 1979; Halsey *et al.*, 1980). The data-sets in the three countries lack a measure of ability or cognitive skills. However, we will use other studies to speculate on the role of ability and cognitive skills in the relationship between social background and education in the last section of this chapter.

In summary, our approach is a multi-dimensional one in two ways. On the background side, three different resources are discernible: economic, social and cultural capital; and on the educational side three different levels of educational attainment are considered: (1) graded schooling, (2) high school diploma, and (3) college attendance in Japan and the United States, and (1) beyond minimum schooling, (2) academic qualifications, and (3) vocational/professional qualifications in Britain. Three levels of educational attainment are introduced because the relationship between social background and education probably differs according to the level of education. The various levels of schooling are not homogeneous with respect to social origin, and failure to distinguish the levels of education would overlook the differential impacts of economic, social and cultural capital. Our approach also involves a cross-national comparison and a cross-cohort comparison; societal difference and temporal variation in the effects of economic, social and cultural capital on educational attainment will be examined.

Before we begin our data analysis, a brief explanation of the measurement of the concepts described above is in order. Economic capital is measured by family income at the age of 16 for OCG, the standard of living at the age of 15 compared to the average family then for SSM, and the possession of various amenities at home when the respondent was aged 14 for OMS. These variables are considered the best representation of the total amount of property and wealth possessed by the family when the respondents were growing up. Social capital is represented by farm upbringing, urban origin, number of siblings, and father's occupational status. These variables are expected to reflect the social environment surrounding the respondents when they were growing up. Cultural capital is measured by the father's and the mother's education. These variables are only a crude proxy for the concept we would like to measure, but they are nonetheless the best available measurements and are the ones used by Bourdieu and by Halsey *et al.* (1980) to test the theory of cultural capital.[5] Finally, race is added in the analysis of the American data. Its net effect will represent the advantages of being a white after all other background characteristics have been controlled for. For detailed explanations of the variables, the readers should consult Section 2.4 on variables in Chapter 2 above.

The following data analysis consists of two parts. The first part will examine the *distribution* of education in the three societies and across cohorts. We will compare the average level of schooling and the degree of inequality of educational attainment. The second part will examine the *allocation* of education – the differences in educational attainment among individuals from different social origins. The relative impacts of economic, social and cultural capital on attainment of various levels of education will be examined. It is important to distinguish inequality of educational distribution and inequality of educational allocation or opportunity of education; the distribution and allocation of education are conceptually independent and should be separated in our comparative analysis (cf. Mare, 1981; Simkus and Andorka, 1982). For example, two societies may have exactly the same extent of inequality in the distribution of schooling – only 10 per cent of youths have access to higher education. However, the allocation of these people to higher education in one society may be random, without any reference to their social origin, while in the other the allocation may be based entirely on social origin. The cross-national difference in the distribution of education is conceptually different from the cross-national difference in the principle of educational allocation. We will try to keep these two issues separate as far as possible in the remaining sections of this chapter.

3.2 DISTRIBUTION OF EDUCATION

Inequality in the distribution of schooling will be examined in two steps: first the cross-national comparison of educational inequality, and second the trends in educational inequality. Table 3.1 describes changes in the distribution of various levels of educational attainment by country among successive cohorts of men born during the first half of the twentieth century. Each birth cohort entered school at different phases of development in the national educational system in the three societies. Moreover, persons with varying levels of schooling

Table 3.1 Educational attainment by age cohort in Japan (SSM), the United States (OCG) and Britain (OMS)

Level of education	Japan			United States		
Age of cohort	Mean	Standard deviation	Coefficient of variation	Mean	Standard deviation	Coefficient of variation
Graded schooling						
20–64	10.26	2.00	0.195	10.55	2.95	0.280
30–34	11.18	1.36	0.122	11.23	2.19	0.195
35–49	10.02	1.98	0.198	10.55	2.88	0.273
50–64	8.86	2.16	0.244	9.54	3.66	0.384
High school completion						
20–64	0.571	0.495	0.867	0.698	0.459	0.658
20–34	0.728	0.445	0.611	0.814	0.389	0.478
35–49	0.506	0.500	0.988	0.686	0.464	0.676
50–64	0.377	0.485	1.286	0.539	0.499	0.926
College attendance						
20–64	0.210	0.408	1.943	0.352	0.478	1.360
20–34	0.272	0.445	1.636	0.421	0.494	1.173
35–49	0.177	0.382	2.158	0.354	0.478	1.350
50–64	0.147	0.355	2.415	0.248	0.432	1.742

Level of education	Britain		
Age of cohort	Mean	Standard deviation	Coefficient of variation
Beyond minimum school leaving age			
20–64	0.559	0.497	0.889
30–34	0.649	0.477	0.735
35–49	0.527	0.499	0.947
50–64	0.481	0.500	1.040
O-level or above			
20–64	0.215	0.411	1.912
20–34	0.321	0.467	1.455
35–49	0.182	0.386	2.121
50–64	0.118	0.322	2.729

continued on p. 58

Table 3.1 *continued*

Level of education	Britain		
Age of cohort	Mean	Standard deviation	Coefficient of variation
ONC or above			
20–64	0.187	0.390	2.086
20–34	0.267	0.443	1.659
35–49	0.176	0.381	2.165
50–64	0.098	0.298	3.041

are homogeneous neither in their social origin nor in their effects. We will therefore examine inequalities in access to three different levels of education. In Japan and the United States, the three levels of schooling are: (1) graded schooling (years of primary and secondary education), (2) high school graduation, and (3) college attendance. Since the British educational system differs markedly from its Japanese and American counterparts, the following three levels are distinguished: (1) schooling beyond the minimum school leaving age (including apprenticeship), (2) attainment of academic qualifications (O-level, A-level and degrees and diplomas from the institutions of higher education), and (3) attainment of vocational/professional qualifications (ONC, HNC, Level C and Level B qualifications).

Cross-national comparison of educational inequality

A direct comparison is made between Japan and the United States because of the similarity in their educational system – the post Second World War educational reforms in Japan made the Japanese system very similar to its American counterpart. The cross-national comparison of graded schooling achievement among all men (see Table 3.1, first row of graded schooling sub-tables) suggests that mean years of schooling are almost identical while a greater variability exists among American men. It is important to note, however, that the almost identical average years of schooling understates the difference in exposure to formal education in the two countries. Due to shorter vacations and a six-day school week, the Japanese educational system demands about 60 more schooling days each year than the American one (Ministry of Education, 1978). In other words, Japanese students receive 3 months more schooling each year than American students, under the five-day week American system. With 10 years of mean graded schooling, an average Japanese man in fact receives slightly more than 3 additional years of exposure to formal education than an American.[6]

The variability and inequality in graded schooling are larger in the United States;[7] the standard deviation and the coefficient of variation are about 1.4 times larger than the Japanese figures. This means that graded schooling is more equally distributed among Japanese men. Since the mean years are almost identical in the two countries, Japanese men are much more likely to cluster around this mean than American men. In fact, the distribution of total years of schooling (not reported here) shows that 95 per cent of all Japanese men lie between 5.4 years and 16.3 years of total schooling while the same American men lie between 4.2 years and 18.9 years.[8]

The cross-national comparison of high school graduation and post-secondary education among all men shows a different picture (see Table 3.1, first row of high school and college education sub-tables). 57 per cent of all Japanese men in SSM completed high school education and 21 per cent attended higher education; 70 per cent of all American men in OCG were high school graduates and 35 per cent received a college education. The percentages are substantially higher in the United States; this reflects the different processes of development in the national educational system in the two societies. The expansion of American secondary education has progressed at a slightly faster rate, and higher education has witnessed an extremely rapid growth rate (Trow, 1961). The 35–49 age cohort clearly demonstrates the uneven development: 51 per cent of the Japanese cohort members completed high school and only 18 per cent of them attended college, while 69 per cent of the American men in the same cohort had high school diplomas and 35 per cent went on to higher education. The variability in high school graduation expressed in standard deviations is almost the same in the two countries. Since the proportion of high school graduates is substantially higher in the United States, the coefficient of variation is 1.3 times higher among Japanese men. Although the variability in attending post-secondary education is higher in the United States, the coefficient of variation is 1.4 times larger in Japan, due to a substantially smaller proportion going to college.

The inequalities in access to various levels of education in Britain show a different picture from that found in Japan and the United States. To begin with, Britain is an undereducated country compared with the other two; there are only 56 per cent of men in the sample who had more than the minimum compulsory education including apprenticeship. In other words, 44 per cent left school immediately after the compulsory completion date without going into the apprenticeship system and obtained no academic or vocational qualifications during their career.[9] The extent of undereducation becomes more apparent when we examine more recent statistics in the 1980s. In United Kingdom in 1985, 73 per cent of the 16-year-olds and 51 per cent of the 17-year-olds were continuing education in secondary schools and institutions of higher education, including part-time students in further education establishments (Central Statistical Office, 1988, Table 5.6). In 1985, in Japan, over 90 per cent of 15–17-year-old youths were enrolled in high schools (Sorifu, 1986, Table 19.5) and in the United States 92 per cent of 16–17 year old youths were enrolled in high schools (US Bureau of the Census, 1988, Table 196).

The attainment of academic and vocational qualifications in Britain also shows that a small proportion of the sample obtained these qualifications: 22 per cent of the sample had O-level or above academic qualifications and 19 per cent had ONC or above vocational and professional qualifications. The attainment of higher levels of qualification is even more difficult: 8 per cent of the sample had A-levels or degrees and 13 per cent had HNC or professional qualifications. The coefficient of variation which is the measure of inequality suggests that the attainment of academic and vocational qualifications in Britain is almost as unequally distributed as college education in Japan. Obtaining an O-level or an ONC in Britain appears to be as scarce a resource as college education in Japan.

Trends in educational inequality

Concerning trends in inequality of educational attainment, all three societies show two major trends regardless of the level of educational attainment. First, a continuous upward trend in all levels of education is evident across cohorts, as shown in changes of the mean. The most dramatic change is found in high school graduation; the total increase – that is, the difference between the oldest and the youngest cohort – in the proportion of high school graduates is 35 per cent in Japan and 28 per cent in the United States.[10] This reflects the fact that one of the major social transformations of the educational systems in these two countries in the twentieth century has been the expansion of secondary education (Trow, 1970; Ushiogi, 1978). In Britain, however, all levels of educational attainment showed a modest increase. The proportion of men who had more than a minimum education rose by 17 per cent to reach 65 per cent in the youngest cohort. Men with academic qualifications increased by 20 per cent and men with vocational qualifications increased by 17 per cent across successive cohorts.

Second, a continuous decline in inequality in distribution of all levels of education is evident across cohorts, as shown in the decreasing coefficient of variation. In Japan and the United States, the coefficient of variation is reduced by about half for graded schooling and high school graduation and by a third for college attendance over the 50-year period. Although the degree of inequality in acquiring a high school diploma and in access to higher education is substantially higher in Japan than in the United States among all cohorts (comparing coefficients of variations across sub-tables), the decline in inequality across cohorts (observed in changes of coefficient of variation across rows) is the same in the two countries. In other words, there is a tendency for Japan to have a more unequal distribution of high school graduation and college attendance than for the United States, and that tendency continues during the 50-year period; but the temporal decline in such inequalities within each society is equally evident in both societies. In Britain, the reduction in the extent of inequalities in academic and vocational qualifications is also substantial; the coefficients of variation are reduced by half. Although men who had academic qualifications are less than a third and those with some vocational qualifications are about one-quarter of men even in the youngest cohort, the distribution of these qualifications has become more equal across successive cohorts.

In summary, two findings emerge from our analysis of inequality in the distribution of education. First, Japan has a much lower degree of inequality in access to graded schooling compared with the United States. As far as the attainment of primary and secondary education is concerned, Cummings's claim (1980, p. 268) that education has become 'constant' in Japan is not far from reality. However, substantially more inequality exists in Japan in terms of acquiring a high school diploma and of access to post-secondary education than in the United States. Due to a more rapid expansion of secondary and higher education in the United States, a higher proportion of American men in our sample obtained a high school diploma and attended college; the consequent result is a decrease in the inequality of these educational attainments. Second, a definite trend toward reduction of inequality in all levels of educational attainment is evident in all three countries. During the 50-year span covered in our cohort analysis, the distribution of educational attainment continues to equalize.

3.3 SOCIAL DIFFERENTIALS IN EDUCATIONAL ATTAINMENT

The primary objective of this section is to focus on the allocation of education by individuals from different social origins. In order to separate cross-national difference and cross-cohort change in the distribution of education from those in the allocation of education, we will examine odds (or log-odds) on completing various levels of education by different social background characteristics using the logistic regression method.[11] For example, the unstandardized logistic regression coefficient for urban background predicting high school graduation in Japan (0.874, see Table 3.2) will indicate the difference in log-odds on completing high school education between men of urban and of rural origin controlling for other background characteristics. If we take the anti-log of the coefficient ($e^{0.874} = 2.40$), we know that men of urban origin have almost two and a half times better odds on completing high school than men of rural origin. In the United States, the same coefficient is 0.173 and, by taking the anti-log ($e^{0.173} = 1.19$), men of urban origin have 1.2 times better odds on completing high school education than men of rural origin. Japanese men of urban origin thus are more advantaged than American men of the same origin even though more men graduate from high schools in the United States. The cross-national difference in the effect of urban origin is independent of the proportion of high school graduates in the two societies. The effect of urban origin on high school completion therefore does not depend upon the distribution of education (Bishop *et al.*, 1975, pp. 9–15). Our presentation focuses first on the cross-national comparison and second on the temporal variation in social background differentials in educational attainment.

Cross-national comparison of the effects of social background on educational attainment

Table 3.2 shows the results of logistic regression analysis of various levels of educational attainment on the set of social background

Table 3.2 Logistic regressions on social background of beyond compulsory education, high school completion and college attendance in Japan (SSM) and the United States (OCG) and of minimum schooling, academic qualifications and vocational qualifications in Britain (OMS)

Independent variables	*Dependent variables*		
	Beyond minimum education	*High school completion*	*College attendance*
Japan			
Family income	0.486**(0.081)	0.660**(0.083)	0.452**(0.102)
Father's education	0.105**(0.031)	0.195**(0.030)	0.168**(0.027)
Mother's education	0.050 (0.032)	0.156**(0.033)	0.202**(0.035)
Urban background	0.105 (0.135)	0.874**(0.135)	0.469**(0.208)
Farm origin	−0.682**(0.124)	−0.512**(0.113)	−0.640**(0.163)
Father's occupation	0.047**(0.008)	0.031**(0.006)	0.027**(0.006)
Siblings	−0.060* (0.029)	−0.155**(0.028)	−0.073* (0.036)
Intercept	-2.063**(0.485)	-5.653**(0.511)	−6.683**(0.679)
R^2	0.115	0.250	0.204
D	7.961	13.207	11.322

Independent variables	*Dependent variables*		
	Beyond minimum education	*High school completion*	*College attendance*
United States			
Family income	0.722**(0.030)	0.571**(0.023)	0.342**(0.020)
Father's education	0.099**(0.009)	0.090**(0.007)	0.087**(0.006)
Mother's education	0.159**(0.009)	0.141**(0.007)	0.112**(0.007)
Urban background	0.349**(0.048)	0.173**(0.040)	0.423**(0.041)
Farm origin	−0.705**(0.051)	−0.354**(0.044)	−0.123* (0.049)
Father's occupation	0.018**(0.003)	0.020**(0.002)	0.030**(0.002)
Siblings	−0.119**(0.007)	−0.135**(0.006)	−0.142**(0.007)
Race	−0.046 (0.063)	0.153**(0.054)	−0.081 (0.061)
Intercept	-2.248**(0.134)	-3.071**(0.109)	−4.455**(0.109)
R^2	0.205	0.235	0.213
D	10.430	9.157	8.468

continued on p. 64

Table 3.2 *continued*

Independent variables	*Dependent variables*		
	Beyond minimum education	*Academic qualifications*	*Vocational qualifications*
Britain			
Family income	0.269**(0.021)	0.386**(0.027)	0.254**(0.026)
Father's education	0.357**(0.065)	0.534**(0.056)	0.065 (0.057)
Mother's education	0.354**(0.062)	0.355**(0.056)	0.156**(0.056)
Urban background	0.159* (0.066)	0.149 (0.088)	0.057 (0.084)
Farm origin	-0.725**(0.101)	-0.348* (0.143)	-1.025**(0.172)
Father's occupation	0.030**(0.003)	0.035**(0.003)	0.015**(0.003)
Siblings	-0.176**(0.011)	-0.254**(0.018)	-0.209**(0.017)
Intercept	-0.619**(0.212)	-3.291**(0.286)	-1.310**(0.290)
R^2	0.148	0.184	0.077
D	7.092	8.485	5.418

Notes:
Approximate standard errors are in parentheses.
* Significant at 0.05 level.
** Significant at 0.01 level.

variables for all men between age 20 and 64. The lowest level of educational attainment in Japan and the United States is now expressed by the odds on staying on at school beyond the minimum compulsory level rather than the number of years of graded schooling.[12] Each column of the table presents the unstandardized regression coefficients estimated from SSM, OCG and OMS. The most remarkable finding is that most background variables significantly affect the attainment of all levels of education. In Japan, the effects of all the background characteristics on high school completion and college attendance are significant, while the effects of urban background and the mother's education on schooling beyond the compulsory level are not. In the United States, the effects of all background variables are significant.[13] In Britain, the odds on staying on at school beyond the minimum leaving age are affected by all background variables. The attainment of academic qualifications is not affected by urban origin, and the attainment of vocational qualifications is not affected by father's education and urban background.

The access to vocational qualifications appears to be relatively independent of background characteristics.

The rows labelled R^2 (goodness of fit statistics) in Table 3.2 show overall measures of predictive power of all social background characteristics in explaining educational attainment.[14] The R^2 figures for schooling beyond the minimum level, high school completion, and college attendance in Japan are 0.115, 0.250 and 0.204 respectively, and the same figures in the United States are 0.205, 0.235 and 0.213 respectively. R^2 values are much lower in Britain; 0.148 for schooling beyond the minimum leaving age, 0.184 for academic qualifications and 0.077 for vocational qualifications. However, R^2 measures are influenced by the difference in distribution of education across nations. The greater R^2 for college attendance in the United States than in Japan, for example, is in part influenced by the greater variance in college attendance (see Table 3.1) in the United States than in Japan. However, we would like to ask the question how social background characteristics affect college attendance – the allocation of education – regardless of the proportion of college goers – the distribution of education. We already know that college attendance is much higher in the United States than in Japan, but American men of less favourable social origin may be equally disadvantaged in attending institutions of higher education as Japanese men of the same origin.

In order to have an intuitive understanding of the magnitude of the overall effect of social background independent of cross-national difference in distribution of education, we can estimate the difference in educational attainment between two individuals who come from very different social backgrounds. For example, we can compute the estimated difference in log-odds on completion of various levels of education between two men who occupy the opposite extremes with regard to background characteristics: (1) a man born in a rural and farm family with a large number of siblings, whose parents had no formal education, and whose father had a job of lowest occupational prestige, and (2) a man born in an urban and non-farm family as a single son, whose parents had a university education, and whose father engaged in a highest-prestige job.[15] The rows labelled *D* in Table 3.2 indicate the difference in log-odds on completion of three levels of education between these two men. The larger the *D* values, the greater the difference between the two, and the greater the overall effect of social background.

These figures suggest the following two points. First, as far as the lowest level of educational attainment (schooling beyond the minimum level) is concerned, the estimated difference between the two men from very different social backgrounds is largest in the United States, followed by Japan and then by Britain. Although the proportion of men who continue schooling beyond the minimum level is higher in the United States (84 per cent) than in Japan (77 per cent) and Britain (56 per cent), the odds on staying beyond the minimum level are more likely to be affected by social origin in the United States than in Japan and Britain. Second, when we examine higher levels of education (high school completion and college attendance in the Japanese and American samples, and the attainment of academic and vocational qualifications in the British sample), the estimated difference in educational achievement between the two men from very different social backgrounds is larger in Japan than in the United States and Britain. The overall impact of social background on the higher levels of education appears to be greatest in Japan.

These results do not seem to lend support to the notion that all Japanese men have an equal chance of obtaining education. In contrast, access to various levels of schooling is restricted by a man's social origin. Furthermore, the extent of the dependence of high school completion and college attendance on social origin in Japan appears to be larger than in the United States and Britain. The empirical evidence does not show that the overall impact of social origin is weaker in Japan.

Economic, social and cultural capital and educational attainment

Next we disaggregate the social background characteristics and analyze the relative importance of three different resources of social background on educational attainment.

Economic capital

Economic capital plays a significant role in the successful attainment of various levels of education in all countries. The amount of family wealth and property, independent of other background characteristics, influences schooling beyond the minimum level, high school completion and college attendance in Japan and the United States, and schooling beyond the minimum leaving age and the attainment of qualifications in Britain. If two men possessed different amounts of economic capital – for example, one from a 'very wealthy family' (the highest category in the family income variable) and the other from a 'very poor family' (the lowest category) but they were identical with respect to social and cultural capital, then the man from the wealthier family would have seven times higher odds on schooling beyond the minimum level in SSM and 18 times in OCG, 14 times higher odds on high school completion in SSM and 10 times in OCG, and six times higher odds on college attendance in SSM and four times in OCG. In Britain, the man from the wealthier family would have three times higher odds on schooling beyond the minimum leaving age, five times on the attainment of academic qualifications, and three times on the attainment of vocational qualifications than the man from the family with least economic capital.[16] The difference between the two men is rather substantial considering that they differ only in their economic capital and that other background characteristics are equal. The dependence of educational success, particularly at the higher levels, on the overall amount of family wealth and property seems to be strongest in Japan followed by the United States, and weakest in Britain. Contrary to the idea of 'Japan as an educational credential society', the relative property and wealth of a family appears to make a larger difference in educational outcomes of the sons in Japan than in the other two nations.

Social capital

The advantages and disadvantages associated with the social environment in which men grow up are evident in all three societies. In the United States, all the variables of social capital exert significant effects on educational attainment. In Japan, the effects of urban origin and the mother's education on schooling beyond the minimum level are absent. In Britain, the attainment of academic and vocational qualifications is not affected by urban background. Taken separately, each influence does not seem to be substantial, but the combined total impact of social capital variables is fairly large.

In order to highlight the effect of social capital, let us compare two men from extremely different social environments. One has a rural and farm background with four brothers and sisters and his father is a farmer. The other man, whose father is a lawyer, comes from an urban non-farm background with no siblings.[17] If the two men have the same amount of economic and cultural capital, the man with greater social capital is estimated to have 11 times better odds on staying beyond the minimum schooling level in Japan and eight times in the United States, 20 times better odds on high school completion in Japan and six times in the United States, and 10 times better odds on attending college in Japan and eight times in the United States. In Britain, the advantaged man is estimated to have 13 times better odds on schooling beyond the minimum school leaving age, 12 times on access to academic qualifications, and 10 times on access to vocational qualifications. By combining individual effects, the overall effect of social capital variables appears to be stronger in Japan than elsewhere.

Among different characteristics of social capital, the father's occupation and the size of the family generally have a substantial impact on all levels of educational attainment in the three societies and thus constitute important sources of differentiating access to educational opportunities. On the other hand, the effect of urban origin seems to be weakest among the effects of social capital variables.

Cultural Capital

Cultural capital, measured by parental education, plays a crucial role in determining the success of sons in Japan and the United States. A one-year increase in the father's and the mother's years of schooling is expected to increase the odds on schooling beyond the minimum level by 1.1 times for the Japanese men and by 1.3 times for the American men and the odds on both high school completion and college attendance by 1.4 times for the Japanese men and by 1.2 times for the American men. In Britain, however, the attainment of vocational qualifications seems to be affected only weakly by cultural capital. The highly-educated parents are probably concerned with the academic success of their children, but not so much with the vocational 'alternative route' to academic education (Raffe, 1979). Our analysis indeed shows that it is the attainment of academic qualifications which is strongly influenced by parental education. If we take the two extreme categories of parental education – that is, parents with minimum education in non-selective secondary schools and those with some qualifications – the odds on obtaining O-level or higher academic qualifications is 5.9 times higher for the sons from the educated family. Similarly, the sons from the educated family have 1.4 times higher odds on staying school beyond the minimum leaving age than those whose parents had minimum education.

In summary, the inequality of educational opportunities for men from different social backgrounds is clearly documented in all three societies. The allocation of education is not random but is affected by the extent of economic, social and cultural capital of the family in which men are brought up.

Trends in the effects of social origins on education

Have the social differentials in educational attainment changed across the cohorts born in the early twentieth century? Has the allocation of education become more equal over the period? These questions can be answered by an examination of trends in the effects of social background on education.[18] Table 3.3 shows the results of logistic regression analysis of educational attainment on social background variables by three age cohorts.[19] Three points stand out in the trend analysis.

First, college attendance shows a tendency of increasing dependence on social background across successive cohorts in Japan and the United States. The difference in log-odds on college attendance between men of extremely different social origin (row *D* in Table 3.3) and the R^2 measure increased from the oldest to the youngest cohort. In particular, in Japan, not only did the overall measure but also the number of social background effects which are significant increase across cohorts; farm origin and the number of siblings exerted significant influence only in the youngest cohort.

Second, the dependence of high school completion on social origin shows different trends in Japan and the United States. The changes in the overall effect of social origin (see rows *D* and R^2 in Table 3.3) suggest that the social background differentials in completing American high school education diminished in the twentieth century. American men experienced a continuous trend of opening up of opportunities for high school graduation. In Japan, however, the changes in the overall impact of social origin suggest that the effects of social background on high school completion increased from the oldest to the middle cohort and then decreased from the middle to the youngest cohort.

The proportion of Japanese high school graduates grew from 38 per cent in the oldest cohort to slightly over 50 per cent in the middle cohort. A high school diploma probably therefore became a critical credential in the labour market for men in the middle cohort, and the attainment of a high school diploma was a battleground of educational

Table 3.3 Logistic regressions on social background of high school completion and college attendance by cohort in Japan (SSM) and the United States (OCG) and of academic qualifications and vocational qualifications by cohort in Britain (OMS)

Independent variables	*Dependent variables and cohort*					
	High school completion			*College attendance*		
	20–34	*35–49*	*50–64*	*20–34*	*35–49*	*50–64*
Japan						
Family income	0.753**	0.472**	0.962**	0.333*	0.356*	0.782**
	(0.147)	(0.130)	(0.185)	(0.167)	(0.171)	(0.216)
Father's education	0.123**	0.233**	0.259**	0.115**	0.207**	0.291**
	(0.044)	(0.055)	(0.068)	(0.036)	(0.051)	(0.072)
Mother's education	0.174**	0.129*	0.028	0.225**	0.226**	0.039
	(0.053)	(0.058)	(0.071)	(0.048)	(0.066)	(0.088)
Urban background	0.436	1.023**	0.404	0.526	0.408	0.539
	(0.277)	(0.208)	(0.274)	(0.442)	(0.313)	(0.405)
Farm origin	–0.369*	–0.636**	–0.500	–0.841**	–0.409	–0.630
	(0.187)	(0.183)	(0.262)	(0.246)	(0.285)	(0.370)
Father's occupation	0.021*	0.054**	0.025	0.037**	0.036**	–0.011
	(0.010)	(0.010)	(0.014)	(0.009)	(0.011)	(0.015)
Siblings	–0.148**	–0.115*	–0.103	–0.175**	0.017	–0.013
	(0.049)	(0.047)	(0.058)	(0.062)	(0.063)	(0.072)
Intercept	–4.177**	-6.496**	-5.831**	-6.038**	-7.884**	–6.210**
	(0.864)	(0.854)	(1.127)	(1.170)	(1.155)	(1.456)
R^2	0.163	0.259	0.251	0.220	0.199	0.163
D	10.978	13.999	7.992	11.768	10.692	7.784

Independent variables	*Dependent variables and cohort*					
	High school completion			*College attendance*		
	20–34	*35–49*	*50–64*	*20–34*	*35–49*	*50–64*
United States						
Family income	0.552**	0.547**	0.471**	0.401**	0.360**	0.483**
	(0.043)	(0.043)	(0.045)	(0.034)	(0.039)	(0.046)
Father's education	0.094**	0.089**	0.094**	0.110**	0.075**	0.094**
	(0.012)	(0.012)	(0.012)	(0.010)	(0.011)	(0.013)
Mother's education	0.157**	0.128**	0.130**	0.139**	0.126**	0.078**
	(0.013)	(0.012)	(0.012)	(0.012)	(0.011)	(0.013)
Urban background	0.008	0.029	0.223**	0.412**	0.465**	0.252**
	(0.068)	(0.068)	(0.074)	(0.062)	(0.071)	(0.091)
Farm origin	0.191	–0.264**	–0.710**	0.329**	–0.277**	–0.517**
	(0.087)	(0.074)	(0.076)	(0.083)	(0.085)	(0.097)
Father's occupation	0.014**	0.025**	0.027**	0.024**	0.028**	0.035**
	(0.003)	(0.003)	(0.004)	(0.002)	(0.003)	(0.004)
Siblings	–0.161**	–0.122**	–0.130**	–0.163**	–0.125**	–0.132**
	(0.011)	(0.010)	(0.010)	(0.011)	(0.011)	(0.013)

Independent variables	*Dependent variables and cohort*					
	High school completion			*College attendance*		
	20–34	*35–49*	*50–64*	*20–34*	*35–49*	*50–64*
Race	–0.179*	0.381**	0.524**	–0.283**	–0.067	0.127
	(0.089)	(0.094)	(0.114)	(0.088)	(0.109)	(0.153)
Intercept	-2.510**	-3.366**	-3.442**	–4.926**	–4.374**	–4.735**
	(0.192)	(0.193)	(0.200)	(0.174)	(0.195)	(0.235)
R^2	0.175	0.209	0.235	0.220	0.198	0.190
D	8.744	8.769	9.456	9.519	8.468	7.801

Independent variables	*Dependent variables and cohort*					
	Academic qualifications			*Vocational qualifications*		
	20–34	*35–49*	*50–64*	*20–34*	*35–49*	*50–64*
Britain						
Family income	0.236**	0.406**	0.487**	0.081*	0.194**	0.361**
	(0.041)	(0.055)	(0.065)	(0.038)	(0.052)	(0.068)
Father's education	0.515**	0.562**	0.549**	0.034	0.205	0.099
	(0.074)	(0.111)	(0.145)	(0.073)	(0.109)	(0.156)
Mother's education	0.374**	0.245*	0.468*	0.144*	0.152	0.293
	(0.073)	(0.111)	(0.143)	(0.071)	(0.109)	(0.151)
Urban background	0.218	0.064	0.147	0.047	0.266	–0.104
	(0.119)	(0.173)	(0.208)	(0.112)	(0.167)	(0.209)
Farm origin	–0.409	–0.076	–0.462	–0.913**	–0.549*	-2.270**
	(0.218)	(0.252)	(0.293)	(0.251)	(0.273)	(0.573)
Father's occupation	0.032**	0.043**	0.036**	0.006	0.027**	0.030**
	(0.004)	(0.006)	(0.007)	(0.004)	(0.005)	(0.007)
Siblings	–0.292**	–0.289**	–0.141**	–0.182**	–0.269**	–0.121**
	(0.029)	(0.035)	(0.031)	(0.026)	(0.032)	(0.032)
Intercept	-2.526**	-3.763**	-3.903**	0.325	-2.420**	-1.179
	(0.403)	(0.537)	(0.637)	(0.405)	(0.527)	(0.805)
R^2	0.186	0.165	0.114	0.038	0.091	0.066
D	7.722	8.923	7.732	3.345	5.770	6.874

Notes:
Approximate standard errors are in parentheses.
* Significant at 0.05 level.
** Significant at 0.01 level.

competition for men from different social origins in this cohort. In the youngest cohort, however, a high school diploma was not sufficient to guarantee success in the labour market because more than a quarter of this age group went on to institutions of higher education. College attendance seems to have become the key to socioeconomic advancement for men in the youngest cohort, and therefore the privileged families would try to ensure that their sons had a college education.

Social background differentials in high school completion consequently decreased while those in college attendance increased in the youngest cohort in Japan.

Third, in Britain, the dependence of vocational qualifications on social origin declined across cohorts. The effect of social origin on academic qualifications appears to have increased from the oldest to the middle cohort but to have declined from the middle to the youngest cohort. However, when the trend in higher levels of academic qualifications – the attainment of A-level or higher academic qualifications – is examined (not reported here), there is a tendency of an increasing effect of social background characteristics from the oldest to the youngest cohort.[20] The opportunities of higher-level academic achievement seem to have become more unequal across successive cohorts in modern Britain.

In summary, our results suggest two contradictory trends in the overall impact of social background on educational attainment in the three societies. The opportunities of education in the lower level – such as high school completion and O-level qualifications – appear to become more equal at least from the middle to the youngest cohort. In contrast, access to higher levels of education – that is, college attendance and A-level or above academic qualifications – seems to have become more dependent on social origins in the twentieth century.

Trends in the effects of economic, social and cultural capital

What is the changing importance of economic, social and cultural capital among successive cohorts? Let us begin with the temporal change in the effect of economic capital.

Economic capital

In all three societies, economic capital plays a significant role in educational attainment across all cohorts. The independent impact of economic capital shows up consistently from the oldest to the youngest cohort. Its impact appears to decline over the 50-year span in Japan and Britain while its impact has been stable throughout the period in the United States.

Economic capital is an important determinant of college attendance across all cohorts in the United States, and its impact appears to remain the same throughout the period. This implies that economic barriers to American higher education persisted throughout the period. In comparison, college attendance among Japanese men appears to be most strongly affected by economic capital in the oldest cohort. This finding suggests that an expensive private college education is probably not the major barrier to college attendance in Japan in recent years. In the light of the increasing importance of the mother's education, the father's occupation, and the number of siblings in recent cohorts, college attendance in Japan has become more dependent on a variety of resources from which men can benefit in their social background, than on the sheer amount of economic property and wealth. Similarly, in Britain, the tendency of a declining effect of economic capital on access to academic qualifications is accompanied by an increasing effect of other background characteristics.

Social capital

Trends in the effects of social capital do not show a uniform pattern across nations and levels of education. In Japan, the temporal change in the effects of social capital variables generally follows that in the overall impact of social background: for high school completion increasing effects from the oldest to the middle cohort and decreasing effects from the middle to the youngest cohort, and for college attendance a general increase from the oldest to the youngest cohort. It is important to notice that Japanese higher education has become more dependent on social capital, especially in the youngest cohort whose members were educated in the post-war educational system. Although Japanese higher education expanded rapidly after the Second World War, opportunities for higher education among men from different social environments seem to have become more unequal. Although the absolute number of college-goers of farm origin and from large families increased from the oldest to the youngest cohort, the relative disadvantage faced by these men appears to have increased over the period.

In the United States, the dominant trend for social capital variables is a general decline in their effects, with the exception of the number of siblings which shows an increasing influence. In particular, high school completion has clearly become less dependent on farm origin and the father's occupational status. In Britain, the dependence of the attainment of academic qualifications on social capital has more or less stayed the same while that of the attainment of vocational qualifications has declined across cohorts. However, the impact of the number of siblings appears to have increased over the period.

The disadvantages associated with larger numbers of siblings seem to have increased across successive cohorts in all three nations. Since the average size of siblings declined in these nations from the oldest to the youngest cohort, large families are becoming more and more rare and the disadvantages of being brought up in a large family seem to have become more salient over the period.[21]

Cultural capital
Trends in the effect of cultural capital vary across nations. In Japan, the father's and the mother's education show opposite trends: the effect of the father's education declined while that of the mother's education increased across cohorts. Although the father's education exerts a significant impact on both high school completion and college attendance even in the youngest cohort, its relative importance has clearly declined over the period. In contrast, the mother's education has become more important in the younger cohorts. These findings may reflect the tendency of the mother's excessive involvement in the educational success of their children in Japan in recent years (White, 1987). Highly-educated women are more likely to withdraw from the labour market during the childrearing period (Amano, 1988, p. 101) and their sons are more likely to have higher educational aspirations than the sons of the low-qualified mothers (Nakayama and Kojima, 1979, p. 305).

The increasing importance of the mother's education in determining the educational outcomes of their offspring seems to be present also in the United States. However, the effect of the father's education has stayed more or less the same across cohorts. These trends together lead to the increasing role of cultural capital in determining educational attainment over the twentieth century in the United States. In Britain, a strong effect of the father's education on the attainment of academic qualifications shows up consistently across cohorts while the trend in the effect of the mother's education is not clear. The father's education seems to be one of the most important social background characteristics in predicting academic success, and its relative importance has not changed over the period in Britain.

In summary, the trends in the effects of economic, social and cultural capital do not readily fall into a uniform pattern across nations and across different levels of education. The changing pattern of association between social origin and educational attainment was described most effectively by disaggregating both social background characteristics and the levels of educational attainment.

3.4 SUMMARY AND CONCLUSION

The first substantive concern guiding this chapter was the issue of the equality of educational opportunities. Our analysis documents that the allocation of education is not random but is affected by social origin in all three societies. Educational opportunities are not equally distributed among men from different social backgrounds.

One of the propositions derived from the thesis of 'educational credentialism' in Japan stated that opportunities for educational advancement are in general open to all the members of Japanese society and that individuals who are talented and work hard will achieve higher levels of education. The results of this chapter do not appear to support this proposition. Various background characteristics do influence the attainment of various levels of education in Japan. Furthermore, cross-national comparison with American and British societies suggests that the dependence of high school completion and college attendance on social origin is probably larger in Japan than in the United States and Britain. The opportunities of educational attainment appear to be more restricted by men's background characteristics in Japan than in the other two societies.

These findings are probably surprising to many Japanese audiences because of the popular belief that the meritocratic principle operates in the Japanese educational system (Dore, 1987, Chapter 11). The Japanese educational system is often characterized by a highly uniform compulsory education (Cummings, 1980) and a highly differentiated high school and college education (Rohlen, 1983). The differentiation, however, is believed to be based on a meritocratic principle, namely the entrance examination to upper-level schooling. The well-known social phenomenon of 'examination hell' (the excessive preparation by high school students for the college entrance examination) in Japan seems to exemplify the peculiar characteristic of the 'meritocratic' Japanese education. It is not uncommon to assume that educational opportunities are open to all individuals regardless of their social origin and that the educational outcome, especially college attendance, is solely determined by the exam-based standard (cf. Reischauer, 1977).

The 'meritocratic' characteristic of Japanese education, however, does not seem to receive much support from our findings. The overall dependence of educational attainment on social background is not particularly small in Japan; Japanese men with limited background resources are at least as equally handicapped in educational advancement as American and British men. If college attendance is solely determined by the result of entrance examinations in Japan, it is surprising to find consistent effects of social origin on college attendance.

The issue of meritocracy is not a simple one. Our analysis does not address itself directly to this issue because we lack a measure of ability or cognitive skill. As long as the difference in educational attainment by social background derives from 'merit' of some sort, the meritocratic principle holds. In other words, if children from advantaged backgrounds had superior IQ genotypes and cognitive skills, then difference in educational attainment would be based on difference in ability. To argue against the meritocratic principle, we need to show that (1) educational attainment is dependent on social background, and (2) difference in cognitive skills among people from various backgrounds will not explain their difference in educational attainment. Our analysis documents the first but not the second point.

Nonetheless, we can use other studies to speculate on the role of ability and cognitive skills in the relationship between social background and education. In the United States, Jencks *et al.* (1972, p. 138) found that at most 10 per cent of the overall correlation between parental economic status and children's years of schooling appeared to be explained by the fact that economically advantaged children had superior IQ genotypes among the American national sample of native non-farm white males.[22] They also claimed (p. 139) that about a third of the difference in years of schooling between economically advantaged and disadvantaged children was explained by differences in their test scores or cognitive skills. In Britain, Halsey, Heath and Ridge (1980, p. 162), using the same OMS data, estimated the effect of IQ on the relationship between social origin and educational attainment: 12 per cent of the overall correlation between familial material circumstances (which are the composite of our family income, the father's occupation, and the number of siblings variables plus the type of housing where the respondent lived at the age of 14) and secondary schooling was accounted for by IQ.

Although no comparable study exists in Japan to estimate the impact of IQ genotypes, the effect of high school test scores and grades on the relationship between father's occupation and college attendance among high school seniors can be estimated from the cross-tabulations presented by Ehara (1984).[23] Our estimate from the

Japanese high school students' sample shows that high school grades explain a very small part (6 per cent) of the difference in the log-odds on college attendance between students of manual and those of non-manual origin. The odds on attending college were 2.03 times higher for students whose father had a non-manual occupation than for those whose father had a manual occupation before controlling for high school grades, and the difference changed very little after controlling for high school grades.

These studies show that the relationship between background and educational attainment cannot be accounted for totally by cognitive skills. IQ genotypes appear to explain very little of the effect of social background on educational attainment, and cognitive skills appear to explain at most a modest portion of the same effect. In other words, in all three societies, social background differentials seem to produce a difference in educational attainment, regardless of IQ genotypes and test scores. Meritocracy appears not to be the sole determinant of educational success; people with the same IQ genotypes and cognitive skills will still end up attaining different levels of education according to their background characteristics.

The second substantive concern governing this chapter pertained to the thesis of industrialism. One of the predictions of this thesis deals with the trend of social background differentials in education: the effect of social origins on educational attainment diminishes as societies industrialize. Since all three societies experienced an increasing level of industrialization in the twentieth century, according to this thesis our cohort analysis should show a declining effect of social origin across successive cohorts. Our empirical findings are not altogether consistent with this prediction.

To begin with, it is clear that in all these societies the distribution of education has become more equal over the 50-year span covered by our analysis. Furthermore, the absolute number of individuals with higher levels of education has increased across cohorts, even among people from a disadvantaged background in these societies. For example, the absolute number of college-goers of farm origin increased from the oldest to the youngest cohort. Nonetheless, the relative access to education for men of disadvantaged social origins did not always improve across successive cohorts in the twentieth century.

Our analysis suggests that the opportunities of high school graduation and the attainment of O-level qualifications became more equal, at least from the 35–49 cohort to the 20–34 cohort in our societies.

However, our analysis also suggests that college attendance and the attainment of A-level or above academic qualifications have become more dependent on social origin. As an increasing proportion of men are attending institutions of higher education and obtaining A-level or above academic qualifications, a high school diploma and a lower academic qualification do not guarantee socioeconomic advancement. College attendance and A-levels are becoming more and more crucial to success in the labour market, and the privileged families will try harder to ensure that their sons have access to these credentials. The relative difference in access to college education and higher academic qualifications by individuals from different social origins consequently increases across cohorts. In other words, institutions of higher education and higher levels of academic certificates are becoming the means of reproducing inequality from generation to generation. Individuals who are at the top of the socioeconomic and cultural hierarchy pass on their advantaged positions to their children by assuring them higher levels of educational credentials.

The third substantive concern regarding the relationship between social background and education dealt with the distinction among different resources from which men can benefit in their social background. Economic capital plays a significant role in the successful attainment of all levels of education in the three societies. The finding that the impact of economic capital persists despite controlling for all other background variables is particularly important. The amount of wealth and property which a family possesses determines the educational success of its children, independent of other advantages. This may imply that a family can literally 'buy' schooling for its children.

The effect of economic capital on educational success, particularly at the higher levels, seems to be stronger in Japan than in the United States and Britain. This finding casts doubt on the thesis of 'educational credentialism' which emphasizes the meritocratic selection process in the Japanese higher education. Contrary to the prediction of this thesis, the overall amount of family wealth and property appears to make a larger difference in college attendance in Japan than in the other two nations. Our finding is consistent with the claim that private tutoring and cram schools, which are often expensive, are critical to success in college entrance examinations.

Social capital – advantages associated with the social environment in which men grow up – influences the attainment of educational credentials in all three societies. The father's occupation and the size of the family are probably the two major sources of social capital; their effects on various levels of education are generally significant and strong. Urban background, in contrast, is probably the weakest source of the effect of social capital.

Cross-national comparison suggests that the dependence of education on social capital is more evident in Japan than in the United States and Britain. Rural and farm origin, in particular, continues to create a disadvantage in access to higher education in Japan, as they have throughout the twentieth century. Despite the official educational policy of the Japanese government to spread the universities outside the metropolitan areas (Aso and Amano, 1983), new universities were mainly built in the local cities, and men who were brought up in rural and farm environment faced handicaps in attending higher education even in the youngest cohort.

Finally, cultural capital, measured by parental education, plays a crucial role in determining the educational success of sons in all three societies. Children of highly-educated parents have substantial advantages in their academic achievement. In Britain, however, cultural capital seems to have a limited effect on the attainment of vocational qualifications. The highly-educated parents appear to be more concerned with the academic success of their sons than in advocating the vocational 'alternative' route to academic education. These findings appear to be consistent with the cultural reproduction thesis advanced by Bourdieu and others (1973, 1974, 1977; Bourdieu and Passeron, 1977, 1979). It is possible that these culturally advantaged children have acquired from their parents the linguistic, communicative and cultural competence which constitutes a crucial means of appropriating what the school has to offer them, and consequently have got ahead of other children in academic achievement. However, it should be noted that if Bourdieu's theory of 'cultural reproduction' is taken literally, our results may not be interpreted as lending support to his theory. In all three societies, educational attainment is not overwhelmingly determined by cultural capital, and there is no perfect reproduction of educational elites between the generations.

In this chapter, we discussed the relationship between social background and education. Chapter 4 will bring in the labour market as the centre of our analysis and examine the effects of education and social background on the distribution of rewards there.

Notes

1. The average total educational expense for the public sector was \$3666 per year and \$5270 for the private sector in Japan (using an appropriate exchange rate). The comparable figures in the United States are \$2487 for the public 4-year institutions and \$5888 for the private ones in 1980.
2. The survey was cited in *The Asahi* newspaper, (6 March 1980).
3. Our definition of 'social capital' is rather broad, encompassing a variety of factors in social environment. Bourdieu and Passeron's notion of 'social capital' (1977; 1979) refers to 'social networks' which are only one of the aspects covered by our definition.
4. Almost 40 per cent of all four-year universities were concentrated in 10 metropolitan areas in 1982 in Japan (Monbusho, 1982a, p. 32). These metropolitan areas include Tokyo (23 districts), Yokohama and Kawasaki, Nagoya, Kyoto, Osaka, Kobe, Hiroshima, Kitakyushu, Fukuoka and Sapporo.
5. Theatre attendance, visits to museums and art galleries and types of magazines subscribed to at home constitute better measurements of cultural capital than those used in this study (Bourdieu, 1977; Bourdieu and Passeron, 1979; DiMaggio, 1982). We can also think of some survey questions which could be used to measure cultural capital in the Japanese context: the frequency of the use of honorific and polite forms of language at home, and terms with which children address their parents. For example, *papa, otosan* and *tochan* all denote 'father' in English, but they imply different levels of politeness. The use of the more polite form will probably develop the children's use of honorific and polite forms of language and awareness of the social relationships between senior and junior position.
6. However, the difference appears to be somewhat exaggerated because many Japanese school days include sports days, cultural festival days, schools excursions and many days of preparing for these events (e.g., Rohlen, 1983, pp. 160–9). Under the American system, many of these events take place outside the normal school days, such as camping organized by volunteer groups during the summer holidays.
7. The standard deviation is used as the measure of variability and the coefficient of variation is used as the measure of inequality in Table 3.1. Standard deviation for proportions is $\sqrt{P(1 - P)}$, where P is the proportion. The coefficient of variation is calculated by dividing the standard deviation by the mean. For graded schooling, the coefficient of variation implies the extent of variability around the mean, regardless of the value of the mean. For high school graduation (and other 0–1 variables), the coefficient of variation approaches positive infinity when the proportion of high school graduates in the sample becomes close to zero while it approaches zero when the proportion becomes close to 1.0. In other words, the measure of inequality decreases as more and more people in the sample graduate from high schools. Our definition of equal distribution of high school graduation (or any 0–1 variable) thus implies universal high school completion in the sample.

8. The 95 per cent confidence interval of the total years of schooling is estimated from the mean of 10.83 years (SSM) and 11.52 years (OCG) and the standard deviation of 2.79 years (SSM) and 3.76 years (OCG). The distribution is assumed to be normal.
9. However, a small number of people in the sample probably have not completed the process of acquiring qualifications.
10. The total increase in educational attainment may be an underestimate since some men in the youngest cohort probably have not completed their schooling. The underestimation is probably more crucial for American men because a non-negligible portion of people in the cohort were in the military and some men return to school after a few years of working experience.
11. The logistic regression estimates are obtained using GLIM (Payne, 1985). The dependent variable is the log of odds on completing various levels of education.
12. In Japan, attendance beyond the old system elementary school and the new system middle school is considered beyond the minimum level. In the United States, the completion of more than 8 years of schooling indicates attendance beyond the minimum level.
13. The effect of race is not significant, but a comparable variable does not exist in Japan and Britain.
14. R^2 is a goodness of fit statistic and is calculated by the following formula (Aldrich and Nelson, 1984, p. 57):

$$-2\log (L_0/L_1)/(N+2\log(L_0/L_1))$$

where L_0 is the maximum of the likelihood function when only the intercept is included and L_1 is the maximum of the likelihood function when all the independent variables are in the model (cf. Maddala, 1983, pp. 38–40).

15. The two extreme categories used to compute the hypothetical difference are as follows: farm origin (0 and 1), urban origin (0 and 1), family income (1 and 5), parents' education (0 and 16 years or 1 and 3 for Britain), siblings (0 and 10), and father's occupation (13 and 78 points). Non-significant effects were omitted in calculation. Race is held constant in the American sample. These two men are, of course, hypothetical examples and do not really exist in our empirical data.
16. These figures are calculated by (1) multiplying the family income coefficient by four because the highest and the lowest categories in the family income variable are separated by four categories, and then (2) taking the anti-log to express the difference between the two men in terms of odds, rather than log-odds.
17. A farmer's standard international prestige score is 40 and a lawyer's is 72. These scores are used to compute the overall effect of social capital. The difference in odds reported below is based on adding significant effects of social capital and taking the anti-log of the accumulated effect.
18. Since the trends of social background differentials in the minimum level

of education resemble those of high school completion and the attainment of O-level or equivalent qualifications, our trend analysis concentrates on two levels of educational attainment.

19. Some men in the youngest cohort probably have not completed their schooling. The effects of social background in this cohort may consequently increase as the cohort ages.
20. The *D* values were 2.08 in the oldest, 7.58 in the middle, and 8.17 in the youngest cohort.
21. The decline in the average size of siblings from the oldest to the youngest cohort was from 4.16 to 2.77 in Japan, from 4.42 to 3.36 in the United States and from 3.51 to 2.21 in Britain.
22. The data mainly come from the OCGI survey. For details about the sample, see Jencks *et al.* (1972, Appendix B).
23. The original data come from the survey of more than 150 000 high school seniors who graduated from Japanese senior high school in 1968. The survey was conducted by the Ministry of Education. Ehara (1984) selected about 20 000 samples from the original survey and analyzed the relationship among social background characteristics, school types, grades and college attendance. Our estimate is based on the sample of male high school graduates from two types of public high school (selective and non-selective vocational schools). 33 per cent of our sample attended college full-time following high school graduation (for details, see Ehara, 1984, Appendix A and Table A.4). The log of odds on attending college was predicted first by the father's occupation (manual and non-manual) and the type of school (selective and non-selective) and then by these two variables plus high school grades. The change in the coefficient of the father's occupation indicates the impact of high school grades on the net effect of the father's occupation on college attendance. No detailed occupational classification was available in the survey. The survey also did not provide information on college quality.

4 The Process of Socio-economic Attainment

4.1 INTRODUCTION

Educational credentials are known to influence socioeconomic status. In the United States, sociologists have been concerned with the relative impact of education on occupational status since the original formulation of the status attainment model (Duncan and Hodge, 1963; Blau and Duncan, 1967). Probably one of the major contributions in the American study of stratification and mobility in the 1960s was the quantitative documentation of the relative impact of education and of the father's occupation on occupational status attainment. The 'effect of education' referred to the achieved and universalistic criteria and the 'effect of the father's occupation' to the ascribed and particularistic criteria for allocation of occupational positions. The supremacy of the former over the latter led to the general conclusion that 'the American occupational structure is largely governed by universalistic criteria of performance and achievement' (Blau and Duncan, 1967, p. 241).

Economists have long been preoccupied with the issue of income return to education. Human capital theorists in the United States (e.g., Mincer, 1974; Becker, 1964) claim that lengthier schooling can be seen as an individual's decision to invest in his own skills, and that differential investment in human capital results in differential productivity which in turn leads to differential earnings. Other economists argue that education does not necessarily produce productive skills, but may serve as a screening device (Arrow, 1973) or a signalling function (Spence, 1974) which presents differences in ability or trainability (Thurow, 1975), or is believed to do so. While there is disagreement about the interpretation of the relationship between education and monetary rewards, income differences as stratified by educational credentials are well documented in the United States. After controlling for experience, measured ability, and family background, Jencks *et al.* (1979, pp. 183–4) found that completing a high school education would probably raise earnings by 15 to 25 per cent, and completing a four-year college education might raise earnings by as much as 40 per cent.

In Britain, individual position in the labour market is often conceived as a class rather than a status (e.g., Goldthorpe, 1987; Marshall *et al.*, 1988). However, there are studies which concern the process of socioeconomic status attainment (Kerckhoff, 1974; Psacharopoulos, 1977; Mayhew and Rosewell, 1981; Greenhalgh and Stewart, 1985). Halsey (1977), for example, has applied the status attainment model to the British survey data using the Hope-Goldthorpe scale of occupation (Goldthorpe and Hope, 1974). He reported the strong effect of education on both the first and the current occupational status, independent of the father's education and occupation. British labour economists (Psacharopoulos and Layard, 1979; Greenhalgh, 1980; Dolton and Makepeace, 1986, 1987) produced a number of studies which showed the effect of various academic and vocational qualifications on earnings. According to Psacharopoulos and Layard's estimate (1979, p. 498), the attainment of an O-level increased annual earnings by about 20 per cent and the possession of an ONC vocational qualification increased it by 45 per cent.

The relationship between education and labour market outcomes is also well documented in Japan. The effect of educational credentials on occupation is evident in the differential opportunities open to youths who obtain different levels of educational credentials. Table 4.1 shows the distribution of first entry occupations among all male high school students and all male university students who graduated and entered the labour force in 1982.[1] The occupational differences are clearly evident: almost 40 per cent of the college graduates obtained professional, technical and managerial jobs, in contrast to 3 per cent of the high school graduates. The majority of the high school graduates were engaged in craft and production work while less than 1 per cent of the university graduates were so occupied. The occupational labour market thus appears to be segregated by educational credentials (cf. Sengoku and Matsubara, 1978).

Educational credentials determine not only the technical division of labour but also its monetary rewards. In 1983, male high school graduates earned 80 per cent of what male university graduates earned at the time of their entry into the labour market (Rodosho, 1984, Table 115). Fujita (1980, p. 169) estimated that the life-time earnings of high school graduates would be 85 per cent of what university graduates obtained. Numerous studies by Japanese economists have documented such 'monetary gaps' arising from differences in educational credentials and differential age–income profiles

Table 4.1 Distribution of first entry occupation among male high school graduates and male college graduates in Japan, 1982

	High school graduates		*College graduates*	
	(*N*)	(%)	(*N*)	(%)
Professional Technical	9 316	3.2	85 597	37.3
Managerial	–[a]	–	669	0.3
Clerical	28 167	9.7	75 418	32.9
Sales	45 584	15.7	57 618	25.1
Farm, Forestry Fishery and Mining	7 501	2.6	605	0.3
Transportation and Communication	15 187	5.2	601	0.3
Craft and Production	147 574	50.9	1 219	0.5
Service	32 227	11.1	5 799	2.5
Other	4 283	1.5	1 789	0.8
Total	289 839	100.0	229 315	100.0

Note:
[a] The figure for 'managerial' was not available. It is included in the 'other' category.

Source: Monbusho (1982a) Table 6 and (1982b) Table 238.

by education (see, for instance, articles in Funahashi, 1967; Shimada, 1974, 1978).

Despite the proliferation of studies on the relationship between education and the labour market, very little work has been done on the cross-national comparison of the effect of education on socioeconomic outcomes. Although some studies (Koike and Watanabe, 1979; Takeuchi and Aso, 1981; Koike, 1988) attempted a cross-national comparison of earnings differentials by educational credentials, these studies suffered from methodological shortcomings and the non-comparable nature of their data-sets.

For example, Koike and Watanabe (1979; cf. Koike, 1988) relied on the 1960 US Census for the American data and the 1971 Wage Census for the Japanese data. As the authors fully acknowledge (1979, pp. 74–5), there are serious differences between the two data-sets. The two most important differences are: (1) income in the American data includes not only wage but also non-wage income, while the Japanese data includes strictly wage income, and (2) the Japanese data are a sample of employees who work in an establishment that employs more than 10 employees in 1970, while the American data come from the 1960 Census which includes all employees, their employers and the self-employed. These differences are too large to be ignored, and we should be cautious of any conclusions drawn in the comparison of income gaps among different societies.

The primary objective of this chapter, therefore, is to conduct a more precise comparative study of the socioeconomic attainment process in Japan, the United States and Britain. Using nationally representative samples and measuring occupational status and income in a comparable way, we will compare the total effect of educational credentials on socioeconomic status in the three countries. Another important cross-national comparison involves the relative effect of educational credentials. The thesis of industrialism suggests that the allocation of socioeconomic position is more likely to be based on achieved criteria (such as education) than on ascribed factors of social background among industrial societies. The importance of educational credentials relative to social background factors in determining socioeconomic status will therefore be compared across all three societies.

The second objective of this chapter is to estimate the net direct effect of educational credentials on socioeconomic attainment. American studies (e.g., Featherman and Hauser, 1978) on the status attainment process have documented that schooling increases occupational status and income, independent of social background. In contrast, none of the studies by Japanese economists on wage differentials by different levels of education controls for social background. The apparent income gaps among men with different levels of education may be due to the fact that better-educated men came from more advantaged backgrounds which influenced both their educational attainment and their socioeconomic status. The income differences by educational credentials may be overestimated due to the spurious effect of social background on education and income.

The third objective of this chapter focuses on the role that social background plays in determining men's socioeconomic success. The effect of social background characteristics on labour market outcomes has been overlooked in the Japanese literature. Japanese social scientists have often analyzed separately the linkages between background and education and between education and labour market outcomes. In contrast to the studies done in the United States, in Japan very little is known about the mechanism by which various characteristics of men's social background affect their later success in the labour market. This chapter will examine such a mechanism in detail by distinguishing three elements of social background: economic, social and cultural capital resources. This chapter will assess both the extent of the direct impact of these three resources on labour market outcomes independent of education, and the extent of the indirect impact through education. The former component refers to 'the direct reproduction mechanism' of social background, and the latter to 'the indirect reproduction mechanism' or 'the transmission function of education'. These two processes through which background affects attainment will be compared among the three societies.

The fourth and last issue concerning the relationship between educational credentials and the labour market is the enduring effect of credentials on men's socioeconomic careers. Japanese researchers (Tomoda, 1977; Ushiogi, 1980; Hashizume, 1976a, 1976b) claim that one of the most serious problems of 'credentialism' in Japan is its long-lasting impact: once men obtain educational credentials they tend to become an ascribed factor which significantly influences later career achievement, independently of what the men actually do in the workplace. It is thus important to assess whether socioeconomic attainment is affected by educational credentials long after people obtain them, and whether the long-lasting effect exists only in Japan.

In order to estimate the long-term effect of education, this study will examine the net effect of educational credentials on current occupational status in the three countries, independent of its effect through initial occupational status. If the net effect on later socioeconomic status is larger than the effect through the first occupation, the results will imply that the effect of credentials lasts long after entry into the labour market. Age–income profiles for different levels of education will also be compared, in order to examine whether the income gaps between levels of education widen as men proceed in their careers.

The empirical analysis of this chapter on the process of status attainment in the three societies will also throw light on the issue of 'educational credentialism' in Japan, discussed in Chapter 1. The thesis of 'educational credentialism' implies that the status attainment process in Japan is distinct in that the role of educational credentials in determining socioeconomic success is maximized. The body of this chapter will empirically assess three propositions derived from this thesis: (1) the socioeconomic benefits of educational credentials are greater in Japan than in the United States and Britain; (2) the relative impact of educational credentials on socioeconomic achievement as against the total effect of social background is more important in Japan than in other societies – that is, the dominance of the universalistic criteria of performance over the particularistic criteria of social origin in determining socioeconomic outcomes is more pronounced in Japan; and (3) the effect of educational credentials is long-lasting in that credentials affect not only a man's initial labour market status at the time of his entry into the labour force, but also his later socioeconomic achievement throughout his entire career in Japan. This chapter will attempt to test these propositions; the thesis of 'educational credentialism' in Japan is therefore the underlying substantive argument guiding the chapter.

The variables included in this chapter build on the variables in Chapter 3. All the social background variables are identical to those used there. We have grouped social background variables under the headings of economic, social and cultural capital. Educational attainment is measured by credentials because it is based on the belief that credentials, rather than simple years of schooling, have consequences in labour market outcomes (cf. Griffin and Alexander, 1978). Obtaining a junior high school degree in Japan and completing 8 years of education in the United States entitles individuals to participate in the labour market with a minimum credential. Obtaining a high school diploma or an O-level qualification in Britain constitutes another important educational qualification. A bachelor's degree (hereafter a BA degree) – that is, graduating from an institution of higher education – provides a passport to enter the labour market for college graduates.[2] The attainment of various vocational and professional qualifications – ONC, HNC, Level C and Level B qualifications – are also important resources in the British labour market. These educational credential dummy variables are thus included in the regression analysis predicting socioeconomic achievement.

Three labour market outcomes are considered in this chapter: the first occupational status, the current occupational status and the current total individual income. The occupational status is measured by the International Occupational Prestige Scores (IPS), so that the same scale is applied to all three societies. The total individual income is used as a measure of economic success in a society.[3] Using an appropriate exchange rate, the income is expressed in US dollars.[4] Variables measuring 'cumulative work experience' and 'decay of work ability' are included in the regression analysis of income; these variables take into account the fact that income increases as experience increases until a certain age and then income stabilizes and declines at older ages as productive abilities of workers 'decay', or are believed to do so (Featherman and Hauser, 1978).

4.2 RELATIVE IMPACT OF SOCIAL ORIGIN AND EDUCATION ON SOCIOECONOMIC INEQUALITY

This first analysis section compares the overall impact of all the social background characteristics (including both the direct effect and the indirect effect as carried through education) with the impact of educational credentials (independent of social background) in explaining socioeconomic inequality. It examines how much of the inequality or variance in occupational status and income can be explained by the variation in social background characteristics and by the variation in educational credentials as distributed independently of the force of social background. The comparison between the explanatory power of social background and that of education corresponds to the comparison between the ascribed and particularistic forces versus the achieved and universalistic factor in explaining socioeconomic inequality. The former refers to the total reproduction function of social background and the latter to the mobility function of education. The ratio of the latter to the former indicates the relative importance of the achieved over the ascribed criteria in determining the distribution of rewards in the labour market.

Table 4.2 presents the proportion of variance in first occupational status, current occupational status and income explained by all social background characteristics and by educational credentials.[5] The total variance in occupational status and income can be decomposed into three components: (1) the total effect of social background (the sum of the direct and indirect effect), (2) the net direct effect of education, and (3) the unexplained variance which is independent of both social background and education.

In Japan, 9.8 per cent of variance in the first occupational status is explained by all social background characteristics and the additional 11.3 per cent is explained by educational credentials. The remaining 78.9 per cent is the unexplained variance which is not related to social background and education. The ratio between the proportion of variance explained by education and that explained by social background is 1.153 : 1.00. The explanatory power of educational credentials is almost identical to that of social background.[6] The ratio for the

Table 4.2 Proportion of variance in first occupation, current occupation and income explained by social background and educational credentials, in Japan (SSM), the United States (OCG) and Britain (OMS)

	First occupational status		
	Japan	**United States**	**Britain**
Social background	0.098 (46%)	0.153 (34%)	0.174 (50%)
Education	0.113 (54%)	0.299 (66%)	0.172 (50%)
Total	0.211 (100%)	0.452 (100%)	0.346 (100%)
Ratio	1.153	1.954	0.989
	Current occupational status		
	Japan	**United States**	**Britain**
Social background	0.105 (53%)	0.140 (38%)	0.161 (44%)
Education	0.095 (47%)	0.228 (62%)	0.205 (56%)
Total	0.200 (100%)	0.368 (100%)	0.366 (100%)
Ratio	0.905	1.629	1.785
	Income		
	Japan	**United States**	**Britain**
Experience	0.082 (42%)	0.068 (31%)	0.048 (18%)
Social background	0.076 (39%)	0.082 (37%)	0.118 (44%)
Education	0.037 (19%)	0.071 (32%)	0.104 (39%)
Total	0.195 (100%)	0.221 (100%)	0.270 (100%)
Ratio	0.487	0.866	0.881

current occupational status (0.905) implies that the proportion of variance explained by educational credentials is slightly smaller than that explained by social background variables. When the relative effects on income inequality are examined, the effect of education is almost half (0.487) of the overall impact of social background net of labour market experience.

These results seem to indicate that, when we take into account various social background characteristics, the dominance of the universalistic criteria (educational credentials) over the particularistic criteria (social background) in explaining socioeconomic inequality is not clearly evident in Japan. In no way is the overall effect of social background substantially less powerful than the achieved education, as the thesis of 'educational credentialism' would suggest.

In the United States, the proportions of variance in the first and the current occupational status which are accounted for by educational credentials are clearly higher than those accounted for by social background characteristics. The explanatory power of education seems to be more important than that of social background. However, educational credentials appear to play a less important role than social background in explaining income inequality. In Britain, educational credentials and social background both explain almost the same proportion of variance in the first occupational status (17 per cent) while a larger proportion of variation in the current occupational status is explained by educational credentials. However, considering the income inequality, the effect of education is smaller than that of social background.

Cross-national comparison of the relative importance of education in explaining socioeconomic inequality (comparing the ratios across nations) seems to suggest that educational credentials play a more important role in the United States and Britain than in Japan. Contrary to the prediction of 'educational credentialism' in Japan, the relative explanatory power of education in determining socioeconomic outcomes appears to be less pronounced there.

It is probably important to add that the relative importance of labour market experience shows cross-national variation. The effect of labour market experience in explaining income inequality relative to other factors appears to be larger in Japan than in the United States and Britain. This finding may reflect the Japanese employment practice that wage tends to increase according to the length of service – the *nenko* system (Cole, 1979; Inagami, 1988).

The increasing importance of education in the twentieth century appears to be documented by the intertemporal change in the effects of social background versus education on occupational and income inequality. Table 4.3 shows the proportion of variance in first occupation, current occupation, and income explained by all social background characteristics and by educational credentials broken down by cohort.[7] The importance of education relative to social background in explaining socioeconomic inequality is shown on the rows labelled Ratio in Table 4.3. This shows the extent of dominance of education over social origin in determining socioeconomic outcomes. The general trend indicated in the ratios is the one of an increasing relative importance of education across successive cohorts in all three societies: the ratios generally increase as we move from the oldest to the youngest cohort.[8] This trend is consistent with the prediction of the industrialism thesis. Since all three societies experienced indus-

Table 4.3 Proportion of variance in first occupation, current occupation and income explained by social background and educational credentials by cohort in Japan (SSM), the United States (OCG) and Britain (OMS)

	First occupation			*Current occupation*		
	20–34	*35–49*	*50–64*	*20–34*	*35–49*	*50–64*
Japan						
Social background	0.076	0.114	0.159	0.062	0.142	0.189
Education	0.108	0.138	0.121	0.114	0.108	0.137
Total	0.184	0.252	0.280	0.176	0.250	0.326
Ratio	1.421	1.211	0.761	1.839	0.761	0.725
United States						
Social background	0.149	0.177	0.160	0.123	0.198	0.188
Education	0.274	0.318	0.275	0.224	0.229	0.182
Total	0.423	0.495	0.435	0.347	0.427	0.370
Ratio	1.839	1.797	1.719	1.821	1.157	0.968
Britain						
Social background	0.154	0.173	0.145	0.167	0.195	0.158
Education	0.190	0.184	0.128	0.241	0.210	0.151
Total	0.344	0.357	0.273	0.408	0.405	0.309
Ratio	1.234	1.064	0.883	1.443	1.077	0.956

	Income		
	20–34	*35–49*	*50–64*
Japan			
Experience	0.064	0.008	0.128
Social background	0.050	0.080	0.078
Education	0.044	0.040	0.024
Total	0.158	0.128	0.231
Ratio	0.880	0.500	0.308
United States			
Experience	0.074	0.044	0.078
Social background	0.067	0.079	0.068
Education	0.071	0.069	0.043
Total	0.212	0.192	0.189
Ratio	1.060	0.873	0.632
Britain			
Experience	0.072	0.029	0.055
Social background	0.087	0.174	0.112
Education	0.062	0.131	0.130
Total	0.221	0.334	0.297
Ratio	0.723	0.752	1.161

trialization in the twentieth century, according to the thesis the universalistic criteria should become more important in allocating socioeconomic position during the period. Since the effect of education is independent of social background, the rising relative importance of educational achievement may be interpreted as an increasing use of the universalistic criteria in socioeconomic attainment.

It should be noticed, however, that intercohort changes in the relative effect of education reflect not only changes in the historical context but also changes in an individual's life-cycle. The attainment of current occupation and income is influenced by a man's life-cycle stage. Previous research (Featherman, 1971; 1973) suggests that the effects of both social origin and education are stronger in the earlier life-cycle, but it is not clear how the relative effect of education is affected by changes in life-stage. Our results on the effects on current occupation and income should therefore be interpreted cautiously. On the other hand, the intercohort analysis of the effects on first occupation does not confound changes in the life-cycle with historical changes because all men, regardless of their cohort, obtained their first job at almost the same life-stage. When we focus on the relative effect of education on first occupation, we still find an increasing relative importance of education across successive cohorts in all three societies. This trend seems to be most apparent in Japan because the ratios increased substantially from 0.761 to 1.421. All these results lead us to suggest that the socioeconomic attainment has become more responsive to educational achievement relative to social origin.

4.3 SOCIAL BACKGROUND AND SOCIOECONOMIC ATTAINMENT

The previous section showed the overall effect of all social background characteristics on the inequality of occupational status and income. This section will examine in detail the linkage between social background and socioeconomic outcomes. As in Chapter 3, we distinguish three resources of social background: economic, social and cultural capital. First, we compare the effects of various forms of capital on occupational status and income. Second, we examine the process through which they affect socioeconomic achievement.

Cross-national comparison of social background effects

Table 4.4 presents the effects of various social background characteristics on the first occupational status and the current occupational status. In order to highlight the effects, two extreme categories of each variable are contrasted and the difference in the international occupational prestige scores between the two categories shown. For example, the effect of family income on the first occupational status in Japan (5.2) indicates that the expected difference between a man from a 'very wealthy family' and a man from a 'very poor family' is 5.2 points on the IPS scale when other background characteristics are identical between the two.[9]

The cross-national comparison suggests several important differences in the effect of social background. First, the effect of economic capital on the attainment of occupational status is stronger among Japanese and British than among American men. The difference between a man from a 'very wealthy family' and a man from a 'very poor family' results in a 5-point difference in both the first occupational status and the current occupational status in Japan. In Britain, the difference between the two men is about the same: 4 points in the first and the current occupation. In contrast, the amount of economic capital does not seem to affect the current occupational status, and its effect on the first occupational status is also limited in the United States. In other words, American families seem to have difficulty in transforming economic resources into occupational status advantage between the two generations.

Second, the effects of cultural capital on occupational attainment are present in all three societies. In the United States and Britain, both the effects of the father's and the mother's education are significant. In the United States, when both father and mother are university-educated, the sons are estimated to have higher occupational status by 9 points than the sons whose parents had no formal education. In Britain, when both parents had some academic qualifications, the sons are expected to have about a 7-point advantage in occupational attainment over the sons whose parents received minimum education in non-selective secondary schools. Among Japanese men, only the effect of the father's education is present; having a parent who is a university graduate as opposed to a parent with no education is worth about a six-point advantage in occupational status. Highly credentialized parents are able to influence their son's occupational performance in all three societies.

Table 4.4 Comparison of the effects of social background variables on first occupational status and current occupational status in Japan (SSM), the United States (OCG) and Britain (OMS)

	First occupation			*Current occupation*		
	Japan	**United States**	**Britain**	**Japan**	**United States**	**Britain**
Economic capital						
Family income	5.2[a]	2.3	4.3	5.2	NS[b]	4.2
Cultural capital						
Father's education	6.0	3.8	3.7	5.1	3.5	4.5
Mother's education	NS	5.8	2.8	NS	5.6	2.5
Social capital						
Father's occupation	12.1	15.9	10.5	15.5	12.6	15.1
Urban background	NS	2.0	NS	NS	2.2	NS
Farm origin	NS	NS	-2.9	-2.4	-1.3	-2.2
Siblings	NS	-6.0	-6.9	NS	-5.5	-8.3
Race	–	2.0	–	–	4.2	–

Notes:
[a] The figures indicate the difference in the international occupational prestige scores (IPS) between the two extreme categories of each independent variable after controlling for other background variables.
[b] NS indicates that the effect is not significant at 0.05 level.

Third, the intergenerational transmission of occupational status is clearly evident and the extent of transmission appears to be almost identical in all three societies. If two men had fathers with very different occupations – for example, a garbage collector and a physician – but other background characteristics were identical, then they would differ in their first occupational status by 12 points in Japan, 16 points in the United States, and 11 points in Britain. Similarly, their current occupational status would differ by 15 points in Japan and Britain and 13 points in the United States. The 16-point difference on the IPS scale refers to the difference in occupational prestige between an accountant (62) and a retail dealer (46). Although there is no perfect reproduction of occupational hierarchy, families of prestigious occupations on the average successfully pass on their advantaged position in all three societies.

Fourth, other social capital had differential impacts on the occupational attainment in all three countries. American men from an urban origin experienced a 2-point advantage in the first and the current occupational status, while Japanese and British men from an urban background did not enjoy any advantage if they were identical with respect to other background characteristics. On the other hand, the disadvantage of farm origin can be found among British men in the attainment of both the first and current occupational status. Among Japanese and American men, farm origin affects only the attainment of current occupational status. Men of farm background scored on the average 2 to 3 points less than their non-farm counterparts in all three societies. The number of siblings appears to be a distinct disadvantage in American and British societies. The consequence of 10 additional siblings resulted in a 6-point reduction in the first and the current occupational status in the United States. The handicap of coming from a larger family appears to be even greater in Britain: 10 siblings will cost a 7-point reduction in the first occupation and an 8-point reduction in the current occupation. Finally, white Americans enjoyed a 2-point bonus in the first occupation and a 4-point bonus in the current occupation, even when other background characteristics were equivalent.

Table 4.5 presents a similar comparison for the social background effects on income. Some important cross-national differences in the effects of various social backgrounds can be found. First, the reproduction of economic capital is much more salient in the United States. The effect of family income in the United States is more than twice as much as the effect in Japan and Britain. The income difference between a man from a 'very wealthy family' and a man from a 'very poor family' is as much as $4469 in the United States, even though these two men are identical with respect to other social background characteristics.

Second, the effects of cultural capital on income show the same pattern found in occupational status. Both the father's and the mother's education exert significant effects in the United States and Britain. The influence of the father's education is apparent only in Japan. The income advantage of having a parent with a BA degree as opposed to a parent with no formal education is rather substantial in the United States and Japan.

Third, the role of the father's occupational status in determining economic success is evident in all three countries. When other background characteristics are identical, a man whose father is a physician and a man whose father is a garbage collector are expected to differ in their absolute income by $4007 in the United States, by $3375 in Japan, and by $1715 in Britain.

Fourth, the income advantage associated with an urban back-

Table 4.5 Comparison of the effects of social background variables on income in Japan (SSM), the United States (OCG) and Britain (OMS)

	Income		
	Japan	**United States**	**Britain**
Economic capital			
Family income	1865[a]	4469	1800
Cultural capital			
Father's education	2634	1653	817
Mother's education	NS[b]	2782	580
Social capital			
Father's occupation	3375	4007	1715
Urban background	660	1328	309
Farm origin	–726	–700	–492
Siblings	NS	–2228	–881
Race	–	1933	–

Notes:
[a] The figures indicate the difference in dollar income between the two extreme categories of each independence variable after controlling for other background variables and experience and decay.
[b] NS indicates that the effect is not significant at 0.05 level.

ground and non-farm origin is present in all three societies. The net benefit of an urban background among American men is substantially larger than its benefit among Japanese and British men. The cost of a farm origin is slightly larger in Japan and the United States than in Britain. As in occupational attainment, family size does not have a significant effect on income attainment in Japanese society, but the handicap associated with large families is present in American and British societies. An additional sibling reduces absolute income by $223 in the United States and by $88 in Britain. Finally, the net cost of being a non-white was $1933 in the United States.

Relative effects of economic, social and cultural capital

Table 4.6 shows the relative importance of economic, social and cultural capital in occupational and income attainment in all three societies. Table 4.6 departs from our previous tables in that the effects of social background are represented by 'composite capital variables'. For example, the father's and the mother's education are

Table 4.6 Relative impacts of economic, cultural and social capital on occupational and income attainment in Japan (SSM), the United States (OCG) and Britain (OMS)

	First occupation		*Current occupation*		*Income*[a]	
	Weights[b]	*Sheaf*[c]	*Weights*	*Sheaf*	*Weights*	*Sheaf*
Japan						
Economic capital	–	0.094	–	0.079	–	0.072
Family income	1.000	–	1.000	–	1.000	–
Cultural capital	–	0.129	–	0.092	–	0.144
Father's education	0.841	–	0.851	–	0.712	–
Mother's education	0.227	–	0.205	–	0.376	–
Social capital	–	0.197	–	0.246	–	0.166
Father's occupation	0.980	–	0.856	–	0.695	–
Urban background	0.055	–	0.070	–	0.352	–
Farm origin	–0.069	–	–0.405	–	–0.460	–
Siblings	–0.009	–	–0.172	–	–0.151	–
United States						
Economic capital	–	0.038	–	NS[d]	–	0.117
Family income	1.000	–	–	–	1.000	–
Cultural capital	–	0.136	–	0.137	–	0.099
Father's education	0.445	–	0.433	–	0.423	–
Mother's education	0.645	–	0.657	–	0.665	–
Social capital	–	0.280	–	0.290	–	0.181
Father's occupation	0.696	–	0.561	–	0.424	–
Urban background	0.239	–	0.263	–	0.383	–
Farm origin	–0.045	–	–0.138	–	–0.180	–
Siblings	–0.419	–	–0.395	–	–0.380	–
Race	0.146	–	0.310	–	0.337	–
Britain						
Economic capital	–	0.132	–	0.104	–	0.217
Family income	1.000	–	1.000	–	1.000	–
Cultural capital	–	0.140	–	0.124	–	0.120
Father's education	0.674	–	0.755	–	0.696	–
Mother's education	0.499	–	0.397	–	0.472	–

	First occupation		*Current occupation*		*Income*	
	Weights	*Sheaf*	*Weights*	*Sheaf*	*Weights*	*Sheaf*
Social capital	–	0.262	–	0.275	–	0.165
Father's occupation	0.641	–	0.719	–	0.660	–
Urban background	0.079	–	0.074	–	0.275	–
Farm origin	–0.277	–	–0.162	–	–0.297	–
Siblings	–0.594	–	–0.549	–	–0.475	–

Notes:
[a] The effects on income are those after controlling for experience and decay.
[b] The weights are the standardized partial regression coefficients attached to composite capital variables.
[c] The sheaf figures are the sheaf coefficients of composite variables.
[d] NS indicates that the effect is not significant at 0.05 level.

'collected' in a single composite variable called 'cultural capital' whose effect on socioeconomic status indicates a 'combined' effect of parental education. The composite capital variable is treated as an unmeasured variable which is completely determined by one or more measured indicators – in our case social background variables. The weights in creating composite capital variables are determined to maximize the relationship between composite variables and the dependent variable.[10] Both the composite and its component variables are included in a single model, and various social background variables exert their influence on socioeconomic status through the composite capital variables. The model allows us to assess (1) the relative weight of social background variables in forming the composite variables, and (2) the relative impact of sets of variables on socioeconomic attainment through the use of 'composite capital variables'.

Figure 4.1 depicts the nature of the model. It shows how social background characteristics affect first occupational status in Japan through three composite capital variables. The data are taken from Table 4.6 and indicate standardized partial regression coefficients. The effect of cultural capital on first occupational status, for example, shows the 'combined' effect of the father's and the mother's education on first occupation, often called a 'sheaf' coefficient (Whitt, 1986). We can also compute the effect of an individual social background variable on first occupation by multiplying coefficients attached to the paths joining two variables. For example, the effect of the father's education on first occupation is 0.108 which is the product of 0.841 and 0.129. By comparing the effects of composite capital variables on first occupation, we find the effect of social capital to be

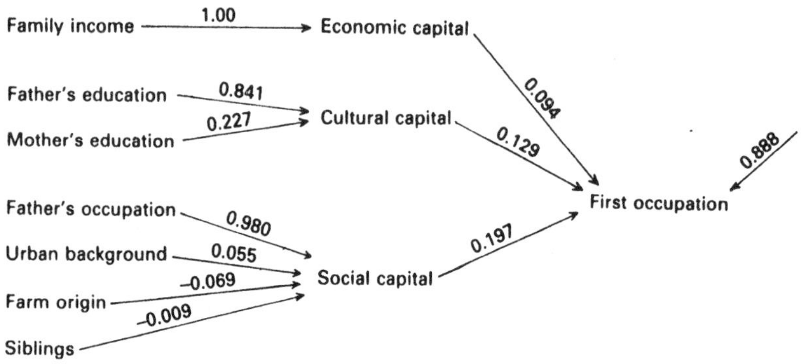

Figure 4.1 Relationship among social background characteristics, composite capital variables and occupational attainment in Japan (SSM)

Note: Correlations among social background characteristics are assumed.

strongest, followed by that of cultural capital and economic capital. By comparing the weights of the social capital composite variable, we find that the father's occupation exerts by far the strongest weight. Figure 4.1 shows how the information provided in Table 4.6 can be drawn on the diagram. With this model in mind, let us go back to Table 4.6 and examine the relative importance of economic, social and cultural capital in the three societies.

As far as the attainment of first and current occupation is concerned, social capital is more important than economic and cultural capital in all three societies; the sheaf coefficients for social capital are generally twice as large as those for economic and cultural capital. This finding is not surprising when we learn that the major determinant of social capital is the father's occupation. In particular, in Japan, the relative weight of the father's occupation in forming the social capital composite is striking: 0.980 in first occupation and 0.856 in current occupation. No other social background characteristics rival the weight of the father's occupation. In the United States and in Britain, the father's occupation no doubt exerts a strong relative weight in shaping social capital, but the effect of the number of siblings cannot be ignored. The relative weight of family size is much larger than those of other background characteristics, and in Britain it is only slightly less than the relative effect of the father's occupation. These findings reveal the importance of social capital in occupational attainment and confirm our observation in the previous section that the intergenerational transmission of occupational status is clearly evident in all three societies.

With regard to income attainment, the relative importance of economic, social and cultural capital shows cross-national variation. In Britain, economic capital appears to be a far more important determinant of economic status than other capital. Relative to other factors determined at birth, family wealth and property seems to be more consequential in economic success in Britain than in the other two nations. In the United States and Japan, social capital exerts a stronger influence on income attainment than other capital. As the weights on the social capital variable indicate, the effect of the father's occupation on income attainment operated through social capital is substantial, especially in Japan. The individual effect of the father's occupation (0.115) is even larger than the effect of economic capital (0.072) in Japan.[11] It is also important to notice that the relative importance of economic capital in determining monetary success is very weak in Japan; this suggests that although the reproduction of economic advantage between generations is present in Japan, the extent of reproduction compared to other forms of transmitting the advantages between generations is probably not as strong as in other nations.

Finally, the comparison of the weights of social background variables in the composite variables shows how each component contributes to the effect of the composite variables. The dominant component of the effect of social capital on socioeconomic attainment is the father's occupation in all three societies: the weight of the father's occupation is by far the strongest. The relative weights of the father's education and the mother's education in the effect of cultural capital are not uniform across nations. In Japan and Britain, the father's education exerts more weight than the mother's education while the opposite seems to be the case in the United States. It is not clear, however, why the effect of the mother's education is more consequential to socioeconomic attainment among American men.

Mechanism of reproduction: direct reproduction *vs* transmission through education

One of the most important issues about the relationship between social background and socioeconomic attainment is the process through which social background influences labour market achievement and the role of education in mediating the effect of social background. Families with considerable resources are able to pass on their advantages directly to their offspring independent of the offspring's own achievement. These families are also able to reproduce their advantaged position by favourably influencing their offspring's school performance and educational achievement. It is therefore particularly important to estimate the extent of the direct reproduction and the extent of the transmission through education. The mechanism of reproduction will be examined separately for the different capital from which men can benefit in their background.

Table 4.7 shows the decomposition of the total effect of economic, cultural and social capital on the first and the current occupational status into the direct reproduction and the indirect transmission through education. The effects of these forms of capital are indicated by the sheaf coefficients – that is, standardized partial regression coefficients for the composite capital variables. The effect of the father's occupation on occupational status is shown separately because it represents the process of occupational transmission between the generations. The structure of the reproductive mechanism among the three countries may be summarized by three points. First, the intergenerational occupational transmission occurs mainly by direct inheritance in Japan, while it takes place through both direct and indirect routes in the United States and Britain. Nearly two-thirds of the total occupational inheritance is independent of education in Japan: men whose father held prestigious occupations are more likely to maintain their occupational advantage through direct inheritance than through education. In comparison, American and British men inherit the occupational advantage of their fathers equally through the means of education and through direct inheritance. The role of education in mediating the mechanism of occupational status reproduction appears to be more prominent in the United States and Britain.

Second, the effect of cultural capital is almost entirely mediated by education in all three countries. Highly credentialized parents tend to insure an advantaged occupational status for their sons by influencing the sons' educational achievement. None of these societies shows significant direct effects of parental education after the indirect route is controlled for.

Third, the effect of economic capital in Japan and Britain goes through both direct and indirect routes. Wealthy families tend to have sons with prestigious occupations, both because they can provide their sons with better education and because they can directly influence the job allocation process. In comparison, in the United

Table 4.7 Decomposition of total effect of economic, cultural and social capital on first occupational status and current occupational status in Japan (SSM), the United States (OCG) and Britain (OMS)

	First occupation			*Current occupation*		
	Total	*Direct*	*Indirect*	*Total*	*Direct*	*Indirect*
Japan						
Economic capital	0.094**[a]	0.051*	0.043[b]	0.079**	0.033	0.046
	(100%)[c]	(54%)	(46%)	(100%)	(42%)	(58%)
Cultural capital	0.129**	0.033	0.096	0.092**	−0.051	0.143
	(100%)	(26%)	(74%)	(100%)	(0%)	(100%)
Social capital	0.197**	0.134**	0.063	0.246**	0.172**	0.074
	(100%)	(68%)	(32%)	(100%)	(70%)	(30%)
Father's occupation	0.194**	0.120**	0.074	0.211**	0.144**	0.067
	(100%)	(63%)	(37%)	(100%)	(68%)	(32%)
United States						
Economic capital	0.038**	0.021	0.017	NS[d]	–	–
	(100%)	(55%)	(45%)			
Cultural capital	0.136**	0.002	0.134	0.137**	0.010	0.127
	(100%)	(1%)	(99%)	(100%)	(7%)	(93%)
Social capital	0.280**	0.131**	0.149	0.290**	0.161**	0.129
	(100%)	(47%)	(53%)	(100%)	(56%)	(44%)
Father's occupation	0.195**	0.100**	0.095	0.163**	0.083**	0.080
	(100%)	(51%)	(49%)	(100%)	(51%)	(49%)
Britain						
Economic capital	0.132**	0.069**	0.063	0.104**	0.036	0.068
	(100%)	(52%)	(48%)	(100%)	(35%)	(65%)
Cultural capital	0.140**	0.041	0.099	0.124**	0.022	0.102
	(100%)	(29%)	(71%)	(100%)	(18%)	(82%)
Social capital	0.262**	0.148**	0.114	0.275**	0.147**	0.128
	(100%)	(56%)	(44%)	(100%)	(53%)	(47%)
Father's occupation	0.168**	0.084**	0.084	0.198**	0.107**	0.091
	(100%)	(50%)	(50%)	(100%)	(54%)	(46%)

Notes:
[a] The coefficients are the standardized partial regression coefficients.
[b] The indirect effect is computed by subtracting the direct effect from the total effect. Thus, the significance of the coefficient is not shown.
[c] The percentage decompositions are shown in parentheses.
[d] NS indicates that the effect is not significant at 0.05 level.
* The effect is significant at 0.05 level.
** The effect is significant at 0.01 level.

States, economic capital exerts only a limited effect on the first occupation and its effect on the current occupation is not significant. Once the effects of cultural and social capital are taken into account, family wealth and property does not seem to help the son's occupational attainment so much. In other words, the transformation of the economic advantage into the occupational status advantage between the two generations is not evident in the United States.

Table 4.8 presents a similar decomposition of the total effect of economic, cultural and social capital on income. The results of the decomposition are not consistent with the findings in occupational status; different mechanisms emerge.

First, the pattern of economic reproduction in Japan differs from that in the United States and Britain. The direct (57 per cent) and indirect (43 per cent) routes account almost equally for the total effect of economic capital in Japan. Economically advantaged families in Japan transmit their economic superiority both by influencing the educational performance of their sons and by direct inheritance. In comparison, the process through which economic capital affects monetary success in the United States and Britain is predominantly independent of education; over 80 per cent of the total effect of economic capital is direct. Affluent American and British families pass on their wealth directly to their offspring, regardless of the offspring's own educational achievement. Reproduction of economic inequality between generations occurs primarily through direct inheritance of wealth and property independent of the sons' educational attainment in the United States and Britain, while economic inequality in Japan is reproduced both by direct inheritance and by transmission through education.

Second, the effect of cultural capital on income is primarily mediated by education in the United States and Britain, although the effect goes equally through both routes in Japan. About two-thirds of the total impact of cultural capital can be accounted for by the indirect effect in American and British societies. In Japan, the indirect route constitutes only half of the total effect of cultural capital on income. Education has more of a mediating effect for cultural capital in the United States and Britain than in Japan.

Third, the effect of social capital on income is more likely to be direct in Japan than in the United States and Britain. 64 per cent of the total effect of social capital is independent of education in Japan while the corresponding figures for the American and British samples are 59 per cent and 51 per cent, respectively. The role of education in

Table 4.8 Decomposition of total effect of economic, cultural and social capital on income in Japan (SSM), the United States (OCG) and Britain (OMS)

	Income		
	Total	*Direct*	*Indirect*
Japan			
Economic capital	0.072**[a]	0.041	0.031[b]
	(100%)[c]	(57%)	(43%)
Cultural capital	0.144**	0.084**	0.060
	(100%)	(58%)	(42%)
Social capital	0.166**	0.106**	0.060
	(100%)	(64%)	(36%)
United States			
Economic capital	0.117**	0.099**	0.016
	(100%)	(85%)	(15%)
Cultural capital	0.099**	0.032	0.067
	(100%)	(32%)	(68%)
Social capital	0.181**	0.107**	0.074
	(100%)	(59%)	(41%)
Britain			
Economic capital	0.217**	0.175**	0.042
	(100%)	(82%)	(18%)
Cultural capital	0.120**	0.046	0.074
	(100%)	(38%)	(62%)
Social capital	0.165**	0.084**	0.081
	(100%)	(51%)	(49%)

Notes:

[a] The coefficients are the standardized partial regression coefficients after experience and decay are controlled for.

[b] The indirect effect is computed by subtracting the direct effect from the total effect. Thus, the significance of the coefficient is not shown.

[c] The percentage decompositions are shown in parentheses.

** The effect is significant at 0.01 level.

mediating the effect of social capital on economic achievement is more important in the United States and Britain.

In summary, the mechanism for reproducing occupational and economic hierarchy from the father's to the son's generation shows a cross-national variation. In Japan, the occupational hierarchy is reproduced primarily through direct inheritance of occupational status, but in the American and British societies occupational status transmission goes through both direct and indirect routes. The mechanism through which the economic hierarchy is reproduced also varies between Japan and the other two societies: among American and British men economic advantages are likely to be passed on to the next generation by direct inheritance of wealth and property, but in Japan the economic hierarchy seems to be regenerated equally by direct inheritance and by the educational attainment of the offspring. When we focus on the indirect route of reproduction, a contrasted role of educational credentials in the reproduction of socioeconomic inequality is found between Japan and the other two societies. Educational credentials tend to reproduce economic inequality in Japan, but they tend to reproduce occupational inequality in the United States and Britain.

4.4 EDUCATIONAL CREDENTIALS AND SOCIOECONOMIC ATTAINMENT

This section focuses on the socioeconomic returns to educational credentials. It compares in detail the effects of various credentials on occupational status and income in Japan, the United States and Britain. It also examines whether the cross-national difference in socioeconomic returns to education can be accounted for by differences in the spread of the distribution of occupational status and income among the three societies.

Overall socioeconomic returns to educational credentials

Table 4.9 presents the occupational benefits of differential educational credentials in Japan, the United States and Britain. Educational credentials are represented by a middle school diploma, a high school diploma, and a BA degree in Japan and the United States. In Britain, the attainments of academic and vocational qualifications are distinguished: an O-level and a BA or an equivalent academic degree, and an ONC, an HNC, a Level C (lower professional), and a Level B (higher professional) qualification.[12] The first line of each sub-table in Table 4.9 (total effect) shows the total advantage of obtaining a particular credential. Let us begin with comparing Japanese and American men. In Japan, a middle school diploma does not confer any occupational status benefits, but American men who have completed 8 years of schooling have a 1-point advantage in their first

Table 4.9 Decomposition of total effect of educational credentials on first occupational status and current occupational status into spurious, causal, direct and indirect effect in Japan (SSM), the United States (OCG) and Britain (OMS)

	First occupation				*Current occupation*			
	Japan	(%)	**United States**	(%)	**Japan**	(%)	**United States**	(%)
Middle school diploma								
Total	NS[a]		1.05[b]		NS		3.29	(100)
Spurious[c]	–		–		–		0.70	(21)
Causal	NS		NS		NS		2.59	(79)
Direct	–		–		–		2.40	(93)[e]
Indirect[d]	–		–		–		0.19	(7)[e]
High school diploma								
Total	4.48	(100)	5.17	(100)	5.81	(100)	4.49	(100)
Spurious	0.09	(2)	0.69	(13)	0.25	(4)	0.66	(15)
Causal	4.39	(98)	4.48	(87)	5.56	(96)	3.83	(85)
Direct	–		–		3.15	(57)	2.33	(61)
Indirect	–		–		2.41	(43)	1.50	(39)
BA								
Total	8.89	(100)	20.20	(100)	8.78	(100)	16.45	(100)
Spurious	0.40	(4)	1.00	(5)	0.77	(9)	0.84	(5)
Causal	8.49	(96)	19.20	(95)	8.01	(91)	15.61	(95)
Direct	–		–		3.36	(42)	9.19	(59)
Indirect	–		–		4.65	(58)	6.42	(41)

	First occupation		*Current occupation*	
	Britain	(%)	**Britain**	(%)
O-level				
Total	7.02	(100)	9.12	(100)
Spurious	1.78	(25)	1.82	(20)
Causal	5.24	(75)	7.30	(80)
Direct	–		5.49	(75)
Indirect	–		1.81	(25)
BA				
Total	10.87	(100)	8.73	(100)
Spurious	1.01	(9)	1.10	(13)
Causal	9.86	(91)	7.63	(87)

continued on p. 108

Table 4.9 *continued*

	First occupation		*Current occupation*	
	Britain	(%)	**Britain**	(%)
Direct	–		4.22	(55)
Indirect	–		3.41	(45)
ONC				
Total	4.07	(100)	4.27	(100)
Spurious	0.82	(20)	0.68	(16)
Causal	3.25	(80)	3.59	(84)
Direct	–		2.46	(69)
Indirect	–		1.13	(31)
HNC				
Total	4.72	(100)	6.49	(100)
Spurious	0.96	(20)	0.87	(13)
Causal	3.76	(80)	5.62	(87)
Direct	–		4.32	(77)
Indirect	–		1.30	(23)
Level C				
Total	5.94	(100)	12.08	(100)
Spurious	0.80	(13)	0.78	(6)
Causal	5.14	(87)	11.30	(94)
Direct	–		9.53	(84)
Indirect	–		1.77	(16)
Level B				
Total	12.03	(100)	17.05	(100)
Spurious	1.02	(8)	1.08	(6)
Causal	11.01	(92)	15.97	(94)
Direct	–		12.17	(76)
Indirect	–		3.80	(24)

Notes:
[a] NS indicates that the effect is not significant at 0.05 level.
[b] The coefficients are the metric regression coefficients.
[c] The spurious effect is the difference between the total and the causal effect.
[d] The indirect effect is the effect through the first occupation, calculated by subtracting the direct from the causal effect.
[e] The percentages for the direct and the indirect effect will sum to 100 per cent.

occupational status and a 3-point advantage in their current occupational status over those who never finished compulsory education. A high school diploma is worth about 5 points on the first and the current occupational status scale in both societies.

The values for higher education, however, show a remarkable difference between Japan and the United States. A BA degree boosts the prestige score of men's initial and current occupation by less than 9 points in Japan, while in the United States the same educational degree increases the prestige score of the initial occupation by 20 points and that of the current occupation by 16 points. The benefit of a BA degree is more than double in the United States.

In Britain, the attainment of an O-level qualification boosts the first occupational status by 7 points and the current occupational status by 9 points. The successful completion of institutions of higher education (a BA or an equivalent degree) adds another 11 points to the first occupation and 9 points to the current occupation. The benefit of a BA degree in Britain is about the same as that in Japan. The occupational returns to some vocational and professional qualifications, however, are substantial. For example, the attainment of a Level C qualification increases the first occupational status by 6 points and the current occupational status by 12 points. The returns to a Level B qualification are even greater: a 12-point increase in the first occupation and a 17-point increase in the current occupation. It is important to notice that the effects of vocational qualifications are generally much stronger on the current than on the first occupation. This suggests that some men who obtained these qualifications probably did so after they had begun full-time employment.[13]

A similar picture arose in the analysis of the effects of educational credentials on income. As shown in the first line of each sub-table in Table 4.10 (total effect), the pattern of overall monetary benefits of educational credentials is similar to the pattern found in the occupational status benefits of education.[14] Completion of compulsory education increases income by $1857 in the United States, but does not have a significant impact in Japan. Obtaining a high school diploma is worth $2412 among Japanese men, while American high school graduates enjoy a $2991 boost over high school dropouts. There is a striking difference in monetary returns to higher education in the two societies. College graduates have a $2162 advantage in Japan and a $6356 advantage in the United States.

In Britain, an O-level qualification is worth $1462 and a BA degree $1572. The attainment of an ONC and an HNC increases income by

Table 4.10 Decomposition of total effect of educational credentials on income into spurious, causal, direct and indirect effect in Japan (SSM), the United States (OCG) and Britain (OMS)

	Income[a]			
	Japan	(%)	**United States**	(%)
Middle school diploma				
Total	NS[b]		1857[c]	(100)
Spurious[d]	–		892	(48)
Causal	NS		965	(52)
Direct	–		937	(97)[f]
Indirect[e]	–		28	(3)[f]
High school diploma				
Total	2412	(100)	2991	(100)
Spurious	533	(22)	858	(29)
Causal	1879	(78)	2133	(71)
Direct	1682	(90)	1830	(86)
Indirect	197	(10)	303	(14)
BA				
Total	2162	(100)	6356	(100)
Spurious	751	(35)	780	(12)
Causal	1411	(65)	5576	(88)
Direct	1041	(74)	4316	(77)
Indirect	370	(26)	1260	(23)

	Income	
	Britain	(%)
O-level		
Total	1462	(100)
Spurious	353	(24)
Causal	1109	(76)
Direct	978	(88)
Indirect	131	(12)
BA		
Total	1572	(100)
Spurious	241	(15)
Causal	1331	(85)
Direct	1083	(81)
Indirect	248	(19)

	Income	
	Britain	(%)
ONC		
Total	516	(100)
Spurious	88	(17)
Causal	428	(83)
Direct	349	(82)
Indirect	79	(18)
HNC		
Total	785	(100)
Spurious	120	(15)
Causal	665	(85)
Direct	573	(86)
Indirect	92	(14)
Level C		
Total	1140	(100)
Spurious	155	(14)
Causal	985	(86)
Direct	857	(87)
Indirect	128	(13)
Level B		
Total	2970	(100)
Spurious	311	(10)
Causal	2659	(90)
Direct	2382	(90)
Indirect	277	(10)

Notes:

[a] All the coefficients are the effects after experience and decay are controlled for.

[b] NS indicates that the effect is not significant at 0.05 level.

[c] The coefficients are the metric regression coefficients.

[d] The spurious effect is the difference between the total and the causal effect.

[e] The indirect effect is the effect through the first occupation, calculated by subtracting the direct from the causal effect.

[f] The percentages for the direct and the indirect effect will sum to 100 per cent.

Table 4.11 Comparative benefit of a BA degree over a high school diploma or an O-level qualification in Japan (SSM), the United States (OCG) and Britain (OMS)

	Japan	United States	Britain
First occupation	1.98	3.91	1.55
Current occupation	1.51	3.66	0.96
Income	0.90	2.13	1.08

$516 and $785, respectively. The income returns to professional qualifications are even larger: a level C qualification yields $1140 and a Level B qualification increases income by as much as $2970.

The comparative benefit of a BA degree over a high school diploma or an O-level qualification highlights the greater returns to higher education in the United States. As shown in Table 4.11, in the United States, the completion of higher education produces an increase in occupational status more than three times as large as the increase produced by a high school diploma, and the monetary boost generated by a BA degree is at least twice as large as the boost generated by a high school diploma. In contrast, in Japan, the monetary benefit of higher education is smaller than the monetary benefit of a high school diploma. In other words, a BA confers a smaller increase in monetary advantage than a high school diploma in Japan. Similarly, in Britain, the increase in current occupational status and income produced by a BA degree is almost equivalent to that generated by an O-level pass. Since the British educational system differs in many respects from its American and Japanese counterparts, the direct comparison of the comparative benefit of a BA degree is not warranted, but our results seem to suggest that American higher education is far more beneficial than its Japanese and British counterparts.

In summary, the pattern of overall socioeconomic returns to education in all three societies shows an important cross-national difference: the returns to higher education in the United States are substantially higher than the returns in the other two societies. This finding casts strong doubt on the popular notion of 'Japan as an educational credential society; the socioeconomic benefits of such credentials, especially college degrees, are much smaller in Japan than in the United States. The cross-national comparison shows that there has been an overemphasis on the socioeconomic returns to a college degree in Japan, despite the highly competitive nature of the Japanese university entrance examination.

Socioeconomic returns to educational credentials among men with the same background

As we have seen in the previous section, families with considerable resources tend to ensure that their sons achieve an advantaged socioeconomic status by providing them with better education. These families also pass on their resources directly, without converting them into educational credentials: even among men of the same level of education, social background correlates with socioeconomic status. The association between a higher level of education and advantaged socioeconomic status can consequently be explained in part by the fact that highly credentialized sons already come from families with a lot of capital. In other words, part of the association between educational credentials and higher socioeconomic status is spurious: highly credentialized men did not achieve higher status due to their educational achievement, but rather due to their better social origin. We may therefore somewhat overestimate returns to educational credentials if we do not take into account the effects of social background on both education and labour market outcomes. We will estimate the effect of educational credentials on occupational status and income among men with the same social background characteristics. The effect is shown as the 'causal' effect in Tables 4.9 and 4.10. The difference between the total effect of education and its effect after controlling for social background is the 'spurious' effect, or the component due to the association with background variables.

Let us first consider socioeconomic returns to a high school diploma. A high school diploma is associated with an advantage of 4.48 points in Japan and 5.17 points in the United States on the prestige scale for the first occupation. Among men with similar social origins, the total advantage of a high school diploma is reduced by 2 per cent to 4.39 in Japan and by 13 per cent to 4.48 in the United States. Similarly, the benefit of a high school diploma in current occupational status is reduced by 4 per cent in Japan and 15 per cent in the United States (see percentages in parentheses in Table 4.9). Although the apparent effect of a high school diploma is slightly more spurious in the United States than in Japan, its effect is largely not due to the difference in background between high school graduates and non-graduates. Japanese and American men with a high school diploma enjoy an advantage in occupational status independent of their social origin.

The apparent income returns to a high school diploma are more inflated by background than the occupational status returns. The total monetary benefit of a high school diploma is reduced by about 22 per cent in Japan and by 29 per cent in the United States, when social background characteristics are controlled for. In real dollar terms, the bonus of a high school diploma is reduced from $2412 to $1879 in Japan and from $2991 to $2133 in the United States. The apparent income difference between high school graduates and non-graduates is in part due to the fact that those who finish high school come from more advantaged homes than those who do not receive a high school diploma. Overall, controlling for social background lowers the income returns to a high school diploma more than it lowers the occupational status returns in both societies.

In Britain, the socioeconomic benefits of an O-level qualification are reduced by 20–25 per cent after controlling for social background. The income and occupational status difference between a man with an O-level pass and a man with no academic qualification is in part due to the better social origin of a man with an academic qualification; the net benefits of an O-level qualification are smaller than the apparent total returns. Similarly, occupational status benefits associated with the attainment of an ONC and an HNC qualification are in part explained by social origin. However, the effects of professional qualifications on occupational attainment are generally independent of social background. Income returns to various vocational and professional qualifications are also generally independent of social origin. The total effects of various qualifications are only moderately reduced, by 10–17 per cent, after controlling for social background.

We now estimate the effect of a BA degree on occupational status and income among men from the same social background. As shown in Table 4.9, the occupational status benefit of a BA degree does not change even after social background has been controlled for in the three societies. Among men with the same social origin, Japanese college graduates continue to enjoy an 8-point advantage, and American graduates benefit by about 17 points. Similarly, the occupational status advantages of British graduates are reduced by only about 10 per cent to 8 points on the occupational prestige scale.[15] The occupational status advantage accorded by higher education seems to have little to do with the background characteristics of college-educated men.

In contrast, the total effect of a BA degree on income is reduced when background characteristics are controlled for, especially in Japan. Table 4.10 shows that more than one-third of the total income returns to a BA degree are spurious in Japan. In real dollars, the apparent benefit of Japanese higher education is $2162. Among men with the same background the benefit is reduced by 35 per cent to $1411. In the United States and Britain, the total effect of higher education on income is at most modestly inflated by social background. When we remove the effect of social background, the advantage conferred by a BA degree decreases by 12 per cent from $6356 to $5576 in the United States and by 15 per cent from $1572 to $1331 in Britain.

These results indicate that the apparent monetary returns to a BA degree appreciably overestimate the net impact of higher education in Japan. Since more than one-third of the total effect is spurious, Japanese men who graduated from a college earn significantly more income than men without a BA degree, in part because they already came from advantaged families which ensures a monetary success regardless of their sons' educational achievement.

The implications of these findings are important. Previous studies by economists on the income gaps between high school graduates and college graduates in Japan suffered from a significant overestimation of the benefit of the higher education. We should not take the apparent income gap by educational credentials at face value; the monetary bonus of a BA degree should probably be reduced by one-third in order to compensate for the spurious bonus due to the advantaged background characteristics of college graduates. On the other hand, the estimation of the BA degree impacts on income in the United States and Britain suffers only moderately from the same problem. The spurious components of benefits of higher education are much smaller, probably about half of the proportion in Japan. The results suggest that American and British higher education improves financial prospects, and that the improvement is mainly independent of the graduates' social background characteristics.

Source of cross-national variation in socioeconomic returns to educational credentials

The most dramatic cross-national difference in the socioeconomic attainment process in Japan, the United States and Britain lies in the effect of educational credentials. In particular, occupational status and income returns to a BA degree are substantially higher in the United States than the other two nations. One of the major reasons for the larger socioeconomic returns to education in the United States is probably the larger spread of the distributions of occupational status and income. Both the distributions of occupational status and income are more unequal in the United States than in Japan and Britain. The variance of the distribution of the current occupational status in the United States is 1.3 times as large as the variance in Japan. The variance of the distribution of the first occupational status is almost twice and that of the income three and a half times greater in the United States than in Japan. Similarly, British distributions of the first and the current occupation are slightly more equal than their American counterparts, and the British distribution of income has almost one-tenth the variance of the American distribution. The income distribution in Britain has less variance than even its Japanese counterpart.[16]

It is therefore clear that the differences in the distributions of occupational status and income have a substantial consequence in the difference in socioeconomic returns to education across nations.[17] We may recalculate the effects of education by assuming that the distributions of occupational status and income were more equal or unequal. In other words, retaining the relationship between education and socioeconomic status, we may substitute a hypothetical variance for the actual variance. For example, if the distributions of occupational status and income in the United States were more equal and had an equally small variance as in Japan, the effect of higher education would be much smaller. On the other hand, if we substitute the income variance in Japan for that in Britain, the effect of a BA degree would be larger because the Japanese income distribution is more unequal than the British.

Table 4.12 shows the causal effects of a high school diploma or an O-level and a BA degree on the first and current occupational status and income in the United States and Britain under the hypothetical condition that the spreads of the distributions of occupational status and income were identical to those in Japan. For comparison, the actual observed effects are shown. As predicted, occupational status and income returns to educational credentials (especially a BA degree) are decreased by a substantial amount under the hypothetical condition in the United States. The causal effect of a BA degree on the first occupational status decreased from 19.2 to 13.7 points, and the same effect on the current occupational status from 15.6 to 13.9

Table 4.12 Hypothetical and observed effects of a high school diploma or an O-level and a BA degree on first occupational status, current occupational status and income in Japan (SSM), the United States (OCG) and Britain (OMS)

	Japan	**United States**		**Britain**	
	Observed	*Hypothetical (observed)*		*Hypothetical (observed)*	
Effect on first occupation					
High school diploma/ O-level	4.39	3.21	(4.48)	4.97	(5.24)
BA	8.49	13.70	(19.20)	9.37	(9.86)
Effect on current occupation					
High school diploma/ O-level	5.56	3.41	(3.83)	6.65	(7.30)
BA	8.01	13.85	(15.61)	6.95	(7.63)
Effect on income					
High school diploma/ O-level	1879	1117	(2133)	2092	(1109)
BA	1411	2913	(5576)	2340	(1331)

points. The causal effect of a BA degree on income is almost a half, decreasing from $5576 to $2913. Consequently, when the American distributions are adjusted to match the Japanese ones, the gap in socioeconomic returns to a BA degree is reduced by almost two-thirds in the case of income and by almost a quarter in the case of the occupational statuses. All these exercises suggest that part of the reason why American higher education is more profitable than its Japanese counterpart is due to the fact that the distributions of occupational status and income are more unequal in the United States than in Japan. Since socioeconomic resources are more unequally distributed in the United States than in Japan, educational credentials exert bigger impacts.

Nonetheless, cross-national differences in the effect of a BA degree still remain. Income returns to American higher education are still twice as large as the same returns to Japanese higher education, even after adjustments have been made for the difference in income distribution in the two societies. Occupational status returns are at least one and a half times greater in the United States than in Japan, even after the adjustment. Therefore, factors other than the differences in the spread of the distributions should account for the remaining cross-national differences in socioeconomic returns to higher education.

The figures for Britain in Table 4.12 tell a different story. The effects of academic qualifications on occupational status changed little after the adjustment, since the variances of occupational distributions in Britain and Japan are not so different. However, the effects of an O-level and a BA degree on income increased substantially after adjusting the spread of income distribution: income returns to an O-level increased from \$1109 to \$2092 and returns to a BA degree from \$1331 to \$2340. Under the hypothetical situation, income returns to a BA degree have therefore become more than one and a half times of those (\$1411) in Japan. In other words, if we take into account the difference in income inequality, the British BA degree is more profitable than the Japanese one.

All these findings lead us to conclude that the socioeconomic benefits of a BA degree in Japan are substantially smaller than those in the United States, and probably smaller than those in Britain, especially when the cross-national difference in income inequality is taken into account. The greater returns to a BA degree in the United States also appear to hold independent of the distributions of occupational status and income.

4.5 ENDURING EFFECTS OF EDUCATIONAL CREDENTIALS

One of the arguments about 'educational credentialism' in Japan is that the effect of credentials persists over men's entire careers, as if, once acquired, they become an ascriptive characteristic. Highly credentialized men tend to be rewarded in pay and promotion regardless of their job performance, and the effect of credentials persists throughout their career, independent of what they actually do at the workplace.

In order to assess the enduring effects of credentials on income attainment, we will examine age–income profiles by different level of educational credentials. The age–income profile describes estimated changes in income throughout the entire career. Men's income generally rises with age until somewhere beyond the age of 45, then levels off, and eventually declines. The profile does not correspond to a real person's profile because it is constructed from aggregates of men working in the labour force at the time of the survey. The profile is estimated from the regression equation predicting income, controlling for social background. The age–income profile generally shows different curves by the level of educational credentials. If the income differential between a high school graduate and a university graduate widens as they age, then this will be consistent with the claim that educational credentials have an enduring impact on income.

Figure 4.2 shows the age–income profile by three levels of education in Japan and the United States and by two levels of academic qualifications in Britain.[18] Three important cross-national differences are evident in the profile in the three countries. First, in Japan income gaps become noticeable only after the age of 35 between high school graduates and middle school graduates, and only after the age of 40 between university graduates and high school graduates. On the other hand, American high school graduates enjoy an income advantage over middle school graduates from their very first entry into the labour market, and American university graduates begin to enjoy their advantage as early as the age of 30. Similarly, in Britain, the income gap between men with an O-level pass and men with a BA degree becomes apparent as early as their early 30s.

Second, the rate of increase in income returns to a BA degree in the mid-career is much greater in the United States than in Japan and Britain. Third, the income advantage of BA degree holders reaches the maximum at about the age of 55 in the United States and Britain, while the advantage of university graduates in Japan continues to grow until the age of retirement (60 years old).

The cross-national comparison suggests that income differentials between different levels of education are much more pronounced as men become older in Japan than in the United States and Britain. Although the absolute income gap between university graduates and high school graduates is much larger in the United States, the gap continues to widen as we move from the youngest to the oldest groups in Japan. These results appear to support the idea that the effect of educational credentials endures throughout the men's entire career in Japan. However, there is an alternative explanation to the apparent difference in age–income profiles.

Since the age–income profile is an estimation using cross-sectional data, the apparent income gap between a high school graduate and a

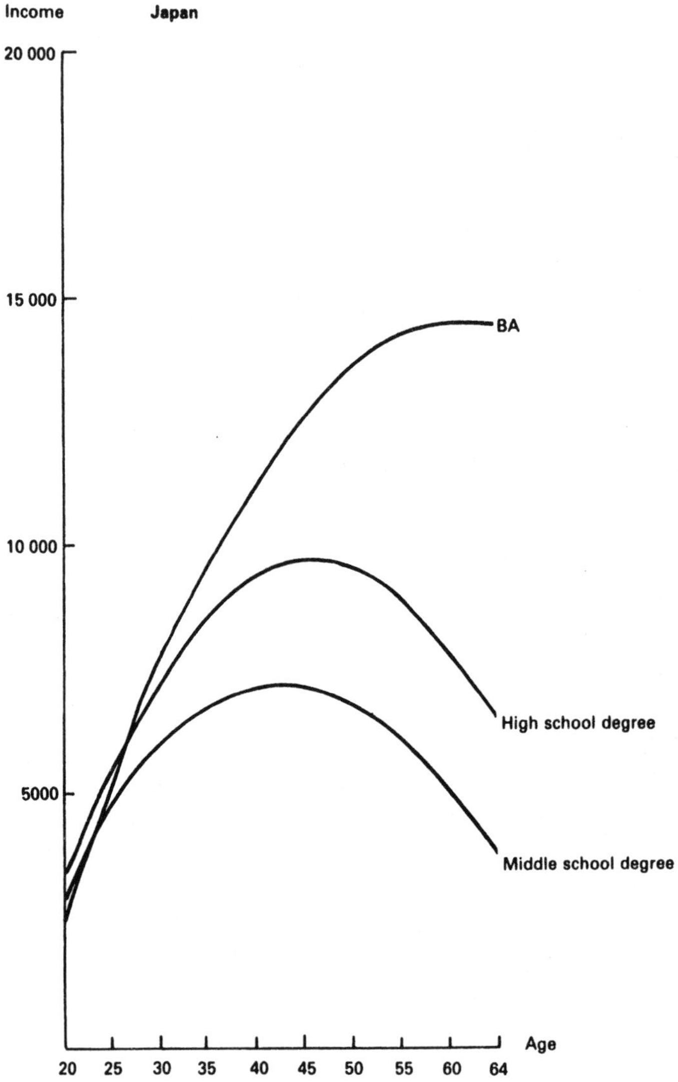

Figure 4.2 Age–income profile by level of education in Japan (SSM), the United States (OCG) and Britain (OMS) with social background controlled for

university graduate may in part be due to the educational distribution of the cohorts. Table 4.13 shows the percentage of high school graduates and university graduates in different cohorts in our datasets. For example, only 7.7 per cent of the 45–49 cohort were BA degree holders in Japan, while 17.9 per cent were in the United

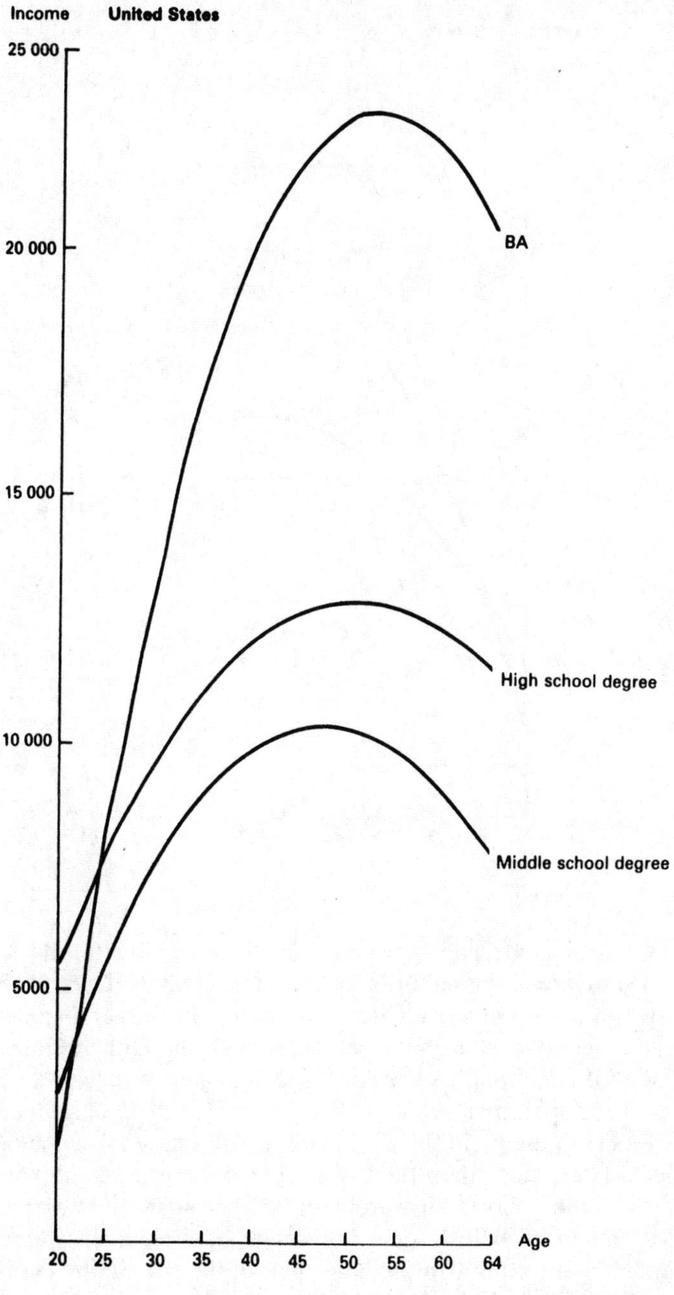

Fig. 4.2 *continued*

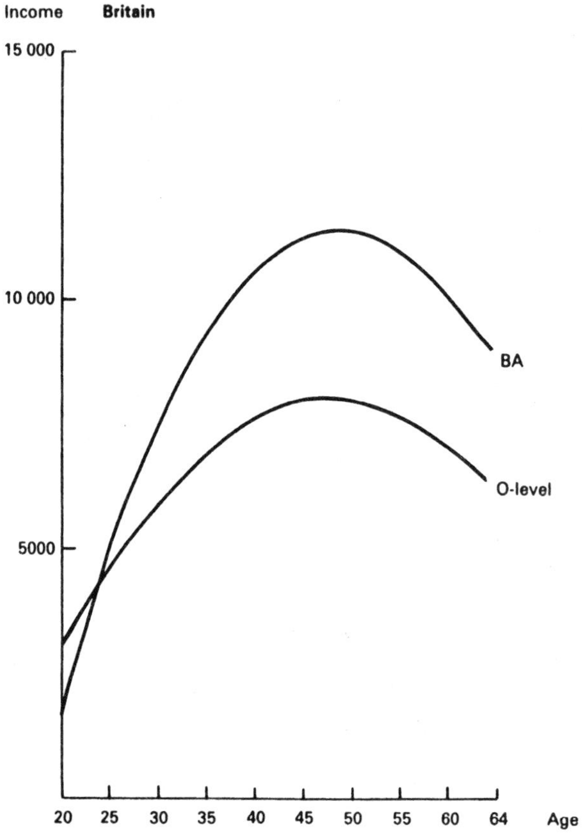

Fig. 4.2 *continued*

States. The income gap between a university graduate and a high school graduate in this cohort may in part be explained by the smaller number of university graduates. Similarly, the larger income gap among older cohorts in Japan compared with the United States may be due to the fact that higher education is available only to a smaller minority in Japan than in the United States. It is not guaranteed that a university graduate in the 20–24 cohort will enjoy the same benefit 25 years later, since then there will be many more people with BA degrees in the cohort. This problem will be much more serious for Japanese than for British society, because Japanese higher education expanded more rapidly in the latter half of the twentieth century, as shown in our data: the proportion of university graduates increased

Table 4.13 Percentage of high school graduates or men with an O-level qualification only and of university graduates by cohort in Japan (SSM), the United States (OCG) and Britain (OMS)

Cohort	*High school graduates or men with an O-level only*			*BA holders*		
	Japan	**United States**	**Britain**	**Japan**	**United States**	**Britain**
20–24	54.4	44.5	20.3	11.2	12.1	3.8
25–29	51.3	40.2	19.3	16.8	22.7	6.0
30–34	40.5	37.6	16.0	15.9	23.1	6.1
35–39	40.4	35.0	15.0	15.7	22.3	5.4
40–44	30.2	34.4	10.4	11.5	21.2	3.8
45–49	28.9	31.7	9.8	7.7	17.9	3.2
50–54	23.8	32.9	9.5	4.7	14.7	1.7
55–59	22.2	32.4	9.2	3.1	12.1	1.9
60–64	23.6	23.3	6.5	3.2	11.8	1.7

from 3.2 per cent in the oldest cohort to 16.8 per cent in the 25–29 cohort. In Britain, only 6.0 per cent of the 25–29 cohort were BA degree holders.

An age–income profile is therefore not in a strict sense the test of 'enduring effect', since both the age effect and the cohort effect are confounded; the apparent income differentiation among different levels of education probably overestimates the enduring effect of education by a significant amount. Thus, while the results are consistent with the notion of enduring effect in Japan, further analysis using longitudinal data is needed truly to test the idea (cf. Koike, 1988).

Educational credentials affect not only future income but also occupational success. In order to assess the enduring effect of credentials on occupational attainment, we will estimate the impact of educational credentials on the current occupational status after the effect of the first occupation is removed. The net effect of credentials on the current occupational status will estimate the enduring effect of credentials after the entry into the labour market. Credentials affect the initial occupational status in the labour market but they also affect the later socioeconomic status, independent of their impact on the initial entry position. If the net impact on the later socioeconomic status is large, this will imply that the effect of credentials lasts long after labour market entry.

The direct effect of educational credentials on the current

occupational status, net of the effect through the first occupation, is shown in Table 4.9 (p. 107). Let us look first at the enduring impact of a high school diploma. Both in the United States and Japan, a high school diploma increases the current occupational status directly, independent of the first occupational status (see rows indicating 'direct' effects in Table 4.9). More than half of the occupational benefit of a high school diploma (after background characteristics have been controlled for) accrues from direct impact without mediation by the first occupational status in both countries: 57 per cent in Japan and 61 per cent in the United States. Similarly, the attainment of an O-level in Britain affects the current occupational status directly without going through the first occupation: 75 per cent is the direct effect. Regardless of the initial labour market position, a high school diploma and an O-level pass appears to certify men's basic skill level and continues to be an important factor in determining later achievement.

In contrast, a cross-societal difference emerges in the effect of a BA degree on the current occupational attainment. The majority of the effect of a BA degree is direct in the United States and Britain: 59 per cent and 55 per cent, respectively. On the other hand, the majority (58 per cent) of the effect in Japan operates through the first occupational status. The occupational status advantage enjoyed by American and British BA degree holders appears to be present not only at the initial stage of men's careers, but continues also to show up in the later stages of working life. Various vocational and professional qualifications in Britain also show strong direct effects on the current occupational status. Since many of those who obtained these qualifications probably did so after they entered the labour market, it is not surprising to see the effects of qualifications on the current occupation independent of the first occupation.

Japanese university graduates enjoy initial access to higher-status first jobs that may serve as stepping stones to later occupational advancement. However, they do not benefit from their higher education in their later career as much as American university graduates. A BA degree bonus in Japan is greatest at the beginning of a career (an eight-point increase) but thereafter it has rather an attenuated impact (a three-point increase) on later occupational attainment. Japanese higher education appears to be most important in the acquisition of a higher-status first occupation, but its value diminishes gradually as men progress in their occupational careers.

Figure 4.3, which shows the interrelationship between educational credentials and occupational attainment, visually highlights the cross-

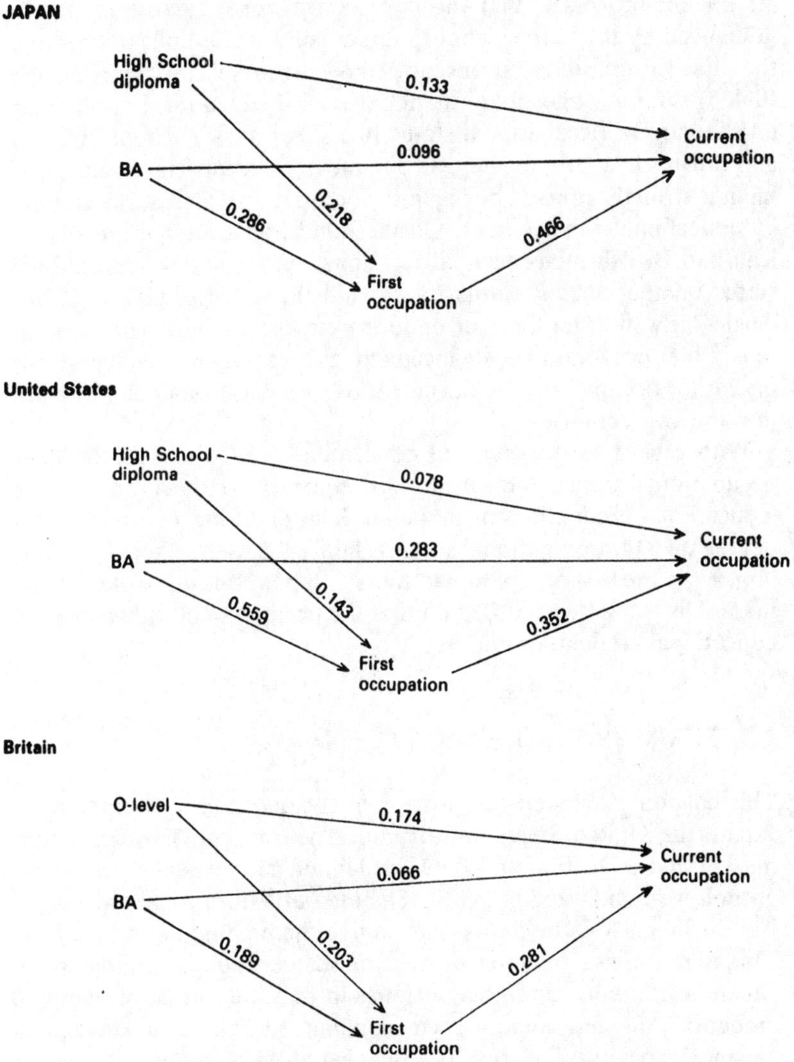

Figure 4.3 Relationship between educational credentials and occupational attainment in Japan (SSM), the United States (OCG) and Britain (OMS)

Note: The numbers are standardized partial regression coefficients after social background variables and other education dummy variables are controlled for.

national difference. The striking feature of the Japanese occupational attainment process is that the later occupational success is largely influenced by the earlier labour market status. The linkage between the first occupational status and the current occupational status (0.466) is far stronger than the net effects of educational credentials on the current occupational status (0.133 for a high school diploma and 0.096 for a BA degree). In Japan, later occupational advancement is strongly affected by the initial occupational status, rather than by educational achievement. On the other hand, among the American and British men the relative impact of the initial occupational status on the current status (0.352 and 0.281, respectively) is not particularly stronger than the enduring effects of educational credentials. Later occupational advancement is almost as equally dependent on earlier occupational achievement as on educational achievement in these two countries.

With regard to the effect of educational credentials on the later occupational status, our results are contrary to the prediction of 'educational credentialism' in Japan. The enduring effect of a BA degree on later occupational status is limited, and the effect functions largely via the first occupational status in Japan. It is more likely to be in the United States and Britain that the occupational status effect of educational credentials endures.

4.6 SUMMARY AND CONCLUSION

This chapter examined the process of socioeconomic attainment in Japan, the United States and Britain. The linkages between labour market and education and between labour market and social background were analyzed in detail. The idea of 'educational credentialism' in Japan was the major substantive theme guiding the chapter. This idea implies that the process of socioeconomic attainment in Japan is different from other societies in that the role of educational credentials in determining socioeconomic success is maximized in Japanese society. The results discussed in this chapter, however, challenge this idea on several grounds.

First, the relative importance of educational credentials as against social background in explaining inequality in socioeconomic achievement does not seem to be greater in Japan than in the United States and Britain. The cross-national comparison suggests that the relative explanatory power of education is more important in the United

States and Britain than in Japan in explaining both occupational and income inequality. However, the intercohort analysis suggests a trend towards an increasing relative importance of education in all three societies in the twentieth century.

Second, the mobility function of education does not overpower the reproduction function of social background in the process of socioeconomic attainment in Japan. The intrasocietal comparison shows that the role of educational credentials in increasing the mobility chances of people does not dominate the reproduction mechanism of social background. When we take into account various social background characteristics, the dominance of universalistic criteria – educational credentials – over the particularistic criteria – social background – in explaining socioeconomic inequality is not clearly evident in Japan. It is not the case that the overall effect of social background is substantially less than the achieved education, as the thesis of 'educational credentialism' would suggest.

Third, social background characteristics affect socioeconomic attainment in Japan both independently of educational credentials (direct reproduction) and through the means of education (indirect reproduction through education). We cannot overlook the importance of social background in the determination of socioeconomic status in Japan and the role of education in transmitting the effect of social background. In particular, the effect of cultural capital is almost entirely mediated by education.

Fourth, occupational and income returns to a BA degree are significantly lower in Japan than in the United States. The occupational status benefit of a BA degree is almost double and the income benefit is almost triple in the United States: American higher education appears to be much more profitable than its Japanese counterpart. Socioeconomic returns to a BA degree from a British institution are about the same as in Japan, but the British men may increase their occupational status and income by obtaining vocational and professional qualifications through further education which are not available in Japan.

Fifth, the apparent monetary benefit of a BA degree in Japan appreciably overestimates the net impact of higher education. Almost one-third of the total monetary benefit is spurious; Japanese men with a BA degree earn significantly more income than men without a degree, in part because they already came from advantaged families, which ensures monetary success regardless of their sons' educational achievement. On the other hand, the spurious component of higher education benefits in the United States and Britain is much less, probably about half of the proportion in Japan.

Sixth, the occupational benefit of a BA degree is greatest at the beginning of the career, but thereafter it has an attenuated impact on later occupational attainment in Japan. Japanese higher education does not appear to exert an enduring occupational status effect. In contrast, American higher education seems not only to provide men with initial access to higher occupational status but also to exercise a continuing direct impact on occupational achievement throughout the career. The effect of British higher education is less enduring than that of American, but the attainment of various vocational and professional qualifications is possible after entry into the labour market and, therefore, has an enduring effect on later occupational attainment.

All these findings are not consistent with the predictions derived from 'educational credentialism' in Japan. In particular, significantly lesser returns to a BA degree in comparison to the United States and the lack of dominance of educational credentials over social background in explaining socioeconomic inequality seem to cast serious doubt on the claim that the role of educational credentials in determining socioeconomic attainment is maximized in Japan.

It is remarkable that 'educational credentialism' in Japan has received so much credence even though the socioeconomic benefits of education are not as large as people believe. In the concluding Chapter 8, we will discuss why Japanese people place so much emphasis on education, and why Japanese students and their parents undergo the educational competition known as an 'examination hell', despite the scanty evidence for great socioeconomic returns to education.

The results of this chapter also place the process of status attainment in the United States and Britain within the comparative framework. First, in comparison to the Japanese and American system of education, the role of vocational and professional qualifications in determining labour market outcomes characterizes the relationship between educational credentials and socioeconomic attainment in Britain. The occupational status and income returns to these various qualifications are as large as those produced by academic qualifications. In case of Level B higher professional qualifications which include medical and law qualifications, the returns are clearly larger than those to a BA degree. These 'alternative routes' to socioeconomic success (Raffe, 1979) do not exist in Japanese society and, therefore, deserve special attention.

Second, the cross-national comparison suggests that the socioeconomic benefits of American higher education are exceptionally high. Even though the proportion of youths who attend institutions of higher learning is the highest in the Western world, the investment in higher education appears to yield large socioeconomic returns. College education increases occupational status more than three times as much as the increase produced by a high school diploma, and the income increase generated by a BA degree is at least one and a half times as large as the increase generated by a high school diploma. These figures are considerably higher than the figures in Japan.

The greater impact of higher education on occupational attainment in the United States than in Japan is also evident in its enduring effect. American higher education influences not only the initial entry occupational status but also later occupational achievement. This long-term effect of college education on occupational attainment was not found in Japan. Higher education appears to hold a key to socioeconomic advancement in American society (cf. Hout, 1988).

Third, the results of this chapter confirm the earlier studies on occupational attainment in the United States in that educational credentials are more important than social background characteristics in determining occupational achievement. The cross-national comparison also suggests that the relative importance of educational credentials in affecting occupational attainment is more pronounced in the United States than in Japan.

Nevertheless, it is important to remember that men's social background characteristics affect educational and socioeconomic attainment in the United States. As we have seen in Chapter 3, the attainment of educational credentials is not independent of social origin, and this chapter showed that background characteristics affect socioeconomic status both directly and indirectly through education. While educational credentials enhance socioeconomic success independently of social background, social background does play a role in affecting socioeconomic achievement. The particularistic criteria in determining labour market success is therefore far from absent in American society.

Notes

1. The figures were reported by the Ministry of Education (Monbusho, 1982a, 1982b).
2. In Japan and the United States, a bachelor's degree means graduating from a four-year college or university. In Britain, it indicates that the respondents either graduated from a university and successfully obtained a first degree or graduated from other institutions of higher education (e.g., polytechnics) and successfully obtained a Diploma of Technology or an equivalent degree.
3. Since the information on income was not available in the British data, we will use the total individual earnings in our analysis. The income variable in Britain is therefore not strictly comparable to that in Japan and the United States.
4. It is possible to use log of income, rather than raw income, as the dependent variable. Although there are some advantages in taking logs, Featherman and Hauser (1978, pp. 288–9), who analyzed the OCG II data, reported an undesirable statistical consequence of the log transformation because it stretched out the lower tail of the distribution and would give an undue weight to a negative skew in the lowest level of education. In view of this disadvantage and the limitation of space here, we do not report the results of log-income. However, these results do not change the substantive conclusions derived from our analysis of raw dollar income (cf. Ishida, 1986).
5. Social background characteristics include seven variables discussed above in Japan and Britain and eight variables including race in the United States. The inclusion of race made little difference in the proportion of variance explained by social background. Educational credentials are represented by a number of dummy variables. It should be noted that the variances in occupational statuses and income vary across nations. The analysis presented here standardized these variances to 1.00.
6. Using the proportion of variance explained to compare the relative impact of social background and education on socioeconomic attainment differs from other approaches. Yasuda (1971) used partial gamma coefficients to estimate the relative impact of the ascribed and achieved factors. The use of sheaf coefficients (Heise, 1972; Whitt, 1986; cf. Alwin, 1988) to summarize the effects of social background variables and of educational credential variables is a useful alternative, but the comparison of the two sheaf coefficients is not equivalent to the comparison of the proportion of variance explained (see, Coleman, 1976, pp. 5–8; Bielby, 1981).
7. Since some men in the 20–34 cohort are still in school (and in the military in the United States), the impacts of both social background and education are likely to be attenuated. The impacts would have been greater if those men had been in the labour force.
8. Intercohort changes in the proportion of variance explained by education and social background are influenced by changes in the variance of socioeconomic outcomes and of independent variables. However, inter-

cohort changes in the ratio of the variance explained are less responsive to changes in the variance of dependent variables.

9. The two extreme categories used in computing the difference are as follows: non-farm and farm origin (0 and 1), rural and urban background (0 and 1), 'very wealthy family' and 'very poor family' (1 and 5), no education and highest level of education (0 and 16 years or 1 and 3 for Britain), no siblings and 10 siblings (0 and 10), and a garbage collector father and a medical doctor father (13 and 78 IPS scores).
10. Details on estimating the weights of individual social background variables on the composite capital variables and computing the 'combined' effects of the composite variables on socioeconomic status are found in Heise (1972), Whitt (1986) and Alwin (1988).
11. The individual effect of the father's occupation is estimated by multiplying the weight (0.695) by the effect of social capital (0.166).
12. Educational credentials in Japan and the United States and academic qualifications in Britain are entered into regression equations as *cumulative* dummy variables. For example, the effect of a high school diploma shows the difference in occupational status between a middle school graduate and a high school graduate, and the effect of a BA degree measures an increase in occupational status over and above a high school diploma. However, vocational qualifications in Britain are entered as non-cumulative dummy variables. The effect of the attainment of vocational qualifications represents the difference in occupational status between those who obtained the qualification and those who had no qualification at all. The socioeconomic benefit of vocational qualifications is always measured against those who had no qualification.
13. It may then be surprising that these vocational qualifications affect the first occupation. There are those who already had qualifications before they entered the labour market on a full-time basis. In addition, many people who obtained qualifications during their careers had first jobs whose job titles were different from dead-end jobs. In other words, a man who was expected to become a qualified skilled worker through the apprenticeship system and the attainment of ONC, HNC, and other qualifications was placed on a different track from the beginning of his career than a man who was expected not to become qualified.
14. The total effect of education is its effect after experience and decay are controlled for. Without the control, the effect of education is substantially underestimated.
15. These figures are the average of the casual effect of a BA degree on the first occupational status and the current occupational status.
16. Part of the reason why the British distribution is more equal is that the annual income excludes non-wage income. If the OMS had asked the respondents the total annual income from all sources including non-wage income, the income distribution would have been more unequal.
17. It is also true that the difference in the distribution of educational credentials across nations affects the cross-national difference in socioeconomic returns to education. Our concern is, however, to evaluate the effect of differential inequality in outcomes, rather than in resources.

18. The three levels of education are represented by middle school graduates, high school graduates and university graduates. In Japan, middle school graduates are those who completed pre-war middle school (*kyusei koto shoggako*) or post-war middle school (*shinsei chuggako*) and had no further education; high school graduates are those who completed pre- or post-war high schools (*kyusei chuggako* and *shinsei koko*) and had no further education; and university graduates refer to those who obtained a BA degree or higher. In the United States, middle school graduates are those who have completed exactly 8 years of schooling; high school graduates are those who have completed exactly 12 years of schooling; and university graduates are those who have completed 16 years or more of schooling. In Britain, men with an O-level qualification are those who passed at least one O-level but had no A-level passes, and men with a BA degree are those who obtained a BA or an equivalent degree.

5 Higher Education and the Labour Market

5.1 INTRODUCTION

Today almost 50 per cent of all American youths attend institutions of higher learning, and almost 36 per cent of all Japanese high school graduates proceed to higher education (US Department of Education, 1982; Monbusho, 1982a, 1982b). These two countries along with Canada are among the leading countries in the Western world in terms of the number of students enrolled in institutions of higher learning and the proportion of college-educated population (Monbusho, 1983). With such a large number of the youth population now proceeding to higher education, two important consequences related to the process of socioeconomic attainment can be expected. The first is that the socioeconomic returns to higher education may decline due to a larger supply of the college-educated population. The second is that stratification in higher education may have a significant impact on labour market outcomes.

This chapter will first examine the issue of 'overeducation' or 'underemployment' of college graduates.[1] Freeman (1971; 1976) contends that the socioeconomic returns to college education declined in the 1970s due to the downturn in the labour market for college graduates in the United States. The supply of the college-going population expanded in the late 1960s because of the 'baby boom', which began in 1946, and because of the increasing percentage of the younger generation who chose to attend higher education. Meanwhile, the rate of increase in demand for college and professional graduates began to slow down in the 1970s. The market value of college education has thus declined, and the college-educated population has become 'overeducated' in the marketplace.

Freeman (1976, p. 26) estimated that the private rate of income return to college education had declined from 11 per cent in 1968 to 7.5 per cent in 1973. The private rate of return on an investment is the rate of interest at which the present value of the income stream yielded by the investment is equal to its cost. Freeman's estimate shows that investment in higher education yields 7.5 per cent per year. Therefore, if one borrows money at 7.4 per cent or less to acquire a higher education which yields 7.5 per cent, one will make a profit: higher education is profitable as long as the rate of return surpasses the market rate of interest.

The more dramatic consequence of the imbalance between supply and demand is unemployment. The unemployment rate of college graduates, still lower than that of workers in general, increased from 0.7 per cent in 1968 to 2.3 per cent in 1974, according to Freeman's estimate (1976, pp. 21–2).

A similar argument has been proposed in Japan by Japanese economists under the rubric of 'employment substitution by college graduates' (Koike and Watanabe, 1979; Watanabe, 1976, 1982; Yano, 1980). The term implies that occupations normally occupied by high school graduates are now filled by college-educated people. The imbalance between the increase in supply of college graduates and that in managerial and professional employment opportunities led to diminishing socioeconomic returns to higher education.

Watanabe (1976, p. 94) found that the private rate of income return to college education had declined from 8.0 per cent in 1968 to 6.2 per cent in 1975. The unemployment rate of college graduates is not available in Japan, but we can use the proportion of college graduates who did not take a full-time job as a crude measure. This figure increased from 10.5 per cent in 1960 to 20 per cent in 1975 (Sorifu, 1983, p. 663).

The issue of 'overeducation' has so far not attracted attention in British society. Although the number of university students increased dramatically in the 1960s, the proportion of students who enrolled in advanced courses in institutions of higher education (including polytechnics and further education establishments) constituted 14 per cent of the 19–20-years-old age group in 1985. If we restrict ourselves to full-time and sandwich course students, the proportion drops to 12 per cent. If we further restrict ourselves to full-time students in universities, excluding those in polytechnics and further education establishments, the proportion becomes only 6 per cent (Central Statistical Office, 1988, Table 5.6). The graduates of the institutions of higher education are therefore still a small minority in contemporary British society, and we should expect that the market value of a higher education would not have declined over the cohorts.[2]

The first part of this chapter (Sections 5.2 and 5.3) will thus examine the issue of the declining market value of a college education, using intercohort analysis. The trends shown in the returns to a college education in first occupational status will permit us to determine whether or not the market value of a BA degree has declined across the cohorts in the three countries.

The second issue which will be examined in this chapter focuses on stratification in higher education and its impact on labour market outcomes. Previous studies on the impact of institutional ranking or college quality in the United States have shown that graduates of prestigious universities are more successful in the attainment of higher socioeconomic status than the graduates of lower-status institutions, and that this effect of college quality persists even after controlling for such factors as social background, ability and aspirations (Speath, 1970; Alwin, 1974, 1976; Solmon and Wachtel, 1975; Solmon, 1975; Griffin and Alexander, 1978; Trusheim and Crouse, 1981; Tinto, 1980; Jencks *et al.*, 1979). Stratification in higher education is likely to have a significant consequence in the labour market, especially for recent cohorts of college graduates, because the pattern of 'overeducation' or 'underemployment' discussed above, (Freeman, 1971; 1976) has continued into the 1980s (Rumberger, 1981; 1982) in the United States.[3]

While college quality independently enhances an individual's bargaining power in the labour market, some argue that elite institutions are disproportionately attended by the offspring of the already advantaged, and that the apparent effect of college quality thus overestimates the independent direct impact (Karabel and Astin, 1975; Useem and Miller, 1975; Karabel and McClelland, 1987). There is therefore some evidence that stratification in American higher education reproduces the inequality between generations.

The impact of stratification in the higher educational system has received much attention in Japan both from the general public and from researchers of education and sociology (Aso, 1983; Koike and Watanabe, 1979; Hashizume, 1976a, 1976b; Iwauchi, 1980; Takeuchi and Aso, 1981). It is believed that the ranking of universities, generally measured by the competitiveness of the entrance examination, has a high correlation with the ranking of the job obtained by graduates. Many prestigious private firms interview only students from top-ranking institutions, and upper managerial positions are often occupied by the graduates of elite institutions. Similarly, upper management positions in the national bureaucracy are heavily dominated by top schools, especially by the University of Tokyo. Rohlen (1983, p. 91), for example, reports that 89 per cent of officials ranked section chief or above in the Ministry of Finance were University of Tokyo graduates.

In Britain, the dominance of two ancient universities, Oxford and Cambridge, over other British universities in access to elite positions in the society has been noted by many observers (e.g., Sampson, 1982). The privileged access appears to be wide-ranging, from the civil service to the commercial and merchant banking field (Stanworth and Giddens, 1974). Thompson (1974) even reports the preponderance of Oxbridge in the Church of England: since the 1880s over 80 per cent of bishops have gone to Oxford or Cambridge for their college education. The role of Oxbridge in producing elites in British society is indeed striking.

This chapter proposes to examine the effect of institutional rankings of higher education on labour market outcomes within a comparative framework. Although studies in all three societies document the impact of stratification in higher education on labour market outcomes, no cross-national studies have been conducted to assess the relative magnitude and strength of its effect. The major purpose of this chapter is to compare the effect of institutional rankings of higher education on the attainment of occupational status and income in Japan and the United States (Sections 5.4 and 5.5). The British OMS survey did not ask the name of the university which the respondents attended, so our analysis is restricted to Japan and the United States. Furthermore, this chapter will compare the extent to which stratification in higher education reproduces socioeconomic inequality between generations in the two societies. While such a reproduction function is reported in the United States, none of the studies on the impact of college quality in Japan controls for the effect of social background. It is thus particularly important to examine whether the apparent college quality effect documented by Japanese social scientists is largely spurious.

Section 5.6 of this chapter will provide some qualitative observations to facilitate the understanding of the process of status attainment of Japanese and American college graduates. It will discuss how college seniors in both societies are employed and allocated to different jobs within a company.

Finally, the last analysis (Section 5.7) of this chapter will examine the relationship between stratification in higher education and the formation of elite segments of society. While the quality of institutions attended may influence socioeconomic returns, one of the most important roles of the institutions of higher learning is to provide pathways to the elite groups within the society. The Japanese higher educational system was originally set up for the purpose of selecting the national elite and providing them with a broad liberal education (Aso and Amano, 1983). We will focus on the linkage between elite institutions and top positions in corporate management and public bureaucracy in Japan, the United States and Britain by examining the educational origins of top corporate elites and bureaucrats.

5.2 TRENDS IN RETURNS TO COLLEGE EDUCATION

Let us first discuss the issue of the declining market value of college education, using intercohort analysis. Intertemporal changes in socioeconomic returns to college education reflect changes in an individual's life-cycle as well as changes in the historical context. The attainment of current occupation and income is heavily contingent on men's life-cycle. The current occupation and income of a man in his late 20s are obviously different from those of a man in his late 40s, due to the different stage he is at in his life-cycle. At the same time, men of different cohorts are affected by differential labour market conditions depending upon the surrounding socioeconomic context of the time (Blau and Duncan, 1967). Intertemporal change of the effects of a college degree on current occupational status and income thus confounds changes in life-cycle and historical changes.

The intercohort analysis of the returns to a BA degree in first occupational status, however, permits us to analyze the effects of historical changes on the linkage between higher education and the labour market. Since all men, regardless of their cohort, obtained their first job at almost the same life-stage, which usually corresponds to the completion of education, the attainment of first occupation is independent of changes in individual life-cycle. We will thus restrict the intercohort analysis to the relationship between college education and initial labour market status.

Table 5.1 presents the effects of a high school diploma or an O-level qualification and a BA degree on first occupational status before and after controlling for background variables in different cohorts in Japan, the United States and Britain.[4] While the purpose of this section is to examine the temporal change in returns to a BA degree, the change in returns to a high school diploma or an O-level qualification is also presented as a reference group.

In Japan, intertemporal change in the returns to a high school diploma shows a clear trend of diminishing value of high school

Table 5.1 Effects of educational credentials on first occupational status by cohort in Japan (SSM), the United States (OCG) and Britain (OMS)

Cohort	**Japan**				**United States**			
	High school		*BA*		*High school*		*BA*	
	Total	*Causal*[a]	Total	Causal	Total	Causal	Total	Causal
20–24	(2.73)[b]	(3.13)	8.72	9.66 (110%)	4.32	3.42 (79%)	16.15	15.16 (94%)
25–29	3.01	2.95 (98%)[c]	7.83	7.33 (94%)	5.96	4.26 (71%)	18.54	16.84 (91%)
30–34	3.22	2.72 (84%)	10.96	9.97 (91%)	5.94	4.79 (81%)	21.53	19.87 (92%)
35–39	4.20	3.98 (95%)	12.33	11.51 (94%)	5.73	4.98 (87%)	22.20	21.04 (95%)
40–44	5.53	5.63 (100%)	8.14	8.63 (106%)	5.47	4.84 (88%)	20.09	19.44 (97%)
45–49	6.83	6.52 (95%)	5.38	(4.04) (75%)	6.22	5.06 (81%)	19.83	18.74 (95%)
50–54	7.02	6.27 (89%)	13.79	13.36 (97%)	5.32	4.68 (88%)	21.47	20.47 (95%)
55–59	9.69	8.27 (85%)	(–[d])	(–[d])	5.24	4.19 (80%)	19.76	18.61 (94%)
60–64	6.19	(4.03)	(–[d])	(–[d])	4.48	4.41 (98%)	18.83	18.13 (96%)

Cohort	**Britain**			
	O-level		*BA*	
	Total	*Causal*	*Total*	*Causal*
20–24	7.80	6.22 (80%)	8.47	7.47 (88%)
25–29	7.21	5.26 (73%)	12.76	11.02 (86%)
30–34	6.54	6.07 (93%)	10.31	9.56 (93%)
35–39	6.03	4.07 (67%)	13.98	12.43 (89%)
40–44	4.44	3.36 (76%)	13.25	13.07 (98%)
45–49	7.97	6.49 (81%)	(5.36)	(4.35)
50–54	7.21	5.78 (80%)	8.30	8.40 (101%)
55–59	5.18	(3.36)	12.19	11.81 (97%)
60–64	(4.90)	(3.31)	(10.37)	(8.61)

Notes:

[a] Causal effect indicates the effect after the background variables are controlled for.

[b] The numbers in parentheses are non-significant effects, and thereby the percentages of non-spurious component are not computed.

[c] The percentages indicate non-spurious component.

[d] The number of BA holders is too small to have a reliable estimate.

education: the total and causal (net of social background) benefit of high school education dropped dramatically from the 55–59 cohort to the 25–29 cohort (from 9.69 to 3.01 for the total effect and from 8.27 to 2.95 for the causal effect), and even became non-significant in the youngest cohort (20–24). In contrast, no clearcut trend is apparent in the effect of college education on first occupational status in Japan. The total returns to a BA degree fluctuate from 13.79 (50–54 cohort) to 5.38 (45–49 cohort), and the causal effect (net of social background) fluctuates from 13.36 (50–54 cohort) to 4.04 (45–49 cohort).[5]

However, the premium of a BA degree seems to have reached its maximum in the 35–39 cohort. These men obtained their first jobs in the late 1950s and early 1960s when the Japanese economy experienced an extremely rapid economic growth. The number of college graduates increased steadily throughout the 1950s and 1960s, as shown in the percentage increase of college graduates from 7.7 per cent in the 45–49 cohort to 16.8 per cent in the 25–29 cohort in Table 5.2 (p. 141). Nonetheless, in the late 1950s and early 1960s, employment opportunity probably expanded more rapidly than the supply of the college-educated population due to economic prosperity. It is thus not surprising that the market value of a college education peaked in this period.

The lower returns in the 40–44 and 45–49 cohort are probably due to Japan's defeat in the Second World War. These men entered the labour force around the period of the defeat in the War and the American Occupation (1945–51), when the old imperial system was destroyed. It is not surprising that a college degree was less likely to be used for the allocation of first jobs in a period of significant social transformation than in more stable times.

It is not clear why the college graduates of the 25–29 cohort suffered lower returns to their degrees. The most probable explanation would be the impact of the student movement. These men entered the labour market around 1968–72 when many Japanese colleges experienced student revolts and a subsequent series of reforms. The context of college training and the role of higher education, including that of providing trained manpower, were questioned from both within and outside the institutions of higher learning. The labour market might have been sensitive to these changes, and many employers may have become reluctant to recruit college graduates for higher-status entry positions, while some graduates may have deliberately obtained lower-status jobs.

The spurious component of the effects of a high school diploma and a BA degree is generally very small across cohorts (see the percentage of non-spurious component in parentheses in Table 5.1). The benefits of both educational credentials are almost totally independent of social background in Japan.

In the United States, the most striking characteristic of the relationship between education and initial occupation is its general historical stability (cf. Featherman and Hauser, 1978). The total effect of a high school diploma on first occupational status is about 5.5 points, and the causal effect after controlling for social background is about 4.5 points. A BA degree increases first occupational status on the average by 20 points without controlling for social background, and it increases the same status by about 19 points among men of statistically equivalent social origin. The premium of a college degree over a high school diploma is about 14.5 points (19 – 4.5) among men of the same social background. The completion of higher education significantly improves prospects for prestigious entry jobs throughout the period.

The non-spurious component of the effects of educational credentials, shown in parentheses in Table 5.1, also exhibits a stable pattern of indifference to historical context. The effects of a high school diploma and a BA degree are virtually independent of social background. The increases in first occupational status are not affected by the background characteristics of high school graduates and BA degree holders.

The general historical stability in both the total and causal (net of social background) effect of education is most striking when we take account of the increasing level of education in the twentieth-century United States. As shown in Table 5.2, the percentage of men with a high school diploma in each cohort increased dramatically from 44.2 per cent in the oldest cohort (60–64) to 81.7 per cent in the youngest cohort (20–24). Similarly, the percentage of men with a BA degree increased from 11.8 per cent in the oldest cohort (60–64) to 22.7 per cent in the 25–29 cohort. Despite the rapid increase in the supply of educated labour and the changing historical and economic contexts in twentieth-century American history, educational credentials performed a stable role of allocating people to initial labour market position.

In Britain, the effects of an O-level qualification and a BA degree on first occupational status are generally stable across cohorts. An O-level increases first occupational status on the average by 6.7

Table 5.2 Percentage of men with a high school diploma or an O-level and of men with a BA degree by cohort in Japan (SSM), the United States (OCG) and Britain (OMS)

Cohort	*High school diploma or O-level*			*BA*		
	Japan	**United States**	**Britain**	**Japan**	**United States**	**Britain**
20–24	68.9	81.7	31.1	11.2	12.1	3.8
25–29	71.2	81.5	30.5	16.8	22.7	6.0
30–34	58.5	76.6	24.2	15.9	23.1	6.1
35–39	58.3	71.7	22.8	15.7	22.3	5.4
40–44	45.3	67.8	16.1	11.5	21.2	3.8
45–49	42.6	61.3	13.7	7.7	17.9	3.2
50–54	39.1	60.4	12.0	4.7	14.7	1.7
55–59	33.3	54.1	12.6	3.1	12.1	1.9
60–64	32.5	44.2	9.2	3.2	11.8	1.7

points before controlling for social background, and by 5.3 points after social background characteristics have been taken into account. A BA degree is worth about 11 points before controlling for social background and 10 points after the control, except for the 45–49 cohort in which the effect of a BA degree is not significant. The non-significant effect in the 45–49 cohort probably reflects the fact that men in this cohort entered the labour market immediately following the end of the Second World War when the linkage between the educational system and the job market was probably looser than in other periods.

Table 5.2 shows that both the proportions of men with an O-level and a BA degree increased steadily in twentieth-century Britain although the increase was less dramatic than in Japan and the United States. Occupational status returns to academic qualifications, none the less, appear to be insensitive to this steady upgrading of educational level and changes in historical and economic contexts.

The spurious components of the effects of an O-level and a BA degree are not substantial. However, the effect of an O-level is in part due to the advantaged background of those who obtained the qualification; its effect decreased on the average 23 per cent after controlling for social background characteristics.

5.3 OVEREDUCATION OF THE COLLEGE-EDUCATED POPULATION?

The intercohort analysis of the returns to educational credentials in first occupational status sheds some light on the issue of 'overeducation'. Freeman (1976) contends that the socioeconomic premium of college education declined in the 1970s due to the downturn in the labour market for college-educated workers in the United States. The United States produced such a large population who went to institutions of higher education that people were 'overeducated' in the marketplace. The returns to a BA degree in the two youngest cohorts (20–24 and 25–29) indeed show weakened effects in the United States: among men of similar background, the benefit of a BA degree decreased from about 19 points (the average of the older cohorts) to 16 points (the average of the two youngest cohorts). While the decline is not dramatic, our result is consistent with Freeman's claim of 'overeducation'.

However, Featherman and Hauser (1978) propose an alternative explanation for the apparent decline in the benefits of a BA degree in the younger cohorts. They claim that prolonging the transition from a student to a full-time worker in the younger cohorts contributes largely to the intercohort reduction in the occupational premium of a BA degree; 'The disappearance of the military draft, higher unemployment rates for younger men, and increased tendencies to combine labor force participation with college enrollment' (Featherman and Hauser, 1978, p. 280) led to delayed full-time entry into the labour force. Thus, if these men who were still in the institutions of higher education in 1973 later engaged in higher-status first jobs than those who were already in the labour force in 1973, then the effect of a BA degree in our analysis would underestimate the returns to college education.

Indeed, as pointed out by Featherman and Hauser (1978, p. 276), substantial minorities of the two youngest cohorts in the OCG data were still students not in the labour force, and were thereby excluded from our analysis; 13 per cent of the 20–24 cohort and 3.4 per cent of the 25–29 cohort were students, while only 0.7 per cent of the 30–34 cohort were enrolled in school. There is a good reason to believe, therefore, that the delayed full-time entry into the labour force contributed to the apparent intercohort decline in the returns to a BA degree for the youngest cohort members. The OCG data, however, does not allow us to preclude the thesis of 'overeducation'. It cannot be guaranteed that the reduction in the effect of a BA degree is explained entirely by the prolongation of the transition from a student to a full-time worker in the younger cohorts.[6]

In Japan, no diminishing market value for college education in recent cohorts is apparent. While the effect of a BA degree in the 25–29 cohort (causal effect is 7.33) appears to be lower than the effect in the previous three cohorts, the youngest cohort (20–24) does not show diminishing returns: the causal effect is 9.66. Furthermore, there is a good reason to believe that this figure underestimates the true premium of a BA degree, since 24 per cent of the 20–24 cohort members were still enrolled in school. The lower returns in the 25–29 cohort are probably due to the impact of the student movement on the recruitment practices of companies and on the job preferences of college students, as discussed above. Our results suggest that until the mid-1970s, when the SSM survey was conducted, no decline in the benefit of a BA degree was evident in Japan.

These findings are contrary to the argument proposed by Japanese economists under the notion of 'employment substitution by college graduates' (Koike and Watanabe, 1979; Watanabe, 1976, 1982; Fujita, 1980). Their idea implies that occupations normally occupied by high school graduates are now filled by college-educated people, and that the occupational returns to college education have declined.

The argument of diminishing returns to college education, however, does not seem to receive much support from other data either. Table 5.3 shows the trend in occupational composition of employees who were newly graduated from college in Japan. The proportion of college graduates who were engaged in professional, technical and managerial occupations stayed about the same from 1956 to 1982, although the proportion in sales occupations increased from 4.8 per cent in 1956 to 20.9 per cent in 1982. Iwauchi (1980) showed that the proportion of high school graduates engaged in sales and clerical occupations as their first entry jobs did not decrease from 1956 to 1979, and thus concluded that 'there is no evidence of employment substitution of high school graduates by college graduates' (p. 95).

Our finding is consistent with Iwauchi's claim. The intercohort analysis suggests that the occupational premium of a BA degree seems to have reached its maximum point around the late 1950s and early 1960s when the 35–39 cohort entered the labour market, but the figure for the youngest cohort does not show any sign of appreciable decline in the market value of college education.

Table 5.3 Occupational composition of employees who are newly graduated from university in Japan, 1956–82 (%)

Year	*Professional, technical and managerial*	*Clerical*	*Sales*	*Other*
1956	47.2	41.5	4.8	6.5
1959	44.8	38.6	9.3	7.3
1962	44.4	37.9	13.2	4.5
1965	45.4	33.9	15.0	5.7
1968	41.0	33.5	17.6	7.9
1971	43.7	33.8	19.3	3.2
1974	39.4	37.2	18.5	4.9
1977	40.1	38.7	17.0	4.2
1979	38.3	37.5	17.9	6.3
1982	41.0	34.2	20.9	3.9

Source: Monbusho, *Gakko Kihon Chosa* (Report on the Basic Survey of Schools), respective years.

5.4 STRATIFICATION IN HIGHER EDUCATION AND LABOUR MARKET OUTCOMES

Let us move to the second issue, examining the relationship between stratification in higher education and labour market outcomes. Our strategy is to assess the effect of institutional rankings or college quality on socioeconomic achievement among college graduates in Japan and the United States.

Table 5.4 reports the effect of college quality on the first occupational status and the current occupational status in Japan and the United States. The effect of college quality is expressed by two categories (dummy variables) representing highly selective and selective institutions; the category for non-selective institutions is used as a base category. The dummy variable for highly selective institutions therefore measures the socioeconomic advantage of graduating from highly selective rather than from non-selective institutions, and the dummy variable for selective institutions measures the advantage of graduating form selective rather than from non-selective institutions (for the details of the college quality variable, refer to Chapter 2).[7] Total effect indicates the effect of college quality without any control, and causal effect is its effect after social background variables have

Table 5.4 Effects of college quality on first occupational status and current occupational status in Japan (SSM) and the United States (OCG)

	First occupation		*Current occupation*	
	Japan (%)	**United States (%)**	**Japan (%)**	**United States (%)**
Highly selective institutions				
Total	NS[a]	3.96 (100)	5.91 (100)	4.74 (100)
Spurious	–	0.30 (8)	1.29 (22)	0.37 (8)
Causal	NS	3.66 (92)	4.62 (78)	4.37 (92)
Direct	–	–	4.42 (96)	2.67 (61)
Indirect	–	–	0.20 (4)	1.70 (39)
Selective institutions				
Total	NS	1.42 (100)	5.06 (100)	1.41 (100)
Spurious	–	0.12 (8)	0.79 (16)	0.08 (6)
Causal	NS	1.30 (92)	4.27 (84)	1.33 (94)
Direct	–	–	3.11 (73)	0.73 (55)
Indirect	–	–	1.16 (27)	0.60 (45)

Note:
[a] NS indicates that the effect is not significant at 0.05 level.

been controlled for.[8] Direct effect shows the effect of college quality independent of social background and the first occupation, and indirect effect refers to the effect through the first occupation.

A striking cross-national difference is evident in the effect of institutional rankings on the first occupational status. In Japan, college quality does not influence the attainment of the first occupational status either with or without control for the social background variables. At entry into the labour market, the stratification in Japanese higher education does not seem to yield occupational status differentiation. In contrast, in the United States college quality shows significant total and causal effects. In particular, alumni of highly selective institutions have a distinct advantage over those of non-selective institutions. A comparison of the total and the causal effects shows that the effect of institutional rankings is largely independent of social background. Graduating from selective institutions independently enhances the chances of prestigious first jobs in the United States.

Both in Japan and the United States, college quality shows significant total and causal effects on the current occupation. However, three cross-national differences are found. First, the effect of institutional rankings in the United States is largely independent of the social background variables: the spurious component of the total effect of college quality is less than 8 per cent. On the other hand, in Japan the spurious component of the college quality effect is 22 per cent for the highly selective institution group and 16 per cent for the selective institution group.[9] The advantaged social background characteristics of the Japanese college graduates from highly selective or selective institutions thus in part explain the occupational advantage later in these men's careers.

Second, in Japan attending either highly selective or selective institutions equally increases the current occupational status by more than four points net of social background; however, in the United States the college graduates from the elite institutions enjoy a significantly larger boost (4.4 points) in the current occupational status than those from the merely selective institutions (1.3 points). This implies that in the United States credentials from the highly selective institutions are necessary for a major improvement in occupational status in the later career, while in Japan the credentials from both highly selective and selective institutions result in a large and significant increase in current occupational status.

Third, a large proportion of the effect of college quality (independent of social background) is mediated by the first occupation in the United States. 39 per cent (for the highly selective college group) and 45 per cent (for the selective college group) of the effect is indirect through the first occupation. In contrast, in Japan only a very small part of the non-spurious effect of college quality operates through the first occupation. In particular, the current occupational boost for the highly selective college graduates is totally independent of the first entry position which these graduates obtain. In other words, there is a lagged effect of college quality on occupational attainment in Japan.

The relationship between college quality and income attainment is shown in Table 5.5. The findings parallel in many ways those for current occupational status attainment. First, in both societies college quality shows significant total and causal effects on income. Stratification in higher education has a significant consequence for the financial prospects of college graduates in the two countries.

Second, as in current occupational status attainment, the graduates from highly selective American institutions of higher learning enjoy a major income improvement: their income return, controlling for social background, is $4131. The same return for the graduates of

Table 5.5 Effects of college quality on income in Japan (SSM) and the United States (OCG)

	Income[a]	
	Japan (%)	**United States (%)**
Highly selective institutions		
Total	2150 (100)	5570 (100)
Spurious	426 (19)	1439 (26)
Causal	1724 (80)	4131 (74)
Direct	1673 (97)	3779 (91)
Indirect	51 (3)	352 (9)
Selective institutions		
Total	1641 (100)	2243 (100)
Spurious	56 (3)	604 (27)
Causal	1585 (97)	1639 (73)
Direct	1430 (90)	1513 (92)
Indirect	155 (10)	126 (8)

Note:
[a] All the coefficients are the effects after experience and decay are controlled for.

selective institutions is only $1639. In Japan, the college graduates from the highly selective institutions and those from selective institutions enjoy almost the same income advantage (about $1600) over those from non-selective schools.

Third, a comparison of the non-spurious causal effect and the direct effect net of the initial occupational status suggests that the effect of college quality on income attainment does not operate through the initial occupation. American and Japanese graduates from highly selective and selective institutions enjoy an income advantage over graduates of non-selective institutions independently of their entry occupations.

Fourth, contrary to the results from the analysis of occupational status attainment, slightly over a quarter of the total effect of institutional rankings in the United States is spurious.[10] The apparent effect of institutional rankings on income in the United States is explained in part by the advantaged background characteristics of college graduates from relatively prestigious institutions. On the other hand, the college quality effect in Japan is less influenced by social background. In particular, the graduates of selective institutions enjoy an income boost over those who graduate from non-selective institutions independently of their background characteristics.[11]

In summary, the most important finding of our analysis is that stratification in higher education in general has a significant impact on socioeconomic attainment in both societies. Although the effect of institutional rankings is not present at the beginning of a career in Japan, it becomes significant in later occupational and income attainment. Stratification in American higher education influences not only entry level occupational position but also later socioeconomic achievement. In particular, the socioeconomic benefit of graduating from highly selective institutions is large.

5.5 CROSS-NATIONAL DIFFERENCES IN THE EFFECT OF COLLEGE QUALITY

Some important cross-national differences deserve special attention. First, the effect of institutional rankings on initial labour market status is absent in Japan. This absence implies that institutional rankings have a lagged impact on the socioeconomic attainment. On the other hand, American college graduates of highly selective and selective institutions enjoy both initial access to a higher-status first job that may serve as a stepping stone to later advancement, and the occupational and income advantages of their later careers.

The lack of the immediate effect of college quality in Japan reflects the characteristic policies of Japanese firms in utilizing newly-recruited members. Japanese firms in general assign newly-recruited college graduates to a variety of clerical jobs in their first few years. The purpose of this policy is to let the newly-recruited members familiarize themselves with various activities of the firm, while at the same time training them on-the-job. Only after spending a few years following their entry into firm are the college graduates recognized as the 'driving force' (*senryoku* in Japanese) of the firm and assigned to responsible positions.

Furthermore, as Yamada (1980, p. 143) pointed out, 'after about three years of work experience, many firms begin to differentiate the college graduates who entered the firm the same year into three groups (the top elite group, the middle management group, and the ordinary group) and in the long run the differentiation affects wage and promotion'. It is therefore not surprising to find that, at the beginning of their careers, there is little differentiation in the kinds of job that college graduates obtain in Japan; the effect of institutional rankings is likely to be suppressed until the employers begin to differentiate the graduates several years later.

The second cross-national difference which deserves special attention is the status of elite institutions. The American college graduates of highly competitive institutions occupy a distinctly advantaged position in the labour market. Their occupational status and income returns are more than double the returns enjoyed by the graduates of selective institutions. In contrast, the occupational and income advantages of graduates from highly selective institutions in Japan are almost identical to the advantages enjoyed by graduates from selective institutions. The labour market consequences of stratification in higher education can probably be explained simply by whether or not men graduated from non-selective institutions in Japan. As far as income benefits are concerned, the American graduates of elite institutions are far more advantaged than their Japanese counterparts.[12] However, as we will see in section 5.7 below, a very small number of Japanese elite institutions are far more likely to produce top corporate management than the American leading institutions.

Finally, stratification in higher education tends to reproduce different kinds of inequality in Japan and the United States. In Japan, the effect of institutional rankings on current occupational status is in part explained by social background. In the United States, the effect of institutional rankings on income is in part explained by social background. In other words, in Japan advantaged families tend to ensure an occupational status advantage by sending their sons to highly-ranked institutions, while in the United States, these advantaged families tend to ensure an income rather than an occupational advantage. Stratification in higher education in Japan therefore tends to reproduce occupational inequality, while the same stratification in the United States tends to reproduce income inequality.

5.6 RECRUITMENT AND ALLOCATION OF COLLEGE GRADUATES

This section provides some qualitative observations which help explain the process of status attainment among Japanese and American college graduates as it takes place within the firm. Interviews with company recruiters and college seniors in Japan and the United States during the summer and autumn of 1984 constitute the basis of the observations reported here. The differences in the process of recruitment and allocation of newly-hired members between Japanese and American firms reflect the cross-national difference in the status attainment process of college graduates.[13]

The Japanese firms generally look for promising but relatively inexperienced students. The personnel manager of one of the largest general trading companies in Japan mentioned: 'what we look for is "raw materials" (*sozai*). We do not want students who have previous job-related experience. If we hire a student with moulding experience, we first have to break him of acquired work habits and re-train him so that he will adjust to our company colour'. This view is supported by college students. One student confessed:

> I worked in a private firm during the summer as a part-time market research assistant. I was very proud of my work experience because students rarely have a chance to work on the actual job setting. So I mentioned my summer job in all the job interviews. But I was not successful. Later I was told by a senior (*senpai*) that job-related experience was not only irrelevant to hiring but harmful. So I changed my strategy. I do not know whether this was the major reason but I certainly had a job offer immediately after I stopped talking about my summer job experience.

One of the 'how-to' books on job search for college students, *How to Win the Job Interview* (Nishi, 1979, pp. 173–4), warns the job applicants: 'the more you emphasize your achievement in part-time work experience, the more disadvantaged you are in the job interview'.

Work experience and job-related skills are generally considered an unimportant and sometimes even disadvantageous factor for Japanese students. Japanese firms appear to favour candidates with minimal job skills and prefer to train them on-the-job in the first few years after they have joined the company. During this period, the newly-recruited members will internalize 'the company's way of handling things', and learn firm-specific skills and firm-specific ways of making decisions. Only after a number of years of experiencing different jobs as a part of extensive on-the-job training are the college graduates assigned to more responsible positions which often have managerial titles. The differentiation among college graduates in terms of their occupational and managerial status therefore occurs some years after they enter the firm.

In contrast, American firms generally favour applicants who already have some knowledge of, and training in, a particular job (cf. Squires, 1979). Recruiters tend to seek job candidates who can immediately contribute to the growth of the company. Work experience and previous work skills acquired in the summer job or jobs between college sessions tend to help American students obtain their first jobs after graduation. The personnel manager of a large food product firm, for example, claims that the company needs people who have 'hands-on experience and can immediately go into work'. The promising candidates are assigned from the very beginning of their career to responsible positions which are often relatively prestigious. Differentiation in status and other kinds of job reward is therefore apparent from the beginning of men's careers in the United States.

In summary, the differences in the ways in which Japanese and American firms select, allocate and train their employees reflect the cross-national differences in the patterns of status attainment among college graduates. The general emphasis on limited work experience and trainability in selecting job applicants combined with the extensive on-the-job training of the Japanese firms lead to a lagged impact of college quality on socioeconomic achievement. In the United States, work experience and job-related skills are generally considered to be favourable characteristics for job candidates, and the college graduates are likely to be allocated to different positions according to their previous work experience and skills. Status differentiation among American college graduates therefore begins early in their careers.

5.7 STRATIFICATION IN HIGHER EDUCATION AND FORMATION OF ELITES

The impact of stratification in higher education on labour market outcomes is generally believed to be maximized at the summit of the organizational hierarchy. Higher occupational status and income do not necessarily imply that the college graduates have joined the 'elite' group; the previous analyses do not shed light on the process of recruitment and formation of the elite. In order to highlight the effect of stratification in higher education on the elite formation, the educational origin of the top corporate and bureucratic elites will now be examined.

In Japan, there are several studies on the relationship between educational credentials and elite formation (Mannari, 1965, 1974;

Table 5.6 Rates of producing business elites by different university background in Japan

University background	*Number of employees*[a]	*Number of directors*	*Production rate*
1. Tokyo	242	52	21.5%
2. Kyoto	131	21	16.0%
3. Hitotsubashi	70	10	14.3%
4. Tokyo Kogyo	45	5	11.1%
5. Hokkaido, Tohoku, Nagoya, Osaka, Kyushu, Kobe, Osaka Ichiritsu	217	18	8.3%
6. Other public institutions	355	4	1.1%
7. Waseda (*p*)[b]	136	10	7.4%
8. Keio (*p*)	140	13	9.3%
9. Chuo, Nihon, Hosei, Meiji, Rikkyo, Kansai, Kangaku, Doshisha, Ritsumeikan (*p*)	160	3	1.9%
10. Other institutions	76	2	2.6%
11. Institution unknown	26	0	0%
Total	1598	138	8.6%

Notes:
[a] The number of college graduates employed in the selected 52 firms in 1951.
[b] (*p*) indicates private institution.
Source: Takeuchi (1981).

Takane, 1976; Aso, 1969). The study by Takeuchi (1981, p. 121) estimated the rate that different universities produced business executives.[14] He calculated how many of the university graduates who had entered private companies in 1951 had reached the top executive positions in 1981. He picked 49 companies which listed the names of undergraduate institutions from which the newly recruited university students had graduated in 1951, and matched the information with the university origins of top executives in these 49 companies. The results are shown in Table 5.6. The three most prestigious and competitive institutions, Tokyo University, Kyoto University and Hitotsubashi University, all of which are national universities, occupy a distinctly advantageous position in producing business executives. Their rates of producing company directors are well above the average rate of 4.8 per cent for all other universities. There

Table 5.7 Educational origin of presidents of companies listed in the First Tokyo Stock Market Exchange, 1985

Institution	*Number of managers*	*(%)*
1. Tokyo	416	22.9
2. Keio (*p*)[a]	158	8.7
3. Kyoto	147	8.1
4. Waseda (*p*)	134	7.4
5. Hitotshubashi	66	3.6
6. Kobe	39	2.2
7. Kyushu	38	2.1
8. Tokyo Kogyo	35	1.9
9. Nihon (*p*)	34	1.9
10. Osaka	32	1.8
11. Tohoku	32	1.8
12. Chuo (*p*)	26	1.4
13. Osaka Ichiritsu	24	1.3
13. Meiji (*p*)	24	1.3
15. Hokkaido	19	1.0
Other universities and non-university graduates	593	32.6
Total	1817	100.0

Note:
[a] (*p*) indicates private institution.
Source: *Nihon Keizai* newspaper (1986).

appears to be a close correspondence between the top of the stratification in higher education and the summit of the managerial hierarchy.

The same pattern can be found among the presidents of the companies listed in the First Tokyo Stock Market Exchange (*Jojo Ichibu*). These companies represent the most competitive and profitable firms in Japan. The *Nihon Keizai* newspaper conducted a survey on the demographic and educational biographies of company presidents;[15] the educational origins of the 1817 presidents are shown in Table 5.7. Again, the dominance of the three most prestigious national universities is evident: almost one-quarter of the presidents graduated from Tokyo University, 8.1 per cent from Kyoto University, and 3.6 per cent from Hitotsubashi University. But two leading private schools, Waseda and Keio, also constituted an important

Table 5.8 Educational origin of successful applicants to higher civil service positions in Japan, 1980

Institution	*Number*	*(%)*
1. Tokyo	519	38.6
2. Kyoto	216	16.1
3. Hokkaido	85	6.3
4. Tokyo Kogyo	53	3.9
5. Waseda (*p*)[a]	51	3.8
6. Kyushu	40	3.0
7. Tohoku	37	2.8
7. Osaka	37	2.8
8. Nagoya	27	2.0
9. Keio (*p*)	18	1.3
10. Chuo (*p*)	13	1.0
10. Tokyo Noukou	13	1.0
Others	235	17.5
Total	1344	100.0

Note:
[a] (*p*) indicates private institution.
Source: Koyama (1981).

educational pathway to the top corporate elites. Keio yielded 8.7 per cent and Waseda 7.4 per cent of all the presidents in the sample. These five institutions accounted for 51 per cent of all the presidents.

The dominance of top national universities is more conspicuous when we examine the educational origins of higher civil servants (*jokyu komuin*) in the national bureaucracies in Japan. These top bureaucrats are recruited from the young candidates who have just completed their education on the basis of the higher civil service examination. As more than 95 per cent of the applicants fail, the civil service examination is highly competitive (Kim, 1988). Table 5.8 shows the educational origins of the applicants who successfully passed the examination in 1980. Over 50 per cent of the successful applicants to higher civil service positions are the graduates of Tokyo and Kyoto Universities. The dominance of these two national universities appears even to have increased in the 1970s, since their share was 42 per cent in 1973 (Koyama, 1981). In contrast, the two leading private schools, Waseda and Keio, have a very small share (5 per cent) in the national bureaucracy. The advantage of these private schools is much more apparent in the private sector. The top civil

Table 5.9 Educational origin of managers and directors in the Useem and Karabel Survey (1986)

Institution	*Number of managers*	*(%)*
1. Yale	145	5.3
2. Harvard	109	4.0
3. Princeton	76	2.8
4. Stanford	74	2.7
5. Dartmouth	51	1.9
6. Cornell	41	1.5
7. Pennsylvania	35	1.3
8. Columbia	33	1.2
9. MIT	28	1.0
10. John Hopkins	11	0.4
11. Williams	11	0.4
Other colleges	1663	60.9
No college or college drop-outs	452	16.6
Total	2729	100.0

Source: Unpublished draft of Useem and Karabel (1986).

service positions in the Japanese national bureaucracy are heavily dominated by the graduates of national universities, in particular of Tokyo University.

In the United States, the pathways to top corporate management are also influenced by stratification in higher education. As early as 1951, Warner and Abegglen (1951) showed that the alumni of elite institutions were overrepresented in top management. Useem and Karabel (1986) examined the educational origin of 2729 corporate managers and directors of 208 large American companies listed in the annual *Fortune* magazine in 1977. Table 5.9 shows the list of undergraduate institutions from which these managers and directors graduated.[16] The top 11 institutions account for 22.5 per cent of all managers and directors. Furthermore, 34.5 per cent of all the managers had MBA or LLB degrees, of whom 62.4 per cent were from the top-ranking MBA and LLB programmes (Useem and Karabel, 1986, p. 188).[17]

Standard and Poor's Corporation conducted a survey on the educational origins of American executives in 1976, 1980, and 1982. The

Table 5.10 University background of executives in Standard and Poor's 1982 Executive College Survey

Undergraduate degree			*Graduate degree*		
Institution	*Number of executives*	(%)	*Institution*	*Number of executives*	(%)
1. Yale	1 679	(3.2)	1. Harvard	3 849	(16.1)
2. Harvard	1 366	(2.6)	2. NYU	1 370	(5.7)
3. CUNY	1 258	(2.4)	3. Columbia	1 223	(5.1)
4. Princeton	1 199	(2.3)	4. Michigan	794	(3.3)
5. NYU	1 093	(2.1)	5. Pennsylvania	742	(3.1)
6. Pennsylvania	1 052	(2.0)	6. Chicago	695	(2.9)
7. Michigan	1 014	(1.9)	7. Northwestern	649	(2.7)
8. Wisconsin	968	(1.8)	8. MIT	566	(2.4)
9. Illinois	945	(1.8)	9. Stanford	551	(2.3)
10. Northwestern	857	(1.6)	10. Rutgers	510	(2.1)
11. Minnesota	827	(1.6)	11. Wisconsin	474	(2.0)
12. Cornell	825	(1.6)	12. Yale	419	(1.7)
All undergraduate degrees	52 837		All graduate degrees	23 959	

Source: Standard and Poor's, *Executive/College Survey* (1982).

1982 survey represented more than 50 000 top executives and directors from more than 38 000 public and private companies in the United States (Standard and Poor's, 1982). The results of the 1982 Executive/College Survey are shown in Table 5.10. Ivy League schools and Big Ten schools account for 28.5 per cent of all undergraduate degrees and 42.7 per cent of all graduate degrees (Standard and Poor's, 1982, p. 2). In the United States, not only the quality of the undergraduate institutions, but also the ranking of the graduate institutions from which the executives obtained higher degrees, appear to have a vast influence. These results show a consistently large overrepresentation of alumni from top-ranking undergraduate and graduate institutions in top managements in American public and private companies.

Stratification in higher education also has a clear impact on the formation of British elites. Fidler (1981, p. 85) reports in his study of the British business elite that 50 per cent of his sample of 111 chief business executives attended Oxford or Cambridge. Only 14 per cent went to other universities and the remaining 45 per cent did not attend universities at all. Fidler's results suggest that chief business

Table 5.11 Educational origin of elites in different sectors of British society, 1970–1

Sector	*Oxbridge*	*Other universities*	*Military academies*	*Other*	*Total*
Civil service	199	50	0	38	287
	(70%)[a]	(17%)	(0%)	(13%)	(100%)
Foreign service	64	7	2	7	80
	(80%)	(8%)	(3%)	(8%)	(100%)
Judiciary	77	8	1	5	91
	(85%)	(9%)	(1%)	(5%)	(100%)
Army	28	10	54	23	115
	(24%)	(9%)	(47%)	(20%)	(100%)
Royal Air Force	14	8	19	39	80
	(18%)	(10%)	(24%)	(49%)	(100%)
Church of England	100	22	0	7	129
	(78%)	(17%)	(0%)	(5%)	(100%)
Clearing banks	81	11	2	40	134
	(60%)	(8%)	(1%)	(30%)	(100%)

Notes:
[a] Row percentages are in parentheses.
Source: Boyd (1973).

executives were not likely to go to university at all if they were not Oxbridge graduates.[18] Whitley (1974, p. 70) also found that 58 per cent of the directors of large financial institutions (Bank of England, clearing and merchant banks and insurance companies) and 40 per cent of the directors of large industrial firms (selected from the *Times 1000* listing for 1970–1) attended either Oxford or Cambridge.

Using various volumes of *Who's Who*, Boyd (1973) studied educational origins of elites in different sectors of British society. The results of his analysis are summarized in Table 5.11.[19] The dominance of Oxbridge is most apparent in the civil and foreign service, the judiciary and the religious sector. Over 70 per cent of elites in these sectors come from Oxford or Cambridge. More than a majority (60 per cent) of the directors of clearing banks have an Oxbridge background. The military sector is least dominated by these ancient universities because military academies, such as Sandhurst and Cranwell, provide important pathways to elite positions in this sector.

All three societies show a strong tendency for stratification in higher education to correspond to the organizational hierarchy. However, the linkage between elite institutions of higher learning and top corporate and public management appears to be much stronger in Japan and Britain than in the United States. According to the

Nihon Keizai newspaper survey, graduates of the top five universities accounted for more than a majority (51 per cent) of all presidents of most competitive and profitable private firms in Japan.

Similarly, in Britain, as Whitley (1974) reported, 50 per cent of 605 directors of large financial institutions and industrial firms were graduates of Oxford and Cambridge. In contrast, Useem and Karabel showed that the top five undergraduate institutions (Yale, Harvard, Princeton, Stanford and Dartmouth) accounted for only 16.7 per cent of all managers and directors in their sample. Even if we combine the managers and directors who had (1) BA degrees only from the 11 top-ranking colleges, and (2) MBA and LLB degrees from the 11 top-ranking programmes, we find that they constituted only a third (32.7 per cent) of all managers and directors. The educational origin of the corporate elite appears to be much more concentrated among a small number of elite institutions in Japan and Britain than in the United States.

5.8 SUMMARY AND CONCLUSION

The first issue discussed in this chapter was the 'overeducation' or 'underemployment' of college graduates. In Japan, intercohort analysis suggests that no diminishing market value for college education in recent cohorts is apparent. The effect of a BA degree on the first occupational status does not seem to have diminished in recent cohorts. At least through the early 1970s, Japanese college graduates enjoyed the benefit of a college degree as much as the older generations had. The increasing size of the college-going population in the 1960s and 1970s does not seem to have had a noticeable effect on the initial labour market position obtained by Japanese college graduates.

In the United States, our results are consistent with Freeman's (1976) claim of 'overeducation'. The effect of a BA degree on first occupational status is weaker in the younger than in the older cohorts. However, the diminished returns to a college education may be the result of the prolongation of the transition from a student to a full-time worker in the youngest cohorts. Both interpretations are equally plausible. It is probably safe to conclude that intercohort analysis on the returns to education cannot rule out the possibility of 'overeducation' in the United States, but that the reduction in market value of a college education is not as large as the advocates of the thesis of 'overeducation' believe.

The second issue examined in this chapter was the effect of stratification in higher education on labour market outcomes. Our results confirm that credentials from elite institutions generally enhance an individual's bargaining power in the labour market in Japan and the United States. In particular, American graduates of highly competitive institutions of higher learning occupy a distinctly advantaged position; their occupational status and income returns are more than double the returns enjoyed by the graduates of merely selective institutions.

Stratification in higher education contributes to the reproduction of inequality between two generations in Japan and the United States. In Japan, the advantaged families are successful in assuring higher occupational status by sending their sons to highly-ranked institutions. In the United States, the privileged families tend to ensure an income, rather than an occupational, advantage.

These results suggest that part of the apparent effect of institutional rankings on socioeconomic outcomes can be traced to the fact that elite institutions are disproportionately attended by the offspring of the already advantaged in Japan and the United States. Previous studies on the impact of college quality in Japan therefore overestimated its direct effect, since none of the studies controlled for social background. Ignoring the role of stratification in higher education in the reproduction of inequality leads to an overemphasis on the fact that higher education facilitates social mobility between two generations in Japan. Similarly, our results suggest that we should not take the apparent socioeconomic benefits of American elite institutions at face value. The reproduction mechanism is at work beneath the relationship between stratification in higher education and labour market outcomes, and thus part of the correlation is spurious.

Some of the cross-national differences in the status attainment process of college graduates in Japan and the United States could be explained by the differing practices of Japanese and American firms in selecting, allocating and training their employees. The lack of college quality effects on the first occupational status in Japan reflects the fact that Japanese firms in general assign newly-recruited college graduates to a variety of clerical jobs as a part of an on-the-job training programme. The differentiation among college graduates begins some years after entry into the firm in Japan. In contrast,

American college graduates of elite institutions tend to enjoy initial access to higher-status occupations.

Institutional rankings of higher education in general appear to have a stronger impact on occupational status and income in the United States than in Japan, but when we focus on the process of elite formation, a different picture emerges. The linkage between the summit of educational stratification and the top of the managerial hierarchy appears to be much stronger in Japan than in the United States. Similarly, in Britain, the preponderance of Oxford and Cambridge graduates securing elite positions in the society is striking. The graduates of these two ancient universities appear to dominate both private and public sectors. Although corporate and bureaucratic elites are disproportionately recruited from a small number of elite institutions of higher learning in all three societies, the concentration of university origin is much greater in Japan and Britain than in the United States. The educational pathway to top corporate elites and higher public servants appears to show a higher degree of closure (Parkin, 1979) in Japan and Britain. The ranking of Japanese universities does differentiate socioeconomic outcomes of university graduates, but the most dramatic impact of stratification in Japanese higher education appears to be on elite formation.

Notes

1. The term 'college graduates' refers to those who graduated from four-year colleges and universities in Japan and the United States and to those who obtained a bachelor's degree or a Diploma of Technology (or an equivalent degree) in Britain. The term 'college graduates' is used interchangeably with the term 'university graduates' in Japan and the United States. However, in Britain, 'college graduates' include both university graduates and those who graduated from other institutions of higher education (e.g., polytechnics) and obtained a Diploma of Technology.
2. Even though the expansion of university education in the 1960s had an effect on returns to a BA degree, we could probably not assess its full impact since the British data were collected in 1972.
3. Hout (1988) also reports that the effect of the father's status on the son's socioeconomic status is absent among college graduates in the late 1970s and 1980s in the United States. The result may imply that the possession of a college degree is not sufficient for passing on the privileged status from one generation to the next and that quality of institution may have become more important in the late 1970s and 1980s.

4. BA degrees include bachelor's degrees and Diplomas of Technology in Britain. The effects represent the direct impact when other education dummy variables (middle school dummy and dummy variables for vocational qualifications in Britain) are present. Background variables include family income, the father's and mother's education, the father's occupation, urban origin, farm background, the number of siblings and race (for OCG). See Chapter 2 and Chapter 4 (Section 4.3) for details.
5. The two older cohorts (the 55–59 and 60–65 cohort) are excluded in the intercohort comparison because there were few BA degree holders (five men and four men, respectively).
6. For the issue of overeducation in late 1970s and 1980s, see Rumberger (1981; 1982) and Smith (1986). Smith (1986) has shown that college graduates did not suffer any loss of relative income in the late 1970s and early 1980s in the United States.
7. Since the analysis of stratification in higher education is restricted to the graduates of four-year institutions of higher learning, the sample size is fairly small: 215 for SSM and 3172 for OCG. It was therefore not possible separately to analyze for each cohort.
8. Social background variables include family income, father's and mother's education, father's occupation, urban origin, farm background, the number of siblings and race (for OCG).
9. The spurious component was computed by the following formula:

   (Total effect − Direct effect) / Total effect.

10. For the highly selective institution group, the spurious effect is (5570 − 4131)/5570 = 0.26. For the selective institution group, the spurious effect is (2243 − 1639)/2243 = 0.27.
11. The spurious component for the selective college group in Japan is (1641 − 1585)/1641 = 0.03. The spurious component for the highly selective college group is (2150 − 1724)/2150 = 0.19.
12. The greater income advantage of the American graduates of elite institutions over their Japanese counterparts can in part be explained by the greater variance in income among American graduates. However, the variances in first and current occupational statuses are not different between the two societies.
13. The recruitment process of Japanese high school students is described in the work of Rosenbaum and Kariya (1989).
14. Business executives are those who are on the board of directors.
15. Among the 1825 firms listed in the First Tokyo Stock Market Exchange (*Jojo Ichibu*) in November 1985, five firms did not have presidents at the time of the survey and three firms had just joined the First Tokyo Stock Market Exchange. The sample thus consists of 1817 presidents. The age of the presidents ranged between 35 and 89, and there was only one female president (*Nihon Keizai Shinbun*, 1986, 1 January, p. 11).
16. This table was supplied by Michael Useem and Jerome Karabel from an unpublished analysis of the same data-set on which their 1986 study was based.
17. The 11 top-ranking MBA programmes include: Columbia, Dartmouth,

Harvard, MIT, Northwestern, Stanford, University of California–Berkeley, UCLA, University of Chicago, University of Michigan and University of Pennsylvania. The 11 top-ranking LLB programmes include: Columbia, Harvard, NYU, Stanford, University of California–Berkeley, University of Chicago, University of Michigan, University of Pennsylvania and Yale University. For details, see Useem and Karabel (1986).

18. It should be noted, however, that 60 per cent of Fidler's sample went to public schools.
19. Boyd (1973) used the 1970 and 1971 *Who's Who* to select elite groups. His definition of elites is as follows: Civil service (Under-Secretaries and above), Foreign service (heads of embassies and legations), Judiciary (high court judges and above), Army (Major-Generals and above), Royal Air Force (Air Vice-Marshals and above), Church of England (assistant bishops and above), and Clearing banks (directors).

6 Class Structure and Class Mobility

6.1 INTRODUCTION

The major focus in this chapter is on class, defined in terms of the social relations of production and marketable skills. The Japanese Marxist economists have long been concerned with the analysis of the class structure of modern Japanese society (e.g., Ohashi, 1971) and the development of Japanese capitalism (e.g., Noro, 1930; Yamada, 1934; Hirano, 1967). Several important studies attempted to estimate the class composition of modern and contemporary Japanese society using the Census and survey data (Hara, 1979; Ohashi, 1971; Shoji, 1977, 1982; Steven, 1983). However, none of these studies on class composition discussed the pattern of class mobility; the nature of the data did not allow investigation of the movement of people within the class structure. Furthermore, the study of mobility was often considered 'bourgeois science', since mobility is generally viewed by Marxists as a factor which weakens class consciousness and collective action among the working class.

Recent quantitative studies on stratification in the United States show a renewal of interest in class (Wright, 1979, 1985; Robinson and Kelley, 1979). These studies focused on the effect of class on the status attainment process; some other studies (Robinson, 1984a, 1984b; Robinson and Garnier, 1985) took up the issue of class mobility within a comparative perspective.

Similarly, in Europe a revival of the study of social mobility from the perspective of class structure and class formation has emerged. Studies on class mobility (Erikson *et al.*, 1979, 1982, 1983; Portocarero, 1983a, 1983b) showed a considerable variation in the patterns of observed mobility. Erikson *et al.* (1979, p. 426), for example, concluded that: 'Sweden shows more total mobility than France, which in turn shows more than England'. This variation was primarily due to 'differing rhythms of their economic histories' (p. 438). In contrast, the same studies showed that the patterns of mobility net of the structural changes in class distribution – often called relative mobility or class fluidity – were remarkably similar among European nations. Erikson and Goldthorpe (1987a) even proposed a model of core class fluidity which characterized the basic pattern of relative mobility among nine European nations.

These studies provide support to the thesis proposed by Featherman, Jones and Hauser (1975) about the similarity in the patterns of social mobility across industrial societies. By refining Lipset and Zetterberg's (1959) hypothesis suggesting that there were no differences in social mobility among industrial societies, they suggest that once differences in the occupational and class structures have been taken into account, 'the genotypical patterns of mobility (circulation mobility) [or what we call class fluidity] in industrial societies with a market economy and a nuclear family system is basically the same' (Featherman, Jones and Hauser, 1975, p. 340).

The examination of the patterns of class mobility in Japan, the United States and Britain will, therefore, be directly relevant to this thesis. Since these societies can be characterized as highly industrialized capitalist societies, this thesis will predict that the three societies show very similar relative mobility patterns but not the observed absolute mobility. The analysis presented here is designed to test this thesis.

Another substantive theme which guides this chapter pertains to the issue of trends in class mobility. The thesis proposed by Featherman, Jones and Hauser (hereafter the FJH hypothesis) recognized that some changes in mobility rates might occur during the initial 'take-off' period into industrialization, but it precluded any further changes once a 'mature' industrial society had been reached (Grusky and Hauser, 1984, p. 20). In contrast, some advocates of the thesis of industrialism (Treiman, 1970; Bell, 1973) predicted a tendency for mobility to increase steadily as the level of industrialization increased.

Treiman (1970) argued that, as societies became economically more developed, meritocratic forms of social selection would replace selection based upon ascriptive criteria, thereby generating a greater 'openness' in industrial societies (cf. Erikson and Goldthorpe, 1987a). Tominaga (1979, p. 63) who applied the thesis of industrialism to the analysis of Japanese occupational mobility, claimed a trend of a 'rapid and consistent increase' both in gross mobility rates and in relative chances of mobility as measured by the Yasuda index (Yasuda, 1964) in post-war Japan. In this chapter, we will examine trends in intergenerational class mobility in Japan in order to evaluate empirically the claim of increasing openness in the class structure of post-war Japan.

This chapter comprises of six parts. First, we will briefly discuss the various definitions and approaches to the concept of class and clarify the class categories used in this study (Sections 6.2 and 6.3). Second, we will present the distribution of class in Japan, the United States and Britain using the social survey data. Both the distribution of the respondents' class and the fathers' class will be examined (Section 6.4). Third, we will examine class mobility in the three nations; the extent of class inheritance and of total mobility will be compared among the societies (Section 6.5). Fourth, we will examine outflow and inflow mobility matrices which indicate the patterns of class trajectory and class recruitment, respectively, among the three nations (Section 6.6). Fifth, we will describe in detail the features of the class fluidity model which fits the data-set for our three nations (Sections 6.7 and 6.8). Finally, we will examine trends in intergenerational class mobility in Japan (Section 6.9).

6.2 DEFINITION OF CLASS

Status attainment research considers socioeconomic status to be the fundamental dimension of stratification in contemporary industrial societies (see, for example, Blau and Duncan, 1967). Status, however, is not class. The crucial distinction between the two notions lies in the quantitative and qualitative nature of the concept. The typical image of stratification and mobility envisioned by status attainment research implies that individuals are ranked from high to low on a unidimensional continuum of status, and that they move up and down this status ladder (Horan, 1978). The differences among the individuals are a matter of quantity: how much they are above or below others in the status scale. Social mobility involves the increase and decrease in a quantity of status along the continuum (Wright, 1979, 1980b; Goldthorpe, 1984).

In contrast, classes are characterized by qualitative differences. They are distinct social collectivities whose differences are not a matter of quantity. Each class occupies a distinct location in the social structure, and may provide individuals who belong to the class with a basis for collective identity (Wright, 1980a). Social mobility involves the departure from a particular social group and attachment to another, which may involve a fundamental change in life-style and socio–political orientation (Goldthorpe, 1987).

Two fundamentally qualitative dimensions are pivotal in determining classes (Wright, 1979): control over the means of production and control over labour.[1] The orthodox Marxist approach claims that classes are defined by the ownership of the means of production; hence class structure in a capitalist society should be viewed as a polarization between two fundamental classes: capitalists and labourers (Marx and Engels, [1848] 1967). This polarized view of the class structure received considerable support from Japanese Marxists. The theory of state monopoly capitalism viewed the Japanese class structure as being polarized between capitalists who controlled the state apparatus and workers, with a small proportion of the population engaged in self-employed, petty bourgeois production (farmers, shop-holders and other members of the traditional petty bourgeoisie).[2]

Defining classes by the possession of, or separation from, the means of production, however, ignores the role of top managers and boards of directors in the corporations; ownership or possession of the means of production is not the only way of controlling the means of production. Control over the means of production implies the capacity to dispose of the means of production. What is produced, how much is produced, when it is produced, and how it is produced are determined by the class which has this control (Wright, 1979).

Under advanced capitalism, the individual form of property ownership has become increasingly rare, if not altogether lost. As more and more business becomes incorporated, the form of ownership is transformed to collective and institutional ownership (Okumura, 1978; 1984). In fact, a significant proportion of the stocks of large corporations are possessed by other institutions, namely financial corporations (Miyazaki, 1976; Kitahara, 1984; Berle and Means, 1932; Useem, 1984). In the advanced capitalist societies, the location of the power of *control* over the means of production resides not only in individual owners, who are very few in number, but also in the top executives who may or may not own stock in the corporations (Scott, 1985; Scott and Griff, 1984). In this study, individual owners and boards of directors are grouped together as a distinct class which possesses control over the means of production.

The second qualitative dimension which defines class involves control over labour. Control over labour implies the capacity to supervise and organize the labour process.[3] Two important aspects of control over labour have been pointed out by many researchers: authority and autonomy (Robinson and Kelley, 1979; Wolf and Fligstein, 1979; Wright, 1979, 1980a, 1980b).

Authority is defined in terms of control over other people's labour.

Managers and supervisors in the organizational hierarchy can determine when and how people work in the production process, specifying individuals' responsibilities, duties and rewards. Depending upon the position in the hierarchy, they often possess the discretionary power of making decisions about sanctioning, firing and hiring. Supervisors and foremen, who are at the lower end of the managerial structure, often perform the direct supervision of subordinate workers. Top and middle managers are often involved in organizing and allocating labour, rather than in directly observing subordinates. However, both have a varying extent of control over other people's labour, and both occupy a dominant position over workers within the social relations of production.

Autonomy is defined in terms of control over one's own labour. Kohn and his associates (Kohn, 1969, 1976; Kohn and Schooler, 1983) have found that occupational self-direction is the most crucial aspect of social position, in that it shows the most potent effect on the psychological well-being of workers. Professional–technical employees are relatively free of direct supervision and able to work independently. They possess a considerable amount of self-direction in the productive process. Because of their relatively high degree of control over their immediate labour process, they occupy a different class location from ordinary workers who do not retain control over their own labour.

Finally, workers are those who have control neither over means of production nor over labour. However, workers can be further differentiated by the nature of their work and the extent of the marketable skills they possess. The manual versus non-manual distinction is an old one in the studies of class and mobility (see, for example, Lipset and Bendix, 1959). Parkin (1971) feels that the 'significant break' in the structure of inequality of modern Western countries lies between the manual and non-manual occupations (cf. Bottomore, 1965). Vanneman and Pampel (1977) show that the manual/non-manual dichotomy is a powerful predictor of voting behaviour and party identification in the United States. Among manual workers, skilled workers who possess recognized skills occupy a significantly advantaged position in the labour market over other semi-skilled and non-skilled workers. As Weberians (Weber, [1922] 1968; Giddens, 1973) indicate, possession of marketable skills secures not only economic returns but also security of employment and a range of fringe benefits. Employees who do not have control over their labour are therefore further broken down into three categories: non-manual workers, skilled workers and semi- and non-skilled workers.[4]

Table 6.1 Criteria for determining class position

Class positions	*Dimensions of social relations of production*			*Working class differentiation*	
	Control over means of production	*Control over labour*			
		Authority	*Autonomy*	*Non-manual*	*Skilled*
Employer class	+	+	+	NA	NA
Petty bourgeois class	+	–	+	NA	NA
Managerial class	–	+	+	NA	NA
Professional class	–	–	+	NA	NA
Non-manual working class	–	–	–	+	–
Skilled working class	–	–	–	–	+
Non-skilled working class	–	–	–	–	–

Notes:
\+ Yes, – No.
NA Not applicable.

In sum, classes are defined by the fundamentally qualitative dimensions of the social relations of production: control over means of production and control over labour. The working class is further differentiated by the nature of work and marketable skills. Table 6.1 presents the summary of class schema used in this chapter.

6.3 OPERATIONALIZATION OF CLASS

We intend to operationalize the class schema in Table 6.1 using the Japanese Social Stratification and Mobility National Survey (SSM), the American Class Structure and Class Consciousness Survey (CSCC), and the Oxford Mobility Survey (OMS).[5] In order to construct class categories, two qualitative relational dimensions have to be measured by survey items: control over means of production and control over labour. Unfortunately no survey questions directly reveal these relational properties, so the following questions have been selected as approximate measures. Employment status is used as a crude measure of control over the means of production, and managerial position is used for measuring control over labour.

First, the employer class is operationalized by employment status and the number of employees. In the British data-set, the self-employed who employ others are classified as the employer class. In the American data-set, individuals who are self-employed and employ others or individuals who are employed by someone else but are owners or part-owners of a profit-making business which employs others are classified as the employer class.[6] In the Japanese data-set, the employer class is composed of owners and small employers (*jieigyosha*) who employ others and members of the boards of directors (*juyaku*) in corporations which employ workers (see Figure 6.1, p. 170). As we have argued above, the power of control over the means of production resides not only in self-employed people but also in the top executives. Grouping the self-employed and employees who are members of the boards in a corporation does not pose a serious problem in defining who controls the means of production.[7] Ideally, we would like to separate the boards of directors who are part-owners of the firm from ordinary managers, and group them into the employer class in the British data-set. However, the survey items did not allow us to separate out employee owners. The employer class in the British data-set therefore includes strictly self-employed people.[8] The employer category is further divided into small employers and large employers by the number of people employed: employers with more than 30 workers are called large employers.[9]

Second, the petty bourgeois class is characterized by the combination of control over the means of production and lack of control over labour. Self-employed individuals who do not employ workers and those who work without pay are called the petty bourgeois class in the American data.[10] In the SSM, self-employed individuals who work on their own account (*tandoku*) and family workers are classified as petty bourgeoisie. The British petty bourgeois class includes individuals who are self-employed without employees and family employees. Since the majority of the Japanese petty bourgeois class are independent farmers, the petty bourgeois class is further divided into two groups: (1) the urban petty bourgeoisie and (2) independent farmers and other self-employed and family workers in primary production.

Third, the managerial and supervisory class is distinguished from the rest of the employees by using the second relational criteria: control over labour. The Japanese and British surveys do not provide data concerning the degree of control over other people's labour so that formal managerial titles are used to arrive at an approximate estimate in all three data-sets. Employees who have any kind of hierarchical titles are assumed to have some control over the labour activities of their subordinates.[11] Individuals who occupy managerial positions (either top, middle, or lower management) are classified as managers and those who occupy supervisory position are classified as supervisors in three data sets.[12]

Fourth, professional and technical employees constitute a separate class characterized by a high degree of autonomy. They are determined by occupational classification and managerial position. Employees who do not hold any managerial positions and engage in professional technical work belong to the professional class.

Finally, the working class is composed of three groups: non-manual, skilled, and semi- or non-skilled workers. They are divided by occupational classification.[13] Figure 6.1 summarizes the operational procedure for constructing the class categories.

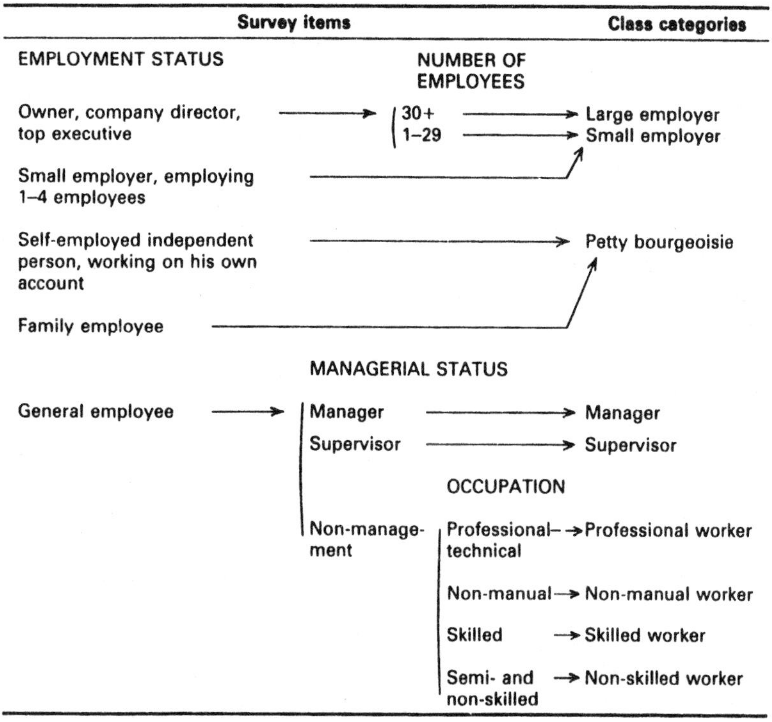

(a)

Figure 6.1 Operationalization of the class schema for (a) the Japanese (SSM), (b) the American (CSCC) and (c) the British (OMS) data.

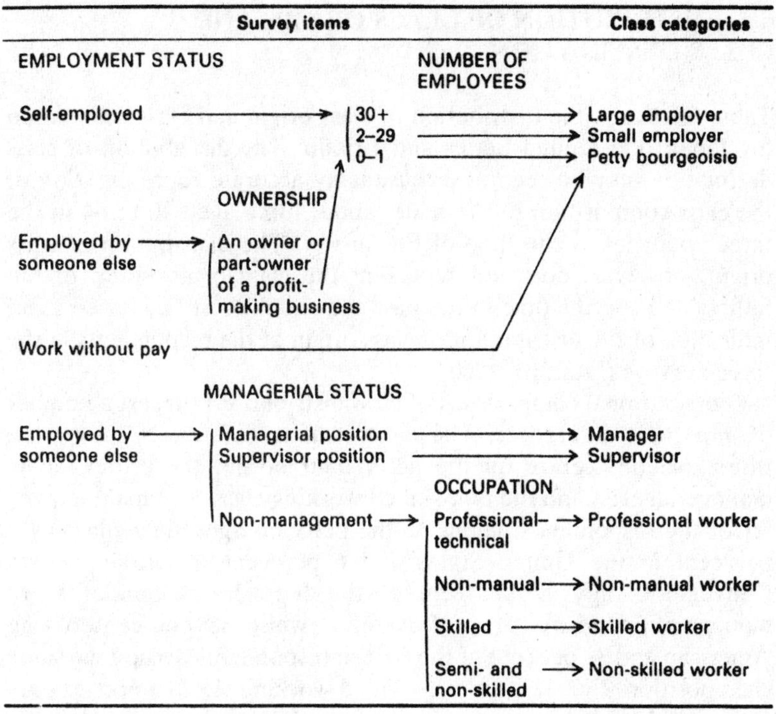
Survey items
Class categories
EMPLOYMENT STATUS
NUMBER OF EMPLOYEES
Self-employed
30+
2–29
0–1
Large employer
Small employer
Petty bourgeoisie
OWNERSHIP
Employed by someone else
An owner or part-owner of a profit-making business
Work without pay
MANAGERIAL STATUS
Employed by someone else
Managerial position
Supervisor position
Non-management
Manager
Supervisor
OCCUPATION
Professional–technical
Non-manual
Skilled
Semi- and non-skilled
Professional worker
Non-manual worker
Skilled worker
Non-skilled worker

(b)

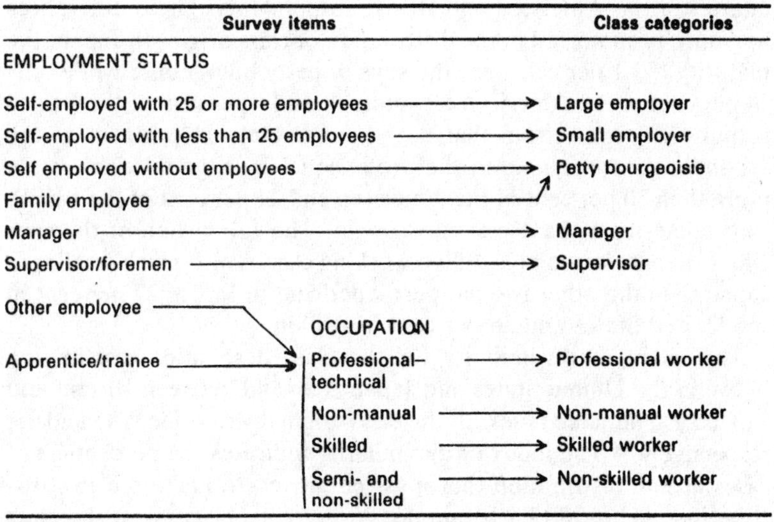
Survey items
Class categories
EMPLOYMENT STATUS
Self-employed with 25 or more employees
Self-employed with less than 25 employees
Self employed without employees
Family employee
Manager
Supervisor/foremen
Other employee
Apprentice/trainee
Large employer
Small employer
Petty bourgeoisie
Manager
Supervisor
OCCUPATION
Professional–technical
Non-manual
Skilled
Semi- and non-skilled
Professional worker
Non-manual worker
Skilled worker
Non-skilled worker

(c)

6.4 DISTRIBUTION OF CLASS ORIGIN AND CLASS DESTINATION

Table 6.2 shows the distribution of class origin and class destination for Japan, the United States and Britain. The distribution of class destination may be seen as a reasonably accurate representation of the class composition of the male labour force aged 20 to 64 in the three countries at the time of the survey. The distribution of class origin, however, does not represent the class composition of the fathers at a specific time in the past and should best be viewed as an indication of the distribution of class origin of the respondents in the three surveys (Duncan, 1966).

Cross-national comparisons of class distributions suggest a number of important differences. The most striking differences among the three societies centre on the petty bourgeoisie, the professional–managerial class and the non-skilled working class. In Japan, a quarter of the respondents belong to the petty bourgeoisie while only 8 per cent in the United States and 6 per cent in Britain do so. Conversely, only 22 per cent of the Japanese respondents are managers/supervisors or professionals, while 38 per cent of the American and 31 per cent of the British respondents occupy the same class position. Further, the non-skilled working class comprises only 15 per cent of all Japanese respondents, while it constitutes almost a quarter of the American and British respondents. These differences are more pronounced in the distribution of class origin. In Japan, the majority (53.1 per cent) are the sons of petty bourgeoisie while only 14 per cent of the American respondents and 6 per cent of the British respondents come from that background. Only 11 per cent of the Japanese sons originate in the professional–managerial class, while more than 30 per cent of the American and 21 per cent of the British sons come from that same class origin. The proportion of the sons who originate in the non-skilled working class is also much smaller in Japan than the other two nations: 9 per cent in Japan, 27 per cent in the United States and 36 per cent in Britain.

The index of dissimilarity for the class destination distribution between the United States and Japan is 26 and between Britain and Japan 29. The same index for the class origin distribution is 45 and 58, respectively.[14] The index of dissimilarity indicates the percentage of cases in one distribution that must be moved to make the two distributions identical. For example, 26 per cent of cases in the class destination distribution and as much as 45 per cent of cases in the

Table 6.2 Class distributions in Japan (SSM), the United States (CSCC) and Britain (OMS) (%)

Class categories	*Class destination*			*Class origin*		
	Japan	**United States**	**Britain**	**Japan**	**United States**	**Britain**
1. Large employer	2.0	1.0	0.5	1.7	13.5 (1–2)	0.8
2. Small employer	11.2	8.2	4.9	16.8		7.7
3. Petty bourgeoisie (urban)	10.8	6.5	5.0	12.0	5.6	4.5
4. Petty bourgeoisie (farm)	13.8	1.3	1.2	41.1	7.9	1.3
5. Manager	7.0	13.7	10.8	5.0	26.9 (5–6)	6.9
6. Supervisor	11.4	17.6	9.7	3.5		10.9
7. Professional	4.0	6.8	10.5	2.5	3.8	3.0
8. Non-manual	14.4	9.1	11.1	5.3	7.3	8.4
9. Skilled	10.2	12.5	20.6	3.4	7.9	20.2
10. Semi- and non-skilled	15.3	23.2	25.7	8.5	27.1	36.3
Total	100.0	100.0	100.0	100.0	100.0	100.0
(*N*)	(2043)	(678)	(8693)	(2043)	(678)	(8693)
Index of dissimilarity between origin and destination	Japan 33.9	United States 13.7	Britain 13.6			
Index of dissimilarity between Japan and the United States	Destination 25.9	Origin 44.7				
Index of dissimilarity between Japan and Britain	Destination 29.4	Origin 57.5				
Index of dissimilarity between United States and Britain	Destination 12.7	Origin 22.5				

class origin distribution must be reclassified in order that Japan and the United States have exactly identical distributions. These indices suggest that the class origin distribution in Japan is substantially different from that in the United States and Britain. Furthermore, the cross-national difference in class origin distribution between Japan and Britain is larger than that between Japan and the United States.

The major differences in the class distribution between Japan and the other two countries reflect in particular the difference in the timing of industrialization. The process of industrialization took place much later in Japan than in Britain and the United States. The largest class origin category (53.1 per cent) in Japan is the petty bourgeoisie, of which over three-quarters are farmers.[15] This percentage stands in a marked contrast with that in Britain: farmers there constitute less than 2 per cent of the entire class origin distribution. In contrast, the manual working classes (skilled and non-skilled combined) have a relatively small share (11.9 per cent) of the Japanese class origin distribution, whereas in Britain these two classes already represent more than a majority (56.5 per cent) of the class origin distribution.

From these findings, it is not difficult to trace the differential courses of industrialization followed by Japanese and British economic history. Britain was the first nation in the world to experience industrialization, and also abandoned agricultural protectionism in the early stage of industrialization. Japan was a late starter in the process of industrialization, and the manual working classes are not yet fully developed in the class origin distribution. In the United States, industrialization took place much earlier than in Japan, but what characterizes the American class origin distribution is the large share taken by the professional–managerial class. It comprises 31 per cent of the entire American class origin distribution, thereby forming the largest class category. This reflects the early development of industrial organizations and their hierarchical structure in the United States (Chandler, 1977; cf. Gagliani, 1985).

Since Japanese society achieved rapid industrialization despite a late start, class destination distributions show much less cross-national variation. However, the 'traditional' petty bourgeois class still has a much bigger share in the distribution in Japan than in the United States and Britain: the proportions of both farmers and non-farm urban petty bourgeoisie are higher in Japan than in the other two societies.

Turning to the comparison of class origin and class destination distribution within society, Japan has experienced more dramatic change between the two generations than the United States and Britain. The major differences between class origin and class destination distribution in Japan lie in the huge contraction of the petty bourgeois class and the increase in the size of the entire working class. The proportion of the petty bourgeois class decreased by half from 53.1 per cent to 24.6 per cent. The reduction is mainly due to the contraction of the farm population. The proportion of supervisor, non-manual, skilled and non-skilled working class each increased by more than 6 per cent. The index of dissimilarity between class origin and class destination distribution in Japan is 34, suggesting that considerable changes have taken place between the two generations.

Similar changes can be found in the United States and Britain on a much smaller scale, except for the contraction of non-skilled workers. The professional–managerial class expanded by more than 7 per cent and the non-manual class expanded by as little as 2 per cent, but the proportion of non-skilled workers decreased from 27.1 to 23.2 per cent in the United States and from 36.3 to 25.7 per cent in Britain. The percentage of cases that must be reclassified to make the two distributions identical is only 14 in both nations.

The larger intra-societal difference between the two class distributions in Japan probably reflects the rapid economic growth in the 1950s and 1960s. The contraction of the agriculture sector and the corresponding expansion of the industrial sector in both blue-collar and white-collar employment had a significant influence on class structure. In particular, the professional–managerial class (22.4 per cent) had become almost as large as the petty bourgeoisie (24.6 per cent) in 1975. The class structures in the three countries in the late 1970s showed a remarkable resemblance, compared with the distribution of class origin in the three countries. Nonetheless, the Japanese class structure is characterized by a relatively higher proportion of the petty bourgeoisie and a lower proportion of the white-collar and blue-collar classes than the American and British class structures.

The test of homogeneity in the class destination distribution and class origin distribution among the three societies is shown in Table 6.3. Although the class destination distributions in the three societies appear to resemble each other, the hypothesis of the homogeneity of class destination is rejected (as shown in line 5 of Table 6.3).[16] The class origin distributions in the three societies are far from identical as shown in the rejection of the hypothesis of the homogeneity of class origin (line 4).

6.5 GROSS CLASS MOBILITY IN JAPAN, THE UNITED STATES AND BRITAIN

Table 6.4 presents the class mobility tables using the sixfold class schema and summarizes the overall gross pattern of class mobility and reproduction – or, as it is often called, absolute mobility – in Japan, the United States and Britain.[17] 'Total' mobility means the proportion of respondents who changed class between two generations

Table 6.3 Text of homogeneity of origin and destination distribution in Japan (SSM), the United States (CSCC) and Britain (OMS)

Model	*Hypothesis and test*	L^2	*df*	*p*	*ID*
1. $(O)(DC)$	Constant origin distribution	4762	85	<0.001	24.8
2. $(D)(OC)$	Constant destination distribution	2572	85	<0.001	19.0
3. $(OC)(DC)$	Different origin and destination distributions	1657	75	<0.001	15.4
4. 1 vs. 3	Test of homogeneity of origin distribution	3105	10	<0.001	9.4
5. 2 vs. 3	Test of homogeneity of destination distribution	870	10	<0.001	3.6

Notes:
O = Origin class.
D = Destination class.
C = Country.

– that is, the number of people in the cells off the main diagonal of the mobility table as a percentage of all respondents. 'Forced' mobility refers to the index of dissimilarity between class origin and class destination distributions – that is, the proportion of all cases that must be reclassified in order to make the two distributions exactly identical. 'Net' mobility is the difference between total mobility and 'forced' mobility. The decomposition of total mobility into 'forced' and 'net' mobility should give us some ideas about the effect of intergenerational change in class structure on total mobility rate.

Two points stand out in Table 6.4. First, the total mobility rate is very high and identical in the three societies: more than two-thirds of the respondents experienced a change of class between the two generations. A substantial amount of total gross mobility is apparent in all three societies. This result has significant implications for the theory of class structure. A naive class reproduction thesis describes none of the societies; change in class position between the two generations is not at all uncommon, and neglecting class mobility would undermine the fluid nature of class structure in the three societies.

Second, the decomposition of total mobility into 'forced' and 'net' mobility shows a dramatic difference among the three societies. In the United States and Britain, net mobility accounts for 80 per cent of total observed mobility. The observed mobility appears to be predominantly the result of mobility which is produced net of the change in class distributions. In Japan, 'forced' and 'net' mobility account for

Table 6.4 Class mobility tables and gross mobility patterns in Japan (SSM), the United States (CSCC) and Britain (OMS)

Class origin	*Class destination*						
	I	*II*	*III*	*IV*	*V*	*VI*	*Total*
Japan							
I Employer	109	72	91	57	20	30	379
II Petty bourgeoisie	105	365	189	125	108	193	1085
III Professional and managerial	28	19	94	49	16	20	226
IV Non-manual	15	10	32	31	8	13	109
V Skilled	4	9	17	11	17	12	70
VI Semi- and non-skilled	8	27	35	21	39	44	174
Total	269	502	458	294	208	312	2043
United States							
I Employer	15	10	35	10	12	9	91
II Petty bourgeoisie	17	15	23	5	12	20	92
III Professional and managerial	19	8	93	19	27	42	208
IV Non-manual	2	2	21	11	5	9	50
V Skilled	2	7	25	3	12	5	54
VI Semi- and non-skilled	8	12	61	14	16	72	183
Total	63	54	258	62	84	157	678
Britain							
I Employer	154	106	254	61	70	96	741
II Petty bourgeoisie	38	90	150	54	69	96	497
III Professional and managerial	106	87	865	222	265	265	1810
IV Non-manual	36	36	281	126	133	121	733
V Skilled	66	84	443	178	490	498	1759
VI Semi- and non-skilled	74	132	700	326	762	1159	3153
Total	474	535	2693	967	1789	2235	8693

	Japan	**United States**	**Britain**
Total mobility	67.7%	67.8%	66.8%
Forced mobility	33.9%	13.7%	13.6%
Net mobility	33.8%	54.1%	53.2%
Counterfactual mobility	–	71.0%	68.5%

about a half of total mobility. According to this decomposition, structural change in class distribution and mobility net of such change contribute equally to the total observed movement. These results are consistent with the examination of the class distribution. Since the distributions of origin and destination are less homogeneous in Japan than in the United States and Britain, a larger proportion of people is 'forced' to be mobile in Japan due to the shifts in class composition between the two generations.

However, the decomposition exercise does not truly separate mobility processes produced by structural change in class distribution between the two generations from mobility processes which are independent of such change (Hauser *et al.*, 1975a, 1975b; cf. Sobel, 1983). When we wish to represent mobility processes which are independent of the marginal distributions of a mobility table by the pattern of odds ratios in that table – that is, what we call class fluidity – the decomposition exercise fails to separate class fluidity from change in marginal distributions. One way to assess the impact on total mobility rates of change in marginal distributions controlling for the patterns of odds ratios is to construct a 'counterfactual' mobility table. We will ask the following question: what would American and British mobility rates be if American and British class distributions were identical to Japanese ones? In other words, we will recalculate the total mobility rates for the United States and for Britain, assuming that these two countries experienced a similar line of development and intergenerational change in class distributions to the ones that actually happened in Japan.

In order to produce a 'counterfactual' table – for example, for the United States – we transform the marginal distributions of the observed American table into the Japanese ones by the method of proportional adjustments of rows and columns of the table (Mosteller, 1968). The new 'counterfactual' table will then have the same marginals as those in the Japanese table, but retain the odds ratios pattern of the observed American table. The total mobility rates calculated from the American and British 'counterfactual' tables are shown at the foot of Table 6.4. These figures suggest that total mobility rates would have been higher if these two countries had experienced changes in class structure that were similar to those found in Japan. However, the impact of cross-national difference in class structure on total mobility rates is much less dramatic than the decomposition exercise would suggest.

6.6 INFLOW AND OUTFLOW PATTERNS OF MOBILITY IN THE THREE SOCIETIES

The inflow mobility matrix shown in Table 6.5 describes the composition of each class destination in terms of the class origin of the respondents – that is, where the members of the class come from. It

Table 6.5 Class composition by class destination: inflow percentage distribution and index of dissimilarity (ID)

Class origin	*Destination I*			*Destination II*			*Destination III*		
	J	*U*	*B*	*J*	*U*	*B*	*J*	*U*	*B*
I	40.5	24.7	32.5	14.3	18.6	19.8	19.9	13.4	9.4
II	39.0	27.1	8.0	72.7	28.1	16.8	41.3	9.1	5.6
III	10.4	29.9	22.4	3.8	14.9	16.3	20.5	36.1	32.1
IV	5.6	2.9	7.6	2.0	3.0	6.7	7.0	8.1	10.4
V	1.5	2.9	13.9	1.8	13.0	15.7	3.7	9.5	16.5
VI	3.0	12.4	15.6	5.4	22.4	24.7	7.6	23.7	26.0

Class origin	*Destination IV*			*Destination V*			*Destination VI*		
	J	*U*	*B*	*J*	*U*	*B*	*J*	*U*	*B*
I	19.4	16.2	6.3	9.6	14.7	3.9	9.6	5.7	4.3
II	42.5	7.3	5.6	51.9	14.1	3.9	61.9	12.7	4.3
III	16.7	31.2	23.0	7.7	31.5	14.8	6.4	26.9	11.9
IV	10.5	17.6	13.0	3.8	6.4	7.4	4.2	5.5	5.4
V	3.7	4.7	18.4	8.2	14.4	27.4	3.8	3.3	22.3
VI	7.1	23.0	33.7	18.8	18.9	42.6	14.1	45.9	51.9

	I	*II*	*III*	*IV*	*V*	*VI*
ID (*J*, *U*)[a]	30.4	44.6	38.7	38.4	37.8	53.6
ID (*J*, *B*)[b]	39.0	55.9	46.2	50.0	53.7	62.9
ID (*U*, *B*)[c]	26.6	11.3	11.5	24.4	37.7	24.9

Notes:
[a] Index of dissimilarity between Japan and the United States.
[b] Index of dissimilarity between Japan and Britain.
[c] Index of dissimilarity between the United States and Britain.

J = Japan, *U* = the United States, *B* = Britain.

I = Employer, *II* = Petty bourgeoisie, *III* = Professional and managerial, *IV* = non-manual, *V* = Skilled, *VI* = Semi- and non-skilled.

shows the extent of class homogeneity of class destination and the pattern of the intergenerational recruitment into each class.

The index of dissimilarity shown on the final three rows of Table 6.5 presents the extent of cross-national variation in recruitment patterns of each destination class. The recruitment patterns appear to be greatly different in all categories of class destination between Japan and the other two societies. In particular, the patterns of the intergenerational recruitment of the non-skilled working class (*VI*) from the indices is that they are much smaller than those of the inflow differ dramatically. The index of dissimilarity between Japan and the United Sates is 54 and between Japan and Britain 63. The American and British non-skilled class is characterized by a very high rate of self-recruitment: 46 per cent of the American and 52 per cent of the British non-skilled working class came from the same class origin. The extent of class closure is extremely high. On the other hand, the Japanese non-skilled workers are heavily recruited from the petty bourgeois class, namely the independent farmers; 62 per cent of the non-skilled workers are of petty bourgeois origin. The dominant class origin of the non-skilled working class shows a large contrast between Japan and the other two nations.

The patterns of intergenerational recruitment into the petty bourgeoisie (*II*) also show a huge difference, mainly due to the high rate of self-recruitment of the Japanese petty bourgeois class: 73 per cent of the Japanese petty bourgeois class came from the same class origin. The extent of class closure appears to be especially high in Japan. A similar closure pattern cannot be found among the American and British petty bourgeois class: only 28 and 17 per cent came from the same class origin, respectively.

The striking characteristic of the recruitment patterns of all classes in Japan is the dominance of the petty bourgeois class. Because of the huge contraction of the independent farmers between the generations, a large proportion of the sons of petty bourgeois origin is found in almost all classes. This feature can be explained by the Japanese experience of late, but rapid, industrialization. A large pool of independent farmers is present in the distribution of class origin because of Japan's 'late developer' status. On the other hand, since the industrialization took place in a relatively compressed period of time, the white-collar industrial sector expanded at almost the same time as the blue-collar industrial sector. Consequently, not only the skilled and non-skilled working classes but also the professional–managerial and non-manual classes are recruited heavily from a petty bourgeois class origin. The sons of the independent farmers are found in both the manual and the white-collar classes.

The outflow mobility matrix shown in Table 6.6 describes the mobility chances of men from a certain class origin – that is, where the members of the class are found in the next generation. It shows the prospects of mobility given class origin and the patterns of the intergenerational class trajectory. The index of dissimilarity shown in Table 6.6 indicates the extent of cross-national variation in class trajectory given class origin. The first conclusion that can be drawn

Table 6.6 Class mobility chances by class origin: outflow percentage distribution and index of dissimilarity (ID)

Class origin		*Class destination*								
		I	*II*	*III*	*IV*	*V*	*VI*	*ID*[a] (*J*, *U*)	*ID*[b] (*J*, *B*)	*ID*[c] (*U*, *B*)
I	Japan	28.8	19.0	24.0	15.0	5.3	7.9	24.2	19.5	10.7
	United States	16.8	10.8	38.0	11.0	13.6	9.9			
	Britain	20.8	14.3	34.3	8.2	9.4	13.0			
II	Japan	9.7	33.6	17.4	11.5	10.0	17.8	23.9	18.2	13.3
	United States	18.4	16.3	25.6	4.9	13.0	21.8			
	Britain	7.6	18.1	30.2	10.9	13.9	19.3			
III	Japan	12.4	8.4	41.6	21.7	7.1	8.8	20.5	19.5	8.7
	United States	8.9	3.8	44.9	9.3	12.8	20.3			
	Britain	5.9	4.8	47.8	12.3	14.6	14.6			
IV	Japan	13.8	9.2	29.4	28.4	7.3	11.9	22.5	24.4	10.2
	United States	3.6	3.2	42.5	22.1	10.9	17.6			
	Britain	4.9	4.9	38.3	17.2	18.1	16.5			
V	Japan	5.7	12.9	24.3	15.7	24.3	17.1	21.5	15.6	28.8
	United States	3.4	12.9	45.9	5.4	22.8	9.7			
	Britain	3.8	4.8	25.2	10.1	27.9	28.3			
VI	Japan	4.6	15.5	20.1	12.1	22.4	25.3	27.4	15.4	18.1
	United States	4.2	6.5	33.5	7.8	8.7	39.4			
	Britain	2.3	4.2	22.2	10.3	24.2	36.8			

Notes:
[a] The index of dissimilarity between Japan and the United States.
[b] The index of dissimilarity between Japan and Britain.
[c] The index of dissimilarity between the United States and Britain.

J = Japan, *U* = The United States, *B* = Britain.

I = Employer, *II* = Petty bourgeoisie, *III* = Professional and managerial, *IV* = Non-manual, *V* = Skilled, *VI* = Semi- and non-skilled.

mobility table. Japan is more similar to the other two countries with respect to patterns of intergenerational class trajectory than to patterns of intergenerational class recruitment. This is because cross-national differences in class origin are much greater than differences in class destination.

Generally the indices comparing Japan and the United States are higher than those comparing Japan and Britain. This is because the patterns of intergenerational class trajectory in the United States are characterized by high outflow rates into the professional–managerial class (*III*) from all class origins. The intergenerational stability of the non-skilled working class (*VI*) and the petty bourgeois class (*II*) deserves special attention. The outflow rates show that the Japanese non-skilled working class has a much lower tendency for immobility (25.3 per cent) than its American (39.4) and British (36.8) counterparts. Many sons of the Japanese non-skilled working class are found not only in the skilled working class (22.4) but also in white-collar employment (32.2) and the petty bourgeoisie (15.5) in the next generation. The intergenerational stability of the Japanese non-skilled working class is therefore clearly weaker than that of the American and British non-skilled workers. In the United States and Britain, the inflow patterns already showed that the non-skilled workers had a homogeneous class origin, namely the tendency for self-recruitment. Both the inflow and outflow patterns therefore suggest the intergenerational stability and closure of the non-skilled working class in the United States and Britain.

The same stability can be found among the petty bourgeois class in Japan. The examination of the inflow patterns already showed a very high rate of self-recruitment among the petty bourgeois class in Japan. The outflow patterns report lesser chances for mobility among Japanese of petty bourgeois class origin than among American and British of similar origin: 34 per cent of petty bourgeois class origin stayed in the same class, whereas only 16 per cent of American petty bourgeois and 18 per cent of British petty bourgeois class origin did so. The extent of class closure therefore appears to be particularly high among the Japanese petty bourgeois class.

In summary, taking both inflow and outflow patterns together, we find some distinctive features of Japanese absolute mobility rates and gross mobility patterns. In particular, a high degree of intergenerational stability and closure of the Japanese petty bourgeois class and a weak extent of such stability and closure of the Japanese non-skilled working class stand out in the cross-national comparison.

6.7 CLASS FLUIDITY IN JAPAN, THE UNITED STATES AND BRITAIN

So far, the analysis has concentrated on gross mobility or absolute mobility patterns in the three countries. The next step is to examine the patterns of class mobility and reproduction,[18] once the differences in class origin and destination distribution have been taken into account. This is the examination of class fluidity.

'Gross mobility' refers to the observed pattern of mobility, and is directly influenced by change in class structure between two generations. 'Class fluidity' or 'relative mobility' refers to the patterns of mobility net of such change. It is important to distinguish the two because we would like to determine whether greater chances of mobility or immobility for a particular class are due to structural shift in class distributions or increase in relative chances of mobility or immobility. An increase in relative chances implies a greater opportunity for mobility or immobility. It is possible for the patterns of class fluidity to be constant, even though the pattern of gross mobility changes dramatically, due to structural shift in the class distribution. Conversely, the patterns of class fluidity may change, resulting in a change in the gross mobility pattern without any shift in the class structure within which the mobility process takes place. The application of loglinear models to the class mobility tables allows us to measure the association between class origin and class destination, net of the influence of the marginals of the mobility table.

Table 6.7 reports the results of fitting various loglinear models to the three-way contingency table: class origin (*O*) by class destination (*D*) by country (*C*). Line 1 shows the fit of the perfect mobility model: origin and destination distributions differ by country (*OC* and *DC*) but origin and destination are independent (no *OD* association). The perfect mobility model does not fit the data as shown in $L^2 = 1657.0$ (likelihood-ratio chi-square) with 75 degrees of freedom. The index of dissimilarity (ID) is 15.4 which implies that 15 per cent of the cases have to be reclassified in order to make origin and destination independent. The lack of fit of the perfect mobility model means that we can reject the hypothesis that class origin and class destination are not related in the three countries. Although the perfect mobility model does not fit the data at all, it will provide a baseline for assessing the fit of other models.

Line 2 in Table 6.7 shows the fit of the common class fluidity model. The common fluidity model implies that: (1) origin distributions are different among the three societies (*OC*), (2) destination distributions are also different (*DC*), (3) origin and destination are associated in the three countries (*OD*), and (4) the association between origin and destination is common across the three countries (no three-way interaction of *ODC*). This model represents the global test of the common pattern of class fluidity and the identical relative mobility rates. The likelihood-ratio test statistic (L^2) for this model is 110.7 which is significant with 50 degrees of freedom. The common

Table 6.7 Selected loglinear models applied to origin (*O*) by destination (*D*) by country (*C*) mobility table

Model	*Fitted marginals and matrices*	L^2	*df*	*p*	*ID*
1. Perfect mobility model	*(OC)(DC)*	1657.0	75	<0.001	15.4
2. Common class fluidity model	*(OC)(DC)(OD)*	110.7	50	<0.001	2.5
3. Quasi-perfect common mobility model	*(OC)(DC)(Q)*	601.1	69	<0.001	8.2
4. Quasi-perfect mobility model	*(OC)(DC)(QC)*	558.7	57	<0.001	7.2
5. Class fluidity model of Figure 6.3	*(OC)(DC)* + Figure 6.3 matrices	84.6	57	0.011	2.2

Notes:
O = Origin class, *D* = Destination class, *C* = Country.
Q = Quasi-perfect common mobility model (Figure 6.2A).
QC = Quasi-perfect mobility model (Figure 6.2B).

fluidity model does not fit the data. The lack of fit suggests significant cross-national variations in relative mobility rates and patterns among Japan, the United States and Britain. The intergenerational class movement, net of the mobility produced by structural influences of marginal distributions, appears to be different in the three societies. However, the common fluidity model accounts for 93.3 per cent of the association under the baseline model of independence, and only 2.5 per cent of all cases are misclassified (see the ID column in Table 6.7). It is therefore possible to claim that the association between origin and destination is very similar among the three countries and that cross-national similarity outweighs cross-national variation in relative mobility.

In considering the differences among the three countries, it is useful to distinguish the common rates of relative mobility from the common patterns. The former requires that identical cells in the mobility matrix in the three countries be assigned to the same level or region, and these cells have exactly the same rate of relative chance of mobility among the three nations. The latter refers to the case where identical cells in the three countries are assigned to the same level but these cells are allowed to have different rates of relative mobility among the three nations. These differences are shown in Figure 6.2*A* and 6.2*B*. Figure 6.2*A* represents quasi-perfect common mobility (Goodman, 1965; 1969). This model assigns each diagonal cell to a special level, and the same diagonal cells in the three

A Quasi-perfect common mobility matrices (*Q*)

	Japan						United States						Britain					
	I	*II*	*III*	*IV*	*V*	*VI*	*I*	*II*	*III*	*IV*	*V*	*VI*	*I*	*II*	*III*	*IV*	*V*	*VI*
I	2	1	1	1	1	1	2	1	1	1	1	1	2	1	1	1	1	1
II	1	3	1	1	1	1	1	3	1	1	1	1	1	3	1	1	1	1
III	1	1	4	1	1	1	1	1	4	1	1	1	1	1	4	1	1	1
IV	1	1	1	5	1	1	1	1	1	5	1	1	1	1	1	5	1	1
V	1	1	1	1	6	1	1	1	1	1	6	1	1	1	1	1	6	1
VI	1	1	1	1	1	7	1	1	1	1	1	7	1	1	1	1	1	7

B Quasi-perfect mobility matrices (*QC*)

	Japan						United States						Britain					
	I	*II*	*III*	*IV*	*V*	*VI*	*I*	*II*	*III*	*IV*	*V*	*VI*	*I*	*II*	*III*	*IV*	*V*	*VI*
I	2	1	1	1	1	1	8	1	1	1	1	1	14	1	1	1	1	1
II	1	3	1	1	1	1	1	9	1	1	1	1	1	15	1	1	1	1
III	1	1	4	1	1	1	1	1	10	1	1	1	1	1	16	1	1	1
IV	1	1	1	5	1	1	1	1	1	11	1	1	1	1	1	17	1	1
V	1	1	1	1	6	1	1	1	1	1	12	1	1	1	1	1	18	1
VI	1	1	1	1	1	7	1	1	1	1	1	13	1	1	1	1	1	19

Figure 6.2 Matrices representing quasi-perfect common mobility (*Q*) and quasi-perfect mobility (*QC*)

countries have the identical rate of relative mobility. The model therefore allows class inheritance (diagonal) cells to exhibit a higher rate than other cells and the extent or rate of class inheritance to be identical in the three societies.

Figure 6.2*B* is referred to as quasi-perfect mobility with non-identical class inheritance rates (Hout, 1983). As in the case of quasi-perfect common mobility, the diagonal cells are assigned special levels, but this time the extent or rate of class inheritance differs from one country to another. The model requires that the three countries have an identical pattern of class fluidity (that is, a quasi-perfect mobility model), but the rates of class inheritance are not identical among Japan, the United States and Britain. For example, the class inheritance rate for employers (that is, cell (1,1)), is assigned to a different level than the off-diagonal cells but cell (1,1) in Japan and the same cell in the United States are also assigned to different levels.

The quasi-perfect common mobility model (see Table 6.7, line 3) improves significantly over the baseline model of independence (the difference in L^2 is 1055.9 and the difference in degrees of freedom is 6) but does not fit the data (L^2 = 601.1, df = 69, $p < 0.001$). The quasi-perfect mobility model with non-identical class inheritance rates (see Table 6.7, line 4) improves significantly over the quasi-perfect common mobility model (the difference in L^2 is 42.4 and the difference in degrees of freedom is 12). The significant improvement over the quasi-perfect common mobility suggests that the rates of class inheritance are probably different among the three societies.[19] However, this model still fails to show an adequate fit to the data ($L^2 = 558.7$, df = 57, $p < 0.001$). These results indicate that although diagonal cells need to receive special attention, there are other cells which significantly depart from the baseline independence model.

The allocation of the cells of the mobility table to different levels should be guided by both sociological theory and the residual patterns. We have already treated diagonal cells as different since these cells represent class inheritance. We will introduce two additional sets of levels which have sociological interest: class boundary and petty bourgeois mobility. The first set attempts to capture the notion of class boundaries. The notion of class boundaries derives from the idea that barriers to mobility exist between classes. Mobility can be viewed as a process of clearing barriers of various heights: some barriers may be higher than others, and some may have a negligible height. For example, crossing the class boundary between the petty bourgeoisie and the professional–managerial class may be more difficult than crossing the boundary between the non-manual and the skilled working class.

Figure 6.3 (p. 187) shows the three sets of class boundary matrices. The first set of matrices (*B*2) indicates the class boundary in relative mobility chances between the petty bourgeoisie and the professional–managerial class. The boundary distinguishes control from non-control over the means of production. The second set of matrices (*B*3) refers to the class boundary between the professional–managerial class and the non-manual working class. Crossing this boundary embodies a change in authority and autonomy. The professional–managerial class as well as the employer class and the petty bourgeois class exercise control over other people's or its own labour, while non-manual workers and the rest of the working classes are excluded from practising such control. The third set of matrices (*B*4) refers to the class boundary between the non-manual working class and the skilled working class. This boundary is the traditional split between non-manual and manual occupations and separates off the skilled and the non-skilled working classes from the rest. The class boundaries at the extremes of the class hierarchy are repre-

A Class inheritance matrices (*IN*)

	Japan						United States						Britain					
	I	*II*	*III*	*IV*	*V*	*VI*	*I*	*II*	*III*	*IV*	*V*	*VI*	*I*	*II*	*III*	*IV*	*V*	*VI*
I	2	1	1	1	1	1	1	1	1	1	1	1	2	1	1	1	1	1
II	1	3	1	1	1	1	1	4	1	1	1	1	1	4	1	1	1	1
III	1	1	5	1	1	1	1	1	6	1	1	1	1	1	6	1	1	1
IV	1	1	1	1	1	1	1	1	1	7	1	1	1	1	1	1	1	1
V	1	1	1	1	1	1	1	1	1	1	8	1	1	1	1	1	1	1
VI	1	1	1	1	1	1	1	1	1	1	1	9	1	1	1	1	1	10

B Class boundary matrices (*B2, B3, B4*)

B2	Japan						United States						Britain					
	I	*II*	*III*	*IV*	*V*	*VI*	*I*	*II*	*III*	*IV*	*V*	*VI*	*I*	*II*	*III*	*IV*	*V*	*VI*
I	2	2	1	1	1	1	3	3	1	1	1	1	3	3	1	1	1	1
II	2	2	1	1	1	1	3	3	1	1	1	1	3	3	1	1	1	1
III	1	1	2	2	2	2	1	1	3	3	3	3	1	1	3	3	3	3
IV	1	1	2	2	2	2	1	1	3	3	3	3	1	1	3	3	3	3
V	1	1	2	2	2	2	1	1	3	3	3	3	1	1	3	3	3	3
VI	1	1	2	2	2	2	1	1	3	3	3	3	1	1	3	3	3	3

B3	Japan						United States						Britain					
	I	*II*	*III*	*IV*	*V*	*VI*	*I*	*II*	*III*	*IV*	*V*	*VI*	*I*	*II*	*III*	*IV*	*V*	*VI*
I	1	1	1	1	1	1	1	1	1	1	1	1	2	2	2	1	1	1
II	1	1	1	1	1	1	1	1	1	1	1	1	2	2	2	1	1	1
III	1	1	1	1	1	1	1	1	1	1	1	1	2	2	2	1	1	1
IV	1	1	1	1	1	1	1	1	1	1	1	1	1	1	1	2	2	2
V	1	1	1	1	1	1	1	1	1	1	1	1	1	1	1	2	2	2
VI	1	1	1	1	1	1	1	1	1	1	1	1	1	1	1	2	2	2

B4	Japan						United States						Britain					
	I	*II*	*III*	*IV*	*V*	*VI*	*I*	*II*	*III*	*IV*	*V*	*VI*	*I*	*II*	*III*	*IV*	*V*	*VI*
I	2	2	2	2	1	1	1	1	1	1	1	1	3	3	3	3	1	1
II	2	2	2	2	1	1	1	1	1	1	1	1	3	3	3	3	1	1
III	2	2	2	2	1	1	1	1	1	1	1	1	3	3	3	3	1	1
IV	2	2	2	2	1	1	1	1	1	1	1	1	3	3	3	3	1	1
V	1	1	1	1	2	2	1	1	1	1	1	1	1	1	1	1	3	3
VI	1	1	1	1	2	2	1	1	1	1	1	1	1	1	1	1	3	3

C Special petty bourgeois mobility (*P1, P2*)

P1	Japan						United States						Britain					
	I	*II*	*III*	*IV*	*V*	*VI*	*I*	*II*	*III*	*IV*	*V*	*VI*	*I*	*II*	*III*	*IV*	*V*	*VI*
I	1	1	1	1	1	1	1	1	1	1	1	1	1	1	1	1	1	1
II	1	1	1	1	1	2	1	1	1	1	1	3	1	1	1	1	1	3
III	1	1	1	1	1	1	1	1	1	1	1	1	1	1	1	1	1	1
IV	1	1	1	1	1	1	1	1	1	1	1	1	1	1	1	1	1	1
V	1	1	1	1	1	1	1	1	1	1	1	1	1	1	1	1	1	1
VI	1	1	1	1	1	1	1	1	1	1	1	1	1	1	1	1	1	1

cont. p. 188

Figure 6.3 Matrices representing the preferred model

P2	Japan						United States						Britain					
	I	II	III	IV	V	VI	I	II	III	IV	V	VI	I	II	III	IV	V	VI
I	1	1	1	1	1	1	1	1	1	1	1	1	1	1	1	1	1	1
II	1	1	1	1	2	1	1	1	1	1	3	1	1	1	1	1	3	1
III	1	1	1	1	1	1	1	1	1	1	1	1	1	1	1	1	1	1
IV	1	1	1	1	1	1	1	1	1	1	1	1	1	1	1	1	1	1
V	1	1	1	1	1	1	1	1	1	1	1	1	1	1	1	1	1	1
VI	1	1	1	1	1	1	1	1	1	1	1	1	1	1	1	1	1	1

Figure 6.3 *continued*

sented by the immobility among the employer class and among the non-skilled working class.

The height of each class boundary will be estimated by the crossing parameters (Goodman, 1972; Pontinen, 1982; Hout, 1983). The heights were initially set differently in the three countries, but some class boundary parameters were later set identically between the two countries when they were not significantly different. The *B*2 boundary is set identically in the United States and Britain, and the *B*3 boundary in Japan and the United States is set to zero because it proved to be statistically non-significant. Figure 6.3 shows the matrix representation of class boundary effects in our preferred model.[20]

A further examination of the residuals from the quasi-perfect mobility model suggests that the petty bourgeois class requires a special treatment. The movements out of the petty bourgeois class into the skilled and the non-skilled working class are relatively more frequent than other mobility chances. When farmers' sons leave farming, they are more likely to be found in manual working class jobs than in white-collar employment.[21] One of the important pools of manual workers appears to be the sons of the petty bourgeoisie who were not able to inherit their fathers' business. Misaki (1979, p. 199), for example, found in his study that manual workers in small firms were recruited heavily from men of farm and petty bourgeois origin. Figure 6.3 shows the matrix representation of the special petty bourgeois mobility.[22]

6.8 FEATURES OF THE CLASS FLUIDITY MODEL

The class fluidity model which fits the data of class mobility in Japan, the United States and Britain has the following features: (1) class inheritance, (2) class boundary, and (3) special petty bourgeois mobility. The model is presented in matrix form in Figure 6.3.[23] The fit of the model is shown in Table 6.7, line 5 ($L^2 = 84.6$, df = 57, $p = 0.011$). Although the model barely fits the data-set, the fit is far better for the Japanese and American data-sets because of the smaller sample sizes. When the model is fitted separately for each country, allowing the parameters to vary across nations, the model fits the Japanese and American data-sets very well: $L^2 = 24.97$, df = 18, $p = 0.125$ for Japan, and $L^2 = 19.99$, df = 17, $p = 0.274$ for the United States. The model does not fit the British data-set under the conventional standard of statistical criteria ($L^2 = 37.6$, df = 16, $p = 0.002$) because of the large sample size. However, if we recalculate the L^2 statistic under the SSM sample size, the fit of the model is satisfactory (L^2 standardized = 21.08, df = 16, $p = 0.175$).[24] The model can therefore be understood as an adequate representation of the mobility tables in the three countries. The following section describes the features of this fitted model.

Class inheritance

Table 6.8 reports the parameter estimates for the diagonal levels. The first striking observation is that not all the diagonals are significantly different from non-diagonal cells. The rates of class inheritance among the non-manual, skilled and non-skilled working classes in Japan, among the employer class in the United States, and among the non-manual and skilled working classes in Britain are not significant. These non-significant diagonals are primarily responsible for the cross-national variation in the rates of class inheritance.

It may appear extremely surprising that the employer class in the United States does not show a tendency toward class reproduction. However, as we will see below section on the class boundary, the employer class and the petty bourgeois class together reproduce themselves. The non-significant diagonal parameter for the employer class in the United States, therefore, does not imply that sons of all class origins have an equal relative chance of becoming an employer. It simply reflects the lack of a barrier between the employer and the petty bourgeois class.

The Japanese and British employer class shows a strong tendency for class inheritance. Class inheritance may be achieved by the transmission of capital in the form of wealth and assets as well as of the cultural kind. Access to top management may be facilitated by the attainment of educational credentials which are affected by family wealth (see Chapter 3).

Table 6.8 Parameter estimates in log-additive form for the fitted loglinear model shown in Figure 6.3

	Japan	*United States*	*Britain*
Parameters for class inheritance			
I Employer	0.705(0.097)[a]	—[b]	0.705(0.097)
II Petty bourgeoisie	0.948(0.133)	0.410(0.136)	0.410(0.136)
III Professional–managerial	0.361(0.158)	0.154(0.066)	0.154(0.066)
IV Non-manual	—	0.939(0.372)	—
V Skilled	—	0.598(0.351)	—
VI Semi- and non-skilled	—	1.082(0.196)	0.385(0.056)
Parameters for class boundary			
*B*2 between II and III	0.283(0.071)	0.463(0.044)	0.463(0.044)
*B*3 between III and IV	—	—	0.165(0.036)
*B*4 between IV and V	0.659(0.085)	—	0.402(0.032)
Parameters for special petty bourgeoisie mobility			
*P*1 mobility to non-skilled	1.240(0.156)	0.600(0.123)	0.600(0.123)
*P*2 mobility to skilled	0.834(0.173)	0.309(0.137)	0.309(0.137)

Notes:
[a] Standard errors under the original sample size are in parentheses.
[b] Non-significant parameters are set zero.

The petty bourgeois class also shows a strong tendency for class inheritance in the three countries. The propensity is stronger in Japan (0.948) than in the United States and Britain (0.410). This is in part related to the fact that more than three-quarters of the petty bourgeois fathers were farmers in Japan whereas 58 per cent in the United States and 22 per cent in Britain were farmers.[25] The independent farmers are able to pass on intergenerationally land capital; a cultural property such as an attachment to land and farming probably also plays an important role in the inheritance of farming.

The propensity for class inheritance among the professional–managerial class is found in all three societies. Control over the labour process seems to be passed on from one generation to the next. The reproduction is probably facilitated by the attainment of educational credentials. Fathers who were engaged in professional and managerial jobs are likely to have a higher level of education, and we have already seen in Chapter 4 that the father's education affects his son's occupational prestige through affecting his son's education. Since the reproduction of the professional–managerial class generally takes place independently of direct transmission of physical capital, the extent of class reproduction is much weaker than that of the employer class and the petty bourgeoisie.

The non-manual working class in Japan and Britain does not seem to show a propensity for class inheritance. However, because the two class boundaries involving this class – the boundaries between the professional–managerial class and the non-manual class and between the non-manual and the skilled working class – are present in Britain (see below), the non-manual class distinguishes itself from neighbouring classes. Further, since the class boundary (*B*3) between the professional–managerial class and the non-manual class is weak (0.165), the sons of the non-manual class have a propensity to stay in white-collar employment in Britain. Similarly in Japan, due to lack of a significant *B*3 class boundary effect, there is a tendency for the sons of the non-manual class to retain white-collar employment.

In contrast, in the United States, not only does the non-manual class but also the skilled working class and the non-skilled working class show a strong propensity for class inheritance. When the strong effect of class inheritance (0.939) among the American non-manual class is interpreted together with the lack of class boundary effects involving this class, the following mobility chances become apparent: the sons of the non-manual class tend to stay in the same class, while when they fail to retain the same class position they tend to have equal mobility chances of moving to the professional–managerial class, the skilled working class and the non-skilled working class. There is also a strong propensity for class inheritance among the sons of the American working classes (in particular, of the non-skilled working class), but when these sons move out of their class origin, their chances of white-collar and blue-collar employment are basically the same.

The non-significant effects of class inheritance among the Japanese skilled and non-skilled working class suggest that the mobility chances of the sons of these class origins are not different. These two classes are disadvantaged in their mobility chances against other classes due to class boundary effects, but the skilled working class are as handicapped as those of the non-skilled working class.

The results of the analysis of class inheritance suggest that the tendency for intergenerational class reproduction within the society is by no means a uniform process. The extent of class inheritance varies according to different classes. Similarly, variations in the effects of class inheritance can be found across three nations.

Class boundary

A significant class boundary between the petty bourgeoisie and the professional–managerial class is present in all three countries. There exists a barrier to class mobility between classes which control and those which do not control the means of production. A powerful tendency for class inheritance can be found within the classes which have control over the means of production.

The class barrier in the United States and Britain is significantly higher than that in Japan (0.463 vs 0.283). The employer class and the petty bourgeois class in the United States and Britain are much more successful in class reproduction and the exclusion of other classes than the Japanese employer and petty bourgeois class. In other words, the relative chance of the sons of employee classes to become an employer or a member of the petty bourgeoisie is much less in the United States and Britain than in Japan. However, as we have seen in the analysis of class inheritance that the employer class in the United States does not have a higher propensity to reproduce itself, there is no class boundary between the employer and the petty bourgeois class in the United States. Both classes have the ability to block the mobility from employee classes, but the employer class cannot block the intrusion of the petty bourgeois class in the United States.

A significant class boundary between the non-manual class and the skilled working class is found in Japan and Britain. This boundary refers to the white-collar and blue-collar distinction or the non-manual/manual division among the working classes. This distinction is more important in Japan than in Britain. Crossing the 'collar-line' appears to be more difficult in Japan than in Britain, and the Japanese skilled and non-skilled working classes together appear to form a blue-collar mobility regime where the tendency for reproduction among the blue-collar classes is strong.

Finally, there is a weak but significant class boundary between the professional–managerial class and the non-manual class in Britain. This suggests that the mobility chances of the professional–managerial class and those of the non-manual class are different in Britain. Not only are their propensities for class inheritance different, but also their chances of mobility into the self-employment sector and into the blue-collar sector.

The absence of class boundaries is an equally important sociological finding. In the United States, no class boundary is present between classes which have control over labour and those which lack such control – that is, between the professional–managerial class and the non-manual class; nor is there a boundary between the non-manual and the manual working classes. In other words, the intergenerational movements involving change of authority and/or autonomy and crossing the non-manual/manual line are not particularly different from other mobility processes in the United States. In Japan, a class boundary separating the two white-collar classes is not present; the differentiation within the white-collar classes in their mobility chances is not apparent in Japan.

The lack of a class boundary pertaining to authority and autonomy has a significant implication for the closure of the professional–managerial class (Ehrenreich and Ehrenreich, 1979). Especially in the United States where the professional–managerial class shows a weak propensity for class inheritance (0.154), there is no strong evidence to support the premise that the professional–managerial class is a distinct class which restricts entry by the other working classes. As far as the intergenerational class fluidity is concerned, the extent of class closure of the professional–managerial class is weak in the United States.

In summary, our results suggest that the class boundary between classes with control over the means of production and classes without such control is present in all three societies. Failure to recognize the class boundary which involves control over the means of production misrepresents the relative mobility patterns in the three societies.

Special petty bourgeois mobility

The intergenerational movements out of the petty bourgeois class into the ranks of manual employment are relatively more frequent than other mobility chances. As shown in Figure 6.3*C* (pp. 187–8), two cells involving the petty bourgeois class deserve special attention in the three countries: first, the intergenerational movement from the petty bourgeois class to the non-skilled working class (*P*1) and, second, the mobility from the petty bourgeois class to the skilled working class (*P*2). In both cases, the parameters in the United States and Britain are set identically because they do not differ significantly from each other. Further, the tendency for intergenerational mobility into the non-skilled working class (*P*1) is stronger than that into the skilled working class (*P*2) in the three societies.

The greater tendency for the sons of the petty bourgeois class to move into the skilled and non-skilled working class can be interpreted as the 'proletarianization' of the petty bourgeoisie.[26] Although the sons of the petty bourgeoisie have a greater propensity to inherit the family business and the farming occupation or to join the employer class, they nonetheless have a high propensity to engage in manual occupations. In this sense, the petty bourgeois class can be characterized by its relative mobility chances as a class to be polarized into two extremes: the reproduction of self-employment and 'proletarianization'.

The tendency for 'proletarianization' is particularly marked in Japan. The two parameters for special petty bourgeois mobility are significantly higher in Japan than in the United States and Britain, and they are also high compared with the parameters representing other mobility processes within the society. The strong propensity for intergenerational mobility into manual employment is in part the result of the composition of the petty bourgeoisie: more than three-quarters of the petty bourgeois fathers were farmers in Japan. The sons of the independent farmers have especially high chances of moving into manual employment when they leave farming. The *P*1 and *P*2 parameters are, in part, reduced when the farm fathers and sons are excluded: *P*1 changed from 1.240 to 1.094 and *P*2 from 0.834 to 0.554.

To conclude, the pattern of class fluidity in the three nations can be characterized by three features: class inheritance, class boundary and special petty bourgeois mobility.[27] In other words, there is a cross-national similarity in the overall pattern of mobility regimes in the three nations. However, cross-national variations are found in the rates associated with the pattern. For example, most diagonal cells require special treatment in all three nations – a cross-national similarity in the pattern – but the rates of class inheritance among some classes are not identical across nations.

The results of our analysis on class fluidity have implications for the 'FJH hypothesis' proposed by Featherman, Jones and Hauser (1975). If we take the FJH hypothesis in its strictest form – that is to say, all industrial societies show not only a similar pattern but also similar rates associated with the pattern – then our empirical results are not in favour of the FJH hypothesis. However, if the hypothesis is modified into a less strict form – that is to say, all industrial nations show a broadly similar pattern of relative mobility chances from which some nation-specific deviations can be found – then our results provide support for this hypothesis (cf. Erikson and Goldthorpe, 1987a).

6.9 TRENDS IN CLASS MOBILITY IN JAPAN

This section focuses on trends in intergenerational class mobility in Japan. In order to derive evidence on trends from a single survey, as we have done in previous chapters, we construct three birth cohorts and compare the mobility experience of men in these cohorts.

Table 6.9 shows class mobility tables by three birth cohorts and gross mobility rates. Total mobility rates consistently increased from the oldest (59.3 per cent) to the youngest cohort (73.8 per cent). The index of dissimilarity between class origin and class destination distribution or 'forced' mobility rate also increased steadily from the oldest (30.2 per cent) to the youngest cohort (37.4 per cent). Total mobility rates which are computed from the 'counterfactual' mobility tables are also shown in Table 6.9. These rates are calculated by adjusting the marginal distributions of the middle-age and old-age mobility tables to those of the young-age table. In other words, the new 'counterfactual' tables will have the same marginal distributions as those in the young-age table but retain the odds ratios patterns in the middle-age and the old-age table. Total mobility rates computed from these 'counterfactual' tables are much higher than the observed rates and come close to the rate in the youngest cohort. This implies that the increase in the observed total mobility rates across cohorts is probably in large part due to the increased dissimilarity between class origin and class destination distribution across successive cohorts.

Table 6.10 reveals the patterns of inflow mobility rates among Japanese men born in three different cohorts. The index of dissimilarity (ID) shows that the indices between the youngest and the oldest cohort are almost always larger than those involving other comparisons. In other words, the patterns of intergenerational recruitment are most dissimilar between the youngest and the oldest cohorts. For example, over 80 per cent of the petty bourgeoisie in the oldest cohort came from the same class origin, but only 60 per cent of the petty bourgeoisie in the youngest cohort did so. On the other hand, only 18 per cent of the non-manual class in the oldest cohort were of white-collar origin while 32 per cent of the non-manual class in the youngest cohort came from the two white-collar classes. These findings are primarily influenced by the difference in the distribution of class origin across cohorts. More than 60 per cent of men in the oldest cohort came from a petty bourgeois class origin while the percentage decreased to 56 per cent of men in the middle-age cohort and further to 46 per cent of men in the youngest cohort. In contrast,

Table 6.9 Class mobility tables by cohorts in Japan (SSM)

Class origin	*Class destination*						
	I	*II*	*III*	*IV*	*V*	*VI*	*Total*
Young 20–34							
I Employer	28	36	15	35	11	8	133
II Petty bourgeoisie	19	88	61	68	50	93	379
III Professional and managerial	8	6	40	38	10	12	114
IV Non-manual	4	6	12	22	6	7	57
V Skilled	0	4	8	8	12	10	42
VI Semi- and non-skilled	1	6	21	18	21	24	91
Total	60	146	157	189	110	154	816
Middle 35–49							
I Employer	59	19	44	13	6	10	151
II Petty bourgeoisie	62	140	92	32	44	70	440
III Professional and managerial	16	9	44	6	6	6	87
IV Non-manual	7	3	13	6	1	4	34
V Skilled	3	2	8	1	4	1	19
VI Semi- and non-skilled	3	13	12	2	14	15	59
Total	150	186	213	60	75	106	790
Old 50–64							
I Employer	22	17	32	9	3	12	95
II Petty bourgeoisie	24	137	36	25	14	30	266
III Professional and managerial	4	4	10	5	0	2	25
IV Non-manual	4	1	7	3	1	2	18
V Skilled	1	3	1	2	1	1	9
VI Semi- and non-skilled	4	8	2	1	4	5	24
Total	59	170	88	45	23	52	437

	Young	**Middle**	**Old**
Total mobility	73.8%	66.1%	59.3%
Forced mobility	37.4%	32.3%	30.2%
Net mobility	36.4%	32.8%	29.1%
Counterfactual mobility	–	71.7%	73.8%

the share of white-collar classes in the class origin distribution increased from 10 per cent in the oldest to 21 per cent in the youngest cohort. The effect of industrialization on reshaping class structure is apparent in cross-cohort variations in inflow rates.

Table 6.11 shows outflow mobility patterns among Japanese men born in different cohorts. The index of dissimilarity shown in Table

Table 6.10 Class composition by class destination for three cohorts: inflow percentage distribution and index of dissimilarity (ID)

Class origin	*Destination I*			*Destination II*			*Destination III*		
	Y	*M*	*O*	*Y*	*M*	*O*	*Y*	*M*	*O*
I	46.7	39.3	37.3	24.7	10.2	10.0	9.6	20.7	36.4
II	31.7	41.3	40.7	60.3	75.3	80.6	38.9	43.2	40.9
III	13.3	10.7	6.8	4.1	4.8	2.4	25.5	20.7	11.4
IV	6.7	4.7	6.8	4.1	1.6	0.6	7.6	6.1	8.0
V	0.0	2.0	1.7	2.7	1.1	1.8	5.1	3.8	1.1
VI	1.7	2.0	6.8	4.1	7.0	4.7	13.4	5.6	2.3

	Destination IV			*Destination V*			*Destination VI*		
	Y	*M*	*O*	*Y*	*M*	*O*	*Y*	*M*	*O*
I	18.5	21.7	20.0	10.0	8.0	13.0	5.2	9.4	23.1
II	36.0	53.3	55.6	45.5	58.7	60.9	60.4	66.0	57.7
III	20.1	10.0	11.1	9.1	8.0	0.0	7.8	5.7	3.8
IV	11.6	10.0	6.7	5.5	1.3	4.3	4.5	3.8	3.8
V	4.2	1.7	4.4	10.9	5.3	4.3	6.5	0.9	1.9
VI	9.5	3.3	2.2	19.1	18.7	17.4	15.6	14.2	9.6

	I	II	III	IV	V	VI
ID (*Y*, *M*)[a]	12.0	18.6	15.4	20.4	13.3	9.8
ID (*Y*, *O*)[b]	15.9	20.8	29.2	21.2	18.6	18.0
ID (*M*, *O*)[c]	6.8	5.9	17.6	6.1	10.3	14.8

Notes:
[a] Index of dissimilarity between young-age and middle-age cohort.
[b] Index of dissimilarity between young-age and old-age cohort.
[c] Index of dissimilarity between middle-age and old-age cohort.

Y = Young-age cohort, M = Middle-age cohort, O = Old-age cohort.

I = Employer, *II* = Petty bourgeoisie, *III* = Professional and managerial, *IV* = non-manual, *V* = Skilled, *VI* = Semi- and non-skilled.

6.11 indicates the extent of cross-cohort variation in class trajectory given class origin. Dissimilarity indices involving the youngest cohort are generally higher than those between the middle-age and old-age cohort. Among men of the youngest cohort, outflow rates into the non-manual class are almost always higher and those into the employer class are always lower than the similar rates among men of other cohorts. These characteristics reflect cross-cohort variations in the distribution of class destination. Men in the youngest cohort,

Table 6.11 Class mobility chances by class origin for three cohorts: outflow percentage distribution and index of dissimilarity (ID)

Class origin		*Class destination*								
		I	*II*	*III*	*IV*	*V*	*VI*	*ID*[a] (*Y*, *M*)	ID[b] (*Y*, *O*)	ID[c] (*M*, *O*)
I	Young	21.1	27.1	11.3	26.3	8.3	6.0	36.5	31.1	16.7
	Middle	39.1	12.6	29.1	8.6	4.0	6.6			
	Old	23.2	17.9	33.7	9.5	3.2	12.6			
II	Young	5.0	23.2	16.1	17.9	13.2	24.5	22.4	32.2	21.8
	Middle	14.1	31.8	20.9	7.3	10.0	15.9			
	Old	9.0	51.5	13.5	9.4	5.3	11.3			
III	Young	7.0	5.3	35.1	33.3	8.8	10.5	31.9	24.6	19.9
	Middle	18.4	10.3	50.6	6.9	6.9	6.9			
	Old	16.0	16.0	40.0	20.0	0.0	8.0			
IV	Young	7.0	10.5	21.1	38.6	10.5	12.3	30.8	32.9	4.8
	Middle	20.6	8.8	38.2	17.6	2.9	11.8			
	Old	22.2	5.6	38.9	16.7	5.6	11.1			
V	Young	0.0	9.5	19.0	19.0	28.6	23.8	39.7	38.1	45.7
	Middle	15.8	10.5	42.1	5.3	21.1	5.3			
	Old	11.1	33.3	11.1	22.2	11.1	11.1			
VI	Young	1.1	6.6	23.1	19.8	23.1	26.4	20.2	42.4	23.6
	Middle	5.1	22.0	20.3	3.4	23.7	25.4			
	Old	16.7	33.3	8.3	4.2	16.7	20.8			

Notes:
[a] The index of dissimilarity between young-age and middle-age cohort.
[b] The index of dissimilarity between young-age and old-age cohort.
[c] The index of dissimilarity between middle-age and old-age cohort.

I = Employer, *II* = Petty bourgeoisie, *III* = Professional and managerial,
IV = Non-manual, *V* = Skilled, *VI* = Semi- and non-skilled.

compared with those in the middle-age and the old-age cohorts, are more likely to be found in the non-manual class and less likely to be found in the employer class. While men in the youngest cohort are more likely to benefit from the expansion of white-collar employment in recent period, they tend to occupy lower-level white-collar positions (namely in the non-manual class) because they have not reached the 'mature' level in their life-stages. The differential outflow patterns across cohorts are therefore probably affected both by life-cycle and by cohort effects.

We now shift our analysis from the patterns of gross mobility or absolute mobility to the patterns of class fluidity which are relative chances of mobility and immobility once the cross-cohort differences in the distributions of class origin and class destination have been taken into account. We will use the Japanese class fluidity model described in Figure 6.3 (pp. 187–8) as a representation of the relative mobility chances in Japan. The model is characterized by (1) class inheritance effects for the employer class, the petty bourgeois class and the professional–managerial class, (2) two class boundary effects (*B*2 and *B*4), and (3) two special petty bourgeois effects. Our interest is to examine whether this model can be fitted to three different cohorts in Japan. When we apply this model to our cohorts without allowing the effect parameters to vary across cohorts, this constant class fluidity model does not produce an acceptable fit to the data ($L^2 = 103.27$, df = 68, $p = 0.004$).[28] In other words, the rates of class fluidity are not constant across successive cohorts. There seem to be some changes in relative chances of mobility and immobility. However, when we allow class inheritance effects for the employer class and the petty bourgeois class to vary across cohorts, our class fluidity model produces an acceptable fit to the data ($L^2 = 90.78$, df = 66, $p = 0.023$).

Table 6.12 shows estimates of effect parameters from the fitted model. It is clear from Table 6.12 that there is a remarkable stability in the relative chances of mobility and immobility across cohorts. The only exceptions to this stability are the propensities for class inheritance among the employer class and the petty bourgeois class, but the trends are in opposite directions.

There is a trend towards a reduction in the effect of class inheritance among the petty bourgeoisie across cohorts. This must be related to changing composition of the petty bourgeois class. Because the propensity for class inheritance is generally greater among the farmers than among the urban petty bourgeoisie, as the proportion of the farmers of petty bourgeois class origin decreases from 80 per cent to 68 per cent from the oldest to the youngest cohort, the overall propensity for class inheritance among the petty bourgeois class is probably reduced. There is an opposite trend of an increasing propensity for class inheritance among the employer class. It is not clear why the employer class in the oldest cohort does not show a propensity for class inheritance. However, because the class boundary effect between the petty bourgeois class and the professional–managerial class is present, the employer class and the petty bourgeois class

Table 6.12 Parameter estimates in log-additive form for the model of class fluidity shown in Figure 6.3 applied to cohort data in Japan (SSM)

	Young-age cohort	*Middle-age cohort*	*Old-age cohort*
Parameters for class inheritance			
I Employer	0.912(0.173)[a]	0.912(0.173)	—[b]
II Petty bourgeoisie	0.596(0.206)	0.931(0.203)	1.537(0.237)
III Professional–managerial	0.432(0.161)	0.432(0.161)	0.432(0.161)
Parameters for class boundary			
*B*2 between *II* and *III*	0.228(0.074)	0.228(0.074)	0.228(0.074)
*B*4 between *IV* and *V*	0.648(0.085)	0.648(0.085)	0.648(0.085)
Parameters for special petty bourgeois mobility			
*P*1 mobility to non-skilled	1.242(0.157)	1.242(0.157)	1.242(0.157)
*P*2 mobility to skilled	0.838(0.175)	0.838(0.175)	0.838(0.175)

Notes:
[a] Standard errors under the original sample size are in parentheses.
[b] Non-significant parameters are set zero.

together have a tendency for reproducing themselves. In the middle-age and the young-age cohort, a strong propensity for class inheritance among the employer class is found.

These results do not provide support for the prediction of an increasing 'openness' in post-war Japan.[29] Treiman's (1970) claim that mobility tends to increase as the level of industrialization increases does not seem to be documented in our analysis. The only empirical evidence in favour of this claim is a decreasing trend in the propensity for class reproduction among the petty bourgeoisie. In contrast, the relative chances of mobility and immobility appear to be extremely stable across successive cohorts in Japan. These findings are consistent with the FJH hypothesis which precludes the possibility of any changes in relative mobility rates among industrial nations.

6.10 SUMMARY AND CONCLUSION

This chapter placed class at the centre of the analysis. Unlike preceding chapters which discussed the status attainment process in Japan, the United States and Britain, here class – defined in terms of social relations of production and marketable skills – and class mobility –

which is the intergenerational movement of people within the class structure – constituted the heart of the analysis. The primary objectives of this chapter were (1) to define class using two qualitative dimensions of social relations of production: control over the means of production and control over labour, (2) to compare the distribution of class origin and class destination within each society and between societies, (3) to compare the patterns of gross or absolute mobility, (4) to discuss the patterns of class fluidity in the three societies, and (5) to examine trends in class mobility in Japan.

The class structures in Japan, the United States and Britain in the 1970s show more resemblance than a generation ago. Nonetheless, the Japanese class structure is characterized by a relatively higher proportion of the petty bourgeoisie and a lower proportion of the professional–managerial class and the non-skilled working class than the American and British class structure. These differences are much more pronounced in the class origin distribution. The comparison of class origin and class destination distribution within each society suggests that Japan has experienced more dramatic changes in the shape of its class structure between the two generations than the United States and Britain – namely, the huge contraction of the petty bourgeois class and the expansion of both the white-collar and the blue-collar classes. The large structural transformation of the class structure in Japan between the two generations has profound implications for our understanding of mobility processes in Japan.

The first major conclusion about class mobility in Japan, the United States and Britain is the cross-national variation in gross or absolute mobility patterns. The cross-national comparison of total mobility, 'forced' mobility, and 'net' mobility shows a striking difference. Although the proportion of people who changed class positions between the two generations is the same in the three countries, the observed total mobility is probably more affected by the change in class distribution in Japan than in the other nations. Inflow and outflow patterns of mobility also show considerable cross-national variation.

Therefore, as far as the patterns of absolute mobility are concerned, distinctive features of the Japanese mobility process do seem to emerge. In particular, the petty bourgeoisie and the non-skilled working class deserve special attention. A high degree of intergenerational class stability and closure (self-recruitment) of the Japanese petty bourgeoisie and the weak extent of such stability and closure in the Japanese non-skilled working class stand out in cross-national comparisons. In other words, if we borrow Goldthorpe's terminology (Goldthorpe, 1984, 1987), the Japanese petty bourgeois class can be characterized by a highly developed 'demographic identity', while the Japanese non-skilled working class appears to possess only a weakly developed one.[30] These mobility characteristics of the Japanese petty bourgeoisie and the Japanese non-skilled working class are probably related to their potential for class-based collective action (see Chapter 8). Furthermore, there may also be a relationship between the weakly developed 'demographic identity' of the non-skilled working class and the much discussed 'middle-strata consciousness' among the Japanese working class (e.g., Murakami, 1984).

The distinctive features of the patterns of absolute mobility in Japan may be traced primarily to the particular course of development followed by Japan, namely *late*, but *rapid*, industrialization. Because of Japan's 'late comer' status, compared with the United States and Britain, a relatively large-sized petty bourgeoisie (namely, independent farmers) and a relatively small-sized non-skilled working class are found in the Japanese distribution of class origin. On the other hand, because of Japan's rapid industrialization, a relatively small-sized non-skilled working class is found in the Japanese distribution of class destination. We therefore observed the tendency for inflow rates to be high from the petty bourgeoisie and low from the non-skilled working class to all class categories, and this pattern was obviously responsible for a high degree of intergenerational stability among the petty bourgeoisie and a low degree of such stability among the non-skilled working class. Similarly, the tendency for outflow rates to be low to the non-skilled working class is related to intergenerational recruitment patterns of the non-skilled working class.

Japan experienced the expansion of the blue-collar as well as of the white-collar sector at about the same time following the decline in the agricultural sector (cf. Cole and Tominaga, 1976). In contrast, in the United States and especially in Britain, the decline of the agricultural labour force was chiefly accompanied by the growth of the manual working class with the white-collar expansion occurring only at a later stage (Gagliani, 1985). There was no stage in the historical development of the Japanese class structure when a stable core of the manual working class reproduced itself for several generations. Japan has been transformed within a very compressed period of time from a society in which most of the labour force is engaged in agricultural production to a highly industrial society in which both white-collar and blue-collar employments form the major part of the labour force.

Japan's experience of late, but rapid, industrialization thus led to a large transformation of the class structure within a generation and produced distinctive inflow and outflow patterns, especially among the petty bourgeois class and the non-skilled working class.

The particular course of industrialization followed by Japan must also have influenced total mobility rates. Although the total mobility rate in Japan is the same as that in the United States and Britain, the extent of total mobility due to intergenerational change in class structure is probably larger in Japan than in the United States and Britain. In other words, if the Japanese class structure had not experienced such dramatic changes between the two generations, the total observed mobility would probably be smaller than the amounts observed in the United States and Britain. We may therefore conclude that the opportunity for mobility net of the structural changes is probably greater and consequently the class structure is more fluid in the United States and Britain than in Japan.

The second major conclusion about class mobility in Japan, the United States and Britain concerns cross-national similarity in the patterns of class fluidity – that is, the chances of mobility and immobility net of the change in class structure between two generations. We already know that the overall *extent* of class fluidity is probably smaller in Japan; however, the *patterns* of class fluidity appear to be very similar. Although the common class fluidity model (which imposes exactly the same pattern of relative mobility chances in the three countries) does not fit the data-set, cross-national similarity heavily outweighs cross-national variation. The patterns of class fluidity in all three societies can be characterized by common features of class inheritance, class boundary and special petty bourgeois mobility.

The two major conclusions from our analyses of class mobility in Japan, the United States and Britain are very similar to those reported in comparative studies of occupational mobility (Erikson *et al.*, 1979, 1982, 1983; Erikson and Pontinen, 1985; Portocarero, 1983a, 1983b; Kerckhoff *et al.*, 1985; Erikson and Goldthorpe, 1987a, 1987b; Grusky and Hauser, 1984): cross-national variations in absolute mobility are mainly due to the effects of the marginal distributions and the patterns of class fluidity are remarkably similar. The conclusions of this chapter are therefore consistent with the thesis proposed by Featherman, Jones and Hauser (1975) about the similarity in the patterns of social mobility among industrial societies. The FJH hypothesis suggests that while the observed absolute mobility may differ among the nations, once the differences in occupational and class distribution are taken into account, the patterns of relative mobility are essentially the same. The two major conclusions of this study – cross-national variation in absolute observed mobility and cross-national similarity in class fluidity – are in accordance with the FJH prediction.

The results of our analysis on trends in class mobility in Japan also provide support to the FJH hypothesis. There was no clear trend towards increasing class fluidity, and the relative chances of mobility and immobility appeared to be extremely stable across successive cohorts. Contrary to the prediction by Treiman (Treiman, 1970; Treiman and Yip, 1987), no trend of a greater 'openness' was found in our data-set, although the level of industrialization increased rapidly across successive cohorts. This stability in class fluidity over time is consistent with the prediction of the FJH hypothesis.

Notes

1. While the class categories proposed in this study are informed by theoretical perspectives (especially Neo-Marxist and Neo-Weberian), they have an eclectic character and should best be regarded as 'working instruments'. There are, of course, different ways of conceptualizing class categories (see, for example, Giddens, 1973; Goldthorpe, 1987; Marshall *et al.*, 1988). For a variety of Marxist definitions of class, see Wright (1980a).
2. For example, Ohashi (1971, Chapter 3) describes the post-war Japanese class structure as the two fundamental classes of capitalists and workers, with two additional classes: the self-employed, and self-defence force members and policemen. See also Kawaguchi (1980) for a similar idea.
3. This line of argument has been introduced in Japan (Tomizawa, 1981; Ichikawa and Sengoku, 1980), but it has never been used in the empirical examination of the Japanese class structure.
4. The semi- and non-skilled working class will be simply called the non-skilled working class in this study.
5. Although social survey data are not the best source to operationalize class categories (especially the employer class, because they are so few in number), these survey data are the only available data which allow the analysis of class mobility.
6. The CSCC survey did not ask the respondents whether their fathers (or the head of the family) were owners or part-owners when they were employed by someone else. These employee owners are probably classified as in the manager/supervisor category in the distribution of class of origin in the United States.

7. The Japanese survey did not ask the members of the board of directors whether they were owner or part-owner of the business. A small number of non-owner executives is therefore probably included in this category.
8. The empirical consequences of not being able to separate out employee owners are that (1) the proportion of the employer class is probably underestimated, and correspondingly the proportion of the managerial class is probably overestimated, and (2) the propensity for class inheritance among the employer class is probably underestimated, and correspondingly the propensity for class inheritance among the professional–managerial class is probably overestimated.
9. In the case of the British data-set, employers with more than 25 workers are called large employers.
10. Erik Olin Wright (1985, p. 150) who was the principal investigator of the CSCC survey, claimed that the questions on the number of employees were not clear. An unknown proportion of the respondents who stated that they had one employee really had none (by counting themselves as an employee). I therefore followed Wright's suggestion of defining the petty bourgeoisie as having no more than one employee. The CSCC survey did not have a category of 'work without pay' in the father's (or the family head's) employment status question. These fathers (or the family heads) are classified as either 'self-employed' or 'worked for someone else' in the American data.
11. Wright *et al.* (1982, p. 715) have shown a close fit between formal hierarchical positions and the measure of authority (sanctioning and task authority). Non-managerial positions are almost entirely excluded from the exercise of sanctioning and task authority. It seems unlikely that employees in non-managerial positions can supervise and control other people's labour without having any formal titles.
12. In the Japanese survey, employees who hold the title of 'chief of the section' (*kacho*) or above are called managers. Supervisors in the Japanese and British data-sets include employees who hold the title of foremen (*kantoku* in Japanese).
13. The American 1970 census occupational classification and the British 1970 Census classification of occupations are recoded into eight major Japanese SSM occupational categories: professional/technical, managerial, clerical, sales, skilled, semi-skilled, non-skilled, and farm.
14. The indices of dissimilarity are computed from the sixfold classification of class categories, so that they are consistent with the figures reported in Table 6.4.
15. Strictly speaking, 75 per cent of the petty bourgeois fathers were farmers and 2 per cent were other self-employed and family workers in primary production.
16. Even the class destination distributions in the United States and Britain are significantly different.
17. The original tenfold class schema is collapsed into a sixfold class schema: (1) large and small employers are combined into one category of the 'employer class', (2) the farming petty bourgeoisie and the urban petty bourgeoisie are combined into the 'petty bourgeois class', and (3) managers, supervisors, and professionals are combined into one category called the 'professional–managerial class'.

18. The term 'reproduction' here refers to the process through which the relative position of individuals in the class structure is maintained between the two generations. Our usage does not refer to the process through which the structure of classes (i.e., marginal distributions of the mobility table) is maintained between the generations, regardless of individuals who occupy the positions (cf. Poulantzas, 1975, p. 33).
19. However, as we will see later in this section, not all diagonals are different among the three societies. The employer class shows identical rates of class inheritance in Japan and Britain. The rates of class inheritance in the United States and Britain are the same for the petty bourgeois class and the professional-managerial class.
20. I have also tried the uniform association model (Duncan, 1979; Goodman, 1979) which assumes an equal spacing between the class categories. The inclusion of the uniform association parameter did not significantly improve the fit of the preferred model discussed below, so the result is not reported in this chapter.
21. Even when the sons remain in farming, an increasing number of them are becoming part-time farmers working simultaneously in manual non-farm jobs in Japan (Kada, 1980; Fukutake, 1967).
22. The propensity for the sons of the petty bourgeoisie to move into the skilled and non-skilled working classes is found to be significantly higher in Japan than in the United States and Britain. The effects of the special petty bourgeoisie mobility in Japan are therefore set at a different level than those in the United States and Britain.
23. These separate matrices are fitted to the data-set simultaneously. For example, fitting the diagonal matrices allows diagonal cells to be different from other (non-diagonal) cells and each diagonal has a different strength of immobility except for some cells where the same numbers are assigned. When the diagonal cell has a number of 1, it means that that cell is treated in the same way as other non-diagonal cells. The different numbers simply mean that the strength of immobility is different; the larger number does not imply greater immobility. These matrices correspond to the input matrices in the GLIM program (Payne, 1985) from which the parameter estimates were obtained.
24. The formula for calculating the standardized L^2 (Erikson and Goldthorpe, 1987b, p. 148) is the following:

$$((L^2 - \text{df}) / N) \times 2043 + \text{df}.$$

25. In fact, the extent of class inheritance in Japan is reduced from 0.948 to 0.704 when we exclude respondents and fathers who were farmers.
26. The tendency for 'proletarianization' is probably more apparent than real because some sons from the petty bourgeois family work as employees and probably have not yet 'inherited' the family business at the time of the survey.
27. These results are not altogether consistent with Yamaguchi's findings (1987) on intergenerational occupational mobility in Japan, the United States and Britain. However, direct comparison is unwarranted because his analysis is based on occupational categories while we have used class

categories which were constructed not only from occupation but also from employment status, managerial status and firm size.

28. When full origin–destination association is used rather than effect matrices, the constant social fluidity model does not produce an acceptable fit either ($L^2 = 79.41$, df = 50, p = 0.005).
29. Our results are not consistent with Yamaguchi's findings (1987) on trends in occupational mobility in Japan. The differences may be due to the fact that he based his analysis on occupation, while we have used class (see n. 27 above). However, our results are in broad agreement with studies on trends in occupational mobility by other Japanese sociologists using the 1955, 1965 and 1975 SSM Surveys (Kojima and Hamana, 1984; Iwamoto, 1985; Tokuyasu, 1986).
30. These distinctive features of the Japanese absolute mobility patterns are also found in the comparison with European nations (Ishida, Goldthorpe and Erikson, 1987).

7 Class Structure, Status Hierarchies and Inequality in the Labour Market

7.1 INTRODUCTION

This chapter focuses on the interplay among class, status and labour market outcomes in contemporary Japan. In the preceding chapters we analyzed separately the status attainment process and the patterns of class mobility. In this chapter, the relationship between class and the process of socioeconomic attainment will be examined. We will (1) investigate the relationship between class and the distribution of status characteristics, (2) compare the effect of class on rewards in the labour market (income, home ownership and stock holdings) with the effects of education and occupational status, and (3) examine the effect of class on the relationship between education and labour market rewards.

Class and status hierarchies

The first point addresses the issue of the relationship between class structure and status hierarchies in contemporary Japan. The Japanese intellectual tradition, especially that of Marxism, emphasizes the centrality of class in the structure of inequality (e.g., Yamada, 1934; Noro, 1930; Ouchi, 1971; Ohashi, 1971). Class constitutes the foundation of society and 'status stratification which shows internal composition of class is meaningful only when analyzed on the basis of class' (Ohashi, 1971, p. 9). However, many social scientists question the centrality of class in the structure of inequality and propose alternative views about the interplay between class and status hierarchies. As discussed in Chapter 1, this chapter will empirically examine four hypotheses related to the relationship between class structure and various dimensions of status hierarchies (such as hierarchy in occupational status, or education, or income). These hypotheses are called the status homogeneity hypothesis, the bipolarity hypothesis, the status inconsistency hypothesis and the dual structure hypothesis.

The status homogeneity hypothesis, which derives from the work of Murakami (1977; 1984), states that a huge intermediate stratum, which belongs neither to the lower nor the upper class and whose members are highly homogeneous in their life-styles and attitudes, has emerged in contemporary Japan. It is increasingly difficult to distinguish classes by their status characteristics; in virtually every dimension of status hierarchies, class boundaries are blurred.[1] This hypothesis therefore predicts that the status composition of various classes is highly homogeneous.

Kishimoto (1977; 1978) endorses the Marxist perspective of bipolarity between capitalists and workers in the structure of inequality. The basis of the distribution of various status characteristics is polarized along the lines of the ownership of the means of production, with capitalists and workers at opposite ends. Kishimoto rejects Murakami's claim of the emergence of a homogeneous middle mass. According to the bipolarity hypothesis, classes are divided into two basic groups with respect to their status attributes.

The hypothesis of status inconsistency is proposed by Tominaga (1977; 1979) who relies on results reported by Imada and Hara (1979). They found that in Japanese society a variety of status characteristics were distributed differently among the population. Using six different status dimensions (occupational prestige, education, income, assets, living style and power), they classified the respondents to a social survey into six different clusters, of which only two were status-consistent. 60 per cent of all respondents belonged to the 'status-inconsistent' clusters. They concluded that the stratification system in Japan could not be represented by upper, middle and lower categories along a unidimensional status scale. The majority of respondents scored high on at least one of the status characteristics while low on the others. The status inconsistency hypothesis predicts that various status characteristics of classes are inconsistent, so that classes cannot be characterized by consistently high or low status attributes.

Finally, the dual structure hypothesis which is found in the work of labour economists (e.g., Ujihara and Takanashi, 1971; Odaka, 1984) focuses upon the differentiation among employees according to firm size.[2] This hypothesis emphasizes the importance of firm size in the labour market stratification of employees (cf. Koike, 1988). Workers in large firms are advantaged in their average wage, working conditions and range of fringe benefits over those who work in small and medium-sized firms. The 'permanent employment' system, in which employers provide their workers with security throughout their working career, and an internal labour market in which promotions are determined from within are believed to be developed more extensively in larger firms (Koike, 1983).

According to the dual structure hypothesis, employees should be differentiated not only by class position but also by firm size. The status characteristics of employees will differ according to the size of the firm in which they are employed; workers in large firms will tend to show more favourable status attributes than those in small and medium-sized firms even though they belong to the same class.

In order empirically to examine these four hypotheses, this chapter will analyze the distribution of various status characteristics – occupational status, education, income, home ownership and stock investment – among classes. The four hypotheses predict four different outcomes about the status composition of classes; the analysis presented below will assess the predictions of these hypotheses in the light of the empirical data set.

In addition, a similar analysis will be performed on the American data-set to provide a comparative reference. The British data-set is not used in this chapter because it does not contain information on home ownership and stock investment. A cross-national comparison is particularly important in the case of the status homogeneity and the status inconsistency hypotheses because their advocates appear to claim that status homogeneity or status inconsistency is more pronounced in Japan than in other societies (cf. Okamoto, 1982).

Class and inequality in the labour market

The second point addresses the issue of the predictive power of class in explaining inequality in labour market rewards. In the United States, many sociologists (Wright and Perrone, 1977; Kalleberg and Griffin, 1980; Griffin and Kalleberg, 1981; Robinson and Kelley, 1979) have documented that class affects income and other job rewards, independent of occupational status. Wright (1979) even showed that the effect of class on income is stronger than that of occupational status.

In Japan, Marxists have been claiming that class constitutes the fundamental dimension of inequality in Japanese society, in that differences in income, non-pecuniary benefits and assets are largely determined by the individual's position in the class structure. However, Murakami (1977) claims that differences in income and living styles between classes appear to have diminished in modern Japan, leading to the emergence of 'the new middle mass'.[3] Kishimoto (1978) and others (Ishikawa *et al.*, 1983) are sceptical of the new middle class idea: the amount of assets, home ownership and stock holdings are still unequally distributed among different classes.

However, none of the Japanese studies showed that the differential distribution of various rewards among classes could not be explained by the difference among these categories in status characteristics, such as education and occupational status.[4] In order to demonstrate the importance of class in determining the distribution of rewards in Japanese society, it is crucial to document that class affects the attainment of income and other rewards in the society, independent of education and occupational status. This chapter will therefore estimate the predictive power of class in explaining inequality of income, home ownership and stock holdings in Japan and the United States, independent of the effect of education and occupational status.

Class, education, and labour market rewards

The third point which will be addressed in this chapter deals with the interplay among class, education and labour market outcomes. Our purpose is to place the process of status attainment within the structural context of class. In other words, the effect of education on attainment of income, home ownership and stock investment is examined separately for different classes; the returns to education may be different from one class to another.

Wright (1979, 1985; Wright and Perrone, 1977) has already shown that, in the United States, individuals who occupy different class positions receive not only a different average income but also different returns to education. Winn (1984) has shown similar differential income returns to education in Sweden. There is therefore reason to believe that the structural effect of class on the relationship between education and labour market rewards is also present in Japan (cf. Hashimoto, 1986).

This analysis has profound implications for the hypothesis of 'educational credentialism' in Japan. One of the implicit assumptions of the thesis of Japan as an educational credential society is that the returns to education are homogeneous across all segments of society: educational achievement will benefit everyone who works hard enough to obtain educational qualifications. The homogeneous socioeconomic benefits of education have been taken for granted among the advocates of 'educational credentialism' in Japan, but we have seen in Chapters 4 and 5 that these benefits are not particularly striking in Japan contrary to what the advocates of 'educational credentialism' have assumed. In this chapter, we will examine whether the benefits of education are constant across all classes. Depending upon class position, the effect of educational credentials on attainment of various labour market rewards may vary in Japan.

The rest of this chapter is composed of six analysis sections which are organized in terms of the three basic issues discussed above. The first issue which focuses on the relationship between class structure and status hierarchies will be discussed in Sections 7.2, 7.3 and 7.4. The second issue of comparing the effect of class with that of education and of occupational status will be dealt with in Sections 7.5 and 7.6. The third issue of the effect of class on the relationship between education and labour market rewards will be discussed in Section 7.7. Finally, it should be noted that this chapter will concentrate upon a comparison of Japanese and American societies. The comparison with British society is not included because the British data-set does not contain detailed information on status characteristics such as home ownership and stock investment.[5]

7.2 STATUS CHARACTERISTICS OF CLASSES

This section provides a descriptive exposition of various status characteristics of classes. The examination of the status composition of classes will test the homogeneity hypothesis that all classes are homogeneous with respect to their status attributes, and the bipolarity hypothesis that classes are divided into two basic groups of capitalists and workers.

The composition of classes is examined along the five different dimensions of status stratification – education, occupational prestige, income, home ownership and stock investment. These five variables are measured as follows: average year of schooling, average occupational prestige score, average total individual income in US dollars, the proportion of individuals owning homes, and the proportion of individuals investing in stocks and bonds (see Chapter 2 for detailed explanations of the variables). The status characteristics of classes thus indicate the socioeconomic make-up of these classes. Table 7.1 shows the status composition of six different classes in Japan and the United States.

Table 7.1 Status composition of classes in Japan (SSM) and the United States (CSCC)

Class	*Education*	*Occupation*	*Income*	*Home ownership*	*Stock investment*
Japan					
Employer	10.93	50.03	10645	0.793	0.562
	(2.92)[a]	(13.62)	(7147)	(0.406)	(0.497)
Petty bourgeoisie	9.43	38.90	6191	0.868	0.238
	(2.40)	(7.15)	(4762)	(0.339)	(0.427)
Professional and	12.13	49.46	8560	0.664	0.410
managerial	(2.75)	(12.81)	(3429)	(0.473)	(0.492)
Non-manual	12.09	40.58	6312	0.636	0.289
	(2.64)	(5.99)	(2361)	(0.482)	(0.454)
Skilled	9.50	37.80	5571	0.573	0.141
	(2.29)	(6.02)	(2261)	(0.496)	(0.349)
Semi- and	9.50	30.42	5579	0.596	0.151
non-skilled	(2.17)	(7.59)	(2377)	(0.491)	(0.358)
Grand mean	10.63	41.53	7167	0.705	0.303
	(2.82)	(11.74)	(4445)	(0.456)	(0.460)
United States					
Employer	12.67	47.11	28708	0.946	0.441
	(3.35)	(10.76)	(28121)	(0.229)	(0.501)
Petty bourgeoisie	12.40	42.91	15646	0.747	0.203
	(2.67)	(10.04)	(16292)	(0.439)	(0.406)
Professional and	13.58	50.92	13679	0.666	0.247
managerial	(2.41)	(12.07)	(9820)	(0.473)	(0.432)
Non-manual	13.05	40.80	11573	0.819	0.294
	(1.89)	(9.77)	(5610)	(0.389)	(0.459)
Skilled	11.47	39.07	11402	0.708	0.111
	(2.43)	(4.44)	(5648)	(0.457)	(0.316)
Semi- and	10.79	29.78	8963	0.563	0.085
non-skilled	(2.37)	(6.64)	(5395)	(0.498)	(0.280)
Grand mean	12.42	42.35	13401	0.692	0.210
	(2.72)	(12.74)	(12587)	(0.462)	(0.407)
Japan					
Petty bourgeoisie	9.94	37.81	6652	0.764	0.253
excluding farmers	(2.95)	(9.99)	(5234)	(0.426)	(0.436)
United States					
Petty bourgeoisie	12.96	44.18	16061	0.749	0.230
excluding farmers	(2.32)	(10.22)	(17899)	(0.438)	(0.426)

Note:
[a] Standard deviations are in parentheses.

Let us first focus on the employer class. The employer class occupies the most advantageous position in the distribution of resources and rewards in both societies. In particular, its members' income and non-pecuniary rewards (home ownership and stock holdings) give them a distinct advantage over other classes in the overall structure of status stratification. In both societies, the employer class has the highest average income, the highest proportion of stock ownership, and a high proportion of home ownership: nearly over 80 per cent have their own homes and over 40 per cent hold stocks in both societies. The only exception to this dominant position is educational attainment: the employer class in both societies has a lower educational standard than the professional–managerial class and the non-manual class.

The petty bourgeois class is far less privileged than the employer class in its position in the structure of status inequality in both Japan and the United States. Its members fare better in home ownership (especially in Japan), but their other status characteristics are consistently lower than those of the employer class and are often lower, too, than those of the professional–managerial class and the non-manual class. Furthermore, the Japanese petty bourgeoisie reveals the lowest level of educational attainment. The low level of average education (9.4 years) and the high rate of home ownership (87 per cent), the two distinct characteristics of the Japanese petty bourgeoisie, can in part be explained by the fact that the Japanese petty bourgeois class includes a much larger proportion (50 per cent) of independent farmers than does the American petty bourgeois class (16 per cent). When we exclude farmers, the status composition of the Japanese petty bourgeoisie becomes closer to that of its American equivalent (see the bottom panel of Table 7.1).

The professional–managerial class is characterized by high educational achievement and occupational prestige, and to some extent by high income. Although the professional–managerial class does not control the means of production, its members' ability to control other people's labour as well as their own appears to give them an advantage over the employer class in status stratification on certain dimensions – namely, educational qualifications and occupational prestige. The American professional–managerial class tends to enjoy these status advantages to a greater degree, since its average education (13.6 years) and prestige scores (51) are higher than in the case of Japanese counterparts (12.1 years and 49, respectively).

The non-manual working class appears to occupy a position midway between the professional–managerial class and other working classes (skilled and non-skilled workers) in both societies. However, the non-manual class is much closer to the professional–managerial class in terms of level of education. Entry into the non-manual class is probably restricted by educational qualifications, although the restriction is likely to be much less severe than that in the case of the professional–managerial class. Furthermore, in the United States the non-manual class appears to occupy a more advantageous position than the professional–managerial class in terms of home ownership and stock investment: 82 per cent of the non-manual class own homes and 29 per cent hold stocks while the corresponding figures for the professional–managerial class are 67 per cent and 25 per cent, respectively. The Japanese non-manual class, however, is located below the professional–managerial class in all dimensions of status stratification.

The lower-status characteristics of the professional–managerial class in the United States is probably due to its age composition. The proportion of the young people in the professional–managerial class is greater than that in the non-manual class: the average age of the professional–managerial class is 37 years and the average age of the non-manual class is 42 years. Young professionals and managers are highly credentialized and earn good incomes, but probably have not yet invested in stocks and housing.

Finally, the skilled working class and the non-skilled working class constitute the bottom of the status hierarchy in both societies. They show consistently lower status scores on all dimensions of status stratification than do other classes. In particular, these classes are disadvantaged as regards share holding: only 15 per cent of both skilled and non-skilled workers in Japan own stocks, as do only 11 per cent of skilled workers and 9 per cent of non-skilled workers in the United States. The results suggest that stock investment is a particularly critical resource in differentiating the manual working classes from the other classes.

Overall, the status composition of classes shows a remarkable resemblance between Japan and the United States. Three important cross-national differences are, however, worth mentioning. First, the American non-skilled working class occupies the very bottom of the status hierarchy while the Japanese non-skilled working class is much closer to the skilled working class, especially in regard to its education and income levels and the extent of home ownership and stock holding. In other words, the American non-skilled working class is particularly disadvantaged in resources and rewards in the labour market: its members' average education, occupational prestige and income are all far below the averages for the skilled working class. In contrast, in Japan there is not much difference between the skilled and the non-skilled working class, except for occupational prestige: status differentiation within the manual working classes appears to be minimal in Japan.

Second, the status advantages of the American employer class are more pronounced than those of the Japanese employer class. The American employer class enjoys a particularly higher average income ($28 708) and a higher proportion of home ownership (95 per cent) than its Japanese counterpart ($10 645 and 79 per cent). A dominant structural position within the class structure – that is, exercising control over the means of production and labour – seems to yield greater returns in the United States than in Japan.[6]

However, the advantageous position of the American employer class over its Japanese counterpart may be overestimated. Japanese employers often use company facilities and assets almost as if they were personal ones, without making a sharp differentiation. In contrast, American employers tend to make a clearer distinction between personal and company property.[7] Lower average income and relative lack of personal wealth may therefore not in fact put Japanese employers at such a disadvantage compared to Americans as may at first sight appear.

Third, as briefly discussed above, the American non-manual class appears to fare better than its Japanese counterpart. While the average occupational prestige and income of American non-manual workers are much lower than those of members of the professional–managerial class, they are much more likely to own homes and stocks. In contrast, the Japanese non-manual class is less advantaged than the professional–managerial class in all dimensions of status stratification. The non-manual class in Japan shares common status characteristics with the skilled and non-skilled working class, except for educational attainment. In other words, the status characteristics among these three classes are more homogeneous in Japan than in the United States.

Table 7.2 shows the further differentiation among classes with respect to land holdings, possession of sports club membership, and air-conditioned homes in Japan. These three items, which are available only in the Japanese survey, can be used as an indicator of total

Table 7.2 Distribution (average proportion) of land holdings, possession of sports club membership and air-conditioned homes among classes in Japan (SSM)

Class	*Land holdings*	*Sports club membership*	*Air-conditioned homes*
Japan			
Employer	0.714	0.246	0.495
	(0.452)[a]	(0.432)	(0.501)
Petty bourgeoisie	0.794	0.026	0.153
	(0.405)	(0.159)	(0.360)
Professional and managerial	0.603	0.090	0.240
	(0.490)	(0.287)	(0.428)
Non-manual	0.562	0.080	0.195
	(0.497)	(0.272)	(0.397)
Skilled	0.462	0.027	0.118
	(0.499)	(0.161)	(0.324)
Semi- and non-skilled	0.545	0.023	0.133
	(0.499)	(0.150)	(0.340)
Grand mean	0.633	0.077	0.217
	(0.482)	(0.267)	(0.412)
Petty bourgeoisie excluding farmers	0.627	0.038	0.267
	(0.485)	(0.191)	(0.443)

Note:
[a] Standard deviations are in parentheses.

assets and wealth. According to Kishimoto (1978), as we have earlier noted, land holdings constitute a crucial asset for becoming 'self-sufficient' especially in the case of sudden change in economic conditions.[8] The possession of membership of golf and tennis clubs is often considered to be a status attribute because such membership is not only very expensive but also provides access to facilities which are reserved exclusively for the inner circle of wealthy people. Having an air-conditioned home conferred a similar status attribute because it was considered to be a luxurious possession in 1975 (Ozawa, 1985).

The composition of classes with respect to these three items in Japan resembles the pattern found in Table 7.1. The employer class shows the highest average proportions of the possession of sports club membership and air-conditioned homes and a high proportion of land holdings. The petty bourgeoisie is characterized by its high level of land holdings while it scores low on the other two items. In contrast, the professional–managerial class and the non-manual class score higher on possession of sports club membership and air-conditioned homes but lower on land holdings than the petty bourgeoisie. The skilled and non-skilled working classes occupy the most disadvantaged position.

What do these findings in Tables 7.1 and 7.2 tell us about the homogeneity and bipolarity hypotheses? The results do not provide support for the hypothesis of the homogeneity of status characteristics in Japan. The status make-up of classes varies considerably. The differences on all dimensions of the status stratification between the employer class and the non-skilled working class, for example, are too large to allow us to accept the claim of status homogeneity.[9] Furthermore, there is no evidence to show that Japanese classes are more status homogeneous than American ones. While status differentiation within the manual working classes (skilled and non-skilled) appears to be much smaller in Japan than in the United States, the overall patterns of status composition show a remarkable resemblance.

Kishimoto's bipolarity hypothesis does not receive much support from the findings, either. While in both societies the employer class occupies the most advantageous position in the distribution of resources and rewards and the two manual working classes constitute the bottom of status hierarchy, the remaining classes do not show any tendency towards polarization. As will become clearer in the next section, polarization is apparent only at the two extremes of the class structure.

7.3 CLASS AND STATUS INCONSISTENCY

Let us turn to the issue of status consistency and inconsistency among classes. Figure 7.1 is a diagram of the composition of classes along five different dimensions of status stratification in Japan and the United States, and Figure 7.2 is a diagram of the composition of classes along three further dimensions in Japan. Each status scale is now standardized by subtracting the mean and dividing by the standard deviation, so that all status dimensions have the same scaling. Figures 7.1 and 7.2 show the extent of status consistency and inconsistency for different classes. If classes are status-consistent, the lines will be relatively straight and run parallel to each other. If classes are status-inconsistent, the lines will show a zigzag pattern and intersect each other. Major features of Figures 7.1 and 7.2 can be summarized in five points.

First, the two manual working classes in both societies score consistently low on all status characteristics. The skilled and non-skilled working classes constitute the bottom of the status hierarchies and show a strong tendency towards 'low-status' consistency.

Second, the most status-inconsistent class is the professional–managerial class. Both in Japan and in the United States, the

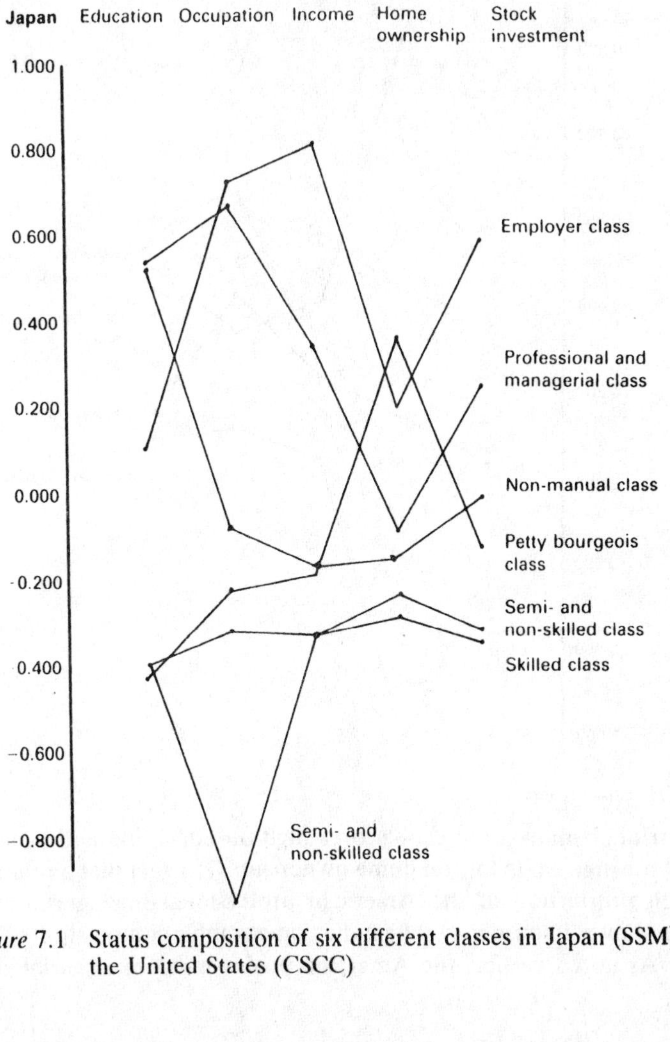

Figure 7.1 Status composition of six different classes in Japan (SSM) and the United States (CSCC)

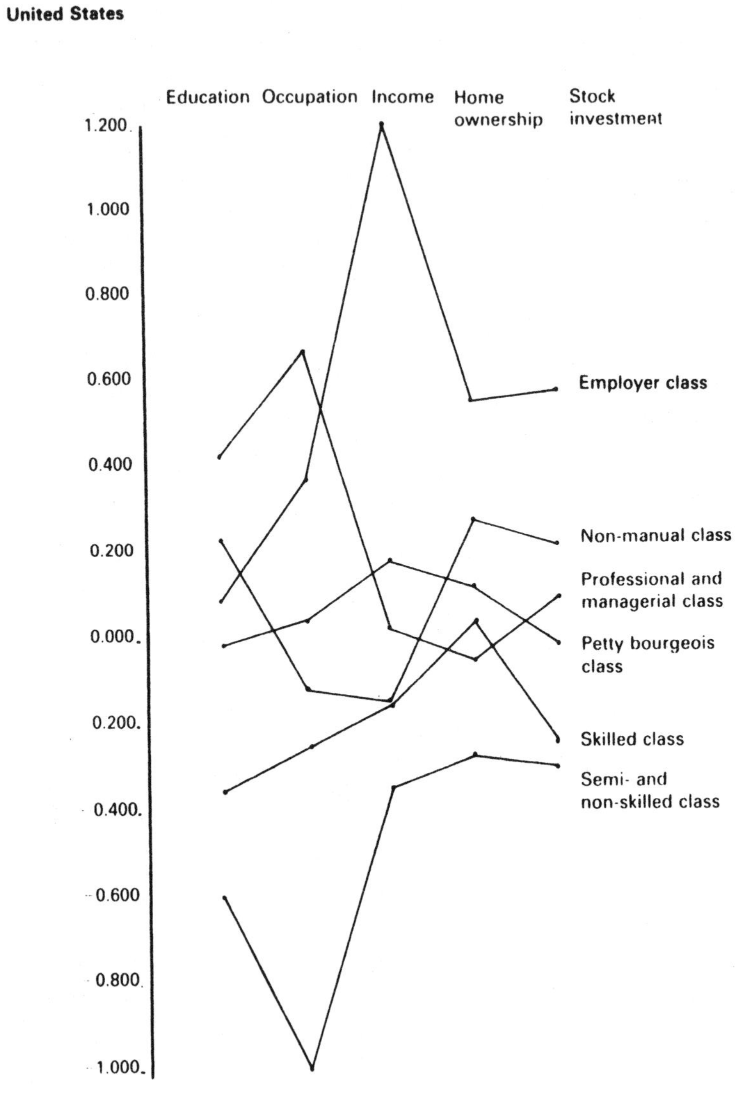

Fig. 7.1 *continued*

professional–managerial class scores high on education and occupational prestige while low on home ownership. The fact that a relatively high proportion of the American professional–managerial class does not own a house may reflect the demographic composition of the class. As noted earlier, the American professional–managerial class

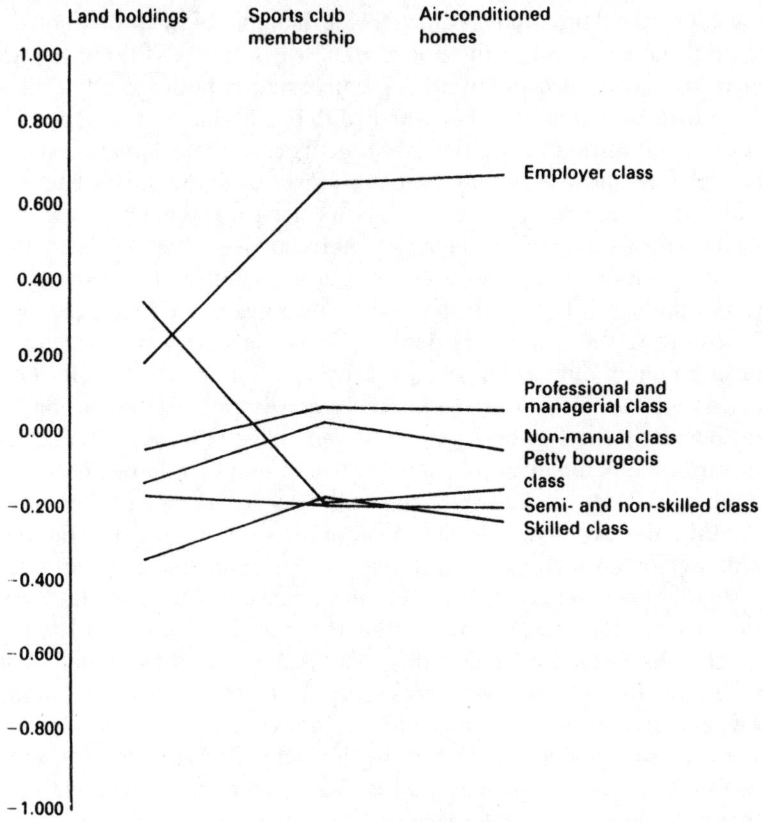

Figure 7.2 Composition of six different classes with respect to land holdings, possession of sports club membership and air-conditioned homes in Japan (SSM)

contains a relatively higher proportion of the young working labour force who may not yet have sufficient financial resources to purchase their own home. In fact, the proportion of home ownership among the American professional–managerial class jumps from 66.6 to 86.6 per cent when the sample is restricted to men aged 35 and over. This increase is far more dramatic than the increase in, for example, the non-manual class (from 81.5 to 89.9 per cent).

Third, in both Japan and the United States the employer class generally occupies the upper end of the status hierarchies. It shows a tendency towards 'high-status' consistency. However, its position in the educational hierarchy is much lower than that of the professional–managerial class and of the non-manual class. There is therefore an inconsistent status element among employers in both societies.

Fourth, a striking cross-national difference can be found in the status composition of the petty bourgeois class. The Japanese petty bourgeoisie shows a strong tendency towards status inconsistency, while its American counterpart shows a strong tendency towards status consistency. The Japanese petty bourgeoisie occupies the lowest position in the educational hierarchy but at the same time shows the highest proportion of home ownership and land holdings. In contrast, the American petty bourgeoisie occupies an average position on all dimensions of status stratification; its relative position across status hierarchies is extremely consistent. The exclusion of farmers from the Japanese petty bourgeois class reduces the tendency towards status inconsistency, but Japanese non-farm proprietors remain more status-inconsistent than the American petty bourgeoisie.

Fifth, the non-manual class also shows cross-national variation, although on a smaller scale. The Japanese non-manual class occupies a slightly low-average position on all dimensions of status stratification, except for educational attainment where it is located at the top of the distribution. In contrast, the American non-manual class fluctuates around the mean status score. Its levels of education, home ownership and stock holdings are well above the mean, but occupational prestige and income fall below the mean. The status composition of the American non-manual class is thus much more inconsistent than that of its Japanese counterpart.

Table 7.3 summarizes the tendencies towards status consistency or inconsistency among the different classes in Japan and the United States. These tendencies are generally similar in the two societies: the employer class, the skilled working class and the non-skilled working class can be characterized as status-consistent classes, while the professional–managerial class is status-inconsistent. However, diverging tendencies are found in the case of the petty bourgeois class and the non-manual class. Status inconsistency is the characteristic of the Japanese petty bourgeoisie, while it is the characteristic of the non-manual class in the United States.

Overall, our results do not support the statement that Japanese classes are more status-inconsistent than American classes; this would apply only to the petty bourgeois class. However, the fact that the majority (50 per cent) of the Japanese petty bourgeoisie are independent farmers accounts in part for the highly inconsistent

Table 7.3 Tendency towards status consistency and inconsistency among various classes in Japan (SSM) and the United States (CSCC)

Class	*Japan*	*United States*
Employer	Consistent	Consistent
Petty bourgeoisie	Strongly inconsistent	Strongly consistent
Professional and managerial	Inconsistent	Strongly inconsistent
Non-manual	Weakly consistent	Inconsistent
Skilled	Strongly consistent	Consistent
Semi- and non-skilled	Consistent	Strongly consistent

status characteristics. The exclusion of farmers clearly reduces the tendency towards status inconsistency.

It is furthermore important to notice that status inconsistency is not a characteristic of the society as a whole, as Imada and Hara (1979) have suggested. At the two extremes of the class structure – that is, among the employers who have control over both the means of production and labour and among the manual working classes who lack such control – status characteristics are either consistently high or consistently low in Japan and the United States. The class which occupies the most dominant position in the social relations of production tends to occupy the most advantageous position within status hierarchies, and those classes which lack crucial resources in the social relations of production are located at the bottom of the status stratification. As far as the extremes of the class structure are concerned, status consistency dominates.

Status inconsistency seems to prevail among the professional–managerial class and to some extent among the non-manual class. These classes are characterized as holding one but not all of the crucial resources in the social relations of production: the professional–managerial class controls labour power; and the non-manual working class holds an advantage in the nature of its work over manual workers. These classes may be viewed as occupying a partially dominant position in the class structure, or to borrow Wright's (1979; 1980a) term, occupying a 'contradictory location' within the social relations of production.[10] The partial dominance and contradictory characteristics of these classes seem to correspond with the inconsistency of their status characteristics. This is particularly true for the professional–managerial class. High educational standard and occupational prestige are probably used by the members of the professional–managerial class to justify exercising authority within organizational hierarchies and enjoying a greater extent of autonomy (Ehrenreich and Ehrenreich, 1979; Bowles and Gintis, 1976). However, their lack of control over the means of production is reflected in their much lower position in the hierarchies of pecuniary and non-pecuniary rewards (income, home ownership and share holdings).

The non-manual class appears to be subject to the same mechanism of correspondence between position in the class structure and position in status hierarchies. The advantage of the non-manual workers over manual workers is probably derived from their superior educational standards. However, other status characteristics of non-manual workers are similar to those of skilled workers, thus suggesting that both are located in similar positions within the class structure.

7.4 STATUS DIFFERENTIATION BY FIRM SIZE AMONG EMPLOYEES

The dual structure hypothesis focuses upon differentiation among employees. It predicts that in Japan employees are not only stratified by class position but also by firm size: workers in large firms tend to have more advantageous status characteristics than those in small and medium-sized firms even though they occupy the same class position. Table 7.4 shows the distribution of status characteristics by class and firm size among employees. Two findings emerge from Table 7.4. First, in Japan workers in large firms have higher levels of education, occupational status and income than those in small and medium-sized firms within each class of employee: all the *t*-statistics testing the difference in means by firm size are significant. In addition, among the professional–managerial class and the skilled working class, workers in large firms are more likely to hold stocks than their counterparts in small and medium-sized firms. Firm size appears to be a powerful factor in differentiating employees within classes.

Second, in the United States the differentiation by firm size appears to be present only among the professional–managerial class. Professional and managerial workers who are employed in a large firm have higher levels of education, occupational status, income and home ownership than those who work in a small and medium-sized firm. However, among non-manual, skilled, and non-skilled workers,

Table 7.4 Distribution of status characteristics among employees by class and firm size in Japan (SSM) and the United States (CSCC)

Class	*Firm size*	*Education*	*Occupation*	*Income*	*Home ownership*	*Stock investment*
Japan						
Professional and managerial	Large	12.75	51.74	9484	0.692	0.486
	Small	11.46	47.04	7554	0.634	0.328
		(t = 5.67)[a]	(t = 4.37)	(t = 6.82)	(t = 1.44)	(t = 3.81)
Non-manual	Large	12.69	41.37	6810	0.651	0.325
	Small	11.53	39.87	5960	0.623	0.257
		(t = 4.19)	(t = 2.36)	(t = 3.81)	(t = 0.53)	(t = 1.41)
Skilled	Large	10.18	39.48	6585	0.638	0.225
	Small	9.20	37.06	5123	0.544	0.104
		(t = 3.23)	(t = 3.04)	(t = 5.04)	(t = 1.41)	(t = 2.61)
Semi- and and non-skilled	Large	9.92	32.16	6368	0.626	0.200
	Small	9.33	29.69	5256	0.583	0.130
		(t = 2.48)	(t = 2.94)	(t = 4.24)	(t = 0.78)	(t = 1.75)
United States						
Professional and managerial	Large	13.84	52.38	14564	0.713	0.239
	Small	12.85	47.02	11181	0.537	0.268
		(t = 2.93)	(t = 3.24)	(t = 2.41)	(t = 2.67)	(t = 0.47)
Non-manual	Large	12.93	40.73	11481	0.807	0.333
	Small	13.57	41.11	12091	0.868	0.132
		(t = 1.06)	(t = 0.12)	(t = 0.29)	(t = 0.49)	(t = 1.37)
Skilled	Large	11.47	39.52	11645	0.770	0.100
	Small	11.49	38.33	11049	0.611	0.129
		(t = 0.04)	(t = 1.25)	(t = 0.47)	(t = 1.61)	(t = 0.42)
Semi- and non-skilled	Large	10.86	29.68	9657	0.607	0.107
	Small	10.69	29.95	7844	0.490	0.050
		(t = 0.45)	(t = 0.25)	(t = 2.10)	(t = 1.48)	(t = 1.26)

Note:
a *T*-statistics testing the difference in means between large firms (500 or more employees) and small firms (less than 500 employees) are shown in parentheses.

firm size does not seem to affect the distribution of status characteristics. The only exception is the income difference among non-skilled workers, in that non-skilled workers who are employed in large firms have a higher average income than those who are employed in small and medium-sized firms.

There is therefore a striking cross-national variation in the role of firm size in explaining differentiation among employees. In Japan, firm size seems to be an important variable in explaining internal differentiation among all classes of employee, whereas in the United States its impact appears to be limited to the professional–managerial class. The significant difference in status attributes by firm size found in Japan supports the dual structure hypothesis.

The importance of firm size, however, does not undermine the effect of class on the distribution of status characteristics in Japan. Class differences in status attributes are found among employees in large firms and those in small and medium-sized firms alike.[11] There is no evidence that firm size *replaces* class in explaining inequality of status attributes among Japanese employees.

However, differentiation among manual workers is more likely to be affected by firm size than by skill level in Japan. Manual workers in large firms have higher average levels of education, income and stock holdings than workers in small firms, but no significant differences in these status attributes are found between manual workers with different skill levels. In other words, firm size appears to be more consequential than skill level in explaining the unequal distribution of status attributes among manual workers in Japan.

7.5 COMPARISON OF THE PREDICTIVE POWER OF CLASS, EDUCATION AND OCCUPATION

The next issue which we will address is the predictive power of class in explaining the inequality of the rewards in the labour market. Among the five different dimensions of status stratification, income, home ownership and stock holdings can be viewed as rewards in the labour market, and education and occupational status can be seen as resources which produce rewards (Coleman and Rainwater, 1978).[12] The distinction between rewards and resources is arbitrary since education, for example, can be both a resource which tends to yield income and other non-pecuniary benefits and a reward in itself. However, the rewards are generally the result of an effective exercise of the resources. The primary focus in this section, therefore, is the comparison between the effect of class and the effect of education and of occupation on the inequality of income, home ownership and stock holdings. It is a comparison of the explanatory power of various resources in determining the rewards in stratified societies. It is particularly important to assess whether class – that is, individual position in the social relations of production – is an equally important determinant of the inequality in income and non-pecuniary benefits as occupational status and education.

Table 7.5 shows the results of change in the explained variance (R^2) when class, education, or occupational status are added to the regression equation predicting income, home ownership and stock holdings.[13] Change in R^2 represents the amount of variance in labour market rewards explained by each labour market resource.

The most striking finding is that class is far more important than education and occupational status in explaining inequality in income, home ownership and stock holdings in Japan and the United States. The percentage of variance explained by class surpasses that by education or occupational status in virtually all aspects of stratification, regardless of controlling and not controlling for other variables. The R^2 values in the column of simple regression (Table 7.5 column 1) show how much of the variance in labour market rewards is explained by class or education or occupational status alone; they can be seen as the total explanatory power of each individual resource. Class shows the strongest total explanatory power. In particular, the inequality in home ownership is primarily affected by individuals' positions in the class structure.

Class shows much stronger explanatory power than education and occupational status even after some controls are added. When class differences in background characteristics are controlled (see Table 7.5, column 2), the predictive power of class is reduced from the total explanatory power. But it is still significant and greater than the impact of education and occupation.[14] Even after controlling for the difference in educational and occupational composition among classes (see Table 7.5, column 3), the net impact of class on income, home ownership and stock holdings is significant and greater than that of education and occupational status, except for the effect of education on stock investment in Japan.

The second crucial finding in Table 7.5 is that the patterns of relative explanatory power of class, education and occupational status are extremely similar in the two societies: (1) the inequality in

Table 7.5 Proportion of variance explained (R^2 adjusted) by class, education and occupation in Japan (SSM) and the United States (CSCC)

	Income			*Home ownership*			*Stock investment*		
	1	2	*3*	*1*	2	*3*	*1*	2	*3*
Japan									
Class	0.147**	0.076**	0.027**	0.060**	0.037**	0.035**	0.086**	0.051**	0.017**
Education	0.039**	0.048**	0.013**	0.008**	0.002*	0.001	0.047**	0.052**	0.022**
Occupation	0.125**	0.076**	0.020**	0.001	0.002*	0.000	0.067**	0.042**	0.005*
United States									
Class	0.161**	0.125**	0.097**	0.047**	0.023**	0.015**	0.066**	0.045**	0.016**
Education	0.059**	0.069**	0.026**	0.000	0.011**	0.003*	0.047**	0.044**	0.011**
Occupation	0.084**	0.050**	0.005**	0.003*	0.005**	0.000	0.051**	0.030**	0.001

Notes:
1 Simple regression with no control.
2 After controlling for background characteristics.
3 After controlling for all other variables.
* The explained variance is significant at 0.05 level with the SSM sample size.
** The explained variance is significant at 0.05 level with the CSCC sample size.

home ownership is explained primarily by class, (2) the inequality in stock investment is explained primarily by class and education, and (3) income differentiation is determined by class and to some extent by education and occupation.

The third finding in Table 7.5 is that the effect of class on income, home ownership and stock holdings is not the result of the status composition of the class. As shown in column 3 of each sub-table, even after controlling for the educational and occupational difference among classes, class remains an important determinant of the inequality in income, home ownership and stock investment. The effect of class is independent of the status characteristics of class.

7.6 SOURCES OF THE EFFECTS OF CLASS ON LABOUR MARKET REWARDS

This section will compare the effect of different class categories on the stratification of various rewards in the society. We have already examined the status characteristics of classes, but this section will further analyze possible sources of rewards differentiation among classes. The primary question asked in this section is: are the differences in rewards between classes due to differences in compositional characteristics of class – namely, social background, education and occupation? The higher average income of the employer class, for example, may be due to its advantageous social background, education and occupational status. The background and status compositions of classes may explain the class differences in rewards in the society. We will therefore compare the impact of class on rewards before and after controlling for background characteristics, education and occupational status.

Table 7.6 presents the effect of individual class categories on income, home ownership and stock holdings. Since the base category is the non-skilled working class, the coefficients indicate the difference in labour market rewards between the non-skilled working class and the class category in question. For example, the first entry for the employer class in Japan (5120) means that the average income difference between the non-skilled worker and the employer is $5120 when no other variables are controlled for.

In both societies, the employer class has a definite advantage over the non-skilled working class in all aspects of stratification in labour market rewards; their income is $5120 more, the proportion of

Table 7.6 Effects (metric regression coefficients) of individual class categories on income, home ownership and stock investment in Japan (SSM) and the United States[a] (CSCC)

	Income			*Home ownership*			*Stock investment*		
	1	2	3	*1*	2	3	*1*	2	3
Japan									
Employer	5120**	3957**	2270**	0.225**	0.218**	0.194**	0.416**	0.344**	0.226**
	(358)	(362)	(392)	(0.038)	(0.039)	(0.043)	(0.038)	(0.039)	(0.043)
Petty bourgeoisie	522	300	–428	0.290**	0.244**	0.234**	0.109*	0.082*	0.031
	(311)	(306)	(307)	(0.033)	(0.033)	(0.034)	(0.033)	(0.033)	(0.033)
Professional and	2883**	2198**	385	0.062	0.068*	0.039	0.271**	0.222**	0.081*
managerial	(315)	(313)	(349)	(0.033)	(0.034)	(0.039)	(0.034)	(0.034)	(0.038)
Non-manual	781*	937*	–119	0.075*	0.114*	0.096*	0.146**	0.129*	0.041
	(347)	(341)	(345)	(0.036)	(0.037)	(0.038)	(0.037)	(0.037)	(0.037)
Skilled	–161	–140	–632	0.005	0.015	0.012	–0.016	–0.017	–0.040
	(383)	(369)	(366)	(0.040)	(0.039)	(0.040)	(0.041)	(0.040)	(0.040)
United States									
Employer	19951**	17565**	12905**	0.384**	0.303**	0.259**	0.367**	0.299**	0.200**
	(1971)	(2007)	(2141)	(0.075)	(0.072)	(0.079)	(0.067)	(0.070)	(0.077)
Petty bourgeoisie	4546**	2779**	–1135	0.190**	0.134*	0.095*	0.093*	0.050	–0.034
	(2200)	(2187)	(2227)	(0.084)	(0.079)	(0.083)	(0.075)	(0.077)	(0.080)
Professional and	4971**	3164**	–1986	0.084*	0.096*	0.049	0.181**	0.143**	0.034
managerial	(1327)	(1348)	(1671)	(0.051)	(0.049)	(0.062)	(0.045)	(0.047)	(0.060)
Non-manual	2505*	97	–3521*	0.220**	0.180**	0.140*	0.224**	0.183**	0.106*
	(1936)	(1924)	(1957)	(0.074)	(0.069)	(0.073)	(0.066)	(0.067)	(0.070)
Skilled	2284*	423	–1078	0.157**	0.133**	0.123**	0.016	–0.020	–0.052
	(1693)	(1685)	(1688)	(0.065)	(0.061)	(0.063)	(0.058)	(0.059)	(0.060)

Notes:
[a] The non-skilled working class is the base category.
1 Simple regression with no control.
2 After controlling for background characteristics.
3 After controlling for all other variables.
* The effect is significant at 0.05 level with the SSM sample size.
** The effect is significant at 0.05 level with the CSCC sample size.

people who own houses is 23 per cent more, and the proportion of people who hold stocks is 42 per cent more than that of the non-skilled working class in Japan. The figures for the United States are more dramatic: $19 951, 38 per cent, and 37 per cent difference, respectively. Moreover, the advantage is not explained by the difference in background characteristics, education and occupational status between the employer class and the non-skilled working class.

Even though the extent of the advantage is slightly reduced by controlling for background factors, education and occupational status, the advantage of the employer class remains substantial. In other words, the privileged position of the employer class over the non-skilled working class is not primarily the result of advantageous background characteristics and superior education and occupational status. Structural location within the social relations of production yields an independent impact on the inequality of income and non-pecuniary rewards.

In contrast, the advantage of the professional–managerial class over the non-skilled working class is primarily due to superior education and occupational prestige in both societies. Average income and proportion of stock investment are significantly higher than that of the non-skilled working class, but once the difference in educational and occupational characteristics between the professional–managerial class and the non-skilled working class is controlled for, the advantage of income and stock investment disappears or is substantially reduced. The same pattern is found among the Japanese non-manual class. An advantage in income and stock investment over the non-skilled working class is primarily due to superior education and occupational prestige. Compositional characteristics explain the privileged position of the Japanese non-manual class.

The Japanese petty bourgeois class differs from the non-skilled working class in home ownership and stock investment patterns. The significantly higher proportion of home ownership is independent of background characteristics, education and occupation. Like the employer class, the Japanese petty bourgeois class derives an advantage in home ownership from its location in the social relations of production.

The American petty bourgeois class differs from the non-skilled working class in all aspects of labour market rewards. Although the sources of higher home ownership are independent of compositional characteristics, the higher income and higher proportion of stock investment are explained by background characteristics, education and occupation. In other words, an advantage over the non-skilled working class in these respects is mainly due to compositional advantages.

The Japanese skilled working class is not significantly advantaged over the Japanese non-skilled working class. In contrast, the American skilled working class shows a higher proportion of home ownership, even after controlling for compositional characteristics.

In sum, the sources of advantage among the professional–managerial class and the Japanese non-manual class appear to come from superior education and occupational status. Similarly, the American petty bourgeois class shows higher income than the American non-skilled working class, primarily because of better education and occupational status. However, in other instances, when the effects of class are present, they are generally independent of compositional characteristics of classes. Social background and status characteristics of class do not generally explain away the influence of class on inequality in rewards in the society. In particular, the distinct advantage enjoyed by the employer class appears to come from its location in the class structure.

7.7 CLASS, EDUCATION AND LABOUR MARKET REWARDS

We have already seen in Chapter 4 how educational attainment affects occupational and income achievement. The purpose of this chapter is to specify this relationship between education and labour market rewards within the structural context of class. The impact of education on income, home ownership and stock investment will be examined within each class category. The analysis will allow us to determine whether the returns to education are homogeneous across all class categories.

Table 7.7 shows the effect of education on income, home ownership and stock investment after controlling for social background variables, labour market experience and decay for different class categories in Japan and the United States.[15] The brackets on the right side of the coefficients present the results of the *t*-test on the difference of the effect of education among different class categories. For example, the brackets for the effect of education on income in Japan shows that the coefficient for the employer class (916) is different from the rest of the class categories while the coefficients of education

Table 7.7 Effects of education on labour market rewards controlling for social background, labour market experience and decay for different class categories in Japan (SSM) and the United States (CSCC)

	Income	*Home ownership*	*Stock in investment*
Japan			
Employer	916	NS	0.069
Petty bourgeoisie	NS	NS	0.042
Professional and managerial	321	NS	0.032
Non-manual	385	NS	0.037
Skilled	250	NS	0.032
Non-skilled	284	NS	0.025
United States			
Employer	4247	NS	0.061
Petty bourgeoisie	3205	NS	0.040
Professional and managerial	1067	NS	0.031
Non-manual	1319	NS	– 0.105
Skilled	532	NS	0.026
Non-skilled	248	0.075	0.022
Japan			
Petty bourgeoisie excluding farmers	NS	NS	0.034
United States			
Petty bourgeoisie excluding farmers	3425	NS	0.053

Note:
NS indicates that the effect of education is not significant at 0.05 level with the SSM sample size.

for the professional–managerial class (321), the non-manual class (385), the skilled working class (250), and the non-skilled working class (284) are not significantly different from one another.

Several important observations can be drawn from Table 7.7. First, home ownership is virtually independent of educational attainment in all class categories in both societies. The only case when educational attainment helps one obtain a home is among the non-skilled working class in the United States, but the effect is not substantial. It therefore appears that educational attainment is not relevant to home ownership for all class categories in both societies.

Second, the effects of education on stock investment appear to be homogeneous across all classes in Japan and the United States, except for the American non-manual class.[16] Educational attainment increases the chance of stock holdings in virtually all class categories, and the effects are not significantly different from each other.[17]

Third, the relationship between education and income attainment is substantially influenced by class position in both societies. In Japan, the effects of education on income are different among three groups: (1) the employer class, (2) the petty bourgeois class, and (3) the remaining working classes. The employer class has the greatest advantage in converting investment in human capital into monetary rewards. The income returns to education ($916) are more than twice as much as the average returns for the entire working class.

In contrast, the Japanese petty bourgeois class does not seem to benefit from education as far as income attainment is concerned. As we have seen in Table 7.1 (p. 213), the average income of the petty bourgeois class ($6191) is slightly higher than that of the skilled ($5571) and the non-skilled ($5579) working class. However, unlike the working classes, education does not seem to help produce financial benefits among the Japanese petty bourgeoisie. The sources of monetary success are independent of educational attainment.

The lack of significant effect of education on income is unaltered even after excluding the farmers. As shown in the bottom panel of Table 7.7, among the non-farm petty bourgeoisie, of whom the majority are small shopholders, income returns to education are not significant. The structural location of the petty bourgeoisie, comprising both farmers and small shopholders, is such that education yields no income returns whatsoever in Japan.

The Japanese professional–managerial class, the non-manual class, the skilled working class and the non-skilled working class show a similar relationship between education and income attainment. The average income increase is about $343. It is important to note that the professional–managerial class and the non-manual class do not show higher income returns to education than the skilled and the non-skilled working class in Japan. We already know that education is used as a major screening device for the entry into the professional–

managerial class and the non-manual class (see Table 7.1). However, after entry, the extent that education differentiates financial rewards among the members of these classes is not noticeably stronger than that among the members of the skilled and the non-skilled classes. The effects of education on monetary returns are modest and identical to those for the skilled and the non-skilled working class in Japan.

The income returns to education appear to be homogeneous across all classes which are excluded from control over the means of production. The results suggest that the difference in income returns to education in Japan derives primarily from control, or lack of control, over the means of production. The differentiation in income returns among the various working classes is negligible in Japan.

Different patterns of the effect of class on the relationship between education and income are found in the United States. As shown in the brackets used on Table 7.7, the effects of education on income are different among three groups: (1) the employer class and the petty bourgeois class, (2) the professional–managerial class and the non-manual class, and (3) the skilled and the non-skilled working class.

Both the employer class and the petty bourgeois class enjoy larger income returns to education than other classes. Each additional year of education increases income on the average by $4247 for the employer class and $3205 for the petty bourgeois class. Unlike the Japanese petty bourgeois class, which showed no relationship between education and income, the American petty bourgeoisie appears to occupy as equally an advantageous location in the labour market as the employer class, as far as the ability to convert education into financial success is concerned.

The professional–managerial class and the non-manual class in the United States appear to occupy a less advantageous position than the employer and the petty bourgeois class but a more advantageous one than the skilled and the non-skilled working class in the financial benefit of education. Each additional year of education produces on the average $1067 increase in income for the professional–managerial class and $1319 increase for the non-manual class. Education seems to be used as a device to allocate monetary rewards among the professional–managerial class and the non-manual class, more so than among the skilled and non-skilled workers in the United States.

Finally, the skilled and the non-skilled working classes in the United States enjoy a modest income increase of $532 and $248, respectively for an additional year of schooling. The differentiation in the income returns to education in the United States occurs not only along the dimension of the control over the means of production but also along the lines of authority, autonomy and the non-manual nature of work.

In summary, the way in which class conditions the relationship between education and labour market rewards is dependent on the kinds of labour market reward. Home ownership is independent of educational attainment in virtually all class categories in both societies. The increase in education leads to higher stock investment in virtually all class categories in both societies. As far as these two labour market rewards are concerned, the effects of education appear to be independent of class position.

In contrast, class conditions the impact of education on income. In both societies, income returns to education are different depending upon class position. An additional year of schooling produces different increases in financial benefits among different classes, and therefore the effects of education on income are not homogeneous across positions in the class structure.

7.8 SUMMARY AND CONCLUSION

This chapter focused on the interplay among class, status and labour market rewards. The first substantive point addressed in this chapter was the issue of the relationship between class structure and status hierarchies in contemporary Japan. Our analysis was aimed at testing four hypotheses about the status composition of classes: the status homogeneity hypothesis, the bipolarity hypothesis, the status inconsistency hypothesis and the dual structure hypothesis.

The results of our analysis are consistent with the prediction of the dual structure hypothesis. Employees in large firms tend to have more favourable status attributes than those in small and medium-sized firms, even though they occupy the same class position in Japan. Firm size appears to be an important source of status differentiation among Japanese employees. In particular, Japanese manual workers are more likely to be stratified by firm size than by skill level.

The results of our analysis also provide partial support for the bipolarity and the status inconsistency hypotheses. At the extremes of the Japanese class structure, the tendency toward status consistency dominates; the employer class is located at the most advantaged positions in the distribution of most status characteristics, while the skilled and the non-skilled working classes are located at the bottom of all status hierarchies. However, classes which occupy partially dominant and 'contradictory' locations in the social relations of production (Wright, 1979; 1980a) tend to show status inconsistency. The professional–managerial class and the petty bourgeoisie are characterized by a combination of high-status scores on some dimensions and low-status scores on other dimensions of status hierarchies. Neither the bipolarity nor the status inconsistency, however, appears to be a generalized feature of Japanese society.

A cross-national comparison of the relationship between class structure and status hierarchies in Japan and the United States suggests that a combination of polarization and inconsistency of status attributes characterizes both Japanese and American class structure. There seems to be little empirical evidence for claiming that status inconsistency is more pronounced in Japan than in the United States (cf. Okamoto, 1982). American class structure can be characterized as being equally status-inconsistent, since the overall status composition of classes is similar in the two countries. However, an important cross-national variation is found in the effect of firm size. Status differentiation by firm size among employees is much more clearly documented in Japan than in the United States. In particular, among Japanese manual workers, firm size seems to be more important than skill level in differentiating status attributes, while American manual workers are stratified by skill level with respect to their status characteristics but not by firm size. The cross-national difference highlights the importance of firm size as a basis of status differentiation in Japan.

The second substantive point addressed in this chapter was the issue of comparing the predictive power of class with that of education and occupational status in explaining inequality in the labour market. The most striking finding is that class is far more important than education and occupational status in explaining inequality in income, home ownership and stock investment both in Japan and the United States. Furthermore, the effect of class is independent of the status characteristics of class; class continues to show a generally stronger explanatory power than education and occupational status, even after controlling for class differences in background characteristics, educational level and occupational prestige.

The results are consistent with earlier studies in the United States (Wright and Perrone, 1977; Wright, 1979, 1985; Kalleberg and Griffin, 1980). Our findings imply that any serious studies of stratification in labour market should take into account structural position in the social relations of production and marketable skills; class appears to be at least as powerful a determinant of financial inequality as education and occupational status in the United States.

The findings cast doubt on the emergence of 'the new middle mass' in Japan (Murakami, 1984). Despite the claim that differences in income and living styles between classes appear to have diminished in Japan, our results indicate that class is the strongest determinant of income inequality as well as home ownership in Japan. Class appears to be a critical variable in explaining inequality in Japanese society, probably more so than educational credentials or occupational status.

The final issue discussed in this chapter was to specify the process of the attainment of labour market rewards within the context of class structure. The effects of education on income, home ownership and stock investment were examined separately within each class category. The results of this chapter suggest that class strongly structures the impact of education on income both in Japan and the United States. Income returns to education are not homogeneous across all class positions. This finding has serious implications for the idea of 'Japan as an educational credentials society'. This idea assumes that once one obtains educational credentials, they will increase socio-economic benefits regardless of position in the society. However, the way in which education is converted into monetary success varies depending upon class position. Among the Japanese petty bourgeoisie, education does not increase the total individual income; education is not relevant for improving the financial prospect of the people who belong to this class. In contrast, the Japanese employer class is able to convert education into monetary rewards most effectively; the rate of income returns to education is highest among the employers. The effect of education on monetary success is therefore not homogeneous across all segments of Japanese society.

Overall, the results of this chapter highlighted the importance of class, defined by the social relations of production and marketable skills. Class not only determines the unequal distribution of rewards in the society regardless of the status composition of classes, but also structures how status characteristics affect labour market rewards. These dual roles of class in the determination of inequality in Japanese society deserve special attention.

Notes

1. Murakami's original argument (1977) emphasizes the homogeneity of status characteristics. However, in his later book (Murakami, 1984), he appears to emphasize 'non-structuration' of various status characteristics, and this view is then much closer to the status inconsistency hypothesis than to his original homogeneity hypothesis. In fact, he cites the work by Imada and Hara (1979) to support his argument.
2. The notion of dual structure was first introduced into academic discourse in Japan in the 1950s (e.g., Arisawa, 1956). This idea paid attention to the differences in productivity, technology and working conditions between large firms and small and medium-sized firms. The notion resembles the dual labour market theory developed in the United States (Doeringer and Piore, 1971), but in Japan the emphasis is on the dual structure created by firm size, rather than on the primary and secondary labour market sectors.
3. This argument is not new but should be distinguished from the idea of the 'new middle class' in the late 1950s which referred to the emerging white-collar 'salary men' (cf. Okouchi, 1960; Vogel, 1963).
4. The only exception is a study by Hashimoto (1986) which showed that income difference by class was not explained by education and occupational status.
5. Because the analysis of the British data-set is not included in this chapter, the age range which is covered in this chapter is 20 to 65 years old, thus making the analysis consistent with my previous work (Ishida, 1986; 1989).
6. Figure 7.1 visually demonstrates the greater returns for the American employer class than for its Japanese counterpart.
7. I am grateful to Professor Ezra Vogel for suggesting this point.
8. Ishizaki (1983) also showed that land assets were more unequally distributed in Japan than individual income.
9. The *t*-statistics testing the difference in means between the employer class and the non-skilled working class are significant on all dimensions of status hierarchies.
10. Wright does not, however, identify the non-manual working class as a separate class. His working class includes my non-manual, skilled and non-skilled workers (see Wright, 1980b). Wright does not model the differentiation among the working class into his class framework.
11. The *t*-statistics testing the effect of class on status attributes were computed separately for employees in large firms and in small and medium-sized firms. Class generally exerted significant effects on all status attributes except for home ownership. The effect of class on home ownership was not significant among all employees regardless of firm size.
12. The distinction between rewards and resources is closely related to the notion of relational and distributive approaches to stratification advocated by Goldthorpe (1972).
13. Since the sample size is small in CSCC and class is represented by five dummy variables using the non-skilled working class as the base category,

R^2 is adjusted by the degrees of freedom. The R^2 values reported in the body of this chapter are, therefore, the values of the adjusted R^2. Similarly, due to the small sample size of CSCC ($N = 514$), I used the SSM sample size ($N = 1953$) to calculate the significance of the coefficients for both samples. Education is measured by years of schooling, and occupation is measured by the international occupational prestige scores (see Chapter 2 for details).

14. The background characteristics include class background (represented by five dummy variables), urban background, farm origin and labour market experience and decay. For the American data, race is added as a control. See Chapter 2 and Chapter 6 for detailed discussion on the variables. The figures indicate the additional proportion of variance explained by class, or education, or occupation over and above the background characteristics.
15. Whenever the figures in Table 7.7 are reported in the body of the paper, the effect indicates the direct effect of education after controlling for social background variables, labour market experience and decay. Education is measured by years of schooling. The figures in Table 7.7 represent unstandardized regression coefficients. For example, the figure for the Japanese employer (916) implied that an additional year of schooling increases income by $916 after controlling for other factors.
16. The negative effect of education on stock investment is found for the American non-manual class. It is not clear why the increase in education leads to the decreasing tendency towards stock investment among the American non-manual workers. Further investigation of the data-set suggests that the attenuated spread of education among the American non-manual class is probably responsible for the negative coefficient: the range of education is between nine and 16 years. The estimate of the effect of education becomes unstable due to a smaller range of educational attainment among the non-manual workers.
17. In Japan, the t-test for the difference between the effect of education for the employer class (0.069) and that for the non-skilled working class (0.025) is significant at the 0.05 level ($t = 2.29$). However, since the t-tests for all other pairs are not significant, the results suggest that (1) all class categories, except the non-skilled working class, appear to have the same effect, and at the same time, (2) all class categories, except the employer class, have the same effect. It is therefore difficult to claim that the effect of the employer class and that of the non-skilled class are different. In the United States, the effect of education for the employer class (0.061) is significantly different from that for the non-skilled working class (0.022): the t-statistic testing the difference in coefficients is 2.05. However, as in Japan, the t-tests for other pairs (excluding the pairs which involve the non-manual class) were not significant. It is therefore more reasonable to claim that the effect of the employer class and that of the non-skilled working class are not different.

8 Conclusions and Prospects

In this final chapter, we return to the substantive themes underlying this study that were spelled out in Chapter 1. These substantive themes have not been dealt with in an ordered fashion nor concentrated in one chapter; It is therefore useful to attempt to bring together the findings from various chapters under a number of headings.[1]

8.1 THE STATUS ATTAINMENT PROCESS AND INDUSTRIALISM

The thesis of industrialism was the underlying theme of this comparative study of social mobility in Japan, the United States and Britain. As stated in Chapter 1, this thesis claims that since industrializing nations are subject to a common set of technological imperatives, in the long run their core structures will become increasingly similar, and that the principles in allocation of social positions will shift from particularistic to universalistic criteria (Kerr *et al.*, 1960; Feldman and Moore, 1962; Treiman, 1970). Furthermore, since the three societies experienced continuous economic growth and an increasing level of industrialization in the twentieth century, the thesis of industrialism also predicts a trend of a declining influence of particularism and a corresponding increase of universalism in the process of status attainment over the period in our societies. With these predictions in mind, we would like to bring together the findings of the various chapters and at the same time provide an overview of the process of status attainment in Japan, the United States and Britain.

Let us begin with the attainment of educational credentials. The findings of Chapter 3, first of all, lead us to conclude that the attainment of educational credentials in all three societies is not independent of social background. Most characteristics of social background significantly affect the attainment of various levels of education in our societies. Secondly, the findings on trends in Chapter 3 show that in all three societies the distribution of education has become more equal over the 50-year span of our analysis. The absolute number of individuals with higher levels of educational attainment has increased across cohorts even among people from disadvantaged backgrounds. Nonetheless, the relative access to education for men of disadvantaged social origins has not always improved across successive cohorts in the twentieth century.

Our cross-cohort analysis suggests that high school graduation and the attainment of O-level/ONC qualifications becomes more equal, at least from the middle-age cohort to the young-age cohort in our societies. However, our analysis also suggests that there is an increasing effect of social origin on college attendance and the attainment of A-level or above academic qualifications across successive cohorts in our societies. College attendance and A-levels are becoming more crucial to success in the labour market across cohorts, due to a general increase in the level of education, and because privileged families try harder to ensure that their sons have access to these credentials. In other words, institutions of higher education and higher levels of academic qualifications are becoming the means of reproducing inequality from generation to generation.

In summary, with regard to the process of educational attainment, our empirical findings are not altogether consistent with the prediction of industrialism; social origin exerts significant effects on educational attainment in all three societies. Although our cohort analysis did show a declining effect of particularism – social origin – on the attainment of lower levels of education in our societies, the access to higher education and higher academic qualifications has become more dependent on social origin. However, it is important to note that these trends in the effects of social origin on educational credentials show a cross-national similarity.

Moving from the attainment of educational credentials to socioeconomic attainment, cross-national variation appears to emerge. The results of Chapter 4 suggest that universalistic criteria – namely, educational credentials – play a more important role in explaining inequality of occupational status and income in the United States and Britain than in Japan. The ratio of the universalistic principle (the net effect of educational credentials) to the particularistic principle (the total effect of social background) in allocation of socioeconomic status is larger in the United States and Britain than in Japan. In other words, the relative weight of education, as compared with that of the overall influence of social background on socioeconomic attainment, is larger in the United States and Britain than in Japan.

The process of socioeconomic attainment, therefore, does not show a clear picture of a cross-national similarity, as the thesis of industrialism would predict.

As far as the trends in the process of socioeconomic attainment are concerned, our results in Chapter 4 find in favour of the prediction derived from the thesis of industrialism. In all three societies, there is a definite trend toward the increasing relative importance of education in socioeconomic attainment. Since the effect of educational credentials is independent of social background, the rising relative importance of education may be interpreted as an increasing use of universalistic criteria in socioeconomic attainment.

However, there is evidence which does not support the prediction of industrialism in all three societies: universalism does not always dominate particularism in allocation of socioeconomic status. In all three societies, income attainment is more likely to be affected by social background characteristics than by education, and the attainment of current occupational status in Japan is also influenced more by social background than by education. In order to determine the weight of particularistic versus universalistic principles in allocation, previous studies (e.g. Blau and Duncan, 1967; Tominaga, 1979) often compared the effect of the father's occupational status with that of education on current occupational status. However, if a wide range of social background characteristics are included, no clear dominance of universalism over particularism can be found at least in the attainment of income. The overall effect of various factors of social background still shows a significant, and often substantial, influence in all three societies.

The issue of universalism versus particularism in allocation of social position is not a simple one and is more complicated than the thesis of industrialism would predict. This is primarily because of the dual role of education in the process of status attainment. Educational credentials serve the function of mobility to the extent that they affect socioeconomic achievement independently of social background. However, at the same time, educational credentials are used by men of privileged background to pass on their advantaged position to the next generation. As argued in Chapter 3, studies on education and social mobility focused on the role of education in reproducing inequality. For example, Berg (1973, p. 183) went as far as to suggest that educational credentials replaced wealth and property in the role of reproducing class advantages over time in the United States:

> Educational credentials have become the new property in America. That nation, which has attempted to make the transmission of real and personal property difficult, has contrived to replace it with an inheritable set of values concerning degrees and diplomas which will most certainly reinforce the formidable class boundaries that remain, even without the right within families to pass benefices from parents to their children.

The findings of Chapter 4 suggest that the effects of various social background characteristics are in fact mediated through educational credentials in all three societies. Specifically, the cultural capital of the family affects the socioeconomic attainment of the son almost entirely through influencing his educational attainment. However, educational credentials do not appear to replace 'real and personal property', as suggested by Berg. No empirical evidence indicates that the direct transmission of economic and social capital is entirely absent in our societies.

Chapter 4 (Section 4.5) discussed in detail the process through which various social background characteristics (economic, social and cultural capital) affected socioeconomic attainment. It is not possible to restate the detailed findings here, but the overall picture suggests that the transmission of socioeconomic advantages between generations occurs through both direct and indirect routes, and that education plays a mediating role in the three societies. The overall mechanism through which social background affects socioeconomic attainment appears to be similar in Japan, the United States and Britain, and the dual roles of education – mobility function and transmission function – are documented in the three societies.

All in all, our empirical results on the process of educational and socioeconomic attainment in Japan, the United States and Britain do not always support the thesis of industrialism. Two basic trends are consistent with the prediction of this thesis: a declining effect of social origin on high school graduation and the attainment of O-level/ONC qualifications and an increasing relative importance of educational credentials in socioeconomic attainment over the period in our societies. However, college attendance and the attainment of A-level or above academic qualifications have become more dependent on social origin across successive cohorts, and educational credentials do not always dominate social origin in allocation of socioeconomic status in our societies. These findings appear to provide evidence against the industrialism thesis.

8.2 SOURCES OF CROSS-NATIONAL VARIATION IN SOCIOECONOMIC ATTAINMENT

The most salient cross-national variation in the process of status attainment pertains to the difference in the socioeconomic benefits of educational credentials. In particular, occupational and income returns to a BA degree are significantly higher in the United States than in Japan: the occupational status benefit of a higher education is almost double and the income benefit almost triple in the United States.

As discussed in Chapter 4, cross-national differences in the socioeconomic benefits of higher education can be explained in part by the difference in the spread of the distribution of occupational status and income. The large differences between Japan and the United States in returns to higher education are reduced almost by two-thirds for income and by one-fourth for occupational status when the difference in the variation of occupational status and income distributions are controlled for. The results suggest that part of the reason why American college education is more profitable than its Japanese counterpart is due to the fact that the distribution of occupational status and income is more unequal in the United States. In other words, if the distribution of occupational status and income had had a larger variance in Japan, the impact of higher education would have been much larger. Nonetheless, the socioeconomic benefits of a BA degree are still smaller in Japan than in the United States even after the adjustment. Factors other than the differences in the spread of the distribution should therefore account for the remaining cross-national differences.

Furthermore, when we adjusted the variance in income distribution in Britain, the effect of a BA degree on income attainment increased rather substantially. Since the British income distribution is much more equal than its Japanese counterpart, income returns to a BA degree become more than one and a half times those in Japan under the hypothetical condition that the British distribution has had the same variance as the Japanese one. The results imply that the socioeconomic benefits of a BA degree in Japan are probably smaller even compared with those in Britain when we take into account the difference in income inequality.

Another factor which may explain the smaller socioeconomic returns to higher education in Japan than in the United States deals with a cross-national difference in recruitment and allocation of college-trained manpower. As discussed in Chapter 5 (Section 5.6), American firms generally favour college applicants who already have some knowledge of and training for the job. Recruiters tend to seek job candidates who can immediately contribute to the growth of the company. In contrast, Japanese firms tend to look for promising but relatively inexperienced students. They appear to favour candidates with minimal skills and train them on-the-job in their first few years with the company.

Because American firms, unlike their Japanese counterparts, often lack extensive training schemes within the firm, they tend to have higher expectations about the skills and training of college graduates than Japanese firms. It is probably not so unrealistic to assume that American college graduates are in fact relatively better trained and equipped with the skills necessary to perform their jobs than Japanese graduates when they leave college. This does not mean that the Japanese college graduates have less potential to become highly productive workers, but that as far as actual skills, work experience and training at the time of entry into the labour market are concerned, American students appear to have a definite advantage. American firms consequently assign promising college graduates to responsible positions which are often prestigious and provide monetary incentives from the beginning of their career. In contrast, Japanese firms tend to train newly-recruited members on-the-job in their first few years, when the new members learn firm-specific skills and firm-specific ways of making decisions. The benefits of higher education become visible only after a relatively long period of service.

This difference in recruitment and allocation of college-trained manpower is most apparent in the cross-national difference in the age–income profiles, discussed in Chapter 4 (Section 4.5). The income advantage of university graduates over high school graduates is apparent from the early stages of a career in the United States, while the same advantage does not become noticeable until much later in the career in Japan. At the aggregate level the total benefit of higher education is therefore much larger in the United States than in Japan because in the United States the returns to higher education are apparent from the beginning of the career and accumulate throughout a man's working life.

The difference in the spread of distribution of income and occupational status and the difference in recruitment and allocation practices between American and Japanese firms do not exhaust the possible explanations for the smaller socioeconomic benefits of a BA degree in Japan. However, they appear to show some of the underlying mechanisms which produce the cross-national variation.

8.3 EDUCATIONAL CREDENTIALISM IN JAPAN RECONSIDERED

The empirical findings of this study do not provide support to the idea of 'Japan as an educational credential society' which suggests a Japanese distinctiveness in the process of status attainment by emphasizing the role of educational credentials. Chapter 1 presented six propositions about the process of status attainment in Japan that can be derived directly or indirectly from this idea of 'educational credentialism'. We will now summarize our findings which are relevant to each proposition.

As to the first proposition about the relationship between social background and education, opportunities for educational advancement are not independent of social background, and various social background characteristics do influence the attainment of education. Men who are born in a rural and farm family with a large number of siblings, whose parents have lower level of education, and whose father engages in a lower-status job are generally disadvantaged in the attainment of educational credentials. The trends in the effect of social background on education suggest that access to higher education has become more dependent on social background in Japan despite the expansion of the higher education sector. Furthermore, cross-national comparison shows no evidence that opportunities for education are more open in Japan than in the United States and Britain. These results in Chapter 3 lead us to conclude that the first proposition is not supported by the empirical analysis.

The second proposition concerns the comparison of the socioeconomic benefits of education between Japan and other societies. The results in Chapter 4 suggest that the socioeconomic benefits of education are much larger in the United States than in Japan, contrary to the proposition derived from the thesis of 'educational credentialism': the occupational status benefit of a BA degree is almost double and the income benefit almost triple in the United States.

The third proposition about the dominance of achieved over ascribed criteria in the allocation of socioeconomic status is the restatement of the thesis of industrialism. As already discussed above, this study cannot find any empirical evidence to support the claim that the universalistic criteria of performance always dominate the particularistic criteria of social origin in allocation of social position in our industrial societies. When a wide range of social background characteristics are included, the overall effect of social background in general surpasses the effect of education on the attainment of socioeconomic status in Japan.

The fourth proposition focused upon the relationship between stratification in higher education and socioeconomic attainment among college graduates. The results in Chapter 5 suggest that the effects of college quality on occupational status and income are by no means greater in Japan than in the United States. The effect of institutional ranking on the first occupational status is absent in Japan while a significant effect exists in the United States. Furthermore, the income difference between the graduates of highly competitive institutions and those of non-competitive institutions is much larger in the United States than in Japan. These results are not in accordance with the prediction of the thesis of 'educational credentialism'.

When the relationship between stratification in higher education and elite recruitment is examined, the institutional origin from which the elite group is recruited appears to be more concentrated in Japan than in the United States. However, British elites also come disproportionately from two ancient universities, Oxford and Cambridge. Although the Japanese top national universities play a dominant role in producing elites, there is no empirical evidence to suggest that their role is more dominant than that played by the ancient British universities. The preponderance of elite institutions in access to elite positions is found in both Japan and Britain.

The fifth proposition concerns the long-lasting effect of educational credentials in Japan. As far as its effect on income is concerned, the results in Chapter 4 are consistent with the claim that educational credentials have an enduring impact on income. The age–income profile shows that the income differential between a high school graduate and a university graduate widens as they age. Furthermore, cross-national comparison suggests that income differentials between different levels of education are much more pronounced as men become older in Japan than in the United States and Britain.

These results appear to support the proposition of 'educational credentialism', but there is an alternative explanation for the apparent differences in age–income profile. Since the profile is estimated using cross-sectional data, the apparent income gap between a high school graduate and a university graduate may in part be due to the educational distribution of the cohorts. For example, only 8 per cent of the 45–49 cohort were BA degree holders in Japan. The income gap between a university graduate and a high school graduate in this cohort may be explained in part by the smaller number of university graduates. It is not guaranteed that a university graduate in the 20–24 cohort will enjoy the same benefit 25 years later, since there will then be many more people with BA degrees in the cohort. The apparent income differentiation among different levels of education therefore probably overestimates the enduring effect of education by a non-trivial amount.

As far as the enduring effect of educational credentials on occupational status is concerned, the results of this study are contrary to the prediction of 'educational credentialism'. In Japan, the occupational benefit of a BA degree is greatest at the beginning of the career, but thereafter it has an attenuated impact on occupational attainment. In contrast, American higher education seems to provide men with initial access to higher occupational status and to exercise a continuing direct impact on occupational achievement throughout the career.

The sixth proposition concerns the homogeneity of the returns to education among people who occupy different class positions. Chapter 7 shows that the effects of education on income are different depending on class position. The employer class enjoys larger income returns to education than any other classes, and among the Japanese petty bourgeois class education does not increase income. The effects of education on income are therefore not homogeneous across all class positions.

In summary, none of the propositions derived from the thesis of 'educational credentialism' is supported by this study. It is indeed remarkable that this thesis has received so much credence both among the public and in scholarly works even though none of its propositions appear to be empirically valid. Why do Japanese people place so much emphasis on education, and why do Japanese students and their parents undergo the educational competition known as an 'examination hell', despite the scanty evidence for the large socio-economic benefits of education?

Finally, we would like to propose some possible explanations for the prevalence of 'educational credentialism' in Japan. First, there is a possibility that people's concern for the attainment of educational credentials is based simply upon the unfounded conception of large socioeconomic benefits of credentials. Although educational credentials do increase socioeconomic status, the extent of the effect of education is probably overestimated by many Japanese. Since there have been very few comparative studies which have estimated relative socioeconomic benefits of educational credentials across different nations, it is not surprising that the benefits of education have been exaggerated in Japan.

Second, the untiring quest for educational credentials in Japan can in part be explained by the 'symbolic and expressive value' of credentials, rather than the socio-economic benefits generating from them. Education plays a role of allocating higher socioeconomic status, but it also represents the status in itself. Credentials do not have to be the means of obtaining socioeconomic status; they constitute an important dimension of the general social standing in a society. Thus, Amano (1983) distinguished the 'status generating function' from the 'status expressing function' of credentials. He claimed that:

> A society where the opportunity for education has been equalized is a society where the equalization of income and consumption has progressed and where the structure of stratified groups cannot be easily distinguished. In such a society, the popular demand for educational credentials as the means of status expression strengthens, rather than vanishes (1983, p. 47).

According to Amano, since the differentiation by income and consumption has become less visible in contemporary Japanese society, educational credentials have come to occupy one of the central roles in differentiating people's social standing. The prevalence of educational credentialism in Japan is due to both the 'status generating function' and the 'status expression function' of credentials.

Third, and perhaps most importantly, the rigid structural barrier between the educational system and the labour market in Japan explains in part the obsession with educational credentials or the 'process of certification' (Dore, 1976). In the United States, it is not unusual to work for a few years before the youths begin their higher education. The transition from schooling to work is not always a clearcut event, and it often occurs over a number of years, involving entry and re-entry into the labour market and marginal entry in the form of part-time work and summer jobs (Osterman, 1980). Furthermore, some professional graduate schools recommend, or even require, that applicants have work experience.

In Britain, while the majority of the youths leave schooling around the minimum school leaving age, institutions of further education provide opportunities for education which lead to the attainment of various vocational and professional qualifications. Concepts such as 'sandwich courses' in which employees spend alternate lengthy periods in college and employment and 'day-release' where students are released for study by their employers for an equivalent of one working day a week are examples of flexible flows of individuals between the educational system and the labour market (Cantor and Roberts, 1983).

In contrast, in Japan, the life-course transition from schooling to work is rarely reversible; it is extremely difficult for Japanese youths to return to education once they have entered the labour market. This is because Japanese youths have to pass a college entrance examination which requires intensive preparation, often possible only when one is still in high school or immediately after high school graduation. The preparation for the college entrance examinations requires total dedication and is almost too demanding for those who are working full-time. The link between educational system and labour market consequently exists only at the time of school completion.

The separation between the educational system and the labour market is also influenced by the way skills are acquired by Japanese workers. Japanese education is known to equip workers with basic competence in reading, writing and arithmetic, but it does not impart vocational skills.[2] As we found among college graduates, work-related experience and skills are unimportant – and even potentially disadvantageous – in searching for the first job. Job-related skills are acquired primarily through on-the-job training and experience of a wide range of related jobs. The process of skill acquisition by passing through a group of related jobs constitutes a career path (Koike, 1981; 1988). Openings in higher-level jobs are consequently likely to be filled by internal promotion of workers who have accumulated work experience within the firm (Sano, 1989). The internal promotion and allocation of the workforce therefore discourages workers from interrupting their working career in order to enrol in educational institutions.[3]

In Britain and the United States, skill acquisition also takes place while holding a job. However, other channels of vocational training are available and ambitious workers often seek training and education outside the workplace. The proliferation of American business schools is one such channel. It is an individual investment to attend a business school and obtain a MBA degree, and the degree will immediately boost salary and enhance job prospects for the graduate. In Britain, institutions of further education also provide opportunities for accumulating skills and obtaining qualifications outside the work setting. Although the training at these institutions is often related to an apprenticeship system, these educational institutions continue to provide crucial resources for skill acquisition. Once British workers are certified with a particular skill and obtain a qualification, they are able to market themselves nationally. Qualifications are recognized nationwide and sometimes entitle certified workers to join professional and technical associations. Using these qualifications and professional memberships, British workers are able to compete for better jobs in the external labour market.

The demanding examination system that characterizes Japanese education and the structure of the Japanese labour market, especially the process of skill acquisition and the internal labour market, lead to the absence of a flexible flow of individuals between labour market and education in Japan. Because of the rigid structural barrier between schooling and the world of work, there is a general concern with assuring the best possible education when the youths go through the educational system for the first and last time. Had the Japanese people a chance to return to school after their first entry into the labour market, and had this further schooling enhanced their opportunities, the popular quest for educational credentials would probably have been weakened. We would therefore suggest that our explanation for the untiring quest for educational credentials in Japan must be sought primarily in the institutional arrangements which characterize the relationship between the educational system and the labour market. It is not always necessary, we would speculate, to seek our explanation in some features of Japanese culture, such as the 'Confucian tradition' or a 'learning culture' (cf. White, 1987).

In summary, the exhausting emphasis on the attainment of educational credentials and the excessive competition for higher levels of schooling in Japan do not necessarily result from the socioeconomic returns to education. As we have seen in this study, there is no reason to believe that the benefits of education are particularly larger in Japan than in the United States and in Britain, or that the mobility function of education surpasses the reproduction function of social background in Japan. While educational credentials do improve socioeconomic well-being independent of social background, the impact of education should not be overestimated.

8.4 CLASS STRUCTURE, CLASS MOBILITY AND INDUSTRIALISM

We now move from the study of the status attainment process to the study of class structure and class mobility. Stimulated by a revival of the tradition of the study of social mobility from the perspective of class structure and class formation, Chapter 6 examined the patterns of intergenerational class mobility in Japan, the United States and Britain.

The investigation of the patterns of observed gross mobility – or, as it is often called, absolute mobility – in Japan, the United States and Britain leads to three major conclusions. First, the total observed mobility rate is very high and identical in the three societies: more than two-thirds of the respondents experienced change of class position between two generations. Second, the extent of total mobility due to intergenerational changes in the class structure seems to be greater in Japan than in the United States and Britain. In other words, if the Japanese class structure had not experienced such dramatic changes between generations, the total observed mobility would probably be smaller than the amounts observed in the United States and Britain. We may therefore conclude that the opportunity for mobility independent of the structural changes is probably smaller, and consequently the class structure is overall less fluid, in Japan than in the United States and Britain.

Third, cross-national variations are found in the patterns of inflow and outflow mobility rates, and some distinctive features of the Japanese mobility process seem to have emerged. In particular, the patterns of intergenerational recruitment and stability among the Japanese petty bourgeoisie and non-skilled working class are different from the American and British patterns. The Japanese petty bourgeoisie have a higher self-recruitment rate and a higher tendency to stay in the same class than their American and British counterparts. The Japanese non-skilled workers, on the other hand, are much more heavily recruited from the farming sector and the sons of these workers are much less likely to stay in non-skilled work than

American and British non-skilled workers. These findings, as we have suggested in the concluding section of Chapter 6 (Section 6.10), reflect the particular course of development followed by Japan – namely, late, but rapid, industrialization.

The sociological significance of the study of mobility from the perspective of class structure and class formation, as Goldthorpe (1984, p. 3) points out, entails 'the implications of mobility for classes as collectivities'. In this respect, distinctive mobility processes – inflow and outflow rates – of the Japanese petty bourgeoisie and non-skilled working class deserve special attention. The Japanese petty bourgeoisie is characterized by a relatively high degree of intergenerational class stability and closure (self-recruitment), and the Japanese non-skilled working class is characterized by the weak extent of such stability and closure. In other words, in Goldthorpe's (1984; 1987) terminology, the Japanese petty bourgeoisie seems to possess a highly developed 'demographic identity' while the Japanese non-skilled working class appears to show a weakly developed one because these two classes clearly have a different extent of demographic continuity among their members.

These mobility characteristics of the Japanese petty bourgeoisie and non-skilled working class probably have significant implications for their socio–political orientation and class consciousness. While the size of the Japanese petty bourgeoisie is shrinking rather dramatically, it does not mean that the class is disintegrating. In contrast, men who are engaged in farming and urban self-employment tend to have a strong attachment to their class position as well as commitment to the survival of the class. This must be related not only to the fact that they are heavily self-recruited and show strong intergenerational stability but also to the observation that they are under threat of further contraction and even elimination. These segments of class structure thus appear to form a relatively 'hereditary' and 'permanent' component (Sorokin, 1959) and also to have a relatively well-defined socio–political orientation. The independent farmers and the urban petty bourgeoisie often form separately strong interest groups which exert pressures on local and national policy formation.[4] For example, the policy of import restriction on rice is the result of the effective mobilization of farmers. It is important to recognize that they possess strong potential for collective action, often in pursuit of their own survival, and cannot be regarded as a disappearing segment of the class structure.[5]

On the other hand, we would speculate that the weakly developed 'demographic identity' of the Japanese non-skilled workers – a low degree of continuity of membership over time – is related to the often-described phenomenon of the 'middle strata consciousness' or a lack of strong working class identity among the Japanese working class (Murakami, 1984). Because of the transient nature of the membership of the non-skilled working class, this class can be hardly described as a cohesive socio–political collectivity. As Goldthorpe (1984; 1987) has pointed out, class formation at the demographic level – that is, involving mobility processes – may be crucial before classes can effectively develop a socio–political cohesion and form a basis for collective action. It is difficult to see how distinctive life-styles and socio–political orientations can emerge among the members of the Japanese non-skilled working class when its membership is no more than temporary. It is even more difficult to see how collective action in order to enhance the class interests of this class can be organized without having permanent class membership.[6] The weakly developed 'demographic identity' of the Japanese non-skilled working class probably undermines not only the development of a strong working class identity but also the possibility of collective action.

Turning to the patterns of class fluidity – relative mobility – we concluded in Chapter 6 that cross-national similarity heavily outweighed cross-national variation. The patterns of relative chances of mobility and immobility net of intergenerational change in class structure are basically similar in Japan, the United States and Britain and can be characterized by common features of class inheritance, class boundary and special petty bourgeois mobility. This conclusion is consistent with the prediction about the patterns of social mobility among industrial nations proposed by Featherman, Jones and Hauser (1975). They suggest that while observed mobility may differ among industrial nations, once the differences in occupational and class distributions are taken into account the patterns of class fluidity are essentially the same.

Our conclusion about trends in intergenerational class mobility in Japan also provides support for the FJH hypothesis. The relative chances of mobility and immobility across successive cohorts appear to be extremely stable. Although the level of industrialization increases rapidly across successive cohorts, there is no clear trend of greater 'openness' in the Japanese class structure (cf. Treiman, 1970).

Overall, it is in the patterns of observed absolute mobility in which cross-national variations are found and Japanese distinctiveness emerges. However, as far as the relative chances of mobility and immobility are concerned, cross-national regularity and cross-cohort stability dominate. The 'generic' form of the mobility regime among industrial nations, as the FJH hypothesis would suggest, emerges in the patterns of class fluidity. In this respect, Japan therefore does not seem to be exceptional among industrial nations.

8.5 STATUS ATTAINMENT AND CLASS MOBILITY IN JAPAN: A SUMMARY

So far, we have attempted to bring together the major findings about the process of status attainment and class mobility in Japan, the United States and Britain around the substantive themes presented in Chapter 1. Before we go on to the next issue of the interrelation among class structure, status hierarchies and labour market rewards, we would like to provide a very brief summary of the process of socioeconomic attainment and class mobility in Japan by tackling the most frequently asked questions about the comparison of social mobility in Japan, the United States and Britain.

Is Japanese society more mobile than American and British societies? There seems to be as much mobility in Japan as in the United States and Britain as far as the total amount of observed mobility is concerned. About two-thirds of the men experienced change in class position between the two generations in all three societies.

Is Japan more open than the United States and Britain? If we equate the notion of 'openness' with the amount of mobility independent of structural change in the society, then Japan appears to be less open than the United States and Britain. Although the total observed mobility rate is the same in all three societies, the extent of total mobility due to intergenerational change in class structure is probably larger in Japan than in the United States and Britain.

Is the Japanese pattern of mobility different from that of the United States and Britain? As far as the patterns of absolute mobility – inflow and outflow rates – are concerned, distinctive Japanese features do seem to emerge reflecting the experience of late, but rapid, industrialization. However, when we focus upon the patterns of relative mobility chances or class fluidity, Japan does not seem to be different from the United States and Britain.

Is Japan more universalistic in the allocation of socioeconomic status than the United States and Britain? If we equate universalistic criteria with educational credentials, then there is no empirical evidence to suggest that Japan is more universalistic than the other two nations. The effect of educational credentials on socioeconomic attainment is no greater in Japan than in the United States and Britain.

Of course, these simple answers require careful and detailed qualification, and such qualification is stated in full in the concluding section of each relevant chapter above. However, these answers reflect a very general summary of the main findings of this study.

8.6 CLASS STRUCTURE, STATUS HIERARCHIES AND LABOUR MARKET INEQUALITY

As stated in Chapter 1, there are two diverging orientations to the study of social mobility: status attainment research, and the study of mobility from a class structure and class formation perspective. The difference between the two orientations lies mainly in the context of stratification within which mobility takes place. Status attainment research defines mobility within the context of status hierarchies. Social mobility is conceived as an upward or downward movement of individuals along the continuum of status hierarchies (Goldthorpe, 1984). The alternative orientation defines mobility within the context of the class structure. The individuals are located within a structure of categorically distinct social collectivities which can be defined by production and market relations. Social mobility is conceived as movements of individuals which involve detachment from, and attachment to, distinguishable social collectivities (Goldthorpe, 1987).

Status hierarchies and class structure, however, are interrelated at the empirical level. This issue of interplay among class structure, status hierarchies and inequality of rewards in society was discussed in Chapter 7,[7] which approached the issue in three basic ways. It (1) examined the relationship between class structure and status hierarchies, (2) compared the predictive power of class with that of status characteristics (education and occupation) in explaining inequality of rewards in labour market, and (3) analyzed the process of status attainment within the structural context of class.

The relationship between class structure and status hierarchies was examined by focusing on the status characteristics of classes. The examination of the status composition of classes provided an empirical test of four hypotheses about the distribution of status characteristics among classes in Japan. The hypothesis of homogeneity of status characteristics predicts that a huge intermediate stratum, which belongs neither to the lower nor the upper class and whose members are highly homogeneous in their life-styles and attitudes, has emerged in contemporary Japan and that the status composition of various classes is highly homogeneous (Murakami, 1977; 1984). The bipolarity hypothesis, endorsed by Kishimoto (1977; 1978), presumes that the basis of distribution of various status attributes is polarized along the lines of ownership of the means of production, forming two extremes of capitalists and workers. The hypothesis of status inconsistency, proposed by Tominaga (1977; 1979) and others (Imada and Hara, 1979), predicts that various status characteristics of classes are inconsistent so that classes cannot be characterized by consistently high or low status attributes. Finally, the dual structure hypothesis which is found in the work of labour economists (e.g., Ujihara and Takanashi, 1971; Odaka, 1984) presumes that status characteristics of employees are differentiated not only by their class position but also by size of firm in which they are employed.

The results in Chapter 7 suggest that the dual structure hypothesis which focuses upon the internal stratification in employees is supported by our analysis. Employees in large firms tend to have more favourable status characteristics than those in small and medium-sized firms, even though they occupy the same class position. The size of the firm where workers are employed appears to be a crucial factor in explaining differentiation among Japanese employees. Our findings are consistent with the thesis of a dual structure in the Japanese labour market which claims that there is a large difference in working conditions and pecuniary and non-pecuniary rewards between workers in large and those in smaller firms.

The bipolarity and the status inconsistency hypotheses also receive partial support from our analysis. Bipolarity in status attributes is evident at the extremes of the Japanese class structure; the employer class occupies the most advantageous position in the distribution of most status attributes while the manual working classes are at the bottom of the all status hierarchies. The employer class enjoys control over both the means of production and the labour power of others while the manual working classes are excluded from such control. This finding may be taken as support for Kishimoto's (1978, p. 118) contention that the fundamental structure of inequality 'lies in the distinction between employers and employees or capitalists and wage-earners'.

However, classes which occupy partially dominant and 'contradictory' locations in the social relations of production (Wright, 1979; 1985) tend to show status inconsistency. The professional–managerial class is the most status-inconsistent class; it scores very high on education and occupational prestige but low on home ownership. The Japanese petty bourgeois class also shows a tendency towards status inconsistency. Here the hypothesis of inconsistency of status characteristics works best.

It can be said, then, that the Japanese class structure is characterized by a combination of polarization and inconsistency of status characteristics with a further differentiation among employees by firm size.[8] It is important to notice also that the American class structure can be characterized by the same combination found in Japan, with the notable exception of the differentiation among employees associated with firm size. At the two extremes of the American class structure – represented by the employer class and the manual working classes – the tendency towards status polarization dominates, and those classes which occupy partially dominant and contradictory locations in the social relations of production – the professional–managerial class and the non-manual class – show status inconsistency.

If we calculate the proportion of people who belong to classes which show status inconsistency, the same proportion (47 per cent) of the male labour force can be called members of status-inconsistent classes in each of the two societies.[9] All these results lend support neither to Imada and Hara's (1979) claim that status inconsistency is a generalized feature of Japanese society, nor to Okamoto's prediction (1982) that status inconsistency is more pronounced in Japan than in any other society.

Finally, it is important to emphasize the differences in the relationship between class structure and status hierarchies in the two societies; differentiation among employees by firm size is much more clearly documented in Japan than in the United States. In particular, among Japanese manual workers, firm size appears to be more consequential than skill level so far as status characteristics are concerned. In contrast, in the United States firm size makes no difference in status composition of the manual working classes. This finding underlines the importance of firm size as a basis for the unequal distribution of various status characteristics in Japan.

Another important issue discussed in Chapter 7 about the interplay among class structure, status hierarchies and inequality of rewards in the society is the comparison of the predictive power of class with that of education and of occupation in explaining inequality in income, home ownership and stock investment. The results in Chapter 7 suggest that class is far more important than education and occupational status in explaining inequality in Japan and the United States. The distributions of income, home ownership and stock holdings are all affected by individuals' positions in the social relations of production, independent of their education, occupational status and social background. In other words, the effect of class on labour market rewards cannot be reduced to an artefact of characteristics of individuals who occupy class positions.

The results of this study are not only consistent with previous studies in the United States on the effect of class on income (Wright and Perrone, 1977; Wright, 1979) and non-pecuniary job rewards (Kalleberg and Griffin, 1980; Griffin and Kalleberg, 1981) but also provide stronger support to the documentation of class effect because we have shown its effect on home ownership and stock investment, in addition to its effect on income. In particular, the decisive role of class in determining home ownership is evident, since home ownership is not affected by education and occupational status once other variables are controlled for.

The results in Chapter 7 cast doubt on the emergence of 'the new middle mass' in Japan (Murakami, 1984). Despite the claim that differences in income and living style between classes have diminished in modern Japan, the findings indicate that class is the strongest determinant of income inequality, let alone home ownership, in Japan. Class appears as a critical variable in explaining inequality in Japanese society, probably more so than educational credentials or occupational status.

The final task concerning the interplay among class structure, status hierarchies and inequality of rewards is to specify the process of status attainment within the context of class structure. The results in Chapter 7 suggest that the way in which class conditions the relationship between education and labour market rewards is dependent on the kinds of labour market reward. Home ownership is not affected by education in virtually any class category in Japan and the United States. Stock investment increases as the level of education increases in virtually all class categories in both societies. As far as these two labour market rewards are concerned, the effects of education appear to be independent of class positions.

In contrast, class strongly structures the impact of education on income in both Japan and the United States. The employer class and the petty bourgeois class showed the highest income returns to education, and the professional–managerial class and the non-manual class had higher returns than the manual working classes in the United States. In Japan, the employer class enjoys larger income returns to education than the remaining classes and the petty bourgeois class shows no effect of education on income.

The results in Chapters 6 and 7 thus highlight the importance of class, defined by the social relations of production and marketable skills. The division between control and no control over the means of production in the distribution of various rewards and in relative mobility chances appears to remain substantial in advanced capitalist societies, such as Japan and the United States. Furthermore, Japan and the United States appear to be similar in patterns of class fluidity, overall status compositions of classes, and the relative predictive power of class.

8.7 FUTURE PROSPECTS

As a concluding remark we would like to point out three possible directions in which this study could be extended. The first is to enlarge the scope of cross-national comparison. Japan, the United States and Britain are highly industrialized countries; none the less they are not the only industrial nations in the world. Fully to test the thesis of industrialism and of the similarity of the patterns of class mobility, more industrial nations should be added to the analysis. In this respect, the CASMIN (Comparative Analysis of Social Mobility in Industrial Nations) project is one of the most promising ongoing research efforts. This project attempts to analyze social mobility data from nine European countries, the United States and Australia. The Japanese data-set (1975 Social Stratification and Mobility National Survey) has also been recoded and included in the CASMIN data file. Only through the painstaking effort of recoding the original data into comparable measurements and the international collaboration of social scientists from various nations will we be able to arrive at firm conclusions about the process of status attainment and class mobility in industrial nations.[10]

The second direction in which this study can be extended involves the impact of class and status on consciousness and attitudes. This study focused on the objective aspect of stratification: the distributions of class, status and labour market rewards and the interplay among them. What was excluded in the analysis is the distributional consequences of class, status and other rewards on the subjective aspects of stratification, namely class consciousness and political attitudes.

Since Japanese public opinion polls show that 90 per cent of Japanese think they belong to middle-strata, it will be particularly interesting to see whether there is class or status differentiation in the class identification.[11] We have speculated about the implications of class mobility (inflow and outflow rates) for socio–political orientation among the Japanese petty bourgeoisie and non-skilled working class. However, we have not shown empirically that class position and intergenerational change in class position affect class consciousness and socio–political orientation. Since many previous discussions on class dealt with the correspondence between class and class consciousness and the rise of class actions (e.g., Wright, 1978, 1985; Ohashi, 1971), one possible direction for extending this study is to examine the impact of class and status on consciousness and political behaviour.

The consequences of mobility should also be recognized as an important topic (Lipset and Bendix, 1959; Goldthorpe, 1987). Long-distance upward mobility, for example, may generate not only personal satisfaction and the acceptance of the status quo but also psychological stress and the rejection of the life-styles of the status quo. Mobility often involves detachment from and attachment to different groups and may have a significant impact on the psychological well-being and socio–political attitudes of individuals who have experienced mobility.

The final direction which could be taken to extend the perspective of this study deals with women. The most serious drawback of this study probably stems from its exclusion of women. It is not our intention to exclude women but it was an inevitable consequence of the limitation of the data-set available for the analysis. The exclusion of women from the analysis may have a serious consequence in the discussion of stratification and mobility in contemporary industrial societies because of increasing rates of women's labour force participation. In particular, an increase in the labour force participation rate among married women has been reported in most industrial societies including Japan. Reflecting these changes, there is a widespread interest in the study of women in more recent American and British research on social stratification and mobility (e.g., Roos,

1985; Reskin, 1984; Reskin and Hartmann, 1986; Dex and Shaw, 1986; Crompton and Mann, 1986; Goldthorpe and Payne, 1986). It now seems an obvious practice to incorporate women in the study of social mobility and compare the process of mobility among women with that among men.

However, in Japan the study of social mobility among women has not been fully developed. Very little has been accomplished in the sociological investigation of women's mobility primarily because of the lack of available data.[12] This problem, however, will soon be solved since the 1985 Social Stratification and Mobility National Survey (1985 SSM), which was conducted by Japanese sociologists in the autumn of 1985, included women for the first time in national surveys of this kind. Although it will require some time before we witness the emergence of a body of research on women's social mobility in Japan, a promising future project has already begun among Japanese sociologists who took part in the 1985 SSM survey (Okamoto, 1989). Therefore, not very far in the future, we can expect the development of mobility research on women in Japan and cross-national studies on patterns of women's mobility.

Notes

1. Readers should be reminded again that the conclusions stated in this chapter are based on the analyses of the Japanese, American and British samples of men aged 20 to 64. The samples do not include women.
2. There are vocational high schools in Japan, but their curriculum emphasizes academic subjects rather than practical vocational skills.
3. It must be added that there are a wide range of skill certificates which workers may obtain by passing national and local tests administered by professional associations. However, these qualifications are closely linked to on-the-job training and increasing the competence of job performance; they are not thought of the means of getting better jobs in the external labour market.
4. The petty bourgeois class is also considered to form an important basis for support for the Japanese conservative party.
5. A similar potential for collective action among the farmers and the urban petty bourgeoisie has been pointed out by Goldthorpe (1984) from the examination of the European experience (cf. Berger and Piore, 1980).
6. These points most forcefully argued by Goldthorpe (1984). The relationship between mobility processes and class formation is also discussed in detail by Parkin (1971) and Giddens (1973).

7. Chapter 7 concentrated upon a comparison of Japanese and American societies. The comparison with Britain was not included because the British data-set does not contain information on home ownership and stock investment.
8. Shoji (1982) arrived at a similar conclusion by re-analyzing the results reported by Imada and Hara (1979).
9. It should be remembered, though, that the petty bourgeois class is characterized as status-inconsistent in Japan but not in the United States, and that the non-manual class shows a tendency towards status inconsistency in the United States but not in Japan. The largest status-inconsistent class in the United States is the professional–managerial class which constitutes 38 per cent of the total male labour force, while it is the petty bourgeois class in Japan which constitutes 25 per cent. The identical proportion of people being status-inconsistent does not therefore imply that they belong to the same class categories in the two societies.
10. A preliminary analysis of the Japanese and the European data sets has already been published as a working paper (Ishida *et al.*, 1987). For the analysis on the European data sets, see Erikson and Goldthorpe (1987a, 1987b).
11. Michiko Naoi (1979) studied the relationship between objective aspect of stratification (e.g., education, occupational status and income) and 'middle-strata consciousness' using the 1975 SSM.
12. However, there are exceptions. Yasuda (1971) analyzed marital mobility among women, and the study by the National Institute of Employment and Vocational Research (Koyou Shokugyo Kenkyujo, 1979) examined career mobility among women (cf. Kojima, 1986).

Appendix

1 STANDARD INTERNATIONAL OCCUPATIONAL PRESTIGE SCORES (IPS) FOR DETAILED JAPANESE OCCUPATIONAL CATEGORIES

Occupation	IPS
Professional and Technical Workers	
Scientific researchers	
001 Natural science researchers	68
002 Cultural and social science researchers	68
Engineers and technicians	
003 Mining engineers	63
004 Metallurgical engineers	60
005 Mechanical engineers	66
006 Electrical engineers	65
007 Chemical engineers	66
008 Architects	72
009 Civil engineers	70
010 Agricultural and forestry engineers	56
011 Computer processing technicians	58
012 Other engineers and technicians	55
Medical and health technicians	
013 Physicians	78
014 Dentists	70
015 Pharmacists	64
016 Midwives	46
017 Public health nurses	48
018 Nutritionists	52
019 Nurses	54
020 Chiropractors, masseurs, acupuncturists and osteopathists	51
021 Other medical and public health technicians	50
Judicial workers	
022 Judges, prosecutors and lawyers	74
023 Other judicial workers	52
Registered accountants	
024 Registered accountants and licensed tax accountants	62
Professors and teachers	
025 Kindergarten teachers	49
026 Primary school teachers	57

027	Secondary school teachers	57
028	High school teachers	64
029	Professors; college and university	78
030	Teachers of blind, dumb and protective schools	62
031	Other teachers	63
Religious workers		
032	Religious workers	54
Authors, reporters and editors		
033	Authors	62
034	Reporters and editors	56
Fine artists, designers and photographers		
035	Sculpture artists and art craftsmen	57
036	Designers	56
037	Photographers and cameramen	46
Musicians, stage artists and professional sportsmen		
038	Musicians	45
039	Actors, stage dancers and performers	57
040	Professional sportsmen	49
Miscellaneous professional and technical workers		
041	Veterinarians	61
042	Kindergarten workers	49
043	Social and welfare workers	52
044	Private teachers	62
045	Professional and technical workers not elsewhere classified	51
Managers and Officials		
Government officials		
046	Government officials	65
047	Members of National Parliament	79
048	Members of Local Parliament	61
Directors of companies and corporations		
049	Directors of companies	65
050	Directors of public enterprises	64
051	Directors of other corporations	64
Other managers and administrators		
052	Station masters and chief operation officers	61
053	Masters of post, telegram, and telephone officers	58
054	Managers and administrators not elsewhere classified	60
Clerical and Related Workers		
General clerical workers		
055	General clerical workers	43

056	Accounting clerks	42
057	Clerical workers in post and communication	44
	Outdoor clerical workers	
058	Bill and account collectors	27
059	Other outdoor clerical workers	27
	Other clerical and related workers	
060	Clerical workers in transportation	37
061	Stenographers and typists	48
062	Key punchers	45
063	Operators of electronic machinery	53
	Sales Workers	
	Sales workers of commodities	
064	Retail dealers	46
065	Wholesale dealers	58
066	Restaurant operators	48
067	Salesmen and sales clerks	32
068	Peddlers and street venders	24
069	Junk dealers	24
	Sales-related workers	
070	Commodity brokers	55
071	Travelling salesmen (except insurance)	46
072	Insurance agents	44
073	Real estate agents and brokers	49
074	Pawnbrokers	39
075	Other sales related workers	28
	Farmers, Lumbermen and Fishermen	
	Farmers and lumbermen	
076	Farmers and sericulturists	40
077	Livestock raisers	26
078	Forest rearers	24
079	Timber fellers and loggers	18
080	Timber collectors and log transporters	24
081	Charcoal makers and firewood choppers	16
082	Gardeners and landscape gardeners	21
083	Other agricultural and forestry workers	19
	Fishermen and kindred workers	
084	Fishermen	28
085	Skippers, seamen, chief engineers and engineers of fishing boats	37
086	Seaweed and shell gathers	28
087	Aquaculture workers	28
088	Other fishery workers	28

Workers in Mining and Quarrying Occupations

Workers in mining and quarrying occupations

089	Metal ore diggers	32
090	Coal diggers	32
091	Quarrymen	24
092	Sand, gravel and clay collectors	24
093	Prop setters	32
094	Mining underground carriers	32
095	Metal ore and coal sorters	32
096	Other workers in mining and quarrying occupations	32

Workers in Transport and Communications Occupations

Workers operating land transport

097	Electrical locomotive engineers and steam locomotive engineers	43
098	Motormen in railways	43
099	Automobile drivers	31

Workers operating marine and air transport

100	Ship captains, navigators and pilots (except fishing boats)	63
101	Chief ship engineers and ship engineers	60
102	Pilots, aircraft navigators, and engineers	66

Other workers operating transport

103	Conductors	32
104	Marshallingmen, signalmen, switchmen and couplers	29
105	Deckhands	29
106	Ship-engine operators	25
107	Workers operating other transport not elsewhere classified	24

Communication workers

108	Radiotelegraphists	37
109	Wiretelegraphists	49
110	Telephone operators	38
111	Mail and telegram deliverers	33
112	Other communication workers	30

Craftsmen, Production Process Workers and Labourers

Metal material workers

113	Iron and steel furnacemen and pourers	45
114	Non-ferrous metal smelters and pourers	45
115	Molders	38
116	Forgers and hammermen	38
117	Metal rolling mill operators	36
118	Wire drawing machine operators	38
119	Tempering workers	38
120	Other metal material workers	38

Metal processing, machine repairing and assembling workers		
121	Metal cutting machine operators	38
122	Metal press machine operators	36
123	Welders and framecutters	39
124	Boiler makers, iron founders and riveters	38
125	Tinsmiths, coppersmiths and sheet metal workers	36
126	Metal engineers	39
127	Galvanizers	28
128	Hand finishers	38
129	Other metal processing workers	38
General machine assembling and repairing workers		
130	General machine assemblers	43
131	General machine repairmen	43
Electric machine assembling and repairing workers		
132	Electrical fitters and repairmen	38
133	Semi-conductor products makers	48
134	Electric lamp and electronic tube assemblers	38
135	Electric wire and cable makers	38
136	Other electric machine assembling and repairing workers	40
Transportation equipment assembling and repairing workers		
137	Automobile fitters	42
138	Automobile repairmen	44
139	Railway car fitters and repairmen	42
140	Shipwrights and repairmen	42
141	Aircraft fitters and repairmen	46
142	Bicycle fitters and repairmen	28
143	Other transportation equipment assembling and repairing workers	30
Meter and optical instrument assembling and repairing workers		
144	Watch makers and repairmen	40
145	Lens grinders and adjusters	41
146	Optical instrument makers and repairmen	47
147	Meter makers and adjusters	47
148	Other meter and optical instrument assembling and repairing workers	42
Silk reel and textile workers		
149	Silk reelers	34
150	Spinners	34
151	Doublers and thread yarn twisters	34
152	Winders	34
153	Loom preparers	30
154	Weavers	30
155	Knitters	29
156	Net and rope makers (except metal and straw)	30

157	Textile and yarn washers and bleachers	25
158	Textile dyers	25
159	Other silk reel and textile workers	26
	Garment and related textile fabrics workers	
160	Tailors	40
161	Kimono makers	40
162	Dressmakers for ladies and kids	40
163	Sewing machinists	26
164	Cutters	41
165	Embroiderers	41
166	Other textile fabrics workers	34
	Wood, bamboo, grass and vine products workers	
167	Sawyers	30
168	Chippermen	30
169	Veneer makers	30
170	Wood workers	30
171	Joiners, cabinet makers and related wood workers	40
172	Ship carpenters	37
173	Coopers	29
174	Bamboo products makers	31
175	Grass and straw products makers	31
176	Other wood, bamboo, grass and vine products workers	31
	Pulp, paper and paper products workers	
177	Pulp makers and paper makers	28
178	Paper millers	28
179	Paper container makers	28
180	Paper products workers	28
181	Other pulp, paper, and paper products workers	29
	Printing and bookbinding workers	
182	General stereotypers	41
183	Type-pickers and type-setters	42
184	Pressmen	41
185	Bookbinders	32
186	Other printing and bookbinding workers	41
	Rubber and plastic products workers	
187	Rubber makers	30
188	Rubber products formers	30
189	Plastic products formers and finishers	30
190	Other rubber and plastic products workers	30
	Leather and leather products workers	
191	Leather tanners	22
192	Shoemakers and shoe repairmen	28
193	Other leather and leather products makers	22

Ceramic, clay and stone products workers		
194	Ceramic raw material workers	30
195	Glass formers	37
196	Potters	25
197	Ceramic decorators	31
198	Brick, tile and earthen pipe makers	25
199	Cement workers	31
200	Cement products makers	31
201	Stone cutters	38
202	Other ceramic, clay and stone products workers	31
Food and beverage manufacturing workers		
203	Grain polishers and millers	33
204	Bakers and confectioners	33
205	Macaroni and other noodle makers	34
206	Tofu (bean-curds), paste of arum root and other allied products makers	34
207	Sugar makers	45
208	Tea processing workers	34
209	Miso makers and soy makers	35
210	Canned and bottled food makers	35
211	Sake, beer and other alcoholic beverage makers	34
212	Non-alcoholic beverage makers	34
213	Dairy products makers	34
214	Aquatic products processing workers	34
215	Oil and fat animals or plants makers	34
216	Other food and beverage manufacturing makers	34
Chemical products workers		
217	Chemical operatives	43
218	Oil and fat processing workers	43
219	Other chemical products workers	43
Construction workers		
220	Construction contractors	53
221	House carpenters	37
222	Roofers	31
223	Plasterers	31
224	Construction assistants (Tobishoku)	37
225	Brick layers and tile setters	34
226	Pipe fitters	34
227	Tatami installers	37
228	Construction labourers	20
229	Trackmen	33
230	Other construction workers	28
Stationary engine and construction machinery operators		
231	Boiler engineers and firemen	34
232	Crane and winch operators	39

233	Construction machinery operators	32
234	Other stationary engine operators	34
	Electrical workers	
235	Electric power station and substation operators	42
236	Linemen	36
237	Electrical equipment fitters	44
238	Telephone and telegraph installers	35
239	Other electrical workers	40
	Miscellaneous craftsman and production process workers	
240	Tobacco workers	34
241	Painters	30
242	Lacquerers	41
243	Upholsters	31
244	Paperhangers	24
245	Japanese umbrella, lantern, and fan makers	28
246	Jewellers, goldsmiths, silversmiths, shell, horn and tusk makers	43
247	Stamp engravers	31
248	Umbrella setters	31
249	Luggage and handbag makers	31
250	Toy makers	31
251	Drawing-men	55
252	Loftsmen	55
253	Package wrapper	31
254	Motion picture projectionists	34
255	Other miscellaneous craftsman and production process workers	30
	Labourers not elsewhere classified	
256	Packers and wrappers	22
257	Warehousemen	20
258	Longshoremen	21
259	Stevedores and carriers	17
260	Railway station labourers	18
261	Carriers	26
262	Other labourers	18
	Protective Service Workers	
	Protective service workers	
263	Members of the self-defence forces	42
264	Policemen including marine and railway	40
265	Fire fighters	35
266	Guards, watchmen and janitors	30
267	Other protective service workers	30
268	Armed forces	42

Service Workers		
Domestic service workers		
269	Domestic maids (resident)	22
270	Housekeepers	28
271	Other domestic service workers	22
Personal service workers		
272	Barbers	30
273	Beauticians	35
274	Bathhouse workers	29
275	Laundry-men and dry cleaners	22
276	Cooks	31
277	Bartenders	23
278	Servants, waiters and waitresses	23
279	Barmaid and cabaret waitresses	20
280	Geisha-girls and hall dancers	39
281	Recreation and amusement place workers	20
282	Temporary keepers, footgear caretakers and lessors	27
283	Other personal service workers	29
Miscellaneous service workers		
284	Masters and Banto (attendants) of hotel, geisha-house, etc.	40
285	Superintendents of lodging, apartment house and matrons	24
286	Fashion models and other advertising workers	28
287	Sweepers and garbage men	13
288	Miscellaneous service workers	29

2 STANDARD INTERNATIONAL OCCUPATIONAL PRESTIGE SCORES (IPS) FOR DETAILED BRITISH OCCUPATIONAL CATEGORIES

	Occupation	*IPS*
1	**Farmers, Foresters, Fishermen**	
001	Fishermen	32
002	Farmers, farm managers, market gardeners	47
003	Agricultural workers n.e.c.	30
004	Agricultural machinery drivers	31
005	Gardeners and groundsmen	21
006	Foresters and woodmen	34
2	**Miners and Quarrymen**	
007	Coal mine – workers underground	32
008	Coal mine – workers above ground	32
009	Workers below ground n.e.c.	32
010	Surface workers n.e.c. – mines and quarries	32
3	**Gas, Coke and Chemicals Makers**	
011	Furnacemen, coal gas and coke ovens	40
012	Chemical production process workers n.e.c.	30
4	**Glass and Ceramics Makers**	
013	Ceramic formers	31
014	Glass formers, finishers and decorators	34
015	Furnacemen, kilnmen, glass and ceramic	31
016	Ceramics' decorators and finishers	31
017	Glass and ceramics production process workers n.e.c.	31
5	**Furnace, Forge, Foundry, Rolling Mill Workers**	
018	Furnacemen – metal	45
019	Rolling, tube mill operators, metal drawers	38
020	Moulders and coremakers (foundry)	38
021	Smiths, forgemen	35
022	Metal making and treating workers n.e.c.	38
023	Fettlers, metal dressers	38
6	**Electrical and Electronic Workers**	
024	Radio and radar mechanics	42
025	Installers and repairmen, telephone	35
026	Linesmen, cable jointers	36
027	Electricians	44
028	Electrical and electronic fitters	43
029	Assemblers (electrical and electronic)	48
030	Electrical engineers (so described)	48

7	**Engineering and Allied Trades Workers n.e.c.**	
031	Foremen (engineering and allied trades)	46
032	Trainee craftsmen (engineering and allied trades)	37
033	Sheet metal workers	36
034	Steel erectors; riggers	32
035	Metal plate workers; riveters	34
036	Gas, electric welders, cutters; braziers	39
037	Turners	37
038	Machine tool setters, setter-operators n.e.c.	40
039	Machine tool operators	38
040	Tool makers, tool room fitters	40
041	Motor mechanics, auto engineers	44
042	Maintenance fitters, maintenance engineers, millwrights	40
043	Fitters n.e.c., machine ejectors, etc.	43
044	Electro-platers, dip platers and related workers	28
045	Plumbers, gas fitters, lead burners	34
046	Pipe fitters, heating engineers	34
047	Press workers and stampers	41
048	Metal workers n.e.c.	38
049	Watch and chronometer makers and repairers	40
050	Precision instrument makers and repairers	47
051	Goldsmiths, silversmiths, jewellery makers	43
052	Coach, carriage, wagon builders and repairers	44
053	Inspectors (metal and electrical goods)	39
054	Other metal making, working; jewellery and electrical production process workers	40
8	**Woodworkers**	
055	Carpenters and joiners	37
056	Cabinet makers	40
057	Sawyers and wood working machinists	33
058	Pattern makers	29
059	Woodworkers n.e.c.	29
9	**Leather Workers**	
060	Tanners; leather, fur dressers, fellmongers	22
061	Shoemakers and shoe repairers	28
062	Cutters, lasters, sewers, footwear and related workers	28
063	Leather products makers n.e.c.	22
10	**Textile Workers**	
064	Fibre preparers	29
065	Spinners, doublers, twisters	34
066	Winders, reelers	34
067	Warpers, sizers, drawers-in	30
068	Weavers	30
069	Knitters	29
070	Bleachers and finishers of textiles	25
071	Dyers of textiles	25

072	Textile fabrics and related products makers and examiners n.e.c.	26
073	Textile fabrics, etc. products process workers n.e.c.	26
11	**Clothing Workers**	
074	Tailors, dress, light clothing makers	40
075	Upholsterers and related workers	31
076	Hand and machine sewers and embroiderers, textile and light leather products	26
077	Clothing and related products makers n.e.c.	34
12	**Food, Drink and Tobacco Workers**	
078	Bakers and pastry cooks	33
079	Butchers and meat cutters	31
080	Brewers, wine makers and related workers	34
081	Food processors n.e.c.	34
082	Tobacco preparers and products makers	34
13	**Paper and Printing Workers**	
083	Makers of paper and paperboard	28
084	Paper products makers	28
085	Compositors	42
086	Printing press operators	41
087	Printers (so described)	42
088	Printing workers n.e.c.	41
14	**Makers of Other Products**	
089	Workers in rubber	30
090	Workers in plastics	30
091	Craftsmen n.e.c.	42
092	Other production process workers	31
15	**Construction Workers**	
093	Bricklayers, tile setters	34
094	Masons, stone cutters, slate workers	34
095	Plasters, cement finishers, terrazzo workers	34
096	Builders (so described); clerks of works	36
097	Bricklayers, etc., labourers n.e.c.	26
098	Construction workers n.e.c.	28
16	**Painters and Decorators**	
099	Aerographers, paint sprayers	31
100	Painters, decorators n.e.c.	30
101	Coach painters (so described)	29
17	**Drivers of Stationary Engines, Cranes, etc.**	
102	Boiler firemen	38

103	Crane and hoist operators; slingers	39
104	Operators of earth moving and other construction machinery n.e.c.	32
105	Stationary engine, materials handling plant operators n.e.c. oilers and greasers	33
18	**Labourers n.e.c.**	
106	Railway lengthmen (labourers and unskilled workers n.e.c.)	33
107	Chemical and allied trades	18
108	Engineering and allied trades	18
109	Foundries in engineering and allied trades	18
110	Textiles (not textile goods)	18
111	Cook ovens and gas works	18
112	Glass and ceramics	18
113	Building and contracting	15
114	Other	18
19	**Transport and Communications Workers**	
115	Deck, engineering officers and pilots, ship	55
116	Deck and engine room ratings, barge and boatmen	29
117	Aircraft pilots, navigators and flight engineers	66
118	Drivers, motormen, second men, railway engine	34
119	Railway guards	30
120	Drivers of buses, coaches	32
121	Drivers of other road passenger vehicles	34
122	Drivers of road goods vehicles	33
123	Inspectors, supervisors, transport	37
124	Shunters, pointsmen	29
125	Signalman and crossing keepers, railways	29
126	Traffic controllers and dispatchers, transport	66
127	Telephone operators	38
128	Telephone and radio operators	47
129	Postmen, mail sorters	33
130	Messengers	26
131	Bus conductors	26
132	Porters, ticket collectors, railway	18
133	Stevedores, dock labourers	20
134	Lorry drivers' mates, van guards	15
135	Workers in transport and communication occupations n.e.c.	31
20	**Warehousemen, Storekeepers, Packers, Bottlers**	
136	Warehousemen, storekeepers and assistants	20
137	Packers, labellers and related workers	22
21	**Clerical Workers**	
138	Office managers n.e.c.	55
139	Clerks, cashiers	38
140	Office machine operators	45
141	Typists, shorthand writers, secretaries	48

142	Civil service executive officers	55
22	**Sales Workers**	
143	Proprietors and managers, sales	47
144	Shop salesmen and assistants	32
145	Roundsmen (bread, milk, laundry, soft drinks)	24
146	Street vendors, hawkers	24
147	Garage proprietors	48
148	Commercial travellers, manufacturers' agents	47
149	Finance, insurance brokers, financial agents	50
150	Salesmen, services; valuers, auctioneers	44
23	**Service, Sport and Recreation Workers**	
151	Fire bridge officers and men	35
152	Police officers and men	40
153	Guards and related workers n.e.c.	30
154	Publicans, innkeepers	34
155	Barmen, barmaids	23
156	Proprietors and managers boarding houses and hotels	40
157	Housekeepers, stewards, matrons and housemothers	37
158	Domestic housekeepers	29
159	Restaurateurs	48
160	Waiters and waitresses	23
161	Canteen assistants, counter hands	21
162	Cooks	31
163	Kitchen hands	22
164	Maids, valets and related service workers n.e.c.	22
165	Caretakers, office keepers	25
166	Charwomen, office cleaners; window cleaners, chimney sweeps	20
167	Hairdressers, manicurists, beauticians	32
168	Launderers, dry cleaners and pressers	22
169	Athletes, sportsmen and related workers	49
170	Hospital or ward orderlies; ambulance men	29
171	Proprietors and managers, service, sport and recreations n.e.c.	38
172	Service, sport and recreation workers n.e.c.	31
24	**Administrators and Managers**	
173	Ministers of the Crown; MPs n.e.c.; senior government officials	78
174	Local authority senior officers	65
175	Managers in engineering and allied trades	65
176	Managers in building and contracting	53
177	Managers in mining and production n.e.c.	64
178	Personnel managers	63
179	Sales managers	63
180	Managers n.e.c.	63
25	**Professional, Technical Workers, Artists**	
181	Medical practitioners (qualified)	78
182	Dental practitioners	70

183	Nurses	54
184	Pharmacists	64
185	Radiographers (medical and industrial)	58
186	Ophthalmic and dispensing opticians	60
187	Chiropodists	50
188	Physiotherapists	67
189	Occupational therapists	57
190	Public health inspection	48
191	Medical workers n.e.c.	50
192	University teachers	78
193	Primary and secondary school teachers	59
194	Teachers n.e.c.	62
195	Civil, structural, municipal engineers	70
196	Mechanical engineers	66
197	Electrical engineers	65
198	Electronic engineers	65
199	Work study, progress engineers	55
200	Planning, production engineers	60
201	Engineers n.e.c.	55
202	Metallurgists	60
203	Technologists n.e.c.	55
204	Chemists	69
205	Physical and biological scientists	71
206	Authors, journalists and related workers	58
207	Stage managers, actors, entertainers, musicians	48
208	Painters, sculptors and related creative artists	57
209	Accountants, professional	68
210	Company secretaries and registrars	62
211	Surveyors	58
212	Architects, town planners	72
213	Clergy, ministers, members of religious orders	54
214	Judges, barristers, advocates, solicitors	72
215	Social welfare and related workers	56
216	Officials of trade or professional associations	50
217	Professional workers n.e.c.	57
218	Draughtsmen	55
219	Laboratory assistants, technicians	46
220	Technical and related workers n.e.c.	46
26	**Armed Forces (British and Foreign)**	
221	Armed forces (UK)	42
222	Armed forces (Commonwealth and foreign)	42

Bibliography

Abercrombie, Nicholas and John Urry (1983) *Capital, Labor and the Middle Class* (London: George Allen & Unwin).

Aldrich, John H. and Forrest D. Nelson (1984) *Linear Probability, Logit, and Probit Models* (Beverly Hills: Sage).

Alwin, Duane (1974) 'College Effect on Educational and Occupational Attainment', *American Sociological Review*, 39: 210–23.

——— (1976) 'Socioeconomic Background, Colleges, and Post-College Achievements', in William H. Sewell, Robert M. Hauser and David Featherman (eds), *Schooling and Achievement in American Society* (New York: Academic Press): 343–73.

——— (1988) 'Measurement and Interpretation of Effects in Structural Equation Models', in J. Scott Long (ed.), *Common Problems/ Proper Solutions* (Beverly Hills: Sage): 15–45.

Amano, Ikuo (1983) 'Kyoiku no Chii Hyoji Kino ni Tsuite' (On the Status Expressing Function of Education), *Kyoiku Shakaigaku Kenkyu*, 38: 44–9.

Amano, Masako (1988) 'Kou-gakureki-ka no Shougeki no Nakade' (In the Midst of High Credentialism), Josei no Raifu Saikuru Kenkyu Iinkai (ed.), *Josei no Raifu Saikuru wa Dou Kawaru* (Tokyo: Tokei Kenkyukai): 61–104.

Ando, Bunshiro (1978) 'Hyohon Sekkei' (Sample Design), in 1975 SSM Survey Committee (ed.), *Shakai Kaiso to Shakai Ido* (Tokyo: 1975 SSM Survey Committee): 16–28.

——— (1979) 'Gakureki Shakai Kasetsu no Kento' (The Examination of Hypotheses of Educational Credential Society), in Ken'ichi Tominaga (ed.), *Nihon no Kaiso Kozo* (Tokyo: Todai Shuppankai): 276–92.

Apple, Michael W. (1978) 'The New Sociology of Education: Analyzing Cultural and Economic Reproduction', *Harvard Educational Review*, 12: 495–503.

——— (1979) *Ideology and Curriculum* (London: Routledge & Kegan Paul).

——— (1982a) 'Reproduction and Contradiction in Education', in Michael W. Apple (ed.), *Cultural and Economic Reproduction in Education* (London: Routledge & Kegan Paul): 1–31.

——— (1982b) *Education and Power* (Boston: Routledge & Kegan Paul).

Arisawa, Hiromi (1956) 'Nihon Shihonshugi to Koyo' (Japanese Capitalism and Employment), *Sekai*, 121 (January): 23–34.

Ariyoshi, Hiroyuki and Haruhiko Hamaguchi (eds) (1982) *Nihon no Shin Chukanso* (The New Middle Class in Japan) (Tokyo: Waseda Daigaku Suppankai).

Arrow, Kenneth J. (1973) 'Higher Education as a Filter', *Journal of Public Economics*, 2: 193–216.

Aso, Makoto (1969) *Erito to Kyoiku* (Elites and Education) (Tokyo: Fukumura Shuppan).

——— (1983) *Gakureki Shakai no Yomikata* (How to Read the Educational Credential Society) (Tokyo: Chikuma Shobo).

——— and Ikuo Amano (1983) *Education and Japan's Modernization* (Tokyo: Japan Times).

Astin, Alexander (1971) *Predicting Academic Performance in College: Selectivity Data for 2300 American Colleges* (New York: Free Press).

Baron, James and William Bielby (1980) 'Bringing the Firms Back In: Stratification, Segmentation, and the Organization of Work', *American Sociological Review*, 45: 737–65.

Beck, E.M., Patrick M. Horan and Charles Tolbert (1978) 'Stratification in a Dual Economy: A Sectoral Model of Earnings Determination', *American Sociological Review*, 43: 704–20.

Becker, Gary (1964) *Human Capital* (New York: National Bureau of Economic Research).

Bell, Daniel (1973) *The Coming of Post-Industrial Society* (New York: Basic Books).

Berg, Ivar (1973) *Education and Jobs: The Great Training Robbery* (Harmondsworth: Penguin Books).

Berger, Suzanne and Michael Piore (1980) *Dualism and Discontinuity in Industrial Societies* (Cambridge: Cambridge University Press).

Berle, Adolf A. and Gardiner C. Means (1932) *The Modern Corporations and Private Property* (New York: Macmillan).

Bernstein, Basil (1977) *Class, Codes and Control*, 2nd edn, vol. 3 (London: Routledge & Kegan Paul).

Bibb, Robert and William H. Form (1977) 'The Effect of Industrial, Occupational, and Sex Stratification on Wages in Blue-collar Markets', *Social Forces*, 55: 974–96.

Bielby, William T. (1981) 'Models of Status Attainment', *Research in Social Stratification and Mobility*, 1: 3–26.

Bishop, Yvonne, Stephen Fienberg and Paul Holland (1975) *Discrete Multivariate Analysis* (Cambridge, Mass.: MIT Press).

Blake, Judith (1985) 'Number of Siblings and Educational Mobility', *American Sociological Review*, 50: 84–94.

Blau, Peter M. and Otis Dudley Duncan (1967) *The American Occupational Structure* (New York: Wiley).

Bottomore, Tom B. (1965) *Classes in Modern Society* (London: Allen & Unwin).

Boudon, Raymond (1974) *Education, Opportunity, and Social Inequality* (New York: Wiley).

Bourdieu, Pierre (1973) 'Cultural Reproduction and Social Reproduction', in Richard Brown (ed.), *Knowledge, Education and Cultural Change* (London: Tavistock): 7–112.

——— (1974) 'The School as a Conservative Force', John Eggleston (ed.), *Contemporary Research in the Sociology of Education* (London: Methuen): 32–46.

——— (1977) 'Cultural Reproduction and Social Reproduction', in

Jerome Karabel and A.H. Halsey (eds), *Power and Ideology in Education* (New York: Oxford University Press): 487–511.
——— and Jean-Claude Passeron (1977) *Reproduction in Education, Society and Culture* (Beverly Hills: Sage).
——— (1979) *The Inheritors* (Chicago: University of Chicago Press).
Bowles, Samuel (1971) 'Unequal Education and the Reproduction of Social Division of Labor', in Jerome Karabel and A.H. Halsey (eds), *Power and Ideology in Education* (New York: Oxford University Press): 137–53.
——— (1972) 'Schooling and Inequality from Generation to Generation', *Journal of Political Economy*, 80: S219–51.
——— and Herbert Gintis (1976) *Schooling in Capitalist America* (New York: Basic Books).
Boyd, David (1973) *Elites and Their Education* (Windsor: NFER Publishing).
Burawoy, Michael (1977) 'Social Structure, Homogenization, and "The Process of Status Attainment in the United States and Great Britain"', *American Journal of Sociology*, 82: 1031–42.
Calvert, Peter (1982) *The Concept of Class* (London: Hutchinson).
Cantor, Leonard and I.F. Roberts (1983) *Further Education Today* (London: Routledge & Kegan Paul).
Central Statistical Office (1988) *Annual Abstract of Statistics*, no. 124 (London: HMSO).
Chandler, Alfred D. (1977) *The Visible Hand* (Cambridge, Mass.: Harvard University Press).
Clark, Burton (1962) *Educating the Expert Society* (San Francisco: Chandler).
Cole, Robert E. (1979) *Work, Mobility, and Participation* (Berkeley: University of California Press).
——— and Ken'ichi Tominaga (1976) 'Japan's Changing Occupational Structure and its Significance', in Hugh Patrick (ed.), *Japanese Industrialization and its Social Consequences* (Berkeley: University of California Press): 53–95.
Coleman, James (1976) 'Regression Analysis for the Comparison of School and Home Effects', *Social Science Research*, 5: 1–20.
Coleman, Richard P. and Lee Rainwater (1978) *Social Standing in America* (New York: Basic Books).
Crompton, Rosemary and Michael Mann (eds) (1986) *Gender and Stratification* (Cambridge: Polity Press).
Cummings, William K. (1980) *Education and Equality in Japan* (Princeton: Princeton University Press).
——— and Atsushi Naoi (1974) 'Social Background, Education, and Personal Advancement in a Dualistic Employment System', *Developing Economics*, 12: 245–73.
Davis, James A. (1982) *General Social Surveys, 1972–1982: Cumulative Code Book* (Storrs: Roper Public Opinion Research Center).
DeVos, George and Hiroshi Wagatsuma (1966) *Japan's Invisible Race* (Berkeley: University of California Press).

Dex, Shirley and Lois B. Shaw (1986) *British and American Women at Work: Do Equal Opportunities Policies Matter?* (London: Macmillan).
DiMaggio, Paul (1982) 'Cultural Capital and School Success', *American Sociological Review*, 47: 189–201.
Doeringer, Peter and Michael Piore (1971) *Internal Labor Market and Manpower Analysis* (Lexington: D.C. Heath).
Dolton, P.J. and G.H. Makepeace (1986) 'Sample Selection and Male–Female Earnings Differentials in the Graduate Labour Market', *Oxford Economic Papers*, 38: 317–41.
——— (1987) 'Marital Status, Child Rearing and Earning Differentials in the Graduate Labour Market', *The Economic Journal*, 97: 897–922.
Dore, Ronald (1976) *The Diploma Disease: Education, Qualification and Development* (Berkeley: University of California Press).
——— (1987) *Taking Japan Seriously* (Stanford: Stanford University Press).
Duncan, Beverly (1968) 'Trends in Output and Distribution of Schooling', in E.B. Sheldon and W.E. Moore (eds), *Indicators of Social Change* (New York: Russell Sage Foundation): 601–72.
Duncan, Otis Dudley (1966) 'Methodological Issues in the Analysis of Social Mobility', in Neil J. Smelser and Seymour Martin Lipset (eds), *Social Structure and Mobility in Economic Development* (Chicago: Aldine): 51–97.
——— (1975) *Introduction to Structural Equation Models* (New York: Academic Press).
——— (1979) 'How Destination Depends on Origin in the Occupational Mobility Table', *American Journal of Sociology*, 84: 793–803.
——— and Robert W. Hodge (1963) 'Education and Occupational Mobility: A Regression Analysis', *American Journal of Sociology*, 68: 629–44.
Ehara, Takekazu (1977) 'Taishuka Katei ni okeru Kotokyoiku Kikai no Kozo' (The Structure of Opportunities for Higher Education under the Mass Process), *Daigaku Ronshu*, 5: 177–99.
——— (1984) *Gendai Koto Kyoiku no Kozo* (The Structure of Contemporary Higher Education) (Tokyo: Todai Shuppan Kai).
Ehrenreich, Barbara and John Ehrenreich (1979) 'The Professional–Managerial Class', in Pat Walker (ed.), *Between Labor and Capital* (Boston: South End Press): 5–45.
Erikson, Robert, John Goldthorpe and Lucienne Portocarero (1979) 'Intergenerational Class Mobility in Three Western European Societies', *British Journal of Sociology*, 30: 415–41.
——— (1982) 'Social Fluidity in Industrial Nations: England, France and Sweden', *British Journal of Sociology*, 33: 1–34.
——— (1983) 'Intergenerational Class Mobility and the Convergence Thesis: England, France and Sweden', *British Journal of Sociology*, 34: 303–43.
——— and John Goldthorpe (1985) 'Are American Rates of Social Mobility Exceptionally High?', *European Sociological Review*, 1: 1–22.
——— and John Goldthorpe (1987a) 'Commonality and Variation in

Social Fluidity in Industrial Nations: A Model for Evaluating the "FJH Hypothesis"', *European Sociological Review*, 3: 54–77.

——— and John Goldthorpe (1987b) 'Commonality and Variation in Social Fluidity in Industrial Nations: The Model of Core Fluidity Applied', *European Sociological Review*, 3: 145–66.

——— and Seppo Pontinen (1985) 'Social Mobility in Finland and Sweden: A Comparison of Men and Women', in Risto Alapuro *et al.* (eds), *Small States in Comparative Perspective* (Oslo: Universitetsforlaget): 138–62.

Featherman, David L. (1971) 'A Social Structural Model for the Socio-economic Career', *American Journal of Sociology*, 77: 293–304.

——— (1973) 'Comments on Models for the Socio-economic Career', *American Sociological Review*, 38: 785–90.

——— (1981) 'Stratification and Social Mobility: Two Decades of Cumulative Social Science', in James F. Short, Jr (ed.), *The State of Sociology* (Beverly Hills: Sage): 79–100.

——— and Robert M. Hauser (1978) *Opportunity and Change* (New York: Academic Press).

———, F. Lancaster Jones and Robert M. Hauser (1975) 'Assumptions of Social Mobility Research in the United States: The Case of Occupational Status', *Social Science Research*, 4: 339–60.

Feldman, Arnold and Wilbert E. Moore (1962) 'Industrialization and Industrialism: Convergence and Differentiation', in Transactions of the Fifth World Congress of Sociology (Washington, D.C.: International Sociological Association).

Fidler, John (1981) *The British Business Elite* (London: Routledge & Kegan Paul).

Freeman, Richard (1971) *The Market for College-Trained Manpower* (Cambridge, Mass.: Harvard University Press).

——— (1976) *The Over-educated American* (New York: Academic Press).

Fujita, Hidenori (1977) 'Gakureki no Shakaiteki Koyo' (Social Returns to Educational Credentials), in Makoto Aso and Morikazu Ushiogi (eds), *Gakureki Koyo Ron* (Tokyo: Yuhikaku): 105–31.

——— (1978) 'Education and Status Attainment in Modern Japan', unpublished Ph.D. dissertation (Stanford University).

——— (1980) 'Kogakureki Shakai no nakano Daisotsu' (College Graduates in the Highly Credentialized Society), in Nobuo Nakanishi *et al.* (eds), *Shushoku* (Tokyo: Yuhikaku): 154–80.

——— (1981) 'Kyoiku Kikai wa Kaihoteki ka' (Are the Educational Opportunities Open?), in Hiroshi Takeuchi and Makoto Aso (eds), *Nihon no Gakureki Shakai wa Kawaru* (Tokyo: Yuhikaku): 27–44.

——— (1983) 'Gakureki no Keizaiteki Koyo no Kokusai Hikaku' (The International Comparison of the Economic and Social Benefits of Educational Credentials), *Kyoiku Shakaigaku Kenkyu*, 38: 76–93.

Fukutake, Tadashi (1967) *Japanese Rural Society* (Ithaca: Cornell University Press).

Funahashi, Yoshimichi (ed.) (1967) *Nihon no Chingin* (Wages in Japan) (Tokyo: Nihon Hyoronsha).

Gagliani, Giorgio (1985) 'Long-term Changes in Occupational Structure', *European Sociological Review*, 1: 183–210.

Galtung, Johan (1971) 'Social Structure, Education Structure and Life Long Education: The Case of Japan', in OECD (ed.), *Reviews of National Policies for Education: Japan* (Paris: OECD): 131–52.

Giddens, Anthony (1973) *The Class Structure of the Advanced Societies* (New York: Harper & Row).

Giroux, Henry A. (1983) 'Theories of Reproduction and Resistance in the New Sociology of Education: A Critical Analysis', *Harvard Educational Review*, 53: 257–93.

Goldthorpe, John H. (1972) 'Class, Status, Party in Modern Britain', *European Archives of Sociology*, 12.

——— (1980) *Social Mobility and Class Structure in Modern Britain*, 1st edn (Oxford: Clarendon Press).

——— (1984) 'Social Mobility and Class Formation: On the Renewal of a Tradition in Sociological Inquiry', Comparative Analysis of Social Mobility in Industrial Nations working paper, no. 1. (Mannheim: CASMIN Project).

——— (1987) *Social Mobility and Class Structure in Modern Britain*, 2nd edn (Oxford: Clarendon Press).

——— and Keith Hope (1974) *The Social Grading of Occupations* (Oxford: Clarendon Press).

——— and Clive Payne (1986) 'On the Class Mobility of Women: Results from Different Approaches to the Analysis of Recent British Data', *Sociology*, 20: 531–55.

Goodman, Leo A. (1965) 'On the Statistical Analysis of Mobility Tables', *American Journal of Sociology*, 70: 564–85.

——— (1969) 'How to Ransack Social Mobility Tables and Other Kinds of Cross-classification Tables', *American Journal of Sociology*, 75: 1–39.

——— (1972) 'Some Multiplicative Models for the Analysis of Cross-classified Data', in J. Neymann (ed.), *Proceedings of the Sixth Berkeley Symposium on Mathematical Statistics and Probability* (Berkeley: University of California Press): 649–96.

——— (1979) 'Multiplicative Models for Analysis of Occupational Mobility Tables and Other Kinds of Cross-classification Tables', *American Journal of Sociology*, 84: 804–19.

Goto, Yasushi (1985) 'Chu-ishiki no Mujun – Kaikyu to Kaiso' (The Contradiction of Middle Consciousness – Class and Stratification), in Rekishigaku Kenkyukai (ed.), *Koza Nihon Rekishi 13* (Tokyo: Todai Shuppankai): 139–64.

Greenhalgh, Christine (1980) 'Male–Female Wage Differentials in Great Britain', *The Economic Journal*, 90: 751–75.

——— and Mark B. Stewart (1985) 'The Occupational Status and Mobility of British Men and Women', *Oxford Economic Papers*, 37: 40–71.

Griffin, Larry J. and Karl L. Alexander (1978) 'Schooling and Socioeconomic Attainments: High School and College Influences', *American Journal of Sociology*, 84: 319–47.

——— and Arne Kalleberg (1981) 'Stratification and Meritocracy in the United States', *British Journal of Sociology*, 32: 1–38.

Grusky, David B. (1983) 'Industrialization and the Status Attainment Process', *American Sociological Review*, 48: 494–506.

——— and Robert M. Hauser (1984) 'Comparative Social Mobility Revisited', *American Sociological Review*, 49: 19–38.

Haller, Archibald O. and William H. Sewell (1957) 'Farm Residence and Levels of Occupational and Educational Aspiration', *American Journal of Sociology*, 62: 407–11.

——— and Alejandro Portes (1973) 'Status Attainment Process', *Sociology of Education*, 46: 51–91.

Halsey, A.H. (1977) 'Towards Meritocracy? The Case of Britain', in Jerome Karabel and A.H. Halsey (eds), *Power and Ideology in Education* (New York: Oxford University Press): 173–86.

——— A.F. Heath and J.M. Ridge (1980) *Origins and Destinations* (Oxford: Clarendon Press).

Hara, Akira (1979) 'Kaikyu Kosei no Shinsuikei' (The New Estimation for the Class Composition), in Yoshio Ando (ed.), *Ryotaisen kan no Nihon Shihonshugi* (Tokyo: Todai Shuppankai): 325–64.

Hashimoto, Kenji (1986) 'Gendai Nihon no Kaikyuu Bunseki' (Class Analysis in Contemporary Japan), *Shakaigaku Hyoron*, 37: 175–90.

Hashizume, Sadao (1976a) 'Gakureki no Koyo to Gakureki Ishiki' (Returns to Educational Credentials and Attitudes toward Credentials), in Sadao Hashizume (ed.), *Gakureki Hencho to sono Kozai* (Tokyo: Daiichi Hoki): 1–68.

——— (1976b) 'Shokuba ni okeru Gakureki Ishiki' (Attitudes toward Credentials in the Workplace), in Sadao Hashizume (ed.), *Gakureki Hencho to sono Kozai* (Tokyo: Daiichi Hoki): 127–92.

Hauser, Robert M. (1970) 'Educational Stratification in the United States', in Edward Laumann (ed.), *Social Stratification: Research and Theory for the 1970s* (New York: Bobbs-Merrill): 102–29.

———, Peter J. Dickinson, Harry P. Travis and John M. Koffel (1975a) 'Structural Changes in Occupational Mobility among Men in the United States', *American Sociological Review*, 40: 585–98.

———, Peter J. Dickinson, Harry P. Travis and John M. Koffel (1975b) 'Temporal Change in Occupational Mobility: Evidence for Men in the United States', *American Sociological Review*, 40: 279–97.

——— and David Featherman (1976) 'Equality of Schooling: Trends and Prospects', *Sociology of Education*, 49: 99–120.

——— and David Featherman (1977) *The Process of Stratification* (New York: Academic Press).

——— and David B. Grusky (1988) 'Cross-national Variation in Occupational Distributions, Relative Mobility Chances, and Intergenerational Shifts in Occupational Distributions', *American Sociological Review*, 53: 723–41.

Heise, David (1972) 'Employing Nominal Variables, Induced Variables, and Block Variables in Path Analysis', *Sociological Methods and Research*, 1: 147–73.

Hirano, Yoshitaro (1967) *Nihon Shihonshugi Shakai no Kiko* (The Structure of the Japanese Capitalist Society), 3rd edn (Tokyo: Iwanami Shoten).

Hirasawa, Yasumasa (1983) 'The Burakumin: Japan's Minority Population', *Integrated Education*, 10: 3–7.

Hodge, Robert W., Donald J. Treiman and Peter H. Rossi (1966) 'Comparative Study of Occupational Prestige', in Reinhard Bendix and Seymour Martin Lipset (eds), *Class, Status and Power*, 2nd edn (New York: Free Press): 309–21.

Hogan, Dennis P. (1978) 'The Variable Order of Events in the Life Cycle', *American Sociological Review*, 43: 573–86.

Horan, Patrick M. (1978) 'Is Status Attainment Research Atheoretical?', *American Sociological Review*, 43: 534–41.

Hout, Michael (1983) *Mobility Tables* (Beverly Hills: Sage).

——— (1988) 'More Universalism, Less Structural Mobility: The American Occupational Structure in the 1980s', *American Journal of Sociology*, 93: 1358–1400.

Ichikawa, Toyo and Yoshiro Sengoku (1980) 'Kaikyu Gakusetsu' (Theories of Class), in Saburo Yasuda *et al.* (eds), *Kiso Shakaigaku: Shakai Kozo*, (Tokyo: Toyo Keizai Shinposha): 120–50.

Imada, Takatoshi and Junsuke Hara (1979) 'Shakaiteki Chii no Ikkansei to Hiikkansei' (Consistency and Inconsistency in Social Status), in Ken'ichi Tominaga (ed.), *Nihon no Kaiso Kozo* (Tokyo: Todai Shuppankai): 162–97.

Inagami, Takeshi (1988) *Japanese Workplace Industrial Relations* (Tokyo: Japan Institute of Labour).

Inkels, Alex and Peter H. Rossi (1956) 'National Comparisons of Occupational Prestige', *American Journal of Sociology*, 61: 329–39.

Ishida, Hiroshi (1986) 'Educational Credentials, Class, and the Labor Market: A Comparative Study of Social Mobility in Japan and the United States', unpublished Ph.D. dissertation (Harvard University).

——— (1989) 'Class Structure and Status Hierarchies in Contemporary Japan', *European Sociological Review*, 5: 65–80.

———, John Goldthorpe and Robert Erikson (1987) 'Intergenerational Class Mobility in Post-war Japan', CASMIN working paper, no. 11 (Mannheim: CASMIN Project).

Ishikawa, Akihiro, Tadashi Umezawa and Takashi Miyajima (1983) *Misekake no Chusan Kaikyu* (A False Middle Class) (Tokyo: Yuhikaku).

Ishizaki, Tadao (1983) *Nihon no Shotoku to Tomi no Bunpai* (The Distribution of Income and Wealth in Japan) (Tokyo: Toyo Keizai Shinposha).

Iwamoto, Takeyoshi (1985) 'Sedaikan Ido no Susei Bunseki' (Trend Analysis of Intergenerational Mobility), in Junsuke Hara and Michio Umino (eds), *Suri Shakaigaku no Genzai* (Tokyo: Suri Shakaigaku Kenkyukai): 215–28.

Iwauchi, Ryoichi (1980) *Gakurekishugi wa Hokai Shitaka* (Did Educational Credentialism Collapse?) (Tokyo: Nihon Keizai Shinbunsha).

Jencks, Christopher S., Marshall Smith, Henry Acland, Mary Jo Bane, David Cohen, Herbert Gintis, Barbara Heyns and Stephan Michelson (1972) *Inequality: A Reassessment of the Effect of Family and Schooling in America* (New York: Basic Books).

———, Susan Bartlett, Mary Corcoran, James Crouse, David Eaglesfield, Gregory Jackson, Kent McClelland, Peter Mueser, Michael Olneck, Joseph Schwartz, Sherry Ward, and Jill Williams (1979) *Who Gets Ahead? The Determinants of Economic Success in America* (New York: Basic Books).

Kada, Ryohei (1980) *Part-time Family Farming* (Tokyo: Centre for Academic Publications, Japan).

Kadowaki, Atsushi (1978) *Gendai no Shusse Kan* (Attitudes towards Getting Ahead in Modern Japan) (Tokyo: Nihon Keizai Shinbunsha).

Kalleberg, Arne and Larry Griffin (1980) 'Class, Occupation, and Inequality in Job Rewards', *American Journal of Sociology*, 85: 731–68.

Karabel, Jerome (1972) 'Community College and Social Stratification', *Harvard Educational Review*, 42: 521–62.

——— and Alexander Astin (1975) 'Social Class, Academic Ability, and College Quality', *Social Forces*, 53: 381–98.

——— and Katherine McClelland (1987) 'Occupational Advantage and the Impact of College Rank on Labour Market Outcomes', *Sociological Inquiry*, 57: 323–47.

Kawaguchi, Kiyoshi (1980) 'Rodosha Kaikyu no Kosei Henka' (Change in Composition of the Working Class), in the Committee on the First Japan–Russo Academic Symposium (eds), *Sengo Nihon no Shakai Kozo no Henka* (Kyoto: Ritsumeikan Daigaku Jinbunkagaku Kenkyusho): 121–40.

Kerckhoff, Alan C. (1974) 'Stratification Processes and Outcomes in England and the U.S.', *American Sociological Review*, 39: 739–801.

———, Richard T. Campbell and Idee Winfield-Laird (1985) 'Social Mobility in Great Britain and the United States', *American Journal of Sociology*, 91: 281–308.

Kerr, C., J.T. Dunlop, F.H. Harbinson and C.A. Myers (1960) *Industrialism and Industrial Man* (Cambridge, Mass.: Harvard University Press).

Kim, Paul (1988) *Japan's Civil Service System* (New York: Greenwood Press).

Kishimoto, Shigenobu (1977) 'Shinchukan Kaisoron wa Kano ka' (Can the New Middle Class Theory be Sustained?), *Asahi Shinbun*, evening edn (9 June).

——— (1978) *Churyu no Genso* (The Illusion of the Middle Class) (Tokyo: Kodansha).

Kitahara, Isamu (1984) *Gendai Shihonshugi ni okeru Shoyu to Kettei* (Ownership and Determination in Contemporary Capitalism) (Tokyo: Iwanami Shoten).

Kohn, Melvin L. (1969) *Class and Conformity* (Homewood, Ill.: Dorsey Press).

——— (1976) 'Occupational Structure and Alienation', *American Journal of Sociology*, 82: 111–30.

——— and Carmi Schooler (1983) *Work and Personality* (New York: Ablex).

Koike, Kazuo (1981) *Nihon no Jukuren* (Skills in Japan) (Tokyo: Yuhikaku).

——— (1983) 'Workers in Small Firms and Women in Industry', in Taishiro Shirai (ed.), *Contemporary Industrial Relations in Japan* (Madison: University of Wisconsin Press): 89–115.

——— (1988) *Understanding Industrial Relations in Modern Japan* (London: Macmillan).

——— and Yukiro Watanabe (1979) *Gakureki Shakai no Kyozo* (The Illusion of the Educational Credential Society) (Tokyo: Toyo Keizai Shinposha).

Kojima, Hideo (1986) 'Josei no Shakai Ido no Nichibei Hikaku Kenkyuu' (A Comparative Study of Women's Social Mobility in Japan and the United States), in Ken'ichi Tominaga (ed.), *Shakai Kaiso no Susei to Hikaku* (Tokyo: SSM Susei to Hikaku Kenkyukai): 41–52.

——— and Atsushi Hamana (1984) 'Shokugyo Ido no Keiko Bunseki' (Trend Analysis of Occupational Mobility), *Ibaraki Daigaku Kyoiku Gakubu Kiyo*, 33: 17–32.

Koyama, Shigeki (1981) 'Kanryo to Gakureki' (Bureaucrats and Educational Credentials), in Hiroshi Takeuchi and Makoto Aso (eds), *Nihon no Gakureki Shakai wa Kawaru*, (Tokyo: Yuhikaku): 62–83.

Koyou Shokugyo Kenkyujo (ed.) (1979) *Nihonjin no Shokugyokeireki to Shokugyo-kan* (Occupational History and Views on Occupation in Japan) (Tokyo: Shiseido).

Lee, Changsoo and George DeVos (1981) *Koreans in Japan* (Berkeley: University of California Press).

Levy, Marion J. (1966) *Modernization and the Structure of Societies* (Princeton: Princeton University Press).

Lie, John (1987) 'Koreans in Japan', *Monthly Review*, 38: 17–23.

Lin, Nan and Daniel Yauger (1975) 'The Process of Occupational Status Attainment: A Preliminary Cross-national Comparison', *American Journal of Sociology*, 81: 543–62.

Lipset, Seymour M. and Reinhard Bendix (eds) (1959) *Social Mobility in Industrial Society* (Berkeley: University of California Press).

——— and Hans L. Zetterberg (1959) 'Social Mobility in Industrial Societies', in Seymour M. Lipset and Reinhard Bendix (eds), *Social Mobility in Industrial Society* (Berkeley: University of California Press): 11–75.

Maddala, G.S. (1983) *Limited-dependent and Qualitative Variables in Econometrics* (Cambridge: Cambridge University Press).

Mannari, Hiroshi (1965) *Bijinesu Erito* (Business Elites) (Tokyo: Chuo Koronsha).

——— (1974) *The Japanese Business Leaders* (Tokyo: University of Tokyo Press).

Mare, Robert D. (1981) 'Change and Stability in Educational Stratification', *American Sociological Review*, 46: 72–87.

——— and Meichu D. Chen (1986) 'Further Evidence on Sibship Size and Educational Stratification', *American Sociological Review*, 51: 403–12.

Marshall, Gordon, Howard Newby, David Rose and Carolyn Vogler (1988) *Social Class in Modern Britain* (London: Hutchinson).

Marx, Karl [1867] (1967) *Capital*, vol. 1 (New York: International Publishers).
——— and Fredrick Engels [1848] (1967) *Manifesto of the Communist Party* (Harmondsworth: Penguin).
Matsuura, Takanori (1978) *Shushoku* (Getting a Job) (Tokyo: Nihon Keizai Shinbunsha).
Mayhew, Ken and Bridget Rosewell (1981) 'Occupational Mobility in Britain', *Oxford Bulletin of Economics and Statistics*, 43: 225–55.
Miller, Herman P. (1971) *Rich Man, Poor Man* (New York: Thomas Y. Crowell).
Miller, S.M. (1960) 'Comparative Social Mobility', *Current Sociology*, 9: 1–89.
Mincer, Jacob (1974) *Schooling, Experience, and Earnings* (New York: National Bureau of Economic Research).
Ministry of Education (1978) *Education in Japan 1978: A Graphic Presentation* (Tokyo: Gyosei).
Misaki, Akira (1979) *Gendai Rodo Shijoron* (Theory of Contemporary Labour Market) (Tokyo: Noson Gyoson Bunka Kyokai).
Miyazaki, Yoshikazu (1976) *Sengò Nihon no Kigyo Shudan* (Corporation Groups in Post-war Japan) (Tokyo: Nihon Keizai Shinbunsha).
Monbusho (Ministry of Education) (1982a) *Gakko Kihonchosa Hokokusho: Koto Kyoiku Kikan* (Report on the Basic Survey of Schools: Higher Education Institutions) (Tokyo: Monbusho).
——— (1982b) *Gakko Kihonchosa Hokokusho: Shoto Chuto Kyoiku Kikan* (Report on the Basic Survey of Schools: Primary and Secondary Education Institutions) (Tokyo: Monbusho).
——— (1983) *Monbu Tokei Yoran* (Digest of Educational Statistics) (Tokyo: Daiichi Hoki).
——— (1988) *Monbu Tokei Yoran* (Digest of Educational Statistics) (Tokyo: Daiichi Hoki).
Morishima, Michio (1977) *Igirisu to Nihon* (Britain and Japan) (Tokyo: Iwanami Shoten).
Mosteller, Frederick (1968) 'Association and Estimation in Contingency Tables', *Journal of American Statistical Association*, 63: 1–28.
Murakami, Yasusuke (1977) 'Shinchukan Kaiso no Genjitsusei' (The Reality of the New Middle Class), *Asahi Shinbun*, evening edn (20 May).
——— (1984) *Shin Chukan Taishu no Jidai* (The Age of New Middle Mass) (Tokyo: Chuo Koronsha).
Nakayama, Keiko and Hideo Kojima (1979) 'Kyoiku Asupireishon to Shokugyo Asupireishon' (Educational Aspirations and Occupational Aspirations), in Ken'ichi Tominaga (ed.), *Nihon no Kaiso Kozo* (Tokyo: Todai Shuppankai): 291–328.
Naoi, Atsushi (1979) 'Shokugyoteki Chiishakudo no Kosei' (The Construction of the Occupational Status Scale), in Ken'ichi Tominaga (ed.), *Nihon no Kaiso Kozo* (Tokyo: Todai Shuppankai): 434–72.
———, Ken'ichi Tominaga and Kazuo Seiyama (1972) 'Shakai Kozo no Hendo' (Changes in Social Structure), in Hiroshi Akuto, Ken'ichi Tominaga and Takao Sofue (eds), *Hendoki no Nihon Shakai* (Tokyo: Nihon Hoso Shuppan Kyokai): 85–158.

Naoi, Michiko (1979) 'Kaiso Ishiki to Kaikyu Ishiki' (Status Consciousness and Class Consciousness), in Ken'ichi Tominaga (ed.), *Nihon no Kaiso Kozo*, (Tokyo: Todai Shuppankai): 365–88.

Nihon Shakai Gakkai Chosa Iinkai (Japanese Sociological Society Research Committee) (1958) *Nihon Shakai no Kaisoteki Kozo* (The Structure of Stratification in Japanese Society) (Tokyo: Yuhikaku).

Nihon Rikuruto Senta (1975) *Gakureki ni Kansuru Kigyo no Ikenchosa* (Opinion Survey on Educational Credentials among Firms) (Tokyo: Nihon Rikuruto Senta).

Nishi, Isao (1979) *Mensetsu ni Katsu Ho* (How to Win the Job Interview) (Tokyo: Goma Shobo).

Noro, Eitaro (1930) *Nihon Shihonshugi Hattatsushi* (The History of the Development of Japanese Capitalism) (Tokyo: Iwanami Shoten).

Odaka, Konosuke (1984) *Rodo Shijo Bunseki* (The Analysis of the Labour Market) (Tokyo: Iwanami Shoten).

OECD (ed.) (1971) *Reviews of National Policies for Education: Japan* (Paris: OECD).

Ogata, Ken (1976) *Gakureki Shinko Shakai* (A Society with a Belief in Educational Credentials) (Tokyo: Jiji Tsushinsha).

Ohashi, Ryuken (ed.) (1971) *Nihon no Kaikyu Kosei* (Japan's Class Composition) (Tokyo: Iwanami Shoten).

Okamoto, Hideo (1982) 'Seikatsu no Kiban toshiteno Seisan to Rodo' (Production and Labour as the Basis of Life), in Haruo Matsubara and Eiji Yamamoto (eds), *Ningen Seikatsu no Shakaigaku* (Tokyo: Kakiuchi Shuppan): 52–71.

——— (ed.) (1989) *1985 Shakai Kaiso to Shakai Ido Zenkoku Chosa Hokokusho: Josei to Shakai Kaiso* (Report on the 1985 Social Stratification and Social Mobility National Survey) (Osaka: 1985 Shakai Kaiso to Shakai Ido Zenkoku Chosa Iinkai).

——— and Junsuke Hara (1979) 'Shokugyo no Miryoku Hyoka no Bunseki' (The Analysis of Prestige Evaluation of Occupations), in Ken'ichi Tominaga *Nihon no Kaiso Kozo* (Tokyo: Todai Shuppankai): 421–33.

Okouchi, Kazuo (1960) *Nihonteki Chusan Kaikyu* (The Japanese Middle Class) (Tokyo: Bungei Shunjusha).

Okumura, Hiroshi (1978) *Kigyo Shudan Jidai no Keieisha* (Managers in the Age of Corporation Groups) (Tokyo: Nihon Keizai Shinbunsha).

——— (1984) *Hojin Shihonshugi* (Corporation Capitalism) (Tokyo: Ochanomizu Shobo).

OPCS (Office of Population Censuses and Surveys) (1970a) *Classification of Occupations 1970* (London: HMSO).

——— (1970b) *Qualified Manpower Tables, Sample Census 1966, Great Britain* (London: HMSO).

Osterman, Paul (1980) *Getting Started* (Cambridge, Mass.: MIT Press).

Ouchi, Tsutomu (1971) *Gendai Nihon Keizairon* (The Theory of the Modern Japanese Economy) (Tokyo: Todai Shuppankai).

Ozawa, Masako (1985) *Shin Kaiso Shohi no Jidai* (The Age of the New Pattern of Consumption by Different Strata) (Tokyo: Nihon Keizai Shinbunsha).

Parkin, Frank (1971) *Class Inequality and Political Order* (New York: Praeger).
——— (1979) *Marxism and Class Theory* (New York: Columbia University Press).
Parsons, Talcott (1951) *The Social System* (Glencoe, Ill.: Free Press).
Passin, Herbert (1965) *Society and Education in Japan* (New York: Teachers College Press).
Payne, Clive (ed.) (1985) *The GLIM System Release 3.77 Manual* (Oxford: Numeric Algorithm Groups).
Pontinen, Seppo (1982) 'Models of Social Mobility Research: A Comparison of Some Log-linear Models of a Social Mobility Matrix', *Quality and Quantity*, 16: 90–107.
Portocarero, Lucienne (1983a) 'Social Fluidity in France and Sweden', *Acta Sociologica*, 26: 127–39.
——— (1983b) 'Social Mobility in Industrial Nations: Women in France and Sweden', *Sociological Review*, 31: 56–82.
——— (1985) 'Social Mobility in France and Sweden: Women, Marriage, and Work', *Acta Sociologica*, 28: 151–70.
Poulantzas, Nicos (1975) *Classes in Contemporary Capitalism* (London: New Left Books).
Psacharopoulos, George (1977) 'Family Background, Education and Achievement', *British Journal of Sociology*, 28: 321–35.
——— and Richard Layard (1979) 'Human Capital and Earnings: British Evidence and a Critique', *Review of Economic Studies*, 46: 485–504.
Raffe, David (1979) 'The "Alternative Route" Reconsidered', *Sociology*, 13: 47–73.
Reischauer, Edwin O. (1977) *The Japanese* (Cambridge, Mass.: Harvard University Press).
Reskin, Barbara F. (ed.) (1984) *Sex Segregation in the Workplace: Trends, Explanations, Remedies* (Washington, D.C.: National Academy Press).
——— and Heidi I. Hartmann (eds) (1986) *Women's Work and Men's Work: Sex Segregation on the Job* (Washington, D.C.: National Academy Press).
Robinson, Robert V. (1984a) 'Reproduction of Class Relations in Industrial Capitalism', *American Sociological Review*, 49: 182–96.
——— (1984b) 'Structural Change and Class Mobility in Capitalist Societies', *Social Forces*, 63: 51–71.
——— and Jonathan Kelley (1979) 'Class as Conceived by Marx and Dahrendorf', *American Sociological Review*, 44: 38–58.
——— and Maurice A. Garnier (1985) 'Class Reproduction among Men and Women in France', *American Journal of Sociology*, 91: 250–80.
Rodosho (Ministry of Labour) (1984) *Rodo Tokei Yoran* (Digest of Labour Statistics) (Tokyo: Daiichi Hoki).
Rohlen, Thomas P. (1980) 'The Juku Phenomenon: An Exploratory Essay', *The Journal of Japanese Studies*, 6: 207–42.
——— (1983) *Japan's High Schools* (Berkeley: University of California Press).
Roos, Patricia (1985) *Gender and Work: A Comparative Analysis of Indust-*

rial Societies (New York: State University of New York Press).
Rosenbaum, James E. and Takehiko Kariya (1989) 'From High School to Work: Market and Institutional Mechanisms in Japan', *American Journal of Sociology*, 94: 1334–65.
Rumberger, Russell (1981) *Overeducation in the US Labor Market* (New York: Praeger).
——— (1982) 'The Structure of Work and the Underutilization of College-Educated Workers', Program Report, no. 82–B7 Institute for Research on Educational Finance and Government (Stanford University).
Sampson, Anthony (1982) *The Changing Anatomy of Britain* (London: Hodder & Stoughton).
Sano, Yoko (1989) *Kigyonai Rodo Shijo* (Intra-firm Labour Market) (Tokyo: Yuhikaku).
Scott, John (1985) *Corporations, Classes, and Capitalism* (London: Hutchinson).
——— and Catherine Griff (1984) *Directors in Industry* (Cambridge: Polity Press).
Sengoku, Tamotsu and Haruo Matsubara (eds) (1978) *Gakureki Shakai no Tsugi ni Kuru Mono* (Things Come Next to the Educational Credential Society) (Tokyo: Gakuyo Shobo).
Sewell, William H. (1964) 'Community of Residence and College Plans', *American Sociological Review*, 29: 24–38.
——— (1971) 'Inequality of Opportunities for Higher Education', *American Sociological Review*, 38: 793–809.
———, Archibald O. Haller and George W. Ohlendorf (1970) 'The Educational and Early Occupational Status Attainment Process: Replication and Revision', *American Sociological Review*, 35: 1014–27.
Shimada, Haruo (1974) 'The Structure of Earnings and Investments in Human Resources: A Comparison between the United States and Japan', unpublished Ph.D. dissertation (University of Wisconsin, Madison).
——— (1978) 'Nenrei-chingin Purofairu no Kokusai Hikaku-Josetsu' (International Comparison of Age–earnings Profiles), in Mikio Sumiya (ed.), *Roshi Kankei no Kokusai Hikaku* (Tokyo: Todai Shuppankai): 117–47.
Shoji, Kokichi (1977) *Gendaika to Gendai Shakai no Riron* (Modernization and Theories of Modern Societies) (Tokyo: Todai Shuppankai).
——— (1982) 'Gendai Shakai no Kaikyu Kozo' (Class Structure in Modern Societies), *Shakaigaku Hyoron*, 33: 20–40.
Siegel, Paul M. (1971) 'Prestige in the American Occupational Structure', unpublished Ph.D dissertation (University of Chicago).
Simkus, Albert and Rudolf Andorka (1982) 'Inequalities in Educational Attainment in Hungary, 1923–1972', *American Sociological Review*, 47: 740–51.
Smith, Herbert L. (1986) 'Overeducation and Underemployment: An Agnostic Review', *Sociology of Education*, 59: 85–99.
Sobel, Michael E. (1983) 'Structural Mobility, Circulation Mobility and the Analysis of Occupational Mobility: A Conceptual Mismatch', *American*

Sociological Review, 48: 721–27.
Solmon, Lewis C. (1975) 'The Definition of College Quality and Its Impact on Earnings', *Explorations in Economic Research*, 2: 537–87.
——— and Paul Wachtel (1975) 'The Effects on Income of Type of College Attended', *Sociology of Education*, 48: 75–90.
Sørensen, Aage (1986) 'Theory and Methodology in Social Stratification', in Ulf Himmelstrand (ed.), *The Sociology of Structure and Action* (Beverly Hills: Sage): 69–95.
Sorifu (Office of the Prime Minister) (1976) *Nihon Tokei Nenkan* (Japan Statistical Yearbook) (Tokyo: Nihon Tokei Kyokai).
——— (1978) *Soshiki de Hataraku Seishonen no Ishiki Chosa* (A Survey on the Attitudes of Working Youth in the Organization) (Tokyo: Sorifu Seishonen Taisaku Honbu).
——— (1982) *Kakeichosa Nenpo* (Annual Report on the Family Income and Expenditure Survey) (Tokyo: Nihon Tokei Kyokai).
——— (1983) *Nihon Tokei Nenkan* (Japan Statistical Yearbook) (Tokyo: Nihon Tokei Kyokai).
——— (1984) *Gekkan Yoron Chosa* (Monthly Public Opinion Survey), vol. 16, no. 9 (Tokyo: Okurasho Insatsu Kyoku).
——— (1986) *Nihon Tokei Nenkan* (Japan Statistical Yearbook) (Tokyo: Nihon Tokei Kyokai).
Sorokin, Pitirim (1959) *Social and Cultural Mobility* (New York: Free Press).
Speath, Joe L. (1970) 'Occupational Attainment among Male College Graduates', *American Journal of Sociology*, 75: 632–44.
Spence, A. Michael (1974) *Market Signaling* (Cambridge, Mass.: Harvard University Press).
Spilerman, Seymour (1977) 'Careers, Labor Market Structure, and Socio-economic Achievement', *American Journal of Sociology*, 83: 531–93.
Squires, Gregory D. (1979) *Education and Jobs: The Imbalance of the Social Machinery* (New Brunswick: Transaction Books).
SSM National Survey Committee (1976) *1975 SSM Survey Code Book* (Tokyo: SSM National Survey Committee).
Standard and Poor's (1982) *Executive/College Survey* (New York: Standard and Poor's).
Stanworth, Philip (1984) 'Elites and Privilege', in Philip Abrams, Richard Brown and Robert Burgess (eds), *UK Society* (London: Weidenfeld & Nicolson): 246–93.
——— and Anthony Giddens (eds) (1974) *Elites and Power in British Society* (Cambridge: Cambridge University Press).
Steven, Rob (1983) *Classes in Contemporary Japan* (Cambridge: Cambridge University Press).
Stolzenberg, Ross M. (1978) 'Bringing the Boss Back In: Employer Size, Employee Schooling, and Socio-economic Achievement', *American Sociological Review*, 43: 813–28.
Takane, Masa'aki (1976) *Nihon no Seiji Erito* (Japanese Political Elites) (Tokyo: Chuo Koron).
Takeuchi, Hiroshi (1981) *Kyoso no Shakaigaku* (The Sociology of Com-

petition) (Tokyo: Sekai Shisosha).

Takeuchi, Hiroshi and Makoto Aso (eds) (1981) *Nihon no Gakurekishakai wa Kawaru* (Educational Credentialism in Japan Will Change) (Tokyo: Yuhikaku).

Thompson, Kenneth (1974) 'Church of England Bishops as an Elite', in P. Stanworth and A. Giddens (eds), *Elites and Power in British Society* (Cambridge: Cambridge University Press): 198–207.

Thurow, Lester C. (1975) *Generating Inequality* (New York: Basic Books).

Tinto, Vincent (1980) 'College Origins and Patterns of Status Attainment: Schooling among Professional and Business–Managerial Occupations', *Sociology of Work and Occupations*, 7: 457–86.

Tocqueville, Alex de [1835] (1969) *Democracy in America* (New York: Knopf).

Tokita, Yoshihisa (1982) *Gendai Shihonshugi to Rodousha Kaikyu* (Contemporary Capitalism and the Working Class) (Tokyo: Iwanami Shoten).

Tokuyasu, Akira (1986) 'Nihon ni okeru Sangyoka to Sedaikan no Susei Bunseki' (Industrialization and Trends in Intergenerational Mobility in Japan), in Ken'ichi Tominaga (ed.), *Shakai Kaiso no Susei to Hikaku* (Trends and Comparisons of Social Stratification) (Tokyo: SSM Susei to Hikaku Kenkyukai): 101–11.

Tolbert, Charles, Patrick M. Horan and E. M. Beck (1980) 'The Structure of Economic Segmentation', *American Journal of Sociology*, 85: 1095–116.

Tominaga, Ken'ichi (1969) 'Trend Analysis of Social Stratification and Social Mobility in Contemporary Japan', *Developing Economics*, 7: 471–98.

——— (1977) 'Shakai Kaiso Kozo no Genjo' (The Current State of Social Stratification), *Asahi Shinbun*, evening edn (27 June).

——— (ed.) (1979) *Nihon no Kaiso Kozo* (The Stratification Structure in Japan) (Tokyo: Todai Shuppankai).

——— (1989) *Nihon Sangyo Shakai no Tenki* (The Change in Japanese Industrial Society) (Tokyo: Todai Shuppankai).

Tomizawa, Kenji (1981) 'Shakai Kosei, Kaikyu Kosei Bunseki no Ichi Shikaku' (A View on the Analysis of Social and Class Composition), *Keizai Kenkyu*, 32: 110–19.

Tomoda, Yasumasa (1977) 'Gakureki Muyoron tai Gakureki Koyoron' (Non-benefits of Credentials versus Benefits of Credentials), in Makoto Aso and Morikazu Ushiogi (eds), *Gakureki Koyoron* (Tokyo: Yuhikaku): 28–48.

Treiman, Donald (1970) 'Industrialization and Social Stratification', in Edward O. Laumann (ed.), *Social Stratification: Research and Theory for the 1970s* (Indianapolis: Bobbs-Merrill): 207–34.

——— (1977) *Occupational Prestige in Comparative Perspective* (New York: Academic Press).

——— and Kermit Terrell (1975) 'The Process of Status Attainment in the United States and Great Britain', *American Journal of Sociology*, 81: 563–83.

——— and Kam-Bor Yip (1987) 'Educational and Occupational Attainment in 21 Countries', a paper presented at the Annual Meeting of

American Sociological Association (Chicago).
Trow, Martin (1961) 'The Second Transformation of American Secondary Education', *International Journal of Comparative Sociology*, 2: 144–65.
——— (1970) 'Reflections on the Transition from Mass to Universal Higher Education', *Daedalus*, 99: 1–42.
Trusheim, Dale and James Crouse (1981) 'Effects of College Prestige on Men's Occupational Status and Income', *Research in Higher Education*, 14: 283–304.
Tsukahara, Shuichi and Junichi Kobayashi (1979) 'Shakai Kaiso to Ido ni okeru Chiiki no Yakuwari' (The Role of Region in Social Stratification and Mobility), in Ken'ichi Tominaga (ed.), *Nihon no Kaiso Kozo* (Tokyo: Todai Shuppankai): 232–71.
Tyree, Andrea, Moshe Semyonov and Robert Hodge (1979) 'Gaps and Glissandos: Inequality, Economic Development, and Social Mobility in 24 Countries', *American Sociological Review*, 44: 410–24.
Ujihara, Shojiro and Akira Takanashi (1971) *Nihon Rodo Shijo Bunseki* (The Analysis of the Japanese Labour Market) (Tokyo: Todai Shuppankai).
US Bureau of the Census (1978) *The Current Population Survey: Design and Methodology*, Technical Paper, no. 40 (Washington, D.C.: US Government Printing Office).
——— (1979) *Statistical Abstract of the United States* (Washington, D.C.: US Government Printing Office).
——— (1983) *Statistical Abstract of the United States* (Washington, D.C.: US Government Printing Office).
——— (1988) *Statistical Abstract of the United States* (Washington, D.C.: US Government Printing Office).
US Department of Education (1982) *Digest of Educational Statistics* (Washington, D.C.: US Government Printing Office).
Useem, Michael (1984) *The Inner Circle* (New York: Oxford University Press).
——— and S. M. Miller (1975) 'Privilege and Domination: The Role of Upper Class in American Higher Education', *Social Science Information*, 14: 115–45.
——— and Jerome Karabel (1986) 'Pathways to Top Corporate Management', *American Sociological Review*, 51: 184–200.
Ushiogi, Morikazu (1975) 'Shinro Kettei Katei no Pasu Kaiseki' (A Path Analysis of the Process of High School Attendance), *Kyoiku Shakaigaku Kenkyu*, 30: 75–86.
——— (1978) *Gakureki Shakai no Tenkan* (A Change of the Educational Credential Society) (Tokyo: Todai Shuppankai).
——— (1980) *Yureru Gakureki Shakai* (The Shifting Educational Credential Society) (Tokyo: Shiseido).
Vanneman, Ree and Fred C. Pampel (1977) 'The American Perception of Class and Status', *American Sociological Review*, 42: 422–37.
Vogel, Ezra F. (1963) *Japan's New Middle Class* (Berkeley: University of California Press).
Warner, Lloyd W. and James Abegglen (1951) *Big Business Leaders in America* (New York: Harper & Brothers).
Watanabe, Yukiro (1976) 'Gakureki wa Hikiau noka' (Do Educational

Credentials Pay Off?), in Sadao Hashizume (ed.), *Gakureki Hencho to Sono Kozai* (Tokyo: Daiichi Hoki): 69–125.
——— (1982) *Kyoiku Keizaigaku no Tenkai* (The Development of the Economics of Education) (Tokyo: Somei Shobo).
Weber, Max [1922] (1968) *Economy and Society* (New York: Bedminster Press).
White, Merry (1987) *The Japanese Educational Challenge* (New York: Free Press).
Whitley, Richard (1974) 'The City and Industry', in P. Stanworth and A. Giddens (eds), *Elites and Power in British Society* (Cambridge: Cambridge University Press): 65–80.
Whitt, Hugh P. (1986) 'The Sheaf Coefficient: A Simplified and Extended Approach', *Social Science Research*, 15: 174–89.
Winn, Stephen Van Zandt (1984) 'Social Class and Income Returns to Education in Sweden: A Research Note', *Social Forces*, 62: 1026–34.
Wolf, Wendy C. and Neil Fligstein (1979) 'Sex and Authority in the Workplace: The Causes of Sexual Inequality', *American Sociological Review*, 44: 235–52.
Wright, Erik Olin (1978) *Class, Crisis and the State* (London: New Left Books).
——— (1979) *Class Structure and Income Determination* (New York: Academic Press).
——— (1980a) 'Varieties of Marxist Conceptions of Class Structure', *Politics and Society*, 9: 323–70.
——— (1980b) 'Class and Occupation', *Theory and Society*, 9: 177–214.
——— (1982) 'The Questionnaire on Class Structure, Class Biography and Class Consciousness'. Comparative Project on Class Structure and Class Consciousness Working Paper Series, No. 2, Department of Sociology (University of Wisconsin-Madison).
——— (1985) *Classes* (London: Verso).
——— and Luca Perrone (1977) 'Marxist Class Categories and Income Inequality', *American Sociological Review*, 42: 32–55.
——— and Joachim Singelmann (1982) 'Proletarianization in the American Class Structure', in Michael Burawoy and Theda Skocpol (eds), *Marxist Inquiries* (Chicago: University of Chicago Press): S176–209.
———, David Hachen, Cynthia Costello and Joey Sprague (1982) 'The American Class Structure', *American Sociological Review*, 47: 709–26.
Yamada, Moritaro (1934) *Nihon Shihonshugi Bunseki* (The Analysis of Japanese Capitalism) (Tokyo: Iwanami Shoten).
Yamada, Yuichi (1980) 'Daisotsusha no Jinji Kanri to Shoshin Patan' (Management and the Patterns of Career Progress Among College Graduates), in Nobuo Nakanishi *et al.* (eds), *Shushoku* (Tokyo: Yuhikaku): 129–52.
Yamaguchi, Kazuo (1983) 'The Structure of Intergenerational Occupational Mobility', *American Journal of Sociology*, 88: 718–45.
——— (1987) 'Models for Comparing Mobility Tables', *American Sociological Review*, 52: 482–94.
Yamamoto, Shinichi (1979) 'Daigaku Singaku Kibou-Ritsu Kitei Yoin no

Bunnseki' (The Analysis of Factors Determining College Plans), *Kyoiku Shakaigaku Kenkyu*, 34: 93–103.

Yamazaki, Hirotoshi, Hiroshi Shimada, Hiroaki Urata, Masashi Fujimura and Takao Kikuchi (1983) 'Gakureki Kenkyu no Doko' (The Trend of Studies on Educational Credentialism), *Kyoiku Shakaigaku Kenkyu*, 38: 94–109.

Yano, Masakazu (1980) 'Gakurekishugi no Kozo to Tenkan' (Structure and Change in Educational Credentialism), in Kunio Amano *et al.* (eds), *Seishonen no Shinro Sentaku* (Tokyo: Yuhikaku).

Yasuda, Saburo (1964) 'A Methodological Inquiry into Social Mobility', *American Sociological Review*, 29: 16–23.

——— (1971) *Shakai Ido no Kenkyu* (The Study of Social Mobility) (Tokyo: Todai Shuppankai).

——— and Junsuke Hara (1982) *Shakai Chosa Hando Bukku* (Handbook of Social Research) (Tokyo: Yuhikaku).

Yoshino, I. Roger and Sueo Murakoshi (1977) *The Invisible Visible Minority* (Osaka: Buraku Kaiho Kenkyusha).

Index